Boris Nicolaievsky
and Otto Maenchen-Helfen

Karl Marx

Man and Fighter

Translated from the German by
Gwenda David and Eric Mosbacher

Allen Lane The Penguin Press

Allen Lane The Penguin Press
74 Grosvenor Street, London W1

● ISBN 0 7139 0342 2

Printed in Great Britain by
Hazell Watson & Viney Ltd,
Aylesbury, Bucks
Set in Linotype Georgian

Publisher's Note

(From the new French edition published by Gallimard in 1970)

A new edition of this work, written in the early thirties by Boris Nicolaievsky with the help of Otto Maenchen-Helfen, is presented to the public herewith. The original German publisher – or intended publisher – put Maenchen-Helfen's name first, to provide a Russian *émigré* with the security of a German name at that time of rising Hitlerism; the order of the names was subsequently reversed, without of course implying any disparagement of Maenchen-Helfen's active contribution. By the time the original German edition was ready in 1933, Hitler was in power, publication had become impossible, and hardly any copies survive. The English version reprinted here was translated from typescript, and these circumstances explain why, when Methuen published it in London a few years later, they described the work as first published in any language in 1936. This version appeared in America in 1937, and a French version was published in the same year. Nicolaievsky died in 1966 and Maenchen-Helfen in 1969.

A few words of explanation seem to be called for on the occasion of this republication.

In the first place, the pre-war editions contain no apparatus of notes and references. Nicolaievsky himself drew attention to this. In an article in the *Proceedings of the American Philosophical Society* of April 1961 he wrote:

> We had no time to dwell on particular questions even when our conclusions were based on unpublished documents and when they differed substantially from the conclusions drawn in other biographies of Marx. Editorial considerations that forced us to exclude the bibliographical material of course limited our possibilities still further. As a result, we could only give our conclusions briefly without explaining how we arrived at them and this despite the fact that we had the materials to justify them ... It should be noted that our book was published in Berlin in 1933, i.e., under Hitler, and was drastically abbreviated by the publishers who were in a hurry to publish it because confiscations and arrests were already in progress.

In the present edition an attempt has been made to reconstitute that apparatus, and in the process to bring it up to date. Footnotes have been provided indicating sources in as brief a form as possible. For fuller information the reader is referred to the bibliography at the back of the book. The dates make it clear which works were available to the authors at the time of writing; the literature on the subject has grown considerably since then, and includes some publications by Nicolaievsky himself.

The authors were well aware of this situation. In the 1963 German re-edition they refer to some of the documents that throw new light on Marx's life: letters written by him to his wife and daughters, correspondence of the Marx family with Kugelmann and between Engels and Kautsky, Lafargue, Turatti, etc. 'Nevertheless', they wrote, 'we have not changed the original text or added anything to it, for the picture that we tried to give remains in broad outline the same'.

Certainly a gieat many of the works concerned are republications, publications of previously unpublished material, or detailed studies of particular periods, and the essentials of the story are not affected. But the reader has a right to be made aware of the new material, and the footnotes, while informing him of the authors' sources, also frequently draw his attention to later research. In regard to five questions in particular it has been considered convenient to sum up the results of such research in the Appendices.

The publisher wishes to express his gratitude to the following scholars who have given their assistance throughout the work: to Arthur Lehning, on the relations between Marx and Bakunin; to Jacques Rougerie, on the period of the First International; to Shlomo Na'aman, on the quotations from Lassalle; and to Émile Bottigelli, Helmut Hirsch and Goetz Langkau on a variety of questions. There is hardly a page of this book that does not owe something to Maximilien Rubel, who provided invaluable information about Marx's and Engels's works. Yvonne Broutin patiently checked a large number of references. The whole was assembled by Louis Evrard, who edited notes, appendices and bibliography.

Contents

Foreword

STRIFE has raged about Karl Marx for decades, and never has it been so embittered as at the present day. He has impressed his image on the time as no other man has done. To some he is a fiend, the arch-enemy of human civilization, and the prince of chaos, while to others he is a far-seeing and beloved leader, guiding the human race towards a brighter future. In Russia his teachings are the official doctrines of the state, while fascist countries wish them exterminated. In the areas under the sway of the Chinese Soviets Marx's portrait appears upon the bank-notes, while in Germany they have burned his books. Practically all the parties of the socialist workers' International, and the communist parties in all countries, acknowledge Marxism, the eradication of which is the sole purpose of innumerable political leagues, associations and coalitions.

The French Proudhonists of the 1860s, the followers of Lassalle in Germany of the 1870s, the Fabians in England before the war produced their own brand of socialism which they opposed to that of Marx. The anti-Marxism of today has nothing in common with those movements. He who opposes Marxism today does not do so because, for instance, he denies the validity of Marx's theory of the tendency of the rate of profit to fall. Similarly there are millions today who acknowledge Marx as their leader, but not because he solved the riddle of capitalist society. Perhaps one socialist in a thousand has ever read any of Marx's economic writings, and of a thousand anti-Marxists not even one. The strife no longer rages round the truth or falsehood of the doctrine of historical materialism or the validity of the labour theory of value or the theory of marginal utility. These things are discussed and also not discussed. The arena in which Marx is fought about today is in the factories, in the parliaments and at the barricades. In both camps, the bourgeois and the socialist, Marx is first of all, if not exclusively, the revolutionary, the leader of the proletariat in its struggle to overthrow capitalism.

This book is intended to describe the life of Marx the fighter. We make no attempt to disguise the difficulties of such an undertaking. Marxism – to use the word in its proper sense, embracing the whole of Marx's work – is a whole. To divide theory from practice was completely alien to Marx's nature. How, then, can his life be understood except as a unity of thought and action?

'The man of science was not even half the man', Engels said in his speech at the grave-side of his dead friend.

For Marx science was an historically moving, revolutionary force. Marx was above all a revolutionary. To cooperate in one way or another in the work of bringing about the downfall of capitalist society and the state institutions which were its creations, to co-operate in the liberation of the modern proletariat, to make it conscious of its situation and its needs, and conscious of the conditions for its own emancipation – that was his real life-work.[1]

Marx was a socialist before he reached real and complete understanding of the laws of development underlying bourgeois society. When he wrote the Communist Manifesto at the age of thirty he did not yet appreciate the many different forms which surplus value could assume, but the Communist Manifesto contained the whole doctrine of the class war and showed the proletariat the historical task that it had to fulfil. We have written the biography of Marx as the strategist of the class struggle. The discoveries made by Marx in the course of his explorations of the anatomy of bourgeois society will only be mentioned in so far as they directly concern our subject. But the word 'directly' need not be taken too literally. A complete picture of Marx's economic doctrines would not be consistent with our theme, which was dictated to us by the time in which we live.

To some periods of Marx's life we have given far more space than others. In writing his biography our standard was not mere length of time but the importance of events in Marx's life. Once, when Marx was asked what his idea of happiness was, his answer was 'to fight'. The years of revolution in 1848–9 and those of the First International are two or three times as important as the rest. We do not believe we have left out anything of importance. To the important things we have given the space that they deserve.

Many new documents have been discovered since the end of the First World War. They put many things in a new light and reveal links and connections the very existence of which was not suspected before. To mention all the sources we have used would take up too much space. Suffice it to say that apart from printed material – incidentally we discovered a great deal of hitherto unsuspected material from old newspapers and periodicals – we have succeeded in extracting a great deal of new matter from archives. In particular the archives of the German Social Democratic Party, which contain the manuscripts Marx and Engels left at their death, as well as those of many of their contemporaries and fellow fighters, and a vast number of documents relating to the history of the First International were put at our disposal. They remained at our disposal even in the present difficult circumstances, when they have been taken abroad, and for this we have to thank the party leaders (at present in Prague). We found a great deal of material in the secret state archives at Berlin-Dahlem and in the Saxon state archives at Dresden.[2]

We were also enabled to use some documents from the archives of the British Foreign Office preserved in the Record Office, more particularly documents regarding the attempt made by the Prussian Government to secure Marx's expulsion from England in 1850. We wish to express our thanks to Mr E. H. Carr, who drew our attention to these documents and sent us copies.

We have intentionally quoted a great deal. We obviously could not recoin phrases coined by Marx which have long become familiar in our everyday speech. We have quoted Marx himself wherever the subject demanded it, and often

let him speak for himself, because the particular turn he gave
his thoughts, the way he fitted his sentences together, the
adjectives he chose, reveal the nature of the man more clearly
than any analysis. For the same reasons we have quoted his
contemporaries whenever possible. Half the contents of a
police agent's report is the way he writes it. To quote a letter
of Bakunin's without using his own words in the important
passages would be to misrepresent him. The fact that we give
the source of our quotations will be welcome to many readers.

B. NICOLAIEVSKY
OTTO MAENCHEN-HELFEN
June 1936

[1]

Origins and Childhood[1]

Trier deservedly enjoys the reputation of being the oldest town in Germany. Its origins are lost in the mists of antiquity. A metropolis under the Roman Empire, it was brought to ruin in the stormy times of the migration of the peoples, but rose and flourished again in the Middle Ages under the mild sway of its bishops, whose diocese extended to Metz, Toul and Verdun. Its position at the extreme edge of German-speaking territory made of it an intermediary between German culture and French. It changed its overlords more than once. It belonged to the German Holy Roman Empire, then to the kingdom of France, then it became German once again. After the outbreak of the French Revolution a stream of French *émigrés* poured into Trier as into other frontier towns, and for some years it was the outpost of the Coblenz reaction. The white detachments were formed in Trier, where conspiracies were hatched and emissaries forgathered going into or coming out of France.

In the autumn of 1793, just a quarter of a century before the birth of Marx, when the allies were retreating to the Rhine before the armies of the revolution, Goethe came to Trier with the Duke of Weimar's troops. 'The town has one striking characteristic', he wrote in his *French Campaign*.

It claims that it possesses more religious buildings than any other place of the same size. Its reputation in this respect could scarcely be denied. For within its walls it is burdened, nay, oppressed, with churches and chapels and cloisters and colleges and buildings dedicated to chivalrous and religious orders, to say nothing of the abbacies, Carthusian convents and institutions which invest, nay, blockade it.

The waves of the Reformation never reached Trier, and the political and economic power of the Church remained

unbroken. For all that its clerical electors did a good deal for
culture and for art. The last, Clement Wenceslaus, who was
forced to flee before the victorious troops of the Convention
in 1794, was a liberal-minded man and his prebendary, Dal-
berg, a vigorous patron of public instruction, belonged to the
order of the illuminati.

Nevertheless the inhabitants of Trier received the French
with enthusiasm. The revolution released the peasants from the
trammels of feudalism, gave the bourgeoisie the administrative and legal apparatus they required for their advancement,
freed the intelligentsia from the tutelage of the priests. The
men of Trier danced round their 'tree of freedom' just like
the inhabitants of Mainz. They had their own Jacobin club.
Many a respected citizen in the 1830s still looked back with
pride to his Jacobin past.

Trier remained French for two decades. But as the novelty
wore off the things wrought by the revolution – the dividing-
up of Church property in particular – and as the burdens that
came in its train increased, the first revolutionary ardour faded,
and indifference grew. In the last years of the Napoleonic
Empire indifference was replaced by open hostility. Every
year the taxes grew more oppressive. The sons of the artisans
of Trier and the peasants of the Moselle bled to death on the
battlefields of Spain, Germany and Russia. In January 1815
Trier greeted the allies as deliverers from an intolerable yoke.

The Congress of Vienna awarded Trier to Prussia.[2] The
Prussian Government appreciated the necessity of handling
its new-won territory with care. It zealously avoided coming
into conflict with the Catholic Church and kept on its guard
against injuring the religious susceptibilities of its newly acquired subjects. But it refrained from laying hands on the possessions of those who had grown rich by the acquisition of
Church property during the revolution. In all its essentials
the Code Napoléon, the French statute-book, remained in
force as far as the Rhineland was concerned. Public and oral
court proceedings were retained. The pick of Prussian official-
dom was sent to the Rhineland provinces, charged with the

duty of scrupulously respecting local idiosyncrasies. For a number of years the Rhineland was sheltered from the full ultra-reactionary blast which set in everywhere else in Prussia immediately after the conclusion of peace.

The Government, tolerant to the Catholic masses, took pains to win over the intelligentsia too. It did a great deal, among other things, for archaeological research. The inhabitants of Trier were proud of the wealth of Roman remains in their town. Scarcely a doctor, lawyer or schoolmaster but was also an historian and archaeologist. The Government provided ample sums of money to subsidize their researches. Instead of agitating against Prussian absolutism, ex-Jacobins burrowed for Mithraic altars and gravestones. In those years the Trier of antiquity, *Augusta Treverorum*, rose once more from its ruins.[3]

The culture of the vine, mainspring then as now of the agricultural economy of the Moselle, flourished mightily, thanks to the tariff which came into force in 1818. High, almost prohibitive duties closed the Prussian market to foreign wines and provided the peasants of the Moselle with a vast and assured outlet for their produce.

Among those who received the Prussians with the greatest enthusiasm were the Rhineland Jews. In 1815 the economic position of the Jews was incomparably more favourable in the kingdom of Prussia than in most of the departments of France.

The Prussian Decree of 11 March 1812 gave them rights that they had enjoyed for only a few years under Napoleon; for practically everything that the revolution had given them was taken away by the 'décret infâme' of 17 March 1808. Extensive restrictions were placed upon their liberty of movement, and their freedom to trade or earn a living as they wished was as good as abolished. The Jews, at any rate economically, were cast back into the ghetto which they had been preparing to leave. And now the yoke they groaned under was heavier than before. Hitherto the Rhineland Jews had been money-lenders, insisting rigorously upon their bond. But Napoleon compelled them to usury that was secret and obscure.

The decree was to last in the first instance for ten years, until 1818. But in 1815 Napoleon fell, and the Jews expected that with him his decree would fall too.

They were disappointed. Article sixteen of the statutes of the new German Federation of Princes specified that legal rights everywhere should remain as they had been before. Prussia, glad at being able to drop the liberal mask she had been forced to adopt in the war of liberation, entered un-abashed upon Napoleon's inheritance insofar as it was suf-ficiently reactionary for her. There was no need whatever to have any consideration for the Jews. So she piled Pelion upon Ossa and superimposed her old Prussian special Jewish regula-tions upon those of Napoleon. Under the French Empire it had been possible in exceptional cases for Jews to enter the service of the state; in Prussia, even after the so-called emanci-pation, it was impossible under any circumstances. So the Rhineland Jews who had entered the state service under Napoleon were compelled to leave it as soon as Friedrich Wilhelm III became their overlord. '

The number of those affected was only three, and one of them was a Trier lawyer, Hirschel Marx, the father of Karl. The chairman of the commission which carried out the trans-fer from French to Prussian authority described him as a 'learned, very industrious and thoroughly conscientious man' and warmly recommended him to be taken over to the Prus-sian service, but this helped him not at all. In June 1815 he wrote a memorial in which he expressed his confidence in Prussian justice in moving terms, but he did not receive so much as a reply. Confronted with the choice of changing his faith or his occupation, he had himself baptized and adopted the name of Heinrich.[4]

To abandon the Jewish faith was no great wrench. He did object to the coercion. He was incensed by the narrow intolerance that forced him to this step. No ties bound him to the synagogue, or, for that matter, to the church either. True, his ancestors, on his father's and his mother's side alike, had been rabbis as far back as his family tree can be traced.

Hirschel's father, Marx Levy, later known as Marx only, who died in 1798, was a Trier rabbi. The family tree of Hirschel's mother, Eva Moses Lvov (1753—1823), included a number of celebrated rabbis, including Meir Katzenellenbogen, head of the Talmud School at Padua, who died in 1565, Joseph Ben Gersen ha-Cohen, who died in 1591, and the honoured teacher, Josua Heschel Lvov (1693-1771). The family lived in Hessia, later emigrated to Poland (Lvov is the Polish name for Lemberg) and had been settled in Trier since the seventeenth century. The eldest of Levy's three sons, Samuel, became a rabbi like his fathers before him. He died in Trier in 1827 in his fiftieth year.[5]

Hirschel Marx was born at Saarlouis in 1782. The scanty indications available point to his having early cut himself adrift from his hereditary environment. In a letter to his son he once wrote that but for his existence itself he had received nothing from his family, 'except, to be fair, my mother's love'. His writings contain no word to indicate even the faintest spiritual link with the Jewish faith. Edgar von Westphalen, who spent many hours of his boyhood in the Marxes' house, remembered Heinrich Marx in his old age as a 'Protestant *à la* Lessing'. A 'real eighteenth-century Frenchman, who knew his Voltaire and Rousseau inside out', a Kantian like most of the educated people of his town, professing 'a pure belief in God, like Newton, Locke and Leibniz', he had nothing whatever in common with the world of rabbinic Jewry. Alienated from his family from his youth up, he had a stony path to tread. In later years he confessed that his 'strong principles' had been his 'only possession'.

His baptism, which took place between the summer of 1816 and the spring of 1817, cut the last loose tie that bound him to his family. If he had hoped before to bring light into the darkness of the ghetto, in spite of being misunderstood, suspected and practically alone, henceforward the task was an impossibility. It was an impossibility not because of his baptism alone. For had the emancipation of the Jews not proved illusory? Was not the dream of their becoming equals among equals over? Now that the door that led from the ghetto to the outer world was once more shut and bolted, the Jews of the ghetto retired into themselves more fanatically than ever. They rejected everything that they had longed for not so long before. They became hyper-orthodox; everything that was traditionally Jewish was sacrosanct, good and bad alike.

We do not know how Marx's father came to terms with it all. But there is an echo in the unwilling words: 'The Hebrew faith is repellent to me', that Marx wrote at the age of twenty-five.[6] What Marx thought in his young years of the Jewry of his time and country we know from what he wrote in 1844 in the *Deutsch-Französische Jahrbücher*.

Let us not search for the secret of the Jews in their religion, but for the secret of their religion in the living Jews [he wrote]. What is the worldly foundation of Jewry? Self-interest and the satisfying of practical wants. What is the worldly worship of the Jews? Huckstering. What is their worldly god? Money. Very well. The emancipation from huckstering and money, that is, from real, practical Jewry, would be the real self-emancipation of our time.[7]

On 24 August 1824 Heinrich Marx's children – Sophie, Karl, Hermann, Henriette, Louise, Emilie and Karoline – were received into the national evangelical church. Their mother, Henriette, waited till her parents were dead before being baptized on 20 November 1825. Her maiden name was Pressburg and she came of a family of Hungarian origin which had been settled in Holland for generations.

In the pages that follow there will be little to say about Marx's mother and his brothers and sisters. His mother was a devoted housewife, lovingly concerned for the minor things of life, engrossed in the health, feeding and clothing of her children, narrow-minded if not actually stupid, without any understanding for the daemon of her son. She never forgave him for not becoming a lawyer like his father. She regarded his activities as suspicious from an early age. Measured by her dreams about his future, he was a failure, a genius maybe, but a scapegrace, incompetent, the black sheep of the family, entirely lacking in sense for the only things that she thought sensible, that is to say, a quiet, comfortable life in a narrow circle, respected by the respectable, the well-to-do and the well-bred. When Marx looked back upon his life at the age of fifty he still remembered her saying, in the execrable German that she spoke all her life: 'If Karl had only *made* capital instead of . . .'[8]

Not very much is known about Marx's brothers and sisters. The first-born, Moritz David, died soon after birth. The next child was Sophie, born on 13 November 1816. She was, as far as we know, the only one of Karl's brothers and sisters who was at all close to him in his youth. In later years, however, he scarcely even kept in touch with this sister, who married a lawyer named Schmalhausen and lived at Maastricht. Karl was born at half past one on the morning of 5 May 1818. Of Karl's two younger brothers, Hermann died at the age of twenty-three and Eduard at the age of eleven. Both succumbed to tuberculosis, the hereditary family disease, as did two other sisters, Henriette and Karoline. Louise, born in 1821, married Jan Karl Juta, a Dutchman, and settled in Cape Town with him. She and her husband twice visited Marx in London, and in 1853 Marx wrote some articles for the *Zuid-Afrikaan,* which his brother-in-law edited. Emilie, born in 1822, married an engineer named Conradi and lived in Trier until her death in 1888.

In 1815, when the Moselle country became Prussian, Heinrich Marx was a lawyer attached to the Trier court. In 1820 he was attached to the newly founded Trier provincial court. Later he acquired the title of *Justizrat* and was for many years *bâtonnier du barreau.* He occupied a respected position in the social life of the town. The family lived in a beautiful old house in the Rhineland baroque style in the Brückenstrasse, one of the best parts of the town.[9] Trier was a small place. In 1818, the year of Marx's birth, it numbered 11,400 inhabitants, of whom the overwhelming majority were Catholic. The Protestant community, to which the Marxes now adhered, consisted of barely 300 souls, mainly officials transferred to the Moselle from other provinces. In these circumstances the origins of the rabbi's son did not matter. 'Here everyone who conducts himself is respected', Ernst von Schiller, the son of Friedrich Schiller, at that time *Landgerichtsrat* at Trier, wrote at the end of 1820.

At the beginning of 1830 Heinrich Marx was the leader of the moderate constitutional party in Trier. He did not share the francophilia which was still fairly widespread in the Rhineland and became accentuated as the old Prussian reaction established itself more and more firmly in the new territories.

'Only the hybrid liberals of today could idolize a Napoleon,' he wrote to his son in 1837.

I assure you that under him no one dared even to think aloud the kind of thing that is daily written in Germany today, without hindrance or impediment, in Prussia in particular. He who has studied Napoleon's history and his crazy system of ideas may rejoice with a good conscience at his fall and the victory of Prussia.

He advised the composition of an ode which should extol the victory of the Belle Alliance. The motif he suggested is interesting. 'Its failure would have laid humanity, and the intellect especially, in everlasting chains.' Heinrich Marx preferred enlightened monarchy to military dictatorship, but he was no defender of absolutism.[10]

As the bureaucratic absolutist Prussian régime increasingly demonstrated its incompetence, his antipathy to it grew. Towards the end of the 1820s the condition of the peasants of the Moselle took a turn for the worse. In 1828 Prussia formed a customs union with Hessia, and in 1834 the German *Zollverein* was formed. The competition of non-Prussian wine-growing peasants deprived the Moselle of the hitherto certain outlet for its produce, and prices rapidly fell, to the accompaniment of rising taxes. The pauperization of the peasants of the Moselle proceeded at such a rate that within a few years contemporaries compared their state with the distress of the weavers of Silesia. Trade slumped, the position of the artisans went from bad to worse. The revolution of July 1830 in Paris, the setting up of the bourgeois kingdom, the September rising in Brussels and the Belgian Declaration of Independence made a profound impression in the Rhineland. In Germany there was unrest in Brunswick, Saxony and Kurhessen. Vintagers from the Moselle area actually took part in the famous Hambacher Fest held by the liberals on 27 May 1832.

In the Rhineland the old francophile tendencies underwent a mighty revival. New, fantastic, shocking and unprecedented ideas came winging their way across the frontier from France. Saint-Simonism gained so many adherents on the Moselle that the Archbishop was compelled to issue an emphatic warning against the new heresy. In 1835 a pamphlet by Ludwig Gall, who has been called the first German socialist, appeared in Trier. In it he declared that labour was the source of all wealth and that millions owned nothing but their power to work. The pamphlet also contained the following phrases: 'The privileged, moneyed class and the labouring classes, sharply divided as they are by diametrically opposing interests, are in sharp conflict. As the position of the former improves, so does that of the latter worsen, become more wretched and distressed.' The police were aware of Gall's 'very suspicious way of thinking' and perceived that he 'required a specially sharp watch to be kept on him'.[11]

At first the local state officials scarcely altered their policy. Better acquainted than the central authorities in Berlin with conditions in the newly acquired territories, they kept them in ignorance of oppositional utterances for fear of intensifying the situation. This went on until events compelled them to intervene, and in these events Heinrich Marx occupied a prominent place.

The Literarische Kasino-Gesellschaft, a club that dated back to the time of French suzerainty, was the hub of the social life of Trier. Differences of social status were of no account in it. 'Any upright and educated man, without regard to rank or occupation', was eligible for membership. The club premises consisted of a big, two-storey house, containing a library, a reading-room, in which the principal French and

German newspapers were kept, a number of social rooms and a hall in which concerts, theatrical performances and balls were given. The Society for Useful Research,[12] which retained strong traditions dating from the time of its foundation in 1802, met at the club. One of its joint founders and most active members was Hugo Wyttenbach, headmaster of Karl Marx's school.

On 12 January 1834 a banquet was held at the club in honour of the deputies to the Rhineland Diet, thus associating the men of Trier with the campaign of banquets which swept South Germany in the winter of 1833-4 under the battle-cry of a constitution. In the opinion of the Prussian authorities this ceremony was quite superfluous; but they did not really become alarmed about it until they discovered that it was not intended to honour all the deputies to the Diet but only the liberal-minded and 'little commendable' Valdenaire, Kaiser and Mohr, while Handel, representative of the Trier nobility, was omitted.

Heinrich Marx was one of the organizers of the banquet and he proposed the toast of the deputies. He paid a glowing tribute to the King 'to whose magnanimity we are indebted for the first institutions of popular representation. In the fullness of his omnipotence he arranged that Diets should assemble so that truth might arrive at the steps of the throne'. He concluded with the words: 'So let us look confidently forward to a serene future, for it rests in the hands of a worthy father, an upright king, whose noble heart will always remain open and well-disposed to the just and reasonable wishes of his people.'[13]

A very loyal speech, to be sure, yet the voice of the opposition was plainly to be discerned in it. The party of ultra-reaction in Berlin wanted to have the Rhenish Diet abolished, or at least have its privileges circumscribed as far as possible. Therefore praising the King for having sanctioned the Diet was equivalent to protesting against the royal plan to suppress it. The president of the administrative district was forced to abandon his previous practice and report the matter to Berlin.

There could be no good purpose behind the banquet, which was a small-scale imitation of similar affairs in the Southern German states. But it was the only one of its kind in Prussia. The Trier Press was not allowed to report it, but the newspapers of Cologne and Coblenz carried detailed descriptive reports of it, and even the Paris *Constitutionnel*, the organ of the left, announced that the inhabitants of Trier had held a 'brilliant banquet' at which 'speeches of the most liberal purport' were delivered. Kamptz, the Minister of Justice, rightly interpreted the pious words. 'They imagine themselves not just deputies to the Diet but representatives of the people, and accordingly receive the civic crown.'[14]

Soon afterwards, to crown the intense disapproval with which the Government regarded the banquet and the speeches made at it, a new sensation arose. On 20 January the club anniversary celebrations were held and became exuberant. The company drank, sang and made merry. They grew overbold and started singing not just German songs but French – the *Marseillaise* and the *Parisienne*. An officer reported the matter. Heinrich Marx was among those who sang and made depreciatory references to the Prussians. At this the whole official apparatus was set in motion. The ministry in Berlin intervened, the Crown Prince, Friedrich Wilhelm, wrote an indignant letter to the burgomaster, describing the songs that were sung as 'heinous, the apotheosis of ancient and modern perfidy', and a detailed report of the matter was made to the King himself. Officers and state officials who had been members of the club resigned and the premises were placed under police supervision. From that day on Heinrich Marx was regarded by the Government as thoroughly unreliable politically. Young Karl, then aged sixteen, cannot have failed to follow these events, in which his father was so closely concerned, with great attention.

Karl Marx was devoted to his father. His daughter Eleanor recalled that he never tired of talking about him.

He always carried with him a photograph of his father which was taken from an old daguerreotype. But he was never willing to show it to strangers, because, he said, it bore so little resemblance to the original. To me the face appeared very fine. The eyes and forehead resembled those of his son, but the part of the face round the mouth and the chin were gentler. His features as a whole were of a definitely Jewish, but fine Jewish type. When Karl Marx started the long, sorrowful journey in search of health after his wife's death, this photograph, an old photograph of my mother on glass and a photograph of my sister, Jenny, went with him. We found them in his breast-pocket after his death. Engels laid them in his coffin.[15]

More detailed knowledge of Marx's boyhood would be welcome, but all that has come down to us are a few meagre, disconnected reminiscences by his sisters. They show him as an unruly companion at play. He seems to have been a fearful tyrant. He drove the girls at full gallop down the Marxberg and insisted on their eating the cakes he made with his dirty hands out of still dirtier dough. But they put up with it all without protest because he told them such marvellous stories in return. His schoolmates loved him and feared him at the same time – loved him because he was always up to tricks and feared him because of the ease with which he wrote satirical verses and lampoons upon his enemies. He retained this ability during the whole of his life.

Karl Marx was sent to the high school in 1830. He was a moderate pupil. The best pupils were singled out at the end of each school year. Marx once received an 'honourable mention' for ancient and modern languages, but he was only tenth on the list. Another time he was singled out for his good performances at German composition. This was not much for five years at school. He passed his examinations without distinction. There is some evidence to indicate that he had the reputation, among schoolfellows and masters alike, of being a poet. After Karl's departure to Bonn University, when his father gave Wyttenbach, his old headmaster, his son's greetings and told him that Karl intended to write a poem in his honour, 'it made the old man happy'.

Whether the poem was ever written is unknown. The inten-

tion alone points to a definite political outlook. Wyttenbach
was the life and soul of a group of Kantians which had been
formed in Trier in the first years of the new century. Marx's
father belonged to it himself. Wyttenbach, scholar, historian,
archaeologist and humanist, educated his pupils in a free, cos-
mopolitan spirit, entirely dissimilar to that prevailing in the
royal Prussian high schools. He had a high conception of his
calling, as is demonstrated by the speeches he made each year
at the ceremonial departure to the university of the pupils
who were leaving. These were always fully reported in the
Trier newspapers. 'A teacher cannot alter a child's individuality,' he said. 'But he can thwart or help it, cripple or develop
it.' The wearisome phrases about throne and altar, prevalent,
nay, actually prescribed at the time, were never used by him.

The police did not concern themselves with the high school
until 1830. The Prussian authorities, in conformity with the
duty incumbent upon them of winning over their new subjects, shut their eyes and let Wyttenbach do as he liked. After
1830 this state of affairs altered. The persecution of the 'demagogues' began. A commission 'for the suppression of politically
dangerous groups' had been established in Berlin. It directed
its attention to Trier. Schnabel, the administrative head of the
district of Saarbrücken, with whom denouncing was a passion,
had all and sundry spied upon by his agent, a degenerate individual named Nohl.

Nohl sent his denunciations to Berlin by way of Schnabel
week by week. No one was safe, neither doctor nor artisan nor
innkeeper nor official, nor even the wife of the president of the
administrative district. All were demagogues and Jacobins.
The Coblenz school committee tried to defend their traduced
colleagues, but it helped them little. The local officials, intimidated, dismayed, unsure what course to steer, admitted that
there were some partially 'ill-disposed' members of the high
school staff. Many of them were said to exercise a 'bad influence' upon the boys. One master, Steininger, who taught Marx
natural science and mathematics, had 'an innate propensity
to opposition' and Wyttenbach was too weak and, moreover,

protected his colleagues when anything against them was ventured upon. A deplorable lack of discipline was to be observed among the pupils. Boys of the top forms were sometimes to be seen sitting about in the taverns until after midnight and, what was far worse, forbidden literature circulated among them. A copy of the speeches made at the Hambacher Fest in 1833 was found in a boy's possession.[16] In 1834 it was discovered that the boys actually wrote poems with political implications. One was arrested and was in the remand prison for months.

Henceforth the Coblenz school committee and the Trier officials kept the school under zealous observation. Between 1833 and 1835 it was the subject of dozens of official reports.

These were Marx's last years at school. There can be no doubt of the interest with which he must have followed these events, which so closely concerned his masters, his schoolfellows and himself. True, his name does not occur in the official correspondence, but the official correspondence contains the names of no schoolboys at all. He is certain to have made rich use of his gift of writing lampoons upon his enemies.

The essays he wrote at his final examination cast a light upon his mentality at the time. The influence of the French liberal intelligence, particularly that of Rousseau, imparted by his father and Wyttenbach, is plain enough. Of greater significance are these phrases from an essay called 'Observations of a young man before choosing a career'.

If we choose the career in which we can do humanity the most good, burdens cannot overwhelm us, since they are nothing but sacrifice for the benefit of all ... Experience rates him as the happiest who has made the greatest number happy, and religion itself teaches us the ideal for which all strive, to sacrifice oneself for humanity.[17]

The only upholders of these ideals at that time were the left, the members of the 'Burschenschaft', and the revolutionaries who hungered in exile. In their appeals to youth the words: 'be ready to sacrifice yourself, renounce your well-being for humanity's sake', constantly recur. They remained the fundamental maxim of Marx's life. Paul Lafargue records that 'to work for humanity' was his favourite motto.[18]

The spy's reports about the masters at his school turned out to be grossly exaggerated. Investigation showed that 'no good spirit was prevalent' among the boys, but that there was nothing tangible against the staff. Wyttenbach was not dismissed, as the more extreme among his enemies demanded. But he was given a joint headmaster, Loers, the Latin master, a 'well-disposed man', whose duty it was to preside over the school discipline.

Loers's appointment became known just as Karl left school. It gave him a welcome opportunity of making a demonstration – an innocuous demonstration, it is true, but the Prussian Government allowed no others. The Government were not blind to the state of mind expressed in such demonstrations, nor were they intended to be.

It was usual for young men just going to the university to call on their old masters to say good-bye. Marx visited every one of them but Loers. 'Herr Loers took it very much amiss that you did not go and see him', Heinrich Marx wrote to his son at Bonn. 'You and Clemens were the only ones.'[19] He told a white lie and said that Karl had gone with him to call on Loers, but unfortunately he had been out.

In the middle of October 1835 Karl Marx went to Bonn.

[2]

A Happy Year at Bonn

IT had long ago been decided by the Marx family council that Karl should go to the university. His father's circumstances were quite comfortable, but he was not rich enough to allow all his sons to study. Hermann, Karl's moderately gifted younger brother, was indentured to a Brussels business house. But, however difficult it might occasionally be, means must be found for Karl, the favourite child, the son in whom his father lived again, the son who should achieve what his father had been denied.

The university he should go to had been chosen too. Most students from Trier went to Bonn as the nearest university town. In 1835 and 1836 the association of Trier students at Bonn numbered more than thirty members. Later Karl was intended to spend a few terms at another university – at Berlin, if it could possibly be managed.

What he should study had also been decided for him. He was to study law; not because at the age of sixteen he was particularly attracted to the subject; he was equally interested in literature, philosophy and science, especially physics and chemistry. As he had no particular preference for any one branch of knowledge, because he wanted to embrace them all, he accepted his father's advice without question. Practical motives were undoubtedly Heinrich Marx's chief consideration in making the choice for his son. New courts were being established in the Trier area, and intending lawyers had excellent prospects of finding good and well-paid posts. Of the seven students from Trier who matriculated at Bonn University in 1834, four studied law.

Parents, brothers, sisters and friends accompanied Karl to the 'express yacht' which left Trier at four o'clock in the morning. Halley's comet was in the sky. The covered boat so grandiosely styled took him down the Moselle – the river was almost the only link with the east of Germany – as far as the Rhine, and then one of the recently introduced Rhine steamers took him upstream to Bonn, where he arrived on Saturday 17 October and entered his name at the university on the same day.

Bonn, a town of nearly 40,000 inhabitants, was distinctly bigger than Trier. Although it did not number many more than 700 students, the university dominated the life of the town. In the 1820s and 1830s the University of Bonn could rightly boast of the great freedom it enjoyed. Students' associations had no need for concealment. This did not apply only to associations of students from the same town or district; it applied equally to the definitely liberal 'Burschenschafter', who drank and duelled and sang, regarded with esteem by the citizens and benevolence by the authorities. 'They act so freely and openly', an examining magistrate later wrote, 'that the existence of the societies is a secret to no one' – least of all to the university authorities, who were not in the least perturbed by them. On the contrary, they practically sanctioned them. As the state officials did not wish to disturb the university, they respected its independence and let things take their course.

A stop, and a very thorough stop, was put to this state of affairs shortly before Marx came to Bonn. In April 1835 a small group of foolhardy young men had attempted to break up the Federal Diet at Frankfurt and set up a provisional government in its place. The rising was undertaken with totally inadequate means and put down without any difficulty whatever. But the governments of Germany were thoroughly alarmed. Though some of them had hitherto had liberal impulses, they now started furiously building at 'the saving dam' which the decisions of the Vienna Conference of spring 1834 – drafted by Metternich – imposed upon them the duty of erecting against the 'rising flood'. The drive descended with especial fury upon the students' associations. Bonn's turn came a little later. When Marx came to Bonn in the autumn of 1835, informers were daily sending 'suspects' to prison. University authorities, police, and spies denounced, arrested, and expelled dozens of Burschenschafter.

Not a single association that was connected in any way with any general purpose, even the most discreet, survived the stress of these severe measures. The only one to remain was the 'Korps', who, as a contemporary protested, regarded 'brawling and carousing as the highest aim of a student's life'. The authorities were glad enough to close their eyes to the activities of the Korps. There were also small tavern clubs, consisting of groups of students from the same towns, from Cologne, Aachen, etc. These were not distinguished for their rich intellectual life either. After most of the boldest, most advanced and liberal-minded students had been eliminated those who remained were too bewildered or too indifferent not scrupulously to avoid all discussion of politics.

Lectures had not yet begun when Marx arrived at Bonn. He had plenty of time to settle down. He took a room quite close to the university, and immediately fell upon the lecture list. The natural sciences were so badly represented at Bonn that Marx resolved to postpone his study of physics and chemistry until going to Berlin, where he would be able to study under the real authorities on those subjects. Sufficient remained for him to do nevertheless. He decided to attend courses of lectures in no fewer than nine subjects. His father, to whom he wrote of his plans, hesitated between pleasure at so much zeal and fear that Karl might overwork. 'Nine courses of lectures seem rather a lot to me', he wrote, 'and I don't want you to undertake more than mind and body can stand. But if you can manage it, very well. The field of knowledge is immense and time is short.'[1]

In the end Marx only attended six courses. According to his professors he was 'industrious' or 'very industrious' at them all. Professor Welcker, under whom Marx studied Greek and Roman mythology, stated that he was 'exceptionally industrious and attentive'. In the summer term Marx attended four courses. This was still a great deal, particularly when compared with his later studies in Berlin, when he only attended fourteen courses of lectures in nine terms. The year at Bonn was the only one in which he took his university studies seriously. Somewhat to his own surprise, Marx discovered a taste for law, his future profession. All the same he seems to have preferred listening to the great Schlegel on Homer or the elegies of Propertius and D'Alton on the history of art.

However industriously he applied himself to them, his studies failed to engross him completely. As he demonstrated at school, he was no bookworm or spoilsport. He joined the Trier tavern club and was one of its five presidents in the summer term of 1836. Marx, a true son of the Rhineland, appreciated a good 'drop' all his life. In June he was condemned to one day's detention by the proctor for being drunk and disorderly. The prison in which he served his sentence was a very jolly one. A contemporary who studied at Bonn a year later than Marx reports that the prisoners were allowed visitors, who practically never failed to turn up with wine, beer and cards. Sometimes the merrymaking was such that the entertainment expenses made a serious inroad into the prisoners' monthly allowance. It was not because of the one day's confinement alone that Karl got into debt, in spite of the ample allowance sent him by his generous father.

Marx joined another club as well. It was called the Poets' Club. If the police records are to be believed, this club of enthusiastic young men was not so entirely innocuous as it seemed. Its founders were Fenner von Fenneberg, who took a very active part in the revolution of 1848 and 1849, first in Vienna and later in Baden, and a Trier student named Biermann, who had come under suspicion while still at school as the author of 'seditious poetry'. He escaped to Paris to avoid arrest, and it was proved that he had been in contact with a Major Stieldorf, whom the police accused of agitating for the annexation by Belgium of the western Trier territory.

Marx appears to have been very active in the Poets' Club. Moritz Carrière, a philosopher and aesthetician of some merit, who at the time was the leader of a similar group at Göttingen, with whom the Bonn club was on friendly terms, remembered Marx as one of the three most important members. The other two were Emanuel Geibel, who later made a reputation as a lyric poet, and Karl Grün, an adherent of the 'true' socialism which Marx was soon so pitilessly to combat and deride.[2]

His father approved of Karl's joining the Poets' Club. He knew his son's stormy nature and was never without anxiety that it might run away with him. He did not like the tavern club, for he feared Karl might become involved in a duel. He was relieved when he learned that Karl had joined the Poets' Club and wrote: 'I like your little group far better than the tavern. Young people who take pleasure in such gatherings are necessarily civilized human beings, and set greater store on their value as future good citizens than those who set most store by rowdiness.'[3]

However, it soon appeared that even this little group was not without its dangers. The police, suspecting treasonable activities everywhere, started taking an interest in the Poets' Club. The club rules and the minutes of their meetings in the winter of 1834–5 fell into the hands of the police spy Nohl, who had now been sent to Bonn, but to their disappointment the police were forced to admit that both the rules and the minutes were politically completely innocuous. According to the rules the members, 'moved by a similar love of *belles lettres*', had decided to unite 'for the reciprocal exercise of their would-be poetical talents'. In spite of this the police remained full of misgivings, and although their inquiries had resulted in nothing tangible, the matter was handed over to the university authorities, whose disciplinary court should institute proceedings.

Marx's name was not mentioned. His father, well-informed about events in Bonn, once more had cause for anxiety about him, and not on account of the Poets' Club alone. In the spring of 1836 a wild conflict broke out among the students, and the association of Trier students was in the midst of the fray. Conflict between the Korps associations and the tavern clubs had begun during the winter. The Korps demanded that the tavern clubs should merge with them. This is the tavern clubs refused to do, and the refusal resulted in hostile encounters with members of the Borussia Korps, who were 'true Prussians and aristocrats', and, under the leadership of Counts von der Goltz, von der Schulenberg and von Heyden, provoked, derided and challenged the 'plebeians' whenever they met them. Their especial hatred was directed to the Trier students. In the conflict of the feudal Borussians with the sons of the bourgeois citizens of Trier there was, in a sense, an element of class war.

In 1858 Lassalle, after some unpleasant fellow had sent him a challenge, wrote to Marx and asked him his opinion of duels. Marx replied that it was obviously absurd to try and decide whether duelling as such was consistent with *the* principle; but within the biased limitations of bourgeois society it might sometimes be necessary to justify one's individuality in this feudal manner.[4] As an eighteen-year-old student at Bonn Marx evidently thought the same. An entry in the records of the university disciplinary court states that Marx was once seen bearing a weapon such as was usually used for duels.

His father in Trier heard of this incident and wrote to his son:

Since when is duelling so interwoven with philosophy? Men fight duels out of respect, nay, rather out of fear of public opinion. And what public opinion? Not always the best – far from it! So little consistency is there among mankind! Do not let this taste – if it is not a taste, this disease – take root. You might, after all, end by robbing yourself and your parents of their finest hopes for you. I do not believe that a reasonable man can so easily disregard these things.[5]

There was foundation for his father's fears. The duels the students fought in the suburbs of Ippendorf and Kessenich were anything but harmless. The young Count von Arnim was killed in a duel in 1834, and soon afterwards a student named Daniels, from Aachen, was killed too. Karl did not heed his father's warnings. He fought a duel, in all probability with a Borussian, in August 1836. He received a thrust over the left eye.

How his father took the news is not known. Before the end of the summer term he had given the Bonn university authorities his consent to his son's transfer to Berlin. He did not 'merely give his consent' but heavily underlined the statement that it was 'his wish'. A longer stay in Bonn would have profited Karl nothing and only threatened duels on the one hand and police persecution on the other.

[3]

Jenny von Westphalen[1]

MARX spent the summer and autumn of 1836 in Trier, where he became secretly engaged to Jenny von Westphalen, his future wife.

Her antecedents were entirely different from his own. She came from a different world. Her grandfather, Philipp Westphalen (1724–92) was adviser and confidential secretary to Duke Ferdinand of Brunswick. A man of middle-class origin, he owed his rise to his abilities alone. His contemporaries spoke of him as a competent administrator and a far-seeing and prudent politician. He never became a soldier but remained a civil official throughout his career, but the victories of Krefeld, Bellinghausen, Warburg, Wilhelmsthal and Minden were his handiwork. Philipp Westphalen was the Duke's real chief of staff during the Seven Years' War. Delbrück, the military historian, describes him as the Gneisenau of the Seven Years' War, and Bernhardi calls him the leading spirit of Ferdinand's staff. He was a gifted writer, and his notes are among the most important historical sources for the period.

The King of England esteemed the German so highly that he appointed him adjutant-general of his army. Westphalen, with the national pride that distinguished him and later frequently brought him into conflict with the fawning courtiers of the Guelf court, declined the honour. In the end he only accepted ennoblement at the hands of the house of Brunswick in order to be able to marry the woman of his choice.

He met her when she was on a visit to her uncle, General Beckwith, commander of the English-Hanoverian army, which helped Duke Ferdinand in the struggle against the French. Jeanie Wishart of Pitarrow came of the family of the Earls of Argyll who played such a big role in the history of Scotland, particularly during the Reformation and the Great Rebellion.

One of her forefathers, George Wishart, was burned at the stake as a Protestant in 1547 and a little later another, Earl Archibald Argyll, mounted the scaffold in Edinburgh as a rebel against King James II.

The younger branch of the family, to which Jeanie Wishart of Pitarrow belonged – she was the fifth child of George Wishart, an Edinburgh minister – also produced a number of prominent men. William Wishart, Jenny's great-grand-father, accompanied the Prince of Orange to England, and his brother was the celebrated Admiral James Wishart. Jenny's grandmother, Anne Campbell of Orchard, wife of the minister, belonged to the old Scottish aristocracy too.

Ludwig von Westphalen, the youngest son of this German-Scottish marriage, was born on 11 July 1770. He was his mother's favourite child. She survived her husband by twenty years and lived with her son until her death. He was an exceptionally learned man. He spoke English, his second native tongue, as well as German, and could read Latin, Greek, Italian, French and Spanish. Marx used to remember with pleasure how old Westphalen would recite whole hymns of Homer by heart. It was from her father that Jenny and Karl learned to love Shakespeare, a love they preserved all their lives and handed on to their children.

Marx was sincerely attached to Jenny's father, his 'paternal friend'. The words with which he dedicated the thesis for his doctor's degree proceeded from a thankful heart. 'May all who are in doubt', he wrote,

have the good fortune that I have had and be able to look up with admiration to an old man who retains his youthful vigour and welcomes every advance of the times with enthusiasm and passion for truth and an idealism which, bright as sunshine and proceed-ing from deep conviction, recognizes only the word of truth before which all the spirits of the world appear, and never shrinks back from the retrograde ghosts which obscure the gloomy sky, but, full of godlike energy and with manly, confident glance, penetrates all the chrysalis changes of the world and sees the empyrean with-in. You, my paternal friend, provided me always with a living *argumentum ad oculos* that idealism is not a figment of the imagination but a truth.[2]

For a man with an outlook of that kind there was not much scope in the German states of his time. Little bound him to the hereditary Brunswick Guelf dynasty. He had no hesitation in entering the service of the Napoleonic kingdom of Westphalen. His son and biographer, Ferdinand von Westphalen, tried to attribute this step to his concern for the well-being of his family, but this cannot be accepted as a satisfactory explanation. His family always had been prosperous and was still prosperous at the time, and, besides, Ludwig von Westphalen proved sufficiently a few years later that he was willing to make greater sacrifices for his convictions than that involved in declining an official position. The kingdom of Westphalia was such a notable advance on the feudal state, and so full of beneficial reforms in every respect, that a man as sensitive to the demands of the time as Ludwig von Westphalen could not hesitate a moment in choosing whether to serve a fossilized petty princeling or the brother of the emperor of the world.

In the realm of King Jerome, just as in the Rhineland, the popularity of the new régime, at first widespread among middle classes and peasants alike, dwindled away, to be replaced by aversion and ultimately bitter hostility. With every increase in the taxes necessary to finance the never-ending war, with every new calling-up of recruits, hostility grew. In 1813 Westphalen, then sub-prefect of the *arrondissement* of Salzwedel in the department of the Elbe, was arrested by order of Marshal Davout because of his hostility to the French régime and confined in the fortress of Gifhorn. He was only freed by the troops of the allies.

He was confirmed in the office of administrative head of the district by the Prussians and remained in Salzwedel for another three years. In 1816 he was promoted and transferred to Trier, which became his and his family's second home.[3]

Westphalen's first wife, Elisabeth von Veltheim, was descended from the old Prussian aristocracy and died young, in 1807, leaving four children. Two daughters were brought up by her relatives. They grew up far from their father and he only went to see them occasionally. Ferdinand, the elder of the two sons, stayed in Salzwedel until he left school and then went to live with his sisters. His father had practically no influence upon his upbringing. He grew up in a thoroughly reactionary environment to be a thorough reactionary himself – arrogant, narrow-minded and bigoted. He actually became Prussian Minister of the Interior, and in the most reactionary cabinet that Prussia ever had he was the most reactionary of them all. Friedrich Wilhelm IV, the 'romantic on the throne', was later very friendly with him.[4]

Ludwig von Westphalen's second wife was Karoline Heubel, daughter of a minor Prussian official from the Rhineland. She was a clever and courageous woman. A picture of her in her old age, with her large, gleaming eyes, enables one to see how beautiful she was in her youth. There were three children of this marriage. Jenny, the eldest, was born at Salzwedel on 12 February 1814. The next child was a daughter, of whom no more is known, and the third was a son, Edgar, born in 1819.

Jenny, who later had to endure poverty in its shabbiest form – for in London there was no money to buy a coffin for her dead child – had a happy and carefree childhood. Her parents were rich.

Ludwig von Westphalen's salary in the early 1820s was 1,600 thalers a year, which was a great deal at that time and place, and in addition there was the yield of a respectable estate. At that time two good furnished rooms could be rented at Trier for from six to seven thalers a month, and the price of a four-course dinner every day for a whole month was from six to seven thalers. The Westphalens occupied a sumptuous house with a big garden in one of the best streets of Trier.

Heinrich Marx and his family lived next door. In a small town like Trier everybody knows practically everybody else. Children living in neighbouring houses know each other best of all. Jenny's favourite playmate was Karl's elder sister, Sophie. Edgar, who was scarcely a year younger than Karl, sat next to him on the same school bench. Westphalen, himself half-German and half-Scottish, had no national or racial prejudices. Lessing was one of his favourite authors. That Heinrich Marx had only recently become a Christian worried him not at all. The children made friends and the fathers followed suit. The Marx children played in the Westphalens' garden, and in his old age Edgar von Westphalen still remembered with pleasure the friendly greeting that old Marx always had for him and his sisters.

A close friendship sprang up between old Westphalen and Karl Marx. The old man – he was in his seventies – used to enjoy wandering 'over our wonderfully picturesque hills and woods' with the young schoolboy. Of the talks that they had on these occasions Marx was fondest of recalling those in which Westphalen awakened in him his first interest in the character and teachings of Saint-Simon. Marx's father was a Kantian. The pedigree of scientific socialism according to Friedrich Engels is well known: 'We German socialists are proud of being descended, not only from Saint-Simon, Fourier and Owen but from Kant, Fichte and Hegel as well.'[5]

Laura Lafargue burned the whole of the correspondence between her parents. We do not know when the love-affair between the two young people first began, and we believe it to be a waste of time to try and find out from the rare and obliterated traces that are left. At the time of Marx's death an old inhabitant of Trier could still remember 'lovely Jenny' and Marx, the young student, whom he recollected as 'practically the ugliest human being whom the sun could ever have shone on'. An older friend of his, he said, still used to speak ardently of the charming, bewitching creature, and neither he nor anybody else could understand how her choice had possibly managed to fall upon Marx. True, he admitted that Marx's early demonstrated talent and force of character and his prepossessing ways with women made up for his ugly exterior. One seems to hear the voice of a spurned suitor in all this.

Karl's father was at first the only person to know of the secret engagement. He knew his son too well not to know

that it was useless to forbid him something which Karl would
certainly not have allowed himself to be forbidden. He expressed what reassured him in his letters to his son. He admonished him in this affair, as in all others, to be as candid
with his father as with a friend, to test himself rigorously and,
above all, to be mindful of man's sacred duty to the weaker
sex. Karl, if he persisted in his decision, must become a man at
once. Six weeks later he wrote again :

> I have spoken to Jenny, and I should have liked to have been able
> to reassure her completely. I did my uttermost, but I could not
> talk everything away. I do not know how her parents will take
> it. The judgement of relatives and of the world is after all no
> trifle ... She is making a priceless sacrifice for you. She is mani-
> festing a self-denial which cold reason alone can fully appreciate.
> Woe betide you if ever in your life you forget it! You must look
> into your heart alone. The sure, certain knowledge that in spite of
> your youth you are a man, deserving the world's respect, nay,
> fighting and earning it, giving assurance of your steadfastness and
> future earnest striving, and imposing silence on evil tongues for
> past mistakes, must proceed from you alone.[6]

At the time of his engagement Karl Marx was an eighteen-
year-old student with numerous inclinations and a highly
uncertain future. As the second son of a numerous family,
with no considerable financial prospects to look forward to,
he would have to fight for his own place in the world, and he
would need a number of years for the purpose. Jenny, four
years older than he, was the daughter of a rich and noble
state official, the 'prettiest girl in Trier', the 'queen of the ball'.[7]
When Marx visited Trier in 1863 he found Jenny still survived
in old people's memories as the 'fairy princess'. The engagement conflicted with all the prejudices of the bourgeois and
noble world.

Karl had to 'become a man at once'. In the middle of October he went to Berlin and plunged head over heels into his
books. In order to marry it was necessary to complete his
studies as quickly as possible, pass his examinations and find
a job. In the meantime all Jenny could do was wait. She was

twenty-two years old. Many of her friends were married, and the rest were engaged. She rejected all her suitors – officers, landed proprietors and government officials. People in Trier started to talk.

As long as Karl had been in Trier what people said did not worry Jenny. When she grew afraid he had been there to support her, full of courage and plans for the future. She believed in him, in his future and hers. But when he went she was alone. Nobody must notice anything, she must laugh gaily, pay visits, go to dances, as behoved a girl of marriageable age belonging to the best society. Karl's father and his sister Sophie were her only confidants. With them she could talk openly of her love and of her anxieties.

The two persons dearest to Marx, Jenny and his father, were often filled with anxiety for the future. His father wrote to him at the beginning of March 1837 and said that though from time to time his heart delighted in thoughts of him and of the future, he could not shake off anxious and gloomy forebodings when the thought struck him: Was Karl's heart in conformity with his head, his capacity? Was there room for the earthly but tender feelings so consolatory to the man of feeling in this vale of tears? Karl's heart was clearly possessed by a daemon it was not granted everybody to be possessed by, but was the nature of this daemon divine or Faustian? Would Karl – and this doubt was not the least painful of those that afflicted his father's heart – ever be susceptible of a true, human, domestic happiness? Would Karl – and this doubt, since he had recently begun to love a certain person not less than his own child, was no less tormenting – ever be in a position to bring happiness into his most immediate surroundings? He felt sorry for Jenny. Jenny, who with her pure, childish disposition was so utterly devoted to Karl, was from time to time a victim, against her will, of a kind of fear, heavy with foreboding, that he could not explain.[8]

In another letter six months later he wrote: 'You can be certain, and I myself am certain, that no prince could estrange her from you. She cleaves to you body and soul, and she is making a sacrifice for you of which most girls are certainly not capable. That is something you must never forget.'⁹

Jenny waited impatiently for Karl's letters. They came rarely. Marx was never a very good correspondent. To make up for it, at Christmas 1836 Jenny received a volume of poems, *The Book of Love,* dedicated to his 'dear, ever-beloved Jenny von Westphalen'. Sophie wrote to her brother that when Jenny came to see Marx's parents on the day after Christmas 'she wept tears of joy and pain when she was given the poems'.

The three volumes of *The Book of Love* have long since vanished. What survives[10] of Marx's poetical attempts – two poems published in a periodical, the *Athenäum*, a volume of poems dedicated to his father, scenes from *Oulanem,* a tragedy, and some chapters from *Scorpion and Felix,* a novel in the manner of Sterne – justify the harsh judgement that Marx himself passed on them. He described them as sentiment wildly and formlessly expressed, completely lacking in naturalness and entirely woven out of moonshine, with rhetorical reflections taking the place of poetical feeling. All the same he granted them a certain warmth and straining after vital rhythm.[11]

Jenny's position became more and more intolerable. She hesitated when his father suggested that Karl should reveal the secret and ask her parents for her hand. She seems to have been worried by the difference in age between herself and Karl. Eventually she agreed to Karl's father's suggestion and Karl wrote to Trier. How the demand for her hand was received we do not know. There seem to have been difficulties and some opposition, the leader of which is sure to have been Ferdinand, the subsequent Prussian Minister of the Interior, who had just been transferred to an official position in Trier, where he was soon noted for his 'great zeal and moderate intelligence'.

Eventually Jenny's parents gave their consent. At the end of 1837, Karl Heinrich Marx, a student nineteen years of age, became officially engaged to Jenny von Westphalen.

[4]

Student Years in Berlin

THERE were 700 students at Bonn, but several thousand in Berlin. Bonn, in spite of spies and informers, was a pleasant, patriarchal provincial town, in which it was not easy to get away from the usual students' round, with its taverns and duels. The University of Berlin, compared to the other universities in Germany, was a 'workhouse' compared to a 'tavern', to quote Ludwig Feuerbach.

At that period Berlin still retained many relics of the times of the Brandenburg electors. The walls still surrounded the old town, and the old towers, only the names of which remain today, were still standing. Gardens, meadows and fields still made deep inroads into the maze of narrow, crooked alleys. Schöneberg was still the wooded 'beautiful mountain', and the unpretentious houses of the Nollendorfs still stood on the Nollendorfplatz, which teems with traffic today. It lagged behind the young industrial towns of the Rhineland in economic and social development, but with its 300,000 inhabitants it was second only to Vienna, the biggest town on German-speaking territory, and was the first big town that Marx became acquainted with.

He matriculated in the faculty of law on 22 October 1837, took a modest room in the Mittelstrasse, not far from the university, and reluctantly proceeded to pay calls upon a few influential friends of his father's to whom he had been given introductions, and then cut himself off from all social intercourse. He saw no one and spoke to no one.

Bonn had taught him that an attractive title to a course of lectures is not always a reliable guide to its contents. In his first term he attended only three courses of lectures – by Steffens, the philosopher, on anthropology, Savigny on jurisprudence and Gans on criminal law.[1]

Gans and Savigny, the two stars of the university, were bitter opponents. Friedrich Karl Savigny was the founder and principal theorist of the school of historical jurisprudence which rejected the conception of natural right as an empty abstraction and regarded law as something concrete arising out of the spirit and historical development of a nation. This boiled down in practice to a simple sanctification of everything handed down from the past. The ideologist of the Christian-German state had discerned the revolutionary implications of the philosophy of Hegel at a time when the ruling powers still regarded it as absolutism's strongest possible support.

His most important adversary was Eduard Gans. Hegel had summoned the young scholar, who possessed a gift of eloquence not granted to other lecturers, to the faculty of jurisprudence. Gans was not a thinker of special originality. All his life he remained faithful to his great teacher's system, but he went his own way in the conclusions he drew from Hegel's fundamental principles. In opposition to the school of historical law that looked towards the past, he set up Saint-Simonistic ideas looking towards the future. He had a glowing enthusiasm for the complete freeing of the human personality, an enthusiasm for all plans which had as their goal the complete reconstruction of society. His controversy with Savigny was more than merely a legal one. It assumed a philosophical, actually a political character.

After the death of Hegel in 1831 Gans lectured on history as well as law, the history of the French Revolution and its salutary effects on the rest of Europe in particular. The big lecture hall was filled to overflowing by his audience. His lectures were attended not only by students but by officials, officers, men of letters, 'the whole of Berlin', in fact everyone who was still concerned for political and social questions in those fusty times. They came to listen to the free speech of a free man.

The fact that the university was freedom's only sanctuary was one of the principal factors in its importance. Gans once took a French scholar round Berlin. In Unter den Linden he showed him the building next to the university. 'Look!' he said. 'The university next to the arsenal. That is the symbol of Prussia.' Prussia was an enormous barracks. A narrow and spiteful censorship waged a pitiless war on intellectual freedom. It was a time when a censor (he was the one with whom Marx was destined to tussle when editor of the *Rheinische Zeitung*) suppressed an advertisement of a translation of Dante's *Divine Comedy* by 'Philalethes', the later King John of Saxony, with the comment that 'no comedy should be made of divine things'. A police régime of the pettiest kind hampered the citizen's activities in every direction and made his life increasingly intolerable. Only at the university was there a modicum of freedom of speech. Gans was one of the few who made real use of his academic freedom. He expressed opinions and praised the French Revolution in his lectures in a way he could not possibly have done in books.

Savigny and Steffens testified to the zeal with which Marx listened to them, and Gans's report on him was that he was 'exceptionally industrious'.

Marx, obliged to study law, felt, to use his own expression, 'above all an urge to wrestle with philosophy'. He made up his mind to combine philosophy and law. He worked through the sources and the commentaries and translated the first two books of the Pandects – 'absolutely uncritically and just like a schoolboy', as he wrote to his father in retrospect. He worked at a 300-page philosophy of law, covering the whole territory of the law, only to see at the end that 'without philosophy nothing could be accomplished'. In addition he made excerpts from works on the history of art, translated Latin classics, started studying English and Italian in order at the end of term 'once more to search for the dance of the Muses and the music of the satyrs'. These poems, he wrote to his father, were the only ones in which he 'caught a glimpse, as if by the touch of a magic wand, of the realm of true poetry as a distant fairy palace', and 'all his creations fell away to nothing'.

'What with all these activities, in my first term I stayed up many nights, fought many battles, experienced much internal and external excitement. In the end I emerged not very much enriched, having neglected nature and art, and rejected friendships.' His health had been seriously affected in the process, but he did not spare himself but cast himself once more into the arms of philosophy. Once more he wanted to 'plunge into the ocean, but with the firm intention of finding mental nature to be necessarily just as concretely and firmly grounded as physical nature . . . my aim was to search for the idea in real things themselves.' Marx had read fragments of the Hegelian philosophy, whose 'grotesque, craggy melody' he had not found to his taste. He wrote a dialogue entitled 'Cleanthes, or the point of departure and necessary progress of philosophy', a philosophical-dialectical treatment of divinity as manifested as an idea in itself, as religion and as history, only to find at the end that his dearest child had been 'nursed in moonshine, and that it was as if a false siren had carried it in her arms and handed it over to the enemy'. His last sentence was the beginning of the Hegelian system. Mortification at finding himself forced to bend the knee to a philosophical system that he hated made him ill. During his indisposition he read Hegel from beginning to end, and most of Hegel's pupils as well, and 'chained himself firmly and more firmly still to the present philosophy of the world from which he had thought to escape'.[2] By the late summer of 1837 he had become an Hegelian.

He was living at the time at Stralau, a country place near Berlin, where the doctor had sent him. Fresh air, plenty of walks and a healthier life enabled him to 'ripen from a pale-faced weakling to robust bodily vigour'. Moreover, it was at Stralau that he met the men who introduced him to the 'Doktorklub' and played a great part in the next stage of his development.

The Doktorklub had been founded a few years previously. There were no tavern clubs or local students' associations in Berlin. Students who were in sympathy with one another met on fixed days at inns and coffee-houses, which in Berlin were also reading-rooms. In one of these inns in the Französischestrasse there met regularly a number of students and young graduates united by a similar interest in literary and philosophical questions. In the course of time these meetings took on the character of an informal club and they were transferred to private premises where there would be no undesired guests and more open speech was possible. 'In this circle of ambitious young men', a member of the Doktorklub wrote in his reminiscences,

there reigned that spirit of idealism, that enthusiastic urge for knowledge, that liberal spirit that still so thoroughly animated the youth of that time. Poems and other work done by us used to be read aloud and criticized at our meetings, but our special interest was the philosophy of Hegel, which was still in its prime and held sway more or less over the whole educated world, though individual voices had already been raised against the system and a split between the right and the left had already become perceptible in the ranks of the Hegelians themselves.[3]

Marx became a frequent visitor to the club, and through it he made numerous acquaintances in Berlin literary and scientific circles including Bettina von Arnim, the last Romantic, in whose *salon* in Unter den Linden the most varied society met – young writers and old generals, liberals and conservatives, ministers and Jewish journalists, believers and atheists. Marx does not seem to have been a frequent guest of Bettina's, and in his poems he wrote a pointed epigram about the 'newfangled Romantic'. Bettina remembered the young student well. When she came to Trier in 1838 (or 1839) he had to accompany her on all her excursions. Marx only had a week to spend in his native town, and was left with practically no time to talk to Jenny at all.[4]

The university became unimportant for Marx. True, he had to attend the prescribed lectures, the lectures essential for a law student if he were to pass his examinations, but more than that he did not do. In the eight terms he spent in Berlin after the summer of 1837 he only attended seven courses of lectures, and for three whole terms he attended no lectures at all. His interests were now confined to philosophy. Some of his notebooks of this period have been preserved. They are full of excerpts from Aristotle, Spinoza, Leibniz, Bacon, and other philosophical classics.[5]

The political undercurrents of the time masqueraded, were forced to masquerade, as philosophical schools of thought. Division appeared in the Hegelian camp. The 'Old' Hegelians remained loyal to the system and conservative ideals of the older Hegel, while the 'Young' Hegelians laid even greater stress on the revolutionary elements in the Hegelian method, on the Hegelian dialectic, which regards nothing as permanent but everything as flowing or becoming, recognizes the contradiction in everything and is thus the 'algebra of the revolution'. The breach between the two schools of thought became wider and wider and the Doktorklub was in the very midst of the rising battle. The challenging Young Hegelian group began to crystallize out of it. Its most important representatives were Adolf Rutenberg, Karl Friedrich Köppen and Bruno Bauer.[6]

Marx met Rutenberg first, and it was probably Rutenberg who introduced him to the Doktorklub. In November 1837 he was calling him his most intimate friend. Rutenberg was a former Burschenschafter, and had served long sentences in Prussian prisons. He became a lecturer in geography and history at the Cadet School but was soon dismissed because of the unfavourable influence he was said to exercise on his pupils and because of the liberal newspaper correspondence he wrote. He became a professional writer. He was somewhat superficial, not overweighted with learning, and an easy and quick writer, and soon came to occupy a foremost position among the publicists of Berlin. Political journalism, properly so-called, did not exist in the Germany of the 1830s. The draconic censorship alone was sufficient to nip it in the bud. An inadequate substitute was provided by the general correspondence with which the journalists of Berlin kept the provincial Press supplied. There was very little in this correspondence. It contained few facts and still fewer ideas, but that left all the more scope for liberal expressions and veiled hints about the remarkable things the writer would be able to disclose were the sword of Damocles, i.e. the censorship, not dangling over his head. During the period in question these letters from the capital fulfilled a definite need. They expressed the elementary interests of society and strengthened the elementary protest against the ruling powers. Rutenberg was one of the most prominent representatives of this type of journalism, and as such he had a certain importance in Marx's life. At the beginning of 1842 he was appointed editor of the *Rheinische Zeitung*. In this position, when he had to prove himself as a genuine publicist for the first time, he was a complete failure. He was not fit for more than writing Berlin letters full of veiled hints. Rutenberg sank lower and lower and ended up in doubtful hole-and-corner journalism.

Karl Friedrich Köppen was a man of entirely different stamp. He, like Rutenberg, was a history master by profession, but was a man of real learning and scholarship, with a solid and extensive knowledge in many fields. At the same time he was of a modest and retiring disposition, with no aptitude whatever for placing himself in the limelight, unlike Rutenberg, who was very skilled at it indeed. Köppen's chief work, an account of Lamaism, has in many respects not been superseded to this day. He was the first German historian to put forward an unprejudiced view of the Terror in the French Revolution. Even some of his letters on transitory themes have preserved their value. Those he wrote about Berlin University are still prized by scholars and specialists. It is only as a politician and a pioneer of the socialist movement that Köppen is still not appreciated according to his deserts. He took an active part in the formatioin of the first workers' organizations in Berlin in 1848 and 1849. When the reaction set in he was one of the few intellectuals who continued working in the workers' clubs in spite of the severe penalties he had to suffer. Köppen remained true to his ideals, and his friendship with Marx survived all the vicissitudes of life. When Marx visited him in Berlin in 1861 he found him 'the old Köppen still'. He wrote to Engels that the two occasions he 'pub-crawled' with him really did him good.[7]

The most important member of the group was Bruno Bauer, a lecturer in theology. A contemporary describes him thus:

Somewhat small in build and of medium height, his demeanour is calm and he confronts you with a confident, serene smile; his frame is compact, and you observe with great interest the fine but definite features of his face, the boldly protruding, angular and finely pointed nose, the high-arched brow, the fine-cut mouth, the almost napoleonic figure.[8]

Generally distracted and absent-minded, with his gaze directed into space – Rutenberg's children always used to say that Uncle Bauer was looking into Africa – he used to liven up in argument. His wide erudition, his gift of precise definition, his irony and the boldness of his thought made Bauer the chosen leader of the Young Hegelian movement. It was not till later, when the time came to proceed from analysis to synthesis and establish positive, practical aims that he failed. He remained the critic; and criticism for criticism's sake, 'absolute criticism', became for him an end in itself. But at the end of the 1830s and the beginning of the forties, when the times demanded criticism of the old and the shattering of ancient idols, Bruno Bauer was in the very forefront of the battle.

In 1837, when Marx joined the group, Young Hegelianism was just coming into existence. David Friedrich Strauss had published his *Life of Jesus* two years before. It was the first Hegelian onslaught on the foundations of official religion. It is somewhat difficult today to realize its full significance. Society of that day was divided into strata. It was a rigid framework, resting solely on the sanction of religion, and reason had to adapt itself to it in all modesty and humility as to something willed by God. As long as the foundation on which it rested, namely the principle of divine revelation, stood intact, all criticism of any detail of the social structure was impotent. But any thrust at that principle that went home shook the whole structure to its depths.

Before Strauss, Hegelian philosophy had peacefully and harmoniously cohabited with religion. Certainly it was only a marriage of prudence, but from the point of view of the old world it was a highly useful and convenient one. Strauss was the first to disturb this harmonious bliss. Everybody immediately realized that it forestalled a general attack on the whole position. Marx wrote a few years later:

Criticism of religion is the hypothesis of all criticism. The foundation of irreligious criticism is that man makes religion and religion does not make man. But man is no abstract being lurking somewhere outside and apart from the world. Man means the world of men, the state, society. Religion, which is a distorted outlook on the world because the world is itself distorted, as the product of the state and of society. Religion is a fantastic materialization of the human entity, because the human entity has no true reality. Hence the fight against religion is a direct fight against a world the spiritual aroma of which it is.[9]

Strauss found anything but support among the Hegelians of Berlin. The essays published by Bruno Bauer in 1835 and 1836 were among the most trenchant of the attacks that were made on him. Bauer flatly denied the right of philosophy to criticize Christian dogma, and he did so with such dogmatism and violence that Strauss confidently predicted that he would end up in the camp of the extreme bigots. Bauer took a different path, however, and it was the bigots who forced him down it. Apart from the fact that their attack was directed at the philosophy of Hegel, which a Hegelian like Bauer was necessarily obliged to defend, the God whom they so martially proclaimed was not the mild Jesus of the Sermon on the Mount but the gloomy, vindictive Jehovah of the Old Testament. Their holy book was the Old Testament far more than the New, and it was this that set Bauer on his critical tack.

He made his début in this direction in 1837 and 1838; at a time, that is to say, when Marx had become a member of the Doktorklub. Marx took part in the development of Young Hegelianism which originated in the club; moreover, he was, as far as we can tell – unfortunately there is no period of Marx's life about which we are so badly informed – one of the most active and progressive spirits in its development. He took his place at the most extreme wing from the start. Ruthless consistency was a characteristic at the very beginning of his independent intellectual life. At the end of 1836 he expressed his views about law in a letter to his father, who replied: 'Your views about law are not without truth, but systematized they would be very calculated to cause storms.'[10] The ageing Trier lawyer had lived through the storms of the French Revolution and the Napoleonic Wars, and yearned for peace and quiet. His son liked storms and looked out for them, though for the time being in the realm of intellectual conflict only.

Most of the members of the Doktorklub were older than Marx, and many of them were much older. That did not prevent them from accepting him as an equal practically from the first. As early as 1837, when he was a student of nineteen and was nursing the idea of founding a literary paper, his friends Rutenberg and Bauer were able to assure him that 'all the aesthetic celebrities of the Hegelian school' were willing to collaborate.[11] The club used to meet often, either in private houses or in small inns in the neighbourhood of the university. For a short time it met every day. The books and essays to which it gave birth demonstrate its breadth of interests and the rapid development through which it passed.

At first the chief subject of discussion was religion. To begin with the battle raged round the question of the distortion of true Christianity by mythology and the assimilation of Christianity to the conclusions of contemporary philosophy, but it quickly developed into an attack on religion itself. Though the members of the club did not definitely emerge as atheists until 1842, most of them had long been aware of what lay at the end of the road they had embarked upon, and occasionally ceremoniously greeted one another with the jesting appellation of 'Your irreverence'.

In the second half of the 1830s the Government started a drive against Hegelianism, and that drove the Doktorklub into political opposition, though an outward fillip was still required. The Doktorklub gave the initiative at the 'serenade' of students on Gans's birthday in 1838. The celebrations were intended to honour in Gans the sturdy champion, not only of the Hegelian tradition, but also of the seven Göttingen professors who, to the applause of the whole of Germany, had preferred sacrificing their office to taking an oath of loyalty to the King of Hanover who had abolished the constitution. But, so far as the club was concerned, being in political opposition was still far from involving them in taking an active part in contemporary life. Rutenberg was the only one who demanded that they should take the plunge into contemporary life. His insistence that the time had come to abandon fruitless 'brooding' and pass from the world of theory to the world of action was answered by Bauer, who maintained that there could be no question yet of their direct participation in the life of the time. Before they could have any practical influence upon the world, and that in the near future, they must, in his view, effect an intellectual revolution in men's minds. There was no other way. Marx shared Bauer's opinion. The old must be intellectually annihilated before it could be annihilated on the material plane. The alteration of the world would necessarily follow from the new interpretation put upon it by philosophers. In other words a virtue was made of impotence. This earned the club the following lampoon in classical metre:

> Unsere Taten sind Worte bis jetzt und noch lang
> Hinter die Abstraktion stellt sich die Praxis von selbst.*

Bruno Bauer was still faithful to this view when he moved from Berlin to Bonn in 1838. In 1840 and 1841 the Berlin group moved faster and faster towards the left. In the summer of 1840 an observer characterized it as 'thoroughly devoted to the idea of constitutional monarchy'. Köppen wrote his book on *Frederick the Great and his Opponents* and dedicated it to 'his friend Karl Heinrich Marx of Trier'.[12] Köppen honoured

---

* So far our deeds are all words and are like to remain so;
  Abstractions we have in our minds are bound to come true of
  themselves.

Frederick, 'in whose spirit we swore to live and die', as the enemy of Christian-German reaction. His basic idea was that the state was embodied in its purest form in a monarchy ruled over by a monarch like Frederick, a philosopher, a free servant of the world spirit. Renewal could only come from the top.

The phase of liberal constitutional monarchism soon ran its course. By the winter of 1840–41 the club were calling themselves 'friends of the people', and their theoretical position was therefore at the extreme left wing of revolutionary republicanism. Rutenberg in his Berlin letters compared the so-called reading rooms of Berlin with the Paris coffee-houses on the eve of the revolution and Köppen wrote his essays on the Terror. The club had begun 'direct' participation in contemporary life.

During this period Marx published nothing, and no manuscripts dating from these years have been preserved. His share in the intellectual life of the club, and it was an important one, was only expressed indirectly in the writings of others. It appears from a letter Köppen wrote to Marx on 3 June 1841 that many of the ideas expressed by Bruno Bauer in his essay on 'The Christian State and Our Times', one of the first in which political deductions were drawn from religious criticism, were Marx's. Köppen remarked that as long as Marx was in Berlin he had no 'personal, so to speak, self-thought thoughts of his own'; which was obviously a very friendly and highly exaggerated piece of self-depreciation, but at the same time gives a clue to how much Marx was able to give his friends. They treasured him as 'a warehouse of thoughts, a workshop of ideas'. Marx lived in their memories as the 'young lion', combative, turbulent, quick-witted, as bold in posing problems as in solving them. In the *Christliches Heldengedicht*, written in 1842, after Marx had left Berlin, Marx appeared as the club remembered him:

> Wer jaget hinterdrein mit wildem Ungestüm?
> Ein schwarzer Kerl aus Trier, ein markhaft Ungetüm.
> Er gehet, hüpfet nicht, er springet auf den Hacken
> Und raset voller Wut und gleich als wollt' er packen
> Das weite Himmelszelt und zu der Erde ziehn

Streckt er die Arme sein weit in die Lüfte hin.
Geballt die böse Faust, so tobt er sonder Rasten,
Als wenn ihn bei den Schopf zehntausend Teufel fassten.*[13]

It must not be supposed that the Doktorklub confined itself to bringing together a collection of academic intellectuals for the purpose of philosophical discussion only. Most of its members were young, exuberant and always ready for mischief. Protest against the crass philistinism that surrounded them and the absurd, petty regimentation of personal life by the police occasionally broke out in unruly forms. Bruno Bauer appears in the police records as a 'heavy drinker' and Rutenberg was reported to have taken part in street fights. Edgar Bauer, a younger brother of Bruno, was punished for ostentatiously smoking in the street, which was forbidden by the police. Liebknecht describes in his memoirs how Marx celebrated a reunion with Edgar Bauer in London in the 1850s. They engaged in a 'pub crawl' and not a single tavern on their route was allowed to remain unvisited. When they could drink no longer they started throwing stones at the street lamps under cover of darkness and went on until the police came and they had to run. Marx developed a turn of speed no one had thought him capable of. He was nearly forty at the time, father of a numerous family, author of works of far-reaching importance. One can imagine what he must have been capable of in his twenties in Berlin.[14]

Marx, once accepted into the ranks of the Young Hegelians, paid practically no more attention to the university. It had been 'purged'. Eduard Gans, Hegel's most important pupil and the only Hegelian in the faculty of law, died young in 1839. Bauer had to leave the university soon afterwards. He

* Who's this approaching who thus rants and raves?
  'Tis the wild fury, black-maned Marx of Treves;
  See him advance, nay spring upon the foe
  As though to seize and never let him go.
  See him extend his threatening arms on high
  To seize the heavenly canopy from the sky;
  See his clenched fists, and see his desperate air,
  As though ten thousand devils had him by the hair.

was unspeakably obnoxious to the pietists, and all that Alten-
stein, Minister of Public Worship and Education, who was
favourably inclined towards the Hegelians, was able to do for
him was to have him transferred to Bonn. Reactionaries were
installed in the Hegelians' places. Gans's chair was filled by
Julius Stahl, theorist of Prussian absolutism, who in the 1850s
became a practitioner of it as well. The extreme bigots, the
people whom Hegel had described a few years previously as
the 'rabble' with whom he had to 'tussle', set the tone in the
university.

With the accession of King Friedrich Wilhelm IV the Chris-
tian-Romantic reaction set in in full force. He who did not bow
and hold peace was visited with exemplary punishment. Of
academic freedom no trace was left. The university became an
annexe of the barracks.

In his first student years Marx had had hopes of becoming
a university lecturer at Berlin. This was impossible now. He
could not even expect to take his doctor's degree at the university. His thesis would have to be submitted to Stahl, against
whom the students – with Marx certainly among them – had
noisily demonstrated when he was appointed to Gans's place.
As Varnhagen noted in his diary, this was the first outward
opposition to the new Government.

Marx's father died in May 1838. During the last year the
family's material position had been worsening. In Trier Jenny
was waiting. And on the other side Bruno Bauer was urging
his friend to hurry. It was time to put a stop to his 'shilly-
shallying' and end his 'wearisome vacillation about the sheer,
nonsensical farce of his examinations'. Marx, he said, should
come to Bonn, where he would find things easy. At Bonn he
would be able to get a lectureship. The professors at Bonn
knew they were no philosophers and that the students wanted
to hear philosophy. 'Come here and the new battle will begin.'
Marx doubted whether everything would turn out to be so
easy at Bonn as Bauer hoped. He was far more engrossed with
a project for founding a philosophical journal, about which he
had been conducting an earnest correspondence with Bauer,

than with the prospect of a lectureship at Bonn. But he was not yet willing to give up hope of overcoming the obstacles and being able to teach at Bonn by his friend's side.

On 30 March 1841 he received his leaving certificate from Berlin University. On 6 April he sent to Jena a dissertation on 'The difference between the natural philosophies of Democrites and the Epicureans'.[15] Certain negotiations appear to have preceded this step. The University of Jena was celebrated at the time for the readiness with which it granted doctors' degrees. It lived up to its reputation. A week later the dean of Jena University presented the candidate Karl Heinrich Marx to the faculty of philosophy. The diploma was dated 15 April. Marx's official student years were at an end.[16]

[5]

Philosophy Under Censorship

THE whole of the politics of an absolute state are embodied in the person of the reigning monarch. The more flagrantly his policy contradicts the interests of the classes excluded from government, the more conscious they are of their impotence to break their ruler's power, the more longingly they direct their gaze towards the heir to the throne. Upon him they rely for the fulfilment of all their hopes. With him, or so they whisper to themselves, the great new era will begin. The greater their expectations, the more bitter their disappointment when the new régime turns out to be nothing but a bare sequel of the old.

As Crown Prince, Friedrich Wilhelm IV had been the hope of many. They had taken seriously the high-sounding phrases concerning liberty and national unity that had flowed so easily from his lips, however vague and indefinite the phrases had been. They had expected that when once he was king the era of long-demanded reforms would open. When he ascended the throne new political life awakened on every side, and everyone sent him petitions and demands, expecting them to be fulfilled overnight.

An Augustan age was to begin for Prussia. Everywhere new, fresh forces seemed to be arising; there was germinating and sprouting, and everywhere long-closed buds seemed to be opening in the warm light of the newly arisen sun. A breath of spring went out from Berlin and seemed to spread throughout the fatherland.[1]

The romantic, pious, waywardly intellectual king fulfilled none of the many expectations that were centred upon him. He had proclaimed that there must be freedom of speech, but the new instructions issued to the censor's office provided for no alleviation of his severity. Things remained as they had been before. It was a time when freeing the individual from his traditional ties was the vogue. People's minds were much occupied with the problem of divorce, but the Government settled the matter in its own inimitable way and decided for the *status quo*.

The left-wing Hegelians had had but little faith in the Crown Prince, but even they had not been entirely without hope, as Köppen's writings show. When he became King they were quickly disillusioned. The first blow struck by the new régime fell upon their shoulders. Friedrich Wilhelm IV was a personal friend of Savigny, and Savigny strengthened him in his resolve once and for all to exterminate the godless forces of Hegelianism. He summoned the philosopher Schelling from Munich to Berlin to enable him at last to bring out into the light of day his long-prepared philosophical system, which was but a metaphysical justification of the police state. When the Hegelians tried to combat him the censor suppressed their literary opposition just as ruthlessly as he had done in the past; and thus the men who still to an extent believed that the battle could be fought out on the peaceful plain of theory were driven a stage farther into 'practice', and 'direct participation in life'.

To the Hegelians the dismissal of Bruno Bauer was a still severer blow. To Marx the blow was a personal one. All the plans he had made in his last years at Berlin had been closely bound up with Bruno Bauer. They had wanted to teach together at Bonn, they had wanted to be joint editors of *The Archives of Atheism*, they had intended to do battle together against the enemies of Hegelianism. It was for this reason that Bauer had urged his friend to join him at Bonn at the earliest possible moment. The end of Marx's studies made the proposition a practical one for the first time, but circumstances intervened to make it impossible.

The University of Bonn had two theological schools, Protestant and Catholic, and they had always been bitterly opposed. Each was always ready to go to the assistance of the enemy of the other. The Catholics always supported the not

completely orthodox Protestants and the Protestants always
rallied behind the liberal Catholics. Bruno Bauer counted on
this. Between the pair of hostile brothers he hoped to find
space for his critical annihilation of Christianity. He was disappointed. Catholics and Protestants forgot their ancient feud
and united against their common foe. Pious students, incited
by their teachers, declined as future ministers of religion to go
on listening to the heresies of the 'atheist' lecturer. A Catholic-
Protestant united front, created specially for the purpose,
started making hostile demonstrations against him, free fights
broke out at lectures, and the university authorities strove to
get rid of the disturber of their peace, whom the Ministry of
Public Worship and Education had foisted upon them because
it wanted him out of Berlin.

In the meantime Bauer's standing with the Ministry had
also been seriously impaired. The department had been purged
of its last pro-Hegelians. In April 1841, when Bauer's *Criticism
of the Synoptic Gospels* appeared, Eichhorn, the minister, had
inquired in Bonn whether it would not be possible to withdraw
his right to lecture. But as long as Bauer refrained from political allusions in the lecture-room it was difficult to take any
active steps against him without tearing the last shreds from
the pretence of academic freedom.

The Government found their long-awaited opportunity in
the autumn of 1841. Bauer tied the rope round his own neck
by taking part in the demonstrations that took place in Berlin
in honour of Welcker, who was a professor at Karlsruhe and
leader of the opposition in the Parliament of Baden. Welcker's
journey through Prussia was the signal for an extraordinary
outburst of enthusiasm. The Government well knew that the
banquets and 'serenades' of which he was the occasion were not
in honour of him personally, but in honour of the cause he
represented, i.e. constitutional government and the struggle
against autocracy. The Berlin celebrations were organized by
Bauer's friends, and Bauer was in Berlin at the time. In his
speech at a banquet held on 28 September he drew a contrast
between the Hegelian conception of the reasonable state, con-

sciously understanding its tasks, and the vague spirit of South German liberalism.

The sensation caused by the demonstrations in Welcker's honour, and more particularly by Bauer's speech, was extraordinary. It was talked about for days. The police busied themselves with the 'scandalous' affair and the King ordered a detailed report to be made to him. On 14 October, after reading the report, he wrote a letter to the Minister for Foreign Affairs, insisting that the organizers of the affair be sought out and removed from Berlin, or at least placed under rigorous police supervision. On no account must Bauer be allowed to continue lecturing at Bonn.

The King's letter did its work. Throughout the winter one report was written after another, the affair was exhaustively discussed in the Press, all the universities in Prussia were consulted, and eventually, on 22 March, the verdict the King wanted was delivered. Bruno Bauer left the University of Bonn in May 1842.

Marx followed Bauer's struggle in Bonn with extreme attention, for his own destiny was at stake beside his friend's. If Bauer had to leave the university, an academic career was closed to him as long as Prussia remained the bigoted, reactionary state that it was.

After leaving Berlin University Marx lived partly at Trier, partly at Cologne, partly at Bonn. Only one of his literary plans was realized. The ever-increasing severity of the censorship made it impossible even to think of founding an atheistic periodical. But Bauer's *Posaune des Jüngsten Gerichts über Hegel den Atheisten und Antichristen* did appear and Marx collaborated in it. It appeared anonymously. The writer gave himself out to be a right-thinking Christian and proceeded to demonstrate that the most dangerous enemy of the Christian state was Hegel, because he demolished it from within; and by Hegel he meant Hegel, and not Hegel as interpreted by his misguided pupils; Hegel who had so long passed as a column of the existing order. The deception was so well carried out that at first even men like Arnold Ruge took it for the real thing.

The cat was only let out of the bag by that section of the Press which was friendly to the Hegelians. Every *peasant*,* one paper wrote plainly enough, would understand that the book had not been written by a religious man at all but by an artful rebel. Marx prepared a sequel intended to demonstrate the revolutionary element in Hegel's art teaching. But the censor made it impossible to continue the series of pamphlets which was planned.

The philosophers, whether they wanted it or not, found themselves assailed on every side by the demands of practical, everyday life. Marx went on working at his essay. He wanted to publish it but it never appeared. He stopped, was forced to stop work on it because everything else had become overshadowed by the importance of the plain, practical, political task of coming to grips with the enemy. Marx's essay, 'Remarks on the New Prussian Censorship', written in January and February 1842, the deadliest attack ever made, the sharpest blow ever struck at the brazen profanity of arbitrary despotism, was intended for Ruge's *Deutsche Jahrbücher* but only appeared a year later in the *Anekdota zur neuesten deutschen Philosophie und Publizistik*, which was published in Switzerland.[2]

In April 1842 Marx went to Bonn, where Bauer's fate had already been decided. 'Irritating the devout', shocking the philistine, bursting into peals of laughter in the deadly religious silence, gave them a pleasure which there was now less reason than ever to restrain. Bauer wrote mockingly about it to his brother. He described how he and Marx one day infuriated the excellent citizens of Bonn by appearing in a donkey-cart while everybody was going for a walk. 'The citizens of Bonn looked at us in amazement. We were delighted, and the donkeys brayed.'

In Bonn Marx wrote his first article for the *Rheinische Zeitung*, which had been appearing in Cologne since 1 January 1842, on 'The Proceedings of the Sixth Rhenish Diet ... debate

---

* The German for peasant is *Bauer*.

on the liberty of the Press and the publication of Diet proceedings'.[3]

The Rhine province was economically and politically the most advanced part of Prussia, and its centre was Cologne. In no other part of Germany had industry developed so rapidly or was modern commerce so disseminated. Consciousness of the anachronism of the feudal state developed sooner and more powerfully here than elsewhere among the confident young bourgeoisie. Their economic demands struck everywhere on political impediments, and they recognized comparatively early that these impediments must be removed. If there were no other way, an end must be put to them by force. They required the unity of Germany, which was carved up into thirty-six 'fatherlands' – big, medium, small and pygmy states, each with its own coinage, its own weights and measures, its own customs. Political freedom, the overthrow of the many petty potentates, the unification of Germany into a single big economic unit was their necessary aim.

The centre of the Rhine province was Cologne, where most of the modern industrial undertakings had their headquarters. The most energetic and progressive representatives of the new world which repudiated old Prussia and was hated by it in turn lived there. Cologne was the headquarters of the young intelligentsia arising with and in the midst of the new economic order.

In the course of 1841 a number of young writers, philosophers, merchants and industrialists had gathered into a small, loosely-knit group in Cologne. Camphausen, Mevissen and other future captains of industry belonged to it, besides representatives of the new intelligentsia such as Georg Jung, a member of a rich Dutch family, whose wife was the daughter of a Cologne banker, and Dagobert Oppenheim, brother of the proprietor of the big banking house of Oppenheim and Co.; and writers such as Moses Hess, who was a gifted and versatile man, if too volatile and unstable to make real contributions to the many branches of knowledge he wished to make his own.

Marx made a tremendous impression on the members of

this group when he met them for the first time. This was apparently in July 1841, when he was on his way from Trier to Bonn. Jung spoke of Marx as being 'a quite desperate revolutionary' and having 'one of the acutest minds' he knew.[4] In September 1841 Moses Hess wrote a letter to Berthold Auerbach which was a positive panegyric of Marx. 'You will be delighted to meet a man who is one of our friends here now, though he lives in Bonn, where he will soon be a lecturer', he wrote.

He is a phenomenon who has made a tremendous impression on me, though my interests lie in an entirely different field. In short, you can definitely look forward to meeting the greatest, perhaps the *only real* philosopher now living. Soon, when he makes his début (as a writer as well as in an academic chair) he will draw the eyes of all Germany upon himself. Dr Marx, as my idol is called – he is still a young man (he is at most twenty-four years old) – will give medieval religion and philosophy their last push. He combines the most profound philosophical earnestness with the most biting wit. Think of Rousseau, Voltaire, Holbach, Lessing, Heine and Hegel fused into one – I say *fused*, not just lumped together – and you have Dr Marx.[5]

About this time the Cologne group conceived the project of having a daily paper of their own. Conditions were favourable. Antagonism between Protestant Prussia and the Catholic Rhineland had scarcely diminished during the bare three decades of their amalgamation. In the course of the 1830s Church and state had come into a whole series of conflicts, which were liable to flare up again at any moment. Since the revolutionary upheaval by which the Catholics of Belgium had secured their independence from Protestant Holland, an example that militant sections of the clerical circles in the Rhineland occasionally felt tempted to imitate, the danger inherent in these conflicts was all the greater. The old and widely circulated *Kölnische Zeitung* propagated the Catholic cause with great skill. The Government tried to counter it with a paper of its own, the *Rheinische Allgemeine Zeitung*, which was started in 1841. It met with little success. It was too feeble in every way to compete with the ably conducted *Kölnische Zeitung*.

The Cologne group decided to take the paper over. The response to the appeal to take up shares in the new undertaking far surpassed expectations. 30,000 thalers were subscribed in a short time. In those days that was a very respectable sum of money. Every section of the public having left-wing sympathies of any kind was represented among the subscribers. As a token of the interest the Government took in an anti-ultramontaine organ, even Gerlach, the president of the local administration, was among the shareholders.

The paper did not immediately find its political line. The first editor was intended to have been Friedrich List, whose *National System of Political Economy* had just appeared. In the field of economic theory, List was the first spokesman on behalf of the young bourgeoisie's aspirations for the protection and advancement of industry in an economically independent Germany. But List was ill and recommended Dr Gustav Höfken, one of his disciples, to fill his place. The first number appeared on 1 January 1842. Höfken's policy was for the expansion of the German *Zollverein*, the development of German trade and trade policy, and the liberation of the German consciousness from everything that hampered unity. This did not satisfy the paper's new proprietors. They all belonged to the prosperous and educated bourgeoisie. On the board of directors Rudolf Schramm, the manufacturer's son, sat side by side with wealthy lawyers and doctors. The chief shareholders were leading Cologne industrialists, the most important being Ludolf Camphausen, later Prime Minister of Prussia, one of the pioneers of the railway in Germany. It had long been clear to them that their economic programme could not be realized without a fundamental reorganization of the state. Jung and Oppenheim, the two managers, were Young Hegelians and helped Hess, who was closely associated with the editorial control from the beginning, in finding Young Hegelians to work for the paper. Variances arose with Höfken and on 18 January he resigned.

K.M.—3

Marx already had considerable influence upon the management, especially upon Jung, and it was on his recommendation that his old friend Rutenberg was appointed editor, a position for which he soon proved utterly unsuitable. He could write Young Hegelian articles, but he was simply not equipped for the task of controlling a great political newspaper, which was what the *Rheinische Zeitung* was increasingly becoming every day. From the middle of February onwards the real editor was Moses Hess.[6]

Changes of editorship did not impede the paper's expansion. Its circulation doubled in the first month and went on increasing steadily.

Close as Marx's connection with the paper was from its first day of publication, for the first three months he did not work for it. He wrote nothing for it until after Bauer's dismissal, when all prospect of an academic career had vanished. The first articles he wrote were a series about the debates in the sixth Rhenish Diet on the freedom of the Press, and the first of the series appeared on 5 May 1842. This was the first work of Marx's to be printed, if one excepts the two poems his friends published, possibly against his will, in the *Athenäum*. Georg Jung thought the article 'exceptionally good'. Arnold Ruge called it 'in short, the best that has ever been written about the freedom of the Press'. Ludolf Camphausen inquired of his brother who the writer of the 'admirable' article might be. (Marx did not sign it, but called it 'by a Rhinelander'.) Extracts were quoted everywhere, and earned the *Rheinische Zeitung* such credit that Marx was promptly asked to send in as many more articles as he could as quickly as he could write them. Marx wrote three more articles in the course of the summer, one of which was suppressed by the censor and another heavily blue-pencilled. In the middle of October Marx was sent for to Cologne. On 15 October he took over the editorship of the *Rheinische Zeitung*.

In spite of all the determination with which Marx fought against feudal absolutism and rejected half-solutions and illusory ones – in a letter to Ruge he described constitutional

monarchy as 'a mongrel riddled with contradiction and para-
dox' – he was soon forced to part from his Berlin friends. They
went on with their 'absolute criticism', completely untroubled
as to whether it were possible or justified in the concrete circumstances in which they found themselves. A dispute that
arose between him and Edgar Bauer is illuminating. In some
essays he sent to Marx, Edgar Bauer criticized the principle of
compromise in political matters. Not satisfied with that, he
made a most violent attack on all who were unwilling in practice to make his uncompromising critical attitude their own.
Marx, in a letter to Oppenheim, emphatically repudiated this
species of pseudo-radicalism. He described Bauer's articles as
'quite general theoretical discussions concerning the constitution of the state, suitable rather for a scientific journal than
for a newspaper', and drew a picture of 'liberal-minded, practical men, who have undertaken the troublesome role of
struggling step by step for freedom within constitutional
limits'.

Marx's constant regard for the concrete facts led him to
taking an interest in social problems. At the time the German
Press was paying particular attention to the Chartist movement in England and the communist aspirations in France
and Switzerland. The *Rheinische Zeitung* took up these questions and printed articles by Hess about the communists and
by Von Mevissen, who had just returned to Cologne from
England, about the Chartists. In August 1842 the management of the *Rheinische Zeitung* and those associated with
them formed a study circle for the discussion of social problems.

Marx took part in it himself. At the beginning of October
he defended his paper against a charge of communism. The
article he wrote demonstrates how slight Marx's knowledge
of social problems still was in 1842. He was still under the
influence of ideas recently elaborated by Hess. Hess was the
first of the Young Hegelian camp to turn his attention to
communism, and Engels says that he was the first of the three
of them to come over to communism. What Marx intended

to write was a 'fundamental critique of communism' based on 'a long-continued and thorough study'. He read the works of the French socialists and communists who were the chief authorities on the subject at the time – Proudhon's *Qu'est-ce que la propriété?*, Dezamy's *Calomnie et politique de M. Cabet*, Leroux, Considérant, and others.[7]

However important social questions may have been, there were immediate political problems to solve. In all these Marx shared the views of the other left-wing Hegelians, and his method was theirs. His position was at the extreme left wing of bourgeois democracy. He was, to repeat the phrase, a 'desperate revolutionary'. A clean sweep must be made of things as they were – but for the time being in the domain of theory only. Victory in the intellectual sphere must precede victory in the world of reality – how was uncertain; the path to it was not yet visible. Marx, in spite of some vacillation and changes of mind, clung as long as possible to the hope of being able to convince the rulers of the necessity of fundamental changes. Should their efforts prove in vain there was but one alternative and that was revolution, the threat of which appears in his writings at this period from time to time. When the ruling powers called on divine inspiration for their defence, Marx replied that English history had sufficiently demonstrated that the conception of divine inspiration from above called forth the counter-conception of divine inspiration from below. 'Charles I mounted the scaffold because of divine inspiratioin from below.'[8] The threat was there plainly enough; but it was held in abeyance, only to apply if all efforts to gain the victory in the intellectual sphere should fail. It was their task to persevere tirelessly with these efforts.

The new newspaper was at first not unwelcome to the Government. Upholding the idea of national unity in opposition to the narrow frontiers of provincialism, it stood by implication for Prussian hegemony in Germany, set its face against ultramontanism and state interference in Church matters, all by virtue of its programme of freeing the national consciousness of everything that hampered the sense of unity.[9]

But even before Marx took over control of the paper it had come into ever-growing conflict with the Government. As early as July Marx wrote to Ruge that the 'greatest obduracy' was required to see a paper like the *Rheinische Zeitung* through. It was censored with 'the most stern and unjust rigour'.[10] The more it criticized the autocracy, the bureaucracy, the censorship, the whole system of the Christian-German reaction, the harder did the Government bear down upon it. If at first it had been a welcome ally against the *Kölnische Zeitung,* its tone very soon became 'even more doubtful' than that of the *Kölnische Zeitung.* In the last resort it was possible, if not easy, to come to terms with the Catholic reaction. With the spirit of liberalism, whose banner was flown more flagrantly in the *Rheinische Zeitung* every day, it was out of the question.

Marx directed its policy far more clearly, more purposefully, more single-mindedly, launched it against the innermost chamber of the old Prussian state. Under his direction the paper made extraordinarily rapid strides. When he took it over it had about 1,000 subscribers. On 1 January 1843 the number had increased to 3,000. Very few German papers could boast as many. It was more widely quoted than all the others, and to write for it was considered a high honour. Letters, articles, poems were sent to it from all parts of Germany. Marx edited it as he had wanted it to be edited when he contributed to it from Bonn. It was essential, he had written to Oppenheim from Bonn, that the *Rheinische Zeitung* should not be directed by its contributors but that the contributors should be directed by it. He was, as friend and foe soon saw, 'the source from which the doctrine flowed'. He concerned himself with every detail. The paper was, as it were, fused all of a piece. Marx himself selected the articles and edited them. Traces of his powerful hand are perceptible in the paper's tone, its style, even in its punctuation.

But this meant that Marx was brought up against the hard facts of reality more sharply than ever. The Prussian state as it actually was could still be measured against the idea of what the true state ought to be. But there was no answer in Hegel to economic questions such as that raised by the debates in the Diet about the wood-theft law or the distress among the wine-growing peasants of the Moselle. Engels wrote later that 'Marx always said that it was his going into the question of the wood-theft law and the position of the Moselle peasants that turned his attention from pure politics to economic conditions and thus to socialism.'[11]

The more deeply Marx plunged into reality, the more his Berlin friends lost themselves in abstraction. Their criticism became ever more 'absolute', and was destined to end up in empty negation. It became 'nihilistic'.

The word 'nihilism', which dates from those times, was coined for them. The Russian writer, Turgenev, who is generally supposed to have invented it, learned it during this period in Berlin, when he met members of Bruno Bauer's circle. He transferred it to the Russian revolutionaries twenty years later.

Berlin 'nihilism' took delight in an occasionally absurd ridiculing of philistinism, and the so-called 'Freien', or 'Free', demonstrated their emancipation by an anti-philistinism which in practice tied them to that very world which they so radically repudiated, and rendered them incapable of genuinely combating it. Their emancipation ended up in sheer buffoonery.

Marx's unwillingness to place the *Rheinische Zeitung* at the disposal of their antics brought their violent wrath down upon his head. The final breach came on account of Herwegh.

Georg Herwegh's poems, *Gedichte eines Lebendigen,* had made him the most popular poet in Germany. They expressed incomparably all the vague, sentimental, often naïve longing for liberty that was rife in German society at the time. Herwegh had been forced to seek refuge abroad. He was able to return to Germany in 1842, and his return developed into a triumphal progress. Herwegh, who was a quite unpolitical poet at heart, was so fêted and honoured that he ended by completely losing all sense of proportion. At Berlin he was invited to see the King. Friedrich Wilhelm IV liked assuming a popular role and courting popularity, and on his side Herwegh felt flattered by the role of Marquis Posa which he hoped to play before the King. The interview, however, gave satisfaction to neither party. Each felt the falseness of his position, and when the Press started discussing this curious audience each party behaved as if the other had come off worse. The extreme left took Herwegh's audience especially amiss, and his meeting with Bruno Bauer's group ended in an abrupt breach. Herwegh wrote a letter to the editor of the *Rheinische Zeitung* about the 'Freien'. He skated quickly over the occasion of his own quarrel with them and attacked them on quite general grounds. 'They compromise our cause and our party with their revolutionary romanticism, their longing to be geniuses and their big talk', he said.

Marx was anything but pleased at receiving Herwegh's letter, but his opinion of the Freien coincided with Herwegh's. He was forced to defend Herwegh against the attacks made upon him from Berlin. They demanded that the *Rheinische Zeitung* print their anti-Herwegh articles, but Marx refused. They sent him an ultimatum, which Marx declined. The Berliners broke off relations with Marx and the *Rheinische Zeitung*. This was Marx's first rupture with the ultra-left.[12]

The paper lost little because of the Freien. Its reputation was growing steadily, its circulation was increasing, and it was on the way to becoming the leading paper in Germany, when the censorship suddenly gave it its death-blow.

As early as the days of Rutenberg's editorship the Government had regretted the goodwill they had shown the *Rheinische Zeitung*. In February 1842 inquiries were made in official circles in the Rhineland as to whether it might not be advisable to withdraw its licence. This danger was at first averted because, though the local officials took exception to a great deal in the paper, they were unwilling to lose an ally against their hereditary clerical foes. But the censorship became more rigorous. It was in the hands of the 'shameless' Dolleschall, the dull-witted official who had forbidden 'making a comedy of divine things'. What he understood he blue-pencilled without rhyme or reason, and he was even more rigorous with what he did not understand, because that he regarded as particularly suspicious. But it was impossible to blue-pencil everything. So much that was subversive remained that the Berlin authorities recognized the insufficiency of their previous instructions. New and even more rigorous instructions were sent to the censor. Marx was for a long time fond of quoting one saying of Dolleschall's: 'Now my living's at stake. I'll cross everything out!'[13] It made no difference. Dolleschall was recalled and a new and more severe censor came and ruled in his stead. It was not long before the newcomer was reprimanded for excessive leniency. This hurt his feelings greatly, and he defended himself. He had suppressed no fewer than 140 articles, but he received no mercy because of that. The censor was given a super-censor to sit by his side, so that one should blue-pencil what the other left. Even this did not suffice. In December the Berlin authorities sent a special envoy to the Rhineland to inquire how the population would take it if the paper were suppressed or whether suppression would cause too much dissatisfaction. The paper's reputation had grown to such an extent that the Government shrank from taking the final step. But it was only a question of time.

Though the order came from Berlin, it was the Tsar, Nicholas I, who really suppressed the *Rheinische Zeitung*. On 4 January the *Rheinische Zeitung* published a violent anti-Russian article. Russia was the prop of Prussian foreign policy. It was an alliance in which Russia gave the orders and Prussia listened and obeyed. The Tsar saw to it that Prussia did not deviate from the straight and narrow path. When Friedrich Wilhelm IV ascended the throne and there were murmurs here and there in the Prussian Press to the effect that perhaps this Russian hegemony over a German state was not entirely in order, Nicholas I was filled with righteous indignation. He read the submissive young King a lecture and did not shrink from giving his very plain opinion as to how Prussia ought to be ruled.

The Prussian Ambassador at the court of St Petersburg had

repeatedly to listen to hard words. On 10 January he reported to Berlin another and if possible a more violent outburst of imperial rage. Nicholas I had engaged Herr von Liebermann in conversation at the ball at the Winter Palace on 8 January and said that he found the liberal German Press infamous beyond all measure, and he could not sufficiently express his astonishment at the reception the King had given the notorious Herwegh. His Imperial Majesty spoke so violently and with such a flood of words that the Ambassador was unable to say anything at all. Moreover, the Tsar had already written Friedrich Wilhelm IV a personal letter. His rebukes became so trenchant and so threatening that Berlin became alarmed.

The anti-Russian article had been read with indignation in Berlin two weeks before the Ambassador's report arrived from St Petersburg. This time there was no more hesitation. On 21 January 1843 the three Prussian ministers concerned with the censorship decided to suspend the *Rheinische Zeitung*. The Government were in such a hurry that they sent a special mounted messenger to Cologne. According to the edict which he carried the newspaper had been guilty of malicious slander of the state authorities, especially the censorship department; it had held up the administration of the Press police in Prussia to contempt and offended friendly foreign powers. In order not excessively to damage the shareholders and subscribers, the paper was to be allowed to continue until 31 March but would be subject to special censorship to prevent it from erring during the course of the reprieve.

A clever, cultured cynic named Wilhelm Saint-Paul came to Cologne as the last censor. In his reports on Marx he called him the living source and fountain-head of the paper's views. He had made Marx's acquaintance, and he was a man 'who would die for his ideas'. Another time he wrote that certain as it was that the views of Dr Marx rested upon a profound speculative error, as he had tried to prove to him, Dr Marx was equally certain of the rightness of his views. 'The contributors to the *Rheinische Zeitung* could be accused of anything rather than lack of principle in that sense. This can only be one more reason', Saint-Paul concluded with shameless logic, 'for removing him, in the event of the paper being allowed to continue, from a position of direct and controlling influence.' [14]

The fear that the ban would rouse ill-feeling turned out to be well-founded. In every town of the province, in Cologne, Aachen, Elberfeld, Düsseldorf, Coblenz and Trier, hundreds of respectable citizens signed petitions to the Government, appealing for the lifting of the ban. The whole of the German Press took up the question of the suspension of the *Rheinische Zeitung*. The authorities in Berlin actually hesitated as to whether it might not be advisable to allow the paper to re-appear under definite restrictions.

But in the last resort the Berlin Government regarded the goodwill of the Tsar as more important than the temper of the Rhinelanders. On 7 February the Ambassador in St Petersburg wrote another report:

Depuis l'expédition de mon dernier très-humble rapport, j'ai eu aussi occasion de rencontrer Mr le Comte de Nesselrode, dans le salon de son épouse, et de lui parler; mais au lieu de me fournir des renseignements qui auraient pu m'être utiles, ou intéressants, sous le rapport de la politique Mr le Vice-Chancelier a saisi cette occasion pour me demander: si j'avais lu déjà l'article véritablement infame, que *la gazette Rhénane*, publiée à Cologne, avait lancé dernièrement contre le Cabinet Russe, – en basant ses déclamations furibondes sur le faux prétexte d'une note qui m'aurait été adressée par lui, relativement à la tendance de la presse Allemande. J'ai répondu à Mr le Comte de Nesselrode, que je ne connaissais pas textuellement cet article, mais que je me rappelais fort bien, que *la gazette d'État* avait publié, il n'y a pas longtemps, une réfutation de quelques articles semblables, en déclarant brièvement, mais assez positivement, que les suppositions sur lesquelles le raisonnement de ces articles avait été basé, manquaient de fondement et de tout motif raisonnable. Cette réfutation n'était point inconnue á Mr le Vice-Chancelier; mais il m'a avvué, qu'elle ne suffisait pas, pour lui faire comprendre, comment un censeur employé par le gouvernement de Votre Majesté avait pu laisser passer un article d'une nature semblable, qui, selon lui, surpassait encore de beaucoup, en perfidie et en violence, tout ce qui avait été publié jusqu'ici dans les feuilles Prussiennes contre le gouvernement Imperial. Il y a ajouté encore qu'afin que je puisse en juger pour moi-même, en toute connaissance de cause, il m'enverait la feuille de *la gazette Rhénane*, qui renfermait l'article en question, et il l'a fait, en effet, encore le même soir. – Je suis donc véritablement heureux d'avoir trouvé, cette nuit, en revenant du bal patriotique, dans le numéro de *la gazette d'État* du 31 janvier, qui venait d'arriver par la poste, l'ordre émané tout récemment des trois Ministères de Votre Majesté qui président aux affaires de censure, et en vertu duquel *la gazette Rhénane* doit cesser de paraître à dater du 1 avril prochain! Aussi me ferai-je un devoir des plus empressés de faire valoir cette mesure énergique auprès de Mr le Comte de Nesselrode aujourd'hui même à l'occasion d'un dîner auquel il m'a engagé. Je crois, du reste, devoir faire observer encore très-humblement à ce sujet, que lors de la conversation que j'ai eu, avant-hier, avec Mr le Vice-Chancelier, il m'avait très expressément assuré, que l'Empereur ne connaissait probablement pas encore l'article en question parce que, pour sa part, il avait hésité jusqu'ici à le placer sous les yeux de sa Majesté Imperiale.* [15]

* 'Since submitting my last humble report I have had the opportunity of meeting Count de Nesselrode at his wife's *salon* and of conversing with him. Instead of giving me information which might have been useful or interesting to me in connection with the general political situation, the Vice-Chancellor used the occasion to ask me whether I had read the really infamous attack which the *Rheinische Zeitung*, published at Cologne, had recently made on the Russian Cabinet, basing its furious denunciations on the false pretext of a note said to have been addressed to me by him relative to the tendencies of the German Press. I replied that I was not acquainted with the text of the particular article but I recollected well that the *State Gazette* had recently published a refutation of some similar articles, declaring, briefly but quite categorically, that the assumptions on which those articles were based were entirely without foundation or reasonable cause. This refutation was certainly not unknown to the Vice-Chancellor; but he confessed to me that he was unable to understand how a censor employed by Your Majesty's Government could have passed an article of such a nature. In his opinion it far surpassed in perfidy and violence all previous attacks made on the Imperial Government in the Prussian Press. He added that in order that I might judge for myself and be fully acquainted with the facts he would send me a copy of the *Rheinische Zeitung* containing

The Prussian Government trembled at the thought that the infamous article might yet come to the eyes of the Tsar. It was decided definitely that the ban should remain. A deputation of shareholders was not even received. Marx, in ignorance of the true ground for the suspension of the paper (which, as a matter of fact, has remained unknown to historians to this day) made a last desperate move. An article, inspired by him, appeared in the *Mannheimer Abendzeitung* attributing the whole of the blame to him. It was he who had given the paper its distinguishing tone, he was its evil spirit, its controversialist *par excellence*, and it was his audacious insolence and youthful indiscretion that were to blame. But that made no difference either. The issue of 18 March contained the following: 'The undersigned announces that he has retired from the editorship of the *Rheinische Zeitung* because of the present censorship conditions. Dr Marx.' But still there was no act of clemency.

The last number of the *Rheinische Zeitung* appeared on 31 March. It was so sought after that as much as from eight to ten silver groschen were paid for a copy. The *Rheinische Zeitung* took its departure with a poem:

> Wir liessen kühn der Freiheit Fahne wehen
> Und ernst tat jeder Schiffmann seine Pflicht,
> War d'rum vergebens auch der Mannschaft Spähen:
> Die Fahrt war schön und sie gereut uns nicht.

---

the article in question, which he did the same evening. Consequently I am very gratified tonight, on returning from the patriotic ball, to find in the *State Gazette* for 31 January, which has just arrived by post, that Your Majesty's three ministers in charge of the censorship have recently issued an order by virtue of which the *Rheinische Zeitung* will cease to appear as from 1 April. I shall make it my most immediate duty to draw Count de Nesselrode's attention to this energetic measure today on the occasion of a dinner to which he has invited me. I believe it to be my duty very humbly to add that during my conversation with the Vice-Chancellor the day before yesterday he assured me definitely that in all probability the Emperor has not yet seen the article in question, because he on his part had hesitated to lay it before His Imperial Majesty's eyes.'

Dass uns der Götter Zorn hat nachgetrachtet
Es schreckt uns nicht, dass unser Mast gefällt.
Denn auch Kolumbus ward zuerst verachtet
Und endlich sah er doch die neue Welt.

Ihr Freunde, deren Beifall uns geworden,
Ihr Gegner, die ihr uns mit Kampf geehrt,
Wir seh'n uns wieder einst an neuen Borden,
Wenn Alles bricht, der Mut bleibt unversehrt.*

---

* 'We boldly flew the flag of freedom, and every member of the crew did his duty. In spite of the watch having been kept in vain, the voyage was good and we do not regret it. Though the gods were angry, though our mast fell, we were not intimidated. Columbus himself was despised at first, but he looked upon the New World at last. Friends who applauded us, foes who fought us, we shall meet again on the new shore. If all collapses, courage remains unbroken.'

[6]

The Germans Learn French

THOUGH the final impulse that led to the suppression of the *Rheinische Zeitung* came from the Tsar, even if it had refrained from commenting on foreign politics it would inevitably have been suppressed a few weeks later just the same. The Prussian Government was determined to make an end of the radical Press once and for all. At the end of 1842 it forbade the circulation in Prussia of the *Leipziger Allgemeine Zeitung*, which had been a mouthpiece of the left-wing Hegelians for the past two years under the editorship of Gustav Julius. At the beginning of January 1843 Friedrich Wilhelm IV obtained from the Government of Saxony the suspension in Dresden of Ruge's *Deutsche Jahrbücher*. Soon afterwards Buhl's *Patriot* was banned in Berlin. The police and the censor forced the *Königsberger Zeitung* to sever its connection with the radicals. At the end of January a decree withdrew all the concessions that had been granted two years before.

The left-wing Hegelians had now lost all the literary positions they had occupied at the beginning of the 1840s. They had been worsted in the struggle for the transformation of the state, for the remodelling into rational form of a world the irrationality of which they had demonstrated. They had fought with intellectual weapons only and had been defeated. Old Prussia had not been able to answer their arguments. Incapable of victory in the theoretical field, it had nevertheless conquered in fact. Its weapons were the police, the censorship and force. Against force, theory – theory, pure, unaided and alone – had failed.

Journalism had been the only method of political activity available, and now it had been taken away. No prospect of the situation changing was in sight. Certainly there were protests here and there, and in the Rhineland they were stronger than elsewhere, but the overwhelming majority of the population, the masses, looked upon the executioner of liberty with indifference. Nothing was to be hoped for from the inert multitude. Bruno Bauer and his followers turned into themselves and away from a reality that was so unreasonable. They isolated themselves, spun a new theory out of their very impotence, made a fetish of individual consciousness, which they regarded as the only battlefield on which victories could be fought and won, and ended up in an individual anarchism which reached its zenith in Max Stirner's ultra-radical and ultra-harmless *Der Einzige und sein Eigentum*.[1]

Marx, Ruge, Hess, all who had not grown weary of the fray, drew a different conclusion from defeat. The physical force of the state had emerged victorious only because philosophy had remained alone, had not been able to answer force with force. One duty above all others was now incumbent upon the philosophers – to find their way to the masses. In the spring of 1843 Marx wrote that politics were the only ally with the aid of which contemporary philosophy could become a reality. At the end of that year he expressed the idea with which he, far more than any of his colleagues, was impressed in the celebrated words: 'The weapon of criticism can certainly never be a substitute for the criticism of the weapon; physical force must be overthrown with physical force; and theory will be a physical force as soon as the masses understand it.'[2]

To speak to the people and make them understand one must talk to them freely. Immediately after the suppression of the *Rheinische Zeitung* Marx decided to go abroad and continue the struggle there.[3] 'It is unpleasant', he wrote to Ruge when the suppression was made public,

to perform menial service even in the cause of freedom and to fight with needles instead of with clubs. I have grown weary of hypocrisy, stupidity, the exercise of brute force and bowing and cringing and back-bending and verbal hair-splitting. The Government has released me ... In Germany there is now nothing I can do. In Germany one can only be false to oneself.[4]

Marx's first intention was to settle in Switzerland and work with Herwegh on the *Deutsche Boten,* which Herwegh edited there. But Ruge invited his collaboration in bringing out the suppressed *Deutsche Jahrbücher* in another form abroad. He held out to Marx the prospect of a fixed income of from 550 to 600 thalers and about 250 thalers extra which could be earned by other writing. Thus, if all went well, he would have an income of 850 thalers. This was more than Marx could have hoped for, and he gladly accepted Ruge's proposal. 'Even if it had been possible to continue the *Jahrbücher*', he wrote to Ruge in answer – Ruge had for a time been hesitating as to whether it might not perhaps be better to stay on in Dresden after all if the minister made concessions –

it would at best be a feeble imitation of the 'dear departed', and that would no longer be good enough. In comparison the *Deutsch-Französische Jahrbücher* would be an enterprise of high principle, a thing of consequence, an undertaking to which one could devote oneself with enthusiasm.[5]

Ruge had considered whether it might not be a good idea to make the proposed review one of more than 320 pages. Books of more than 320 pages were not subject to censorship in Germany at the time. Marx rejected the idea. Such books were not for the people. The most one dared offer them was a monthly.

A monthly would be suitable for the problem which now had to be solved, i.e. that of making contact with the masses. The name that Marx chose, the *Deutsch-Französische Jahrbücher,* was an indication of the intended contents. Ludwig Feuerbach had urged that the philosopher who should identify himself with life and mankind should be of Franco-German blood; his heart French and his head German. The head reformed, the heart revolutionalized. For the German radicals the head meant German philosophy. 'We Germans are contemporary with the times in philosophy without being contemporary with the times in history.' The French were contemporary with the times in history. Paris was the 'new capital of the new world'. The review was intended to bring

Germans and French, the most advanced in theory and the most advanced in practice, together into an 'intellectual alliance'.[6]

Negotiations with Julius Fröbel, the prospective publisher, progressed favourably. Marx went to Dresden to make final arrangements. It was impossible for the paper to appear in Switzerland, which was becoming increasingly subservient to orders from Berlin and had started expelling radicals and banning newspapers and books. Brussels, or better still, Paris, held out brighter prospects for the new venture. By the end of May all arrangements were complete, and Marx was able to realize his 'private plans' and marry.

'As soon as we have signed the contract I shall go to Kreuznach and get married', he wrote to Ruge in March.

I can assure you, without being at all romantic, that I am head-over-heels in love. I have been engaged now for more than seven years, and my fiancée has had to fight the hardest battles for my sake, almost shattering her health in the process, partly with her bigoted, aristocratic relations, whose twin objects of worship are the 'Lord in Heaven' and the 'Lord in Berlin', and partly with my own family, into the bosom of which some priests and other enemies of mine have insinuated themselves. For years my fiancée and I have had to engage in more unnecessary and exhausting conflicts than many who are three times as old as we and prate continually of their 'experience of life' (which is one of the favourite expressions in our home circle).[7]

Since the death of Karl's father there had been an element of strain in Jenny's relations with his family. The few letters that survive from the years 1839 to 1843 do not cast a very clear light on the reason. Karl's mother complained in the middle of 1840 that her son had become quite a stranger to his family and wrote in her Dutch-German that he had 'renounced everything which had formerly been valuable and dear to him'. The Westphalen family took no notice of her, humiliated her, annoyed her, behaved haughtily and distantly, were eccentric, and 'had no family feeling at all'. There was much talk of a Herr Schlink, who somehow seems to have encouraged these dissensions.[8] What they were more particularly about cannot now be discovered.

Marx had 'fallen out with his family' since 1842. He told Ruge that he had no claim to his father's estate until after his mother's death. After his 'failure' in his career as the editor of a paper – according to all the well-disposed people whose opinion his mother prized so highly the *Rheinische Zeitung* was a 'fiasco' – his family put obstacles in his way and, although they were comfortably off, he was left in most pressing financial straits. His mother never became reconciled to him. She refused to help him even during his years of acute distress in London. When she died in 1863 Jenny wrote to Frau Liebknecht that it would be hypocrisy for her to say she had been sentimental at the news of her mother-in-law's death.

As long as old Westphalen lived he held a protecting hand over his daughter's engagement to Karl. Hostilities only broke out again after his death. True, no one raised objections to Marx's origin. Many years later, when Charles Longuet, in an obituary on Frau Marx, mentioned racial prejudice as having had to be overcome, Marx described it as 'pure moonshine'.[9] To Jenny's relatives Marx seemed strange and hostile not because of his racial antecedents but because he was a pupil of Hegel, a follower of Feuerbach, a friend of the notorious Bruno Bauer, the atheist. Jenny's half-brother, Ferdinand, was the leader of the religious opposition. Jenny despised him. In her letters she never referred to him as her brother but as the 'Minister of State', the 'Minister of the Interior', and so on.[10] When her daughter Laura became engaged to Lafargue, Jenny Marx observed that their 'agreement about fundamentals, particularly in the religious respect', was 'a singular piece of good fortune'. She added, thinking of her own youth, 'And so Laura will be protected from all the struggles and the suffering inevitable for a girl with her opinions in the environment in which she is to live.' Jenny Marx preserved a bitter hatred of the 'bigots' for the whole of her life.

Though Jenny needed all her determination to overcome the opposition, an open rupture with her family did not take place. On 13 June 1843 there took place the marriage of 'Herr Carl Marx, doctor of philosophy, resident in Cologne, and of Fräulein Bertha Julia Jenny von Westphalen, no occupation, resident in Kreuznach'.

The young couple spent the next few months at Frau von Westphalen's house at Kreuznach, where they had two visitors. The first was Esser, a *Revisionsrat* and a friend of Karl's father, who had the naïve effrontery to offer him work for the Government which had just suppressed the *Rheinische Zeitung*. The attempt to buy him met with a point-blank rebuff.[11]

At the end of July, Ruge passed through Kreuznach on his way to Brussels to find out what prospects it offered for the publication of his periodical. They did not turn out to be very hopeful. The German colony in Brussels was small, and was only moderately interested in philosophy and politics. Though the Press enjoyed greater freedom in Belgium than in France, intellectual life in Belgium, insofar as it could be called such, was only a feeble echo of the French. Ruge went on to Paris.

In the words of the young Engels, Paris was the place where 'European civilization had reached its fullest bloom'. It was the 'nerve-centre of European history, sending out electric shocks at regular intervals which galvanized the whole world'. The bourgeois kingdom was tottering. Ruge, accustomed from Germany to detecting the slightest signs of opposition, found the tension in the city very great. Guizot's majority in the Chamber had sunk to three.

> The bourgeois King's loss of prestige among the people is demonstrated by the many attempts to assassinate that dynastic and autocratic prince. He will not allow himself to be 'hampered' in any way with the promised 'republican institutions'. One day when he dashed by me in the Champs Elysées, well hidden in his coach, with hussars in front and behind and on both sides, I observed to my astonishment that the outriders had their guns cocked ready to fire in earnest and not just in the usual burlesque style. Thus did he ride by with his bad conscience![12]

France was the home of revolution, and in France the inevitable new revolution must start again. Everywhere that revolutionaries lived, waiting impatiently for their hour to strike, they lived in expectation of the 'crowing of the Gallic cock'.[13]

At the end of October 1843 Marx and his wife went to Paris. Ruge and the publisher Fröbel had already approached the leading radicals and members of the opposition with a view to enlisting their support. The journal was intended to be bilingual, the Germans writing in German and the Frenchmen in French. Ruge's opinion was that everybody could read French, a view which accorded ill with the paper's proposed popular appeal. However, they were unsuccessful in securing the collaboration of a single Frenchman. Lamennais turned them down. Lamartine considered that his contributing to the journal would constitute an unwarrantable interference in German affairs. Louis Blanc had misgivings on account of the Young Hegelians' defiantly acknowledged atheism. He was anti-clerical, of course, but as an admirer of Robespierre and an heir of the Jacobins he was a deist. Leroux was for the time being entirely occupied with the invention of a printing machine. Cabet and Considérant also refused to associate themselves with the new journal, and Proudhon was only occasionally in Paris. The new enterprise became the *Deutsch-Französische Jahrbücher* all the same. It taught the Germans 'to talk French', i.e. to be revolutionaries.

All the German contributors were *émigrés*. Not a single contributor wrote from Germany. Feuerbach's reason for declining Marx's invitation to contribute was not very plausible. Even Bakunin in Zürich, with whom Ruge and Marx had already corresponded – the letters were published in the *Jahrbücher* – withdrew. The poets Herwegh and Heine were the only contributors, apart from Marx, whose names were known.

The money for the journal was supplied by Fröbel, who put up 3,000 francs, and Ruge, who put up 6,000 thalers. Ruge and Marx shared the editorship, but Ruge did little. At first he was away from Paris and soon after he came back he was taken ill. All the work devolved upon Marx. The first and only double number appeared at the end of February.

Two essays by Marx appeared in it. One was 'On the Jewish Question',[14] and was in reply to two essays of Bruno Bauer. Marx had written it at Kreuznach. The other, 'Critique of the Hegelian Philosophy of Law',[15] he had started at Kreuznach and finished at the end of the year in Paris. After the suspension of the *Rheinische Zeitung* Marx 'withdrew' from the public stage into the study to solve the doubts that assailed him'.[16] He had to come to terms in his own mind with the Hegelian philosophy of law under the guidance of which he had fought his journalistic battle. In that battle it had been smashed to pieces. According to Hegel the state was the creator and guardian of a rational social and political order. The social organization proceeded from the state. But in dealing with the distress among the wine-growing peasants of the Moselle Marx had been forced to acknowledge that 'there are circumstances which are decided as much by the actions of private individuals as by individual officials, and are as independent of them as the method of drawing one's breath'.[17] The more Marx examined the 'circumstances' which the actions of 'individual officials' determined, the wider the scope they seemed to include. The 'circumstances' turned out to be the special interests of quite definite social groups, and the 'individual officials' ended by becoming identified with the state itself. Marx found it necessary to inquire whether the relations of state and society were not just the reverse of what Hegel had conceived them to be.

Ludwig Feuerbach's *Introductory Theses to the Reform of Philosophy* appeared in March 1843. In this work the doubts which assailed Marx in his own special domain of Hegelian philosophy were exposed in their most general form and solved by a complete reversal of the Hegelian system. 'The true relation of thought to being is only this', wrote Feuerbach.

Being is subject, thought predicate. Thought arises from being, not being from thought. All speculations about law, about will, freedom, personality, without man, beside him or above him, are speculations without unity, necessity, substance, basis or reality.

Man is the existence of personality, the existence of liberty, the existence of law.

Ideas have their origin in reality, they never realize themselves in reality. Applied to the philosophy of law, it follows from this reversal that it is not the idea of the state, the idea realizing itself in the state, which creates and directs society, but society which conditions the state. In 1859 Marx summarized the result of his inquiries at this time in the classical sentences:

Legal conditions, like state forms, are neither to be explained as things in themselves nor from the so-called general development of the human spirit. They have their roots rather in the material conditions of life, the whole of which Hegel, following the example of eighteenth-century Englishmen and Frenchmen, included under the name of 'civil society'.[18]

Feuerbach recognized man to be the creator of ideas which Hegel externalized into independent entities. But even in Hegel man is still an abstraction, a generic being, still 'languishing quite outside the world, having no history'. Marx went farther than Feuerbach; he went into the world of concrete reality. 'Man is the world of men, the state, society.'[19]

Criticism of the state became at the same time criticism of the social order. It reached farther and penetrated to the foundations of society; those foundations were private property. Logically, Marx took the final step. Only one social class could fulfil the task of shaking off barbarism; that class was the proletariat. 'The revolution requires a material foundation. Theory is only realized in a people insofar as its realization is a practical necessity. It is not enough that thought presses for realization, reality itself must press for thought.'[20] The answer to the question as to where the possibility of emancipation in practice lay was as follows:

It lay in the formation of a class with radical chains, a class in bourgeois society, which is yet not of bourgeois society, a social rank which is the abolition of all social ranks ... a sphere of society which cannot emancipate itself without emancipating it-self from all other spheres of society and thus emancipating all other spheres of society at the same time, which, in a word, is the complete loss of man, and which can only attain itself again by the complete winning of man. This social catalyst is the prole-tariat.

Philosophy had emerged into economics. At the end of the road taken by political radicalism in its criticism of the irra-tional Prussian state lay communism, the abolition of private property, the proletarian revolution.

The *Deutsch-Französische Jahrbücher* was the last product of the Young Hegelians. It was the last not only in the sense that after it the Young Hegelians were spoken of no more, but also in another sense. There was nothing left for them to say. Young Hegelianism had become communism. Or rather Young Hegelianism as such shrank back from its consequences, revised its premises and disintegrated; whether into narrow petty-bourgeois philistinism or 'absolute' criticism or indi-vidual philosophy or any other petty-bourgeois manifesta-tion is in the last resort immaterial.

Ruge was not entirely satisfied with the contents of Marx's first number. He considered some of Marx's 'epigrams' too artificial, others too crude. 'Some unpolished things were also served up which otherwise (that is to say, if I had not been ill) I should have corrected, but as it is they got by in the rush.'[21] Nevertheless he considered that the issue also contained a number of remarkable things which would attract a great deal of attention in Germany.

They did indeed attract a great deal of attention. The few copies that entered Germany were secretly passed from hand to hand. They caused astonishment, admiration, execration and disgust among Marx's former comrades. Those who were frightened stopped their ears, shut their eyes, dazzled by the new light. All were greatly affected.

The other side of this political and literary success was material failure. The police grasped the fact that the *Jahr-bücher* were incomparably more dangerous than anything they had had to concern themselves with before. In April the Prussian Government informed the provincial authorities that the *Jahrbücher* came within the definition of attempted high treason and *lèse-majesté*. The police were directed to place Ruge, Marx, Heine, Bernays and their collaborators under arrest immediately they should set foot on Prussian soil. The head of the Austrian police and censorship department described the *Jahrbücher* as a publication 'whose loathsome and disgusting contents surpass everything previously published by the revolutionary Press'. Metternich was afraid it might be 'smuggled into the Austrian realm'. The whole official apparatus was set in motion, right down to the administrators of the town wards. Booksellers were warned against buying this monster of a book and 'notified of the severe penalties involved'. An exhaustive search was ordered to be made for it at all second-hand bookshops.

A hundred copies fell into the hands of the police on a Rhine steamer and 230 were confiscated by the Bavarians at the frontier of France and the Palatinate. Ruge described later how Bernays, who accompanied the parcel on its ill-fated journey, came back very gaily with the information that he had disposed of the whole lot at once. The customs officials had almost doubled up with laughter over Heine's verses about King Ludwig; a pleasure, Ruge added, that Heine and they could have had much more cheaply.

Fröbel refused to continue with the undertaking. Ruge, who was properous – he had only recently increased his fortune by successful speculations – though it was his encouragement that had brought Marx to Paris and though he had guaranteed him a definite income for his work as editor, withdrew likewise. Publication ceased after the first number, and Marx was left in a very difficult situation. He urged Ruge to keep his promise, but Ruge declined. The most he consented to was paying Marx in kind. He left him the unsold copies of the *Jahrbücher* to dispose of as best he could.

A violent quarrel between Marx and Ruge resulted. It would not, however, have ended in a definite rupture had not other

personal differences, especially on fundamental matters of
principle, been developing between them for some time.[22]

Emma Herwegh relates that Ruge proposed to Marx and
Herwegh that they should go and live with him and found a
kind of Fourierist *phalanstère*, a communal household which
the women should take it in turn to manage, doing the cooking
and sewing and all the other domestic work required.

Frau Herwegh rejected the idea at once. How could a nice little
Saxon woman like Frau Ruge possibly get on with the highly
intelligent and even more ambitious Madame Marx, who knew
so much more than she? And how could the so recently married
Frau Herwegh, who was the youngest of them all, possibly feel
attracted to this communal life? Surely enough, Herwegh and his
wife declined Ruge's invitation. Ruge and Marx and their wives
went to live together in the rue Vanneau. A fortnight later they
parted.[23]

Marx and Ruge differed far too much in character, temperament and outlook on life for their collaboration to have endured, even if these external conflicts had not arisen. Ruge was
a radical petty-bourgeois, a narrow-minded moralist, a tedious
censor of morals, a careful, calculating businessman, even if he
was not altogether averse to sacrificing some fraction of his
money for a cause – provided certain definite limits were not
overstepped. Marx was a revolutionary. Ruge, as Marx was
forced to recognize in Paris, rejoiced in 'a fundamental and
universal ignorance'. He could not understand that Marx
'reads so much, works with such extraordinary intensity,
sometimes actually does not go to bed for four nights running,
and keeps on plunging anew into an oceon of books.' [24]

The final and open rupture came because of Ruge's opinion
of Georg Herwegh. There is no record of Marx's side of the
case, but what Ruge stated in his own justification is sufficient.
Herwegh was married to a rich Berlin banker's daughter and
was very fond of luxury. It is not necessarily true that he was
absurdly extravagant in clothes, flowers, food, furniture, car-
riages and horses, although he certainly overdid some things.

Herwegh was very friendly with the Countess d'Agoult, a
friendship which gossip turned into a highly immoral and
dissolute love affair. 'One evening', Ruge wrote to his mother,

the conversation turned to this topic ... I was incensed by Herwegh's way of living and his laziness. Several times I referred to
him warmly as a scoundrel, and declared that when a man gets
married he ought to know what he is doing. Marx said nothing
and took his departure in a perfectly friendly manner. Next morning he wrote to me that Herwegh was a genius with a great future.
My calling him a scoundrel filled him with indignation, and my
ideas on marriage were philistine and inhuman. Since then we
have not seen each other again.[25]

Marx defended Herwegh on another occasion; this time
against Heine. The *Jahrbücher* group had hailed Heine with
joy. He was a new man, with new ideas. His arrival was like
a blast of fresh air, a burst of stormy movement. He made
friends with the *Jahrbücher* group, having quarrelled with
practically all the other German *émigrés* and being lonely and
in bad health. He soon took a dislike to Ruge, of whom he
said that though he had freedom in his mind, he would not let
it sink into his limbs; however enthusiastic he might be for
Hellenic nudity, he was quite incapable of bringing himself to
cast off his barbaric modern trousers, or even the Christian-
German pants of convention. Eleanor Marx remembered hear-
ing from her parents that there was a time when Heine came
to Marx's house day in and day out, to read his verses to the
young couple and obtain their opinion of them. Heine and
Marx would go through a little poem of eight lines a countless
number of times, continually discussing one word or another
and working away at it until everything was perfectly smooth
and no trace of the workshop and the file was left.[26] An infinite
amount of patience was required for all this, because Heine was
morbidly sensitive to criticism. Sometimes he would come to
Marx, literally weeping because of an attack by some obscure
reviewer. Marx's only way of dealing with the situation was
to send him to his wife, whose wit and charm soon brought the

desperate poet round to reason. Heine did not always come seeking for help. Sometimes he brought it. One example of this the Marx family had particular cause to remember.

When little Jenny Marx – she was born on 1 May 1844 – was a baby of only a few months, she was seized with violent cramps which seemed to be threatening her life. Marx and his wife stood by the child in despair, not knowing what to do. Heine arrived, looked at the child and said: 'The baby must be given a bath.' He prepared the bath himself, put the child in it, and as Marx said, saved Jenny's life.[27]

It was certainly more than a coincidence that Heine wrote *Germany: A Winter's Tale* during the year in which he and Marx were friends. He sent parts of it to Marx from Hamburg for serialization in the Paris *Vorwärts* before publication of the whole. He ended the accompanying letter with the words: 'Farewell, dear friend, and excuse my terrible scrawl. I cannot read over what I have written – but we need but few tokens to understand each other.'

Heine's *Weavers' Song* also appeared for the first time in *Vorwärts*, and Marx wrote about the rising of the Silesian weavers in the same paper.[28] If in 1843, when he recognized as latent in the proletariat the power which should carry his philosophy into practice, he had regarded the proletarian revolution as necessary and inevitable though for the time lying in the indefinite future, he now believed he saw communism actually coming into being before his eyes. However he overestimated the desperate revolt of the Silesian weavers. They were not, as he then believed, ahead of the English and French workers' movements in class consciousness and clarity of purpose. On the contrary, they were a long way behind them. This was no rising of organized industrial workers against the capitalists but wild rioting by desperate, impoverished home-workers, who smashed machines as they had done in England half a century before. The philosophic foundation of communism was manifestly insufficient to grapple with the facts. So Marx threw all his energy into the study of political economy.[29] He read and made excerpts from the French economists, J.-B. Say, Frédéric Skarbek, Destutt de Tracy, P. le Pesant de Boisguillebert, besides the great English economists, Adam Smith, David Ricardo, J. R. McCulloch and James Mill, whom he read in French translations. He studied history, especially that of the French Revolution. For a time he planned to write a history of the Convention. And he sought and found contact with the German artisans, the real proletariat, whom so far he had scarcely seen face to face, and with the French secret societies, who were the real revolutionaries. For the time being he was free from material worries. Former shareholders of the *Rheinische Zeitung* sent him 1,000 thalers in March and in July Georg Jung sent him 800 francs as compensation for the 100 confiscated copies of the *Jahrbücher*.

[7]

The Communist Artisans of Paris

SEVERAL tens of thousands of Germans were living in Paris in the mid-1840s. This large colony was divided into two sections having practically no contact with one another. One consisted of writers and artists and the other of artisans. Some trades were almost exclusively in the hands of Germans. This applied particularly to the cobbler's trade. In fact in Paris 'German' and 'cobbler' had almost become synonymous.

Many German artisans went to Paris to improve themselves in the city which dictated the fashions and the taste of Europe, and after a year returned to Germany. Most of them learned but little French, and in Paris they lived a life of their own. This also applied to the great majority of those who had been driven from their native land by sheer hunger and want. The latter class remained in France. Both classes alike depressed the wages of French workers, and for a number of years French and German workers were bitterly hostile. Fierce encounters often took place in the faubourg Saint-Antoine, which was then a working-class district. French workers would attack the Germans and there would be regular street battles.

The tension did not diminish until various revolutionary organizations started their activities among the workers. Quite a number of political *émigrés* had gathered in Paris after the failure of the revolt of the German Burschenschafter in 1833. It appears from the dossiers of the Paris Prefecture of Police that the first secret societies among German *émigrés* were formed in the mid-1830s. At first they consisted exclusively of intellectuals, but they soon attracted workers too. Dr Ewerbeck, a physician, one of the first to go among the workers with revolutionary propaganda, describes how he once took Ludwig Börne to a meeting. Börne listened to the speeches, looked at the faces about him, and burst into tears of pleasure as he left.

The revolutionary intelligentsia had found its way to the people.[1]

The German conspirators soon made contact with the French secret societies. The most active, alert-minded German workers lived the life of their French class comrades. Soon there was no French secret society without a German member. The Blanquist groups actually had special German sections. This joint work did more and more to heal the breach between the French and German workers, and thus enhanced the reputation of the revolutionaries among their German fellow countrymen.

After the Congress of Vienna, Europe was full of secret societies. At first they were most widespread in the Latin countries. The carbonari kept the ideals of the Jacobins alive during the years of reaction, and the Blanquist leagues were their French form. As working-class influence in these organizations increased – for workers tended more and more to form the predominating majority of their members – socialist ideas gradually crept in. Socialist influence was predominant from the middle of the 1830s.

For a long time secret societies in Germany continued to be almost exclusively composed of students and professional men. Out of the 'League of Exiles' there had arisen the 'League of the Just'. The League of Exiles consisted originally of *émigré* intellectuals and it had increased its numbers by admitting workers to its ranks. In this society intellectuals and workers did not hold together as they managed, though not without occasional friction, to do in others. The workers in the League of Exiles cut themselves adrift from the intellectuals and formed a new society of their own – the League of the Just. Hardly any educated men belonged to it. The League of the Just entirely dissociated themselves from the radical literary groups, with whom they wished to have nothing whatever to do. They regarded the 'humanists' with the greatest possible suspicion. Weitling remarked that their humanism did not come from *homo*, a man, but from Humaine, which was the name of one of the leading Paris tailors. All humanists had to

have a suit from Humaine, Weitling maintained. The League
of the Just, the members of which belonged almost exclusively
to the working classes, very soon started adopting socialist
ideas. After the failure of the rising attempted by the Paris
Blanquists in 1839, in which members of the League of the
Just took part, this process was completed. In London, whither
they fled, socialist intellectuals lived like proletarians. Schapper, their leader, a former student of forestry, had worked as a
compositor in Paris.

The spiritual leader of the League of the Just was Wilhelm
Weitling.[3] Weitling was born in Magdeburg in 1808. He was
the illegitimate son of a French officer and a German laundress.
Being 'tainted' for that reason, driven from pillar to post, often
subjected to humiliation, this young, brooding, talented and
gifted tailor's assistant had become a rebel early. He wrote
Humanity as it is and as it ought to be in 1835,[4] and in 1842
there appeared his *Guarantees of Harmony and Freedom*, an
important landmark in the history of criticism of contemporary society. It pointed to a future society to be founded on the
law of nature and love. In 1841 he fled from France to Switzerland and issued a pediodical called *Der Hülferuf der deutschen Jugend* from Geneva. Seven hundred of the 1,000 copies
that were printed went to France, according to the Paris police
estimate.[5]

To Marx, Weitling was the ideologist of the first, still crude
proletarian movement which culminated in the Silesian
weavers' rising. In the article in *Vorwärts* already mentioned
Marx wrote:

Where could the bourgeoisie – including the scribes and the
philosophers – boast of a work like Weitling's *Guarantees of Harmony and Freedom* regarding the emancipation of the bourgeoisie – political emancipation, that is to say? If one compares the
jejune, timid mediocrity of German political literature with the
unbounded brilliance of the literary début of the German worker;
if one compares the gigantic footprints of the proletariat, still in
its infancy, with the diminutive political traces left by the German

bourgeoisie, one can prophesy a truly athletic, powerful form for the German Cinderella.[6]

Propaganda by the communist workers was now intensified. The aim was no longer merely that of holding a small group of revolutionaries together. The object now was to win over all similarly-minded men. In the process their propaganda came up against revolutionary undercurrents with tendencies similar to their own. In many places in Germany, particularly in the Harz Mountains and in Silesia, a number of Christian sects had managed, in spite of all persecution, to keep together and continue teaching a crude kind of primitive Christian communism. Emigrants to America were constantly founding anabaptist groups, which linked up with those who stayed at home. Thoughtful, brooding Silesian and Saxon working men, having no connection with one another, relying entirely upon themselves, independently worked out communist utopias, founded upon the Bible, the only book they knew. Such knowledge of them as occasionally came the way of the educated world caused either irritation, amusement or contempt. The idea of the communalization of women arose among the anabaptists. 'The whole bourgeois world denounces us for wishing to introduce the communalization of women,' is a phrase in the Communist Manifesto. Georg Weerth, a friend of Marx's and a colleague of his on the *Neue Rheinische Zeitung*,[7] wrote this comic poem:

> Auch nach Weibergemeinschaft steht ihr Sinn,
> Abschaffen woll'n sie die Ehe,
> Dass alles in Zukunft ad libitum
> Miteinander zu Bette gehe:
> Tartar und Mongole mit Griechenfrau'n,
> Cherusker mit gelben Chinesen,
> Eisbären mit schwedischen Nachtigall'n,
> Türkinnen und Irokesen.
> Tranduftende Samoyedinnen soll'n
> Zu Briten und Römern sich betten,
> Plattnasige düstre Kaffern zu
> Alabasterweissen Grisetten.

Ja, ändern wird sich die ganze Welt
Durch diese moderne Leitung –
Doch die schönsten Weiber bekommen die
Redakteure der *Rheinischen Zeitung*.*

The influence on the secret societies of the primitive Christian communism of the various sects also came out in phraseology. In the League of Exiles a unit, following the practice of
the carbonari, was called a 'hut' and the members were 'comrades'. In the 1840s the League of the Just used the terms
'communes' and 'brothers'. In Switzerland members met for
common love feasts, like the apostles and disciples of Christ.
All these undercurrents and more were mingled in the communism of the German artisans. The ideals of primitive Christianity jostled with the ideas of Saint-Simon, Owen and
Fourier. The communism of these men, as can be well imagined from the situation in which they found themselves, was
essentially a longing for a return to a transfigured pre-capitalist
world rather than the forward-looking will of a new class for a
new world of which they were to be the expression. The idea
that industry itself creates the conditions for and the possibility of a social revolution, and that the proletariat has a historical task to fulfil was remote from the minds of the German
artisan communists. They could not conceive of the evils under
which they suffered as being other than the consequences of
the machinations of bad and egoistical men.

This 'utterly crude and unintelligent communism' was repudiated by Marx. He saw 'its central motive as want'. He
rebelled against the 'bestial' idea of the communalization of

---

* 'They are also minded to communalize women; they want to
abolish marriage, so everybody in the future may go to bed with one
another *ad libitum*; Tartars and Mongols with Greek women; Cherus-
cans with yellow Chinese; polar bears with Swedish nightingales,
Turkish girls and Iroquois; oil-scented Samoyed women shall bed with
Britons and Romans, and swarthy flat-nosed Kaffirs with alabaster-
white *grisettes*. Yes, we shall alter the whole world under this modern
management, but the most beautiful women will be reserved for the
editorial staff of the *Rheinische Zeitung*.'

women. This kind of communism 'denied personality' and 'physical possessions were the only aim of its life and being'.[8] The elements in it that Marx valued were its criticism of the existing state of things and its will to overthrow it by force. The French secret societies with whom the German communist associations were in touch were animated by the same revolutionary ardour. Since the time of the French Revolution, from Gracchus Babeuf through Buonarotti to Blanqui, they had remained faithful, though in the most multifarious forms, to the single idea of a violent popular revolution. They believed that the people could not be freed from their tormentors and exploiters and that ultimately justice could not be obtained for the poor unless they rose and shattered their enemies to pieces.

The identity of the leaders of the secret societies of French workers with whom Marx came into personal contact has not yet been established. He was introduced to the German communist group by Dr Ewerbeck. According to reports of Prussian secret agents, with whom Paris swarmed in the summer of 1844, Marx was a frequent guest at workers' meetings at the Barrière du Trône, rue de Vincennes. He did not join either the League of the Just or any of the French secret societies. The gulf between him and them was too great. As men and fighters Marx valued them highly. In 1844 he wrote that 'at the communist workers' meetings brotherhood is no phrase but a reality, and a true spirit of nobility is reflected in the faces of these men hardened by labour'.[9] He admired in them 'their studiousness, their thirst for knowledge, their moral energy, their restless urge for development'.[10]

Marx had no easy task in gaining the ear of the communist workers. Most of those who had ever made contact with bourgeois revolutionary writers regretted the experience. When Weitling's friends were collecting money to pay for printing his works, Ewerbeck asked Ruge for a contribution, and Ruge angrily refused. He was filled with righteous indignation at the German communists, 'who wanted to make all men free by making them workers and proposed replacing private property by communal property and the just division of wealth, themselves laying all stress on property and money in particular'.[11] Marx did not meet Weitling personally until the summer of 1845.

Besides the French and German communists with whom he was in touch, Marx kept in contact with the French socialists. He did not share their faith in the possibility of transforming bourgeois society by gradual reforms, belief in which separated them from the communists. He was unable to share their hope of persuading the possessing classes by the force of argument to search into their hearts and turn over a new leaf. But from socialist criticism of existing society he learned a great deal. The communists *a priori* rejected this world as an evil world of evil men. The hatred that filled them sharpened their sight for social contradictions and gave their criticism a moral force which made that of the socialists seem feeble in comparison. But the socialists did not just see the division of the world into rich and poor. They observed the rich growing richer and the poor growing poorer, they watched a historical process developing before their eyes, the downfall of the middle strata, the growing accumulation of capital. They stood in the midst of their times and sought to understand them. The communists who followed Weitling were citizens of the kingdom of Utopia on leave.

In July 1844 Marx met Proudhon, with whom he kept in contact as long as he remained in Paris. He had long discussions with him, which often lasted all night long, and 'infected' him with Hegelianism.[12] Marx did not meet Louis Blanc till towards the end of his stay in Paris. Marx said in 1853 that they formed 'a kind of friendship, if not a specially close one'.[13]

After the collapse of the *Deutsch-Französische Jahrbücher* Marx no longer had a mouthpiece through which he could work, although in Paris it was more important to have one than ever. 'C'est surtout à Paris', a report of the Ministry of the Interior stated,

que les communistes allemands ont établi le foyer et le point de départ de leurs intrigues; c'est par la France qu'ils espèrent agir;

en dehors de ce royaume, si ce n'est en Angleterre, ils n'osent affronter avec une égale audace la sévérité des lois et celle des magistrats.*

The possibility of creating a popular paper which should be intelligible to the German communist workers presented itself in *Vorwärts*.[14] The founder of this weekly was Heinrich Börnstein, who was a translator and an acute businessman. The money for founding the paper had been put up by Meyerbeer, the composer. Like the few other German papers that had been established in Paris before it, it met with only meagre success as long as it was more concerned with tittle-tattle and theatrical gossip than with the questions that agitated the minds of all the Germans in Paris who read a newspaper at all. But Börnstein could also write for the left. On 1 July 1844 he appointed Bernays editor of *Vorwärts*. Bernays was an exceptionally witty and nimble-minded man and had contributed to the *Deutsch-Französische Jahrbücher*.

All *émigrés* of all political leanings started by making use of the opportunity of writing for *Vorwärts*. They did so less out of enthusiasm for the paper than because they had no choice. Börnstein writes in his reminiscences:[15]

There soon gathered round *Vorwärts* a group of writers such as no other paper anywhere could boast, particularly in Germany, where the state of the Press at that time, before the lively assault of 1848, was appalling. Besides Bernays and myself, who were the editors, there wrote for the paper Arnold Ruge, Karl Marx, Heinrich Heine, Georg Herwegh, Bakunin, Georg Weerth, G. Weber, Fr. Engels, Dr Ewerbeck and H. Bürgers. It can well be imagined that these men wrote not only very brilliantly but very radically. *Vorwärts*, as the only uncensored radical paper appearing in the German language anywhere in Europe, soon had a new appeal and increased in circulation. [Börnstein omits to mention that he was the only one to whom it mattered.]

* 'The German communists have made Paris their headquarters and the centre from which all their intrigues radiate. It is through France that they hope to act. Outside the kingdom of France there is no country, except, perhaps, England, where they dare affront the severity of the laws and the magistrates with such audacity.'

I still remember with pleasure [he continued], the editorial conferences, which often took place weekly, at which all these men gathered in my office. I had rented the first floor of the corner house of the rue des Moulins and the rue Neuve des Petits Champs ... From twelve to fourteen men used to gather for these editorial conferences. Some would sit on the bed or on the trunks, others would stand or walk about. They would all smoke terrifically, and argue with great passion and excitement. It was impossible to open the windows, because a crowd would immediately have gathered in the street to find out the cause of the violent uproar, and very soon the room was concealed in such a thick cloud of tobacco smoke that it was impossible for a newcomer to recognize anybody present. In the end we ourselves could not even recognize each other.

Marx's first article in *Vorwärts* appeared on 7 August, and from the middle of August onwards his influence on the paper steadily increased. *Vorwärt's* attacks on Friedrich Wilhelm IV as the most exalted and most assailable representative of reaction became more and more violent. Heine wrote his verses about the 'new Alexander'. The Prussian Government, angry but powerless in the matter, did not decide to intervene in Paris until *Vorwärts* extolled Burgomaster Tscech's attempted assassination of the King. Ernst Dronke describes

how the dicta of the Press went home in Prussian official circles in spite of their pretended bureaucratic indifference. At a meeting to commemorate the introduction of municipal government in Berlin, the minister, Arnim, could actually not refrain from mentioning with abhorrence the praises of regicide which are understood here to have appeared in *Vorwärts*, the forbidden Paris paper.

The language of *Vorwärts* had indeed been very strong. An attempt on the life of a German king, it stated, was Germany's only argument against German absolutism. All others had failed. Absolutism lost its divine infallibility as soon as it was shown to be assailable. Its assailability must be shown on the person of a German king, because neither the fate of

Charles I nor of Louis XVI nor the many attempts on the life
of Louis Philippe had taught Germany its lesson.

The draconic penalties for introducing the 'dregs' of German journalism no longer sufficed. So the King of Prussia appealed to the professional solidarity of kings. The Ambassador,
von Arnim, made representations to the Prime Minister,
Guizot. Guizot was not particularly inclined to do what Arnim
asked. True, he had Bernays brought up before a summary
court and sentenced to two months' imprisonment and a fine
of 300 francs because *Vorwärts* had not paid the fee for the
prescribed licence. A charge based on the anti-Prussian article
would, however, have to be tried by a jury. This prospect did
not suit the Ambassador, and he declined it. Such a trial would
in effect became a political demonstration, and the accused,
as in so many trials at that time, would have too good an
opportunity of giving the widest publicity to their propaganda.
The Prussian Government would attach no value whatever
to a trial of that kind. So Friedrich Wilhelm IV sent Alexander
von Humboldt to Louis Philippe as a special envoy. On 7
January 1845 Humboldt presented His Majesty with 'a beautiful porcelain vase' together with a long letter from his master,
Friedrich Wilhelm IV. Louis Philippe was delighted at the
cordial greetings of the Prussian King. He assured Humboldt
of his firm determination to rid Paris of the German atheists.

The Prussian Government had got what it wanted. Its secret
agents had been on Marx's tracks for a whole year. His name
appears constantly in their reports. They trailed him even
into modest working-class taverns. They denounced him as
the leading spirit behind *Vorwärts* and his name headed the
list of evil-doers whose expulsion Prussia demanded.

On 11 January the Minister of the Interior ordered the expulsion of Marx, Ruge, Börnstein and Bernays. Their presence
in the country, the so-called reasons adduced for the decision
stated, was calculated to disturb public order and security.
They must leave Paris within twenty-four hours of receiving
the order and must leave France within as short a time as
possible. Their return was forbidden under threat of penalties.

The expulsion order was not unconditional. Its recipients were discreetly given to understand that they could remain if they gave an undertaking to refrain from agitating against friendly governments in the Press. To be sure, this hint was given them after the liberal Press had violently protested against this act of French servility to Prussia and after the Government step had been condemned in the Chamber even by many of its own supporters.

Bernays was in prison. Börnstein protested his political innocuousness and was allowed to stay. He gave his promise to suspend *Vorwärts* all the more readily because he found a new occupation. He entered the service of the French political police. Ruge moved heaven and earth, proved that he had nothing whatever to do with the *Vorwärts* people, and that, moreover, he was a subject of Saxony. He remained in Paris too. Marx was the only one to leave.

Heinrich Bürgers, in his *Reminiscences of Ferdinand Freiligrath,* writes:

In Lent of the year 1845 two young men might have been seen travelling towards the Belgian frontier in the *Messagerie,* on their way to Brussels. They were alone in the small coach and beguiled the tedious journey through Picardy with lively conversation, and an occasional song which the younger of the two struck up in order to dispel the reflections which the other tried in vain to master. Their journey was not entirely voluntary, although it was made of their own choice. Karl Marx – for he was the elder of the two young German travellers – had been served with an expulsion order by the Paris Prefecture of Police ... It conflicted with his pride to place himself voluntarily under police supervision, and he decided rather to transplant himself to Brussels, leaving his wife and child behind. He took me with him as his travelling-companion, as the punishment inflicted on the man who was my friend and faithful guide in my studies had disgusted me with the prospect of staying any longer in the French capital.[16]

Marx arrived in Brussels on 5 February 1845. His wife followed him soon afterwards with his daughter, who was barely one year old.

[8]

The Lifelong Friend[1]

In the fifteen months of Marx's stay in Paris he had met Proudhon and Louis Blanc, Heine and Herwegh, German communists and members of French secret societies. Some of them crossed his path again, few encouraged him, he remained friendly with none. His meeting with Friedrich Engels was decisive. From October 1844 until he closed his eyes for the last time, in victory and defeat, in the storm of revolution and the misery of exile, always struggling and always fighting, he trod by Engels's side and Engels trod by his, along the same path towards the same goal.

Friedrich Engels was born in Barmen on 28 November 1820, the eldest son of Friedrich Engels senior. His father was a merchant. Engels's great-grandfather, Johann Caspar Engels, had, on very slender capital, started a lace factory, connected with a bleaching works and a ribbon manufactory, which had developed by the time of his death into one of the biggest undertakings in the Wuppertal and went on expanding under the energetic management of his sons and grandsons. When the brothers parted in 1837, Friedrich Engels senior established the cotton-spinning firm of Engels and Ermen in Manchester. Later it extended to Barmen. The firm survives to this day.

The environment in which Engels grew up was as different as it could possibly have been from that in which Marx passed his boyhood years. In the Wuppertal bigotry reigned in its most repulsive form – a narrow, gloomy, moping 'fundamentalism' which wanted all the world, like it, to go about in sackcloth and ashes, thinking everlastingly of its sins. No songs other than hymns must be sung, no books other than devotional books must be read. Science and art were considered vanities of the Evil One. When a boy at Engels's school asked

one of the masters who Goethe was, the peevish and reproach-
ful answer was that he was 'an atheist'. At the age of eighteen
Engels described his native town as the 'Zion of obscurantism'.

Engels's mother had preserved a cheerful disposition from
her happy childhood in Berlin, but his father not only adhered
to the most rigorous observances of the devout but brought
up his children in strict accord with the oppressive spirit of
the prevalent bigotry. Engels was fond of his mother but became alienated from his father at an early age and actually
hated him.

Trier was a beautiful old town living on the cultivation of
the vine, Bonn was a friendly conglomeration of students,
landladies and artisans, and even in Berlin Marx saw practically nothing of modern industry. Engels grew up among
factories and slums. From his earliest years he was surrounded
by poverty and distress; sick children who 'breathed more
smoke and dust than oxygen' into their lungs in the squalid
rooms in which they lived; men, women and children who
worked at the loom for fourteen or sixteen hours a day, half-
starved, consumptive, their only friend the brandy bottle
which occasionally allowed them to forget the dreariness of
their existence; all the horror of early capitalism, which celebrated its maddest orgies in this part of the Rhineland.

The lively boy rebelled against the grim existence that
surrounded him. When his father found the 'otherwise excellent youth' reading chivalrous romances instead of pious books
in spite of severe punishments, he reproached him for flip-
pancy and lack of principle. There was a small group of young
poets at his school, and young Engels wrote poems entirely in
the manner of Ferdinand Freiligrath, who was then a clerk
in the counting-house of a Barmen business house, writing his
verses 'between the journal and the ledger'. His poems sang
of the free life of the sons of the desert, of lion hunts and Moor-
ish kings. Revulsion from Europe and the present was the first
feeble, passive sign of revolt against the Europe of the time.[2]

As long as Engels lived in Barmen only faint echoes of the
noises of the battle without came to his ears. The bigots of his

K.M.—4*

native town barely knew the names of Börne, Heine, and the poets of Young Germany, and they would have been revolted at the idea of one of their pious community soiling himself by reading such heathenish and sinful stuff. They ignored the movements abroad among the people, and took no interest in politics, literature or philosophy. Engels may have heard older schoolfellows of his talking when they came back to Barmen for their holidays, and this could not have failed to give wings to his longing to escape from his hateful, cramped surroundings. But he did not escape yet.

Engels left school a year early. He was an excellent pupil. He learned easily and quickly, and was particularly good at languages. His father's reason for abandoning the idea of making his son a lawyer and making a merchant of him instead is unknown. He took him first into his own business, and a year later sent him to Bremen for wider experience. He took care that the youth should be preserved from temptation when away from home. The export house young Engels entered was on excellent terms with Engels and Ermen, and the young man lived in the family of a pastor besides. Bremen was another stronghold of bigotry like his native town.

It was also a trade centre, with relations to the outside world that were far different from those of the Wuppertal. In spite of the patriarchal nature of the state that set its imprint upon it, it allowed its subjects incomparably more freedom than was allowed by the timid bureaucracy of Prussia. The censorship was milder, and allowed many things to pass that in Prussia would have been strictly forbidden. A new world was suddenly unfolded before young Engels's eyes. It attracted and repelled him, he sought it and then fled from it, it shook him to the foundations of his being.

The writings of Börne made him a political radical. The step he thus took over the boundaries imposed upon him seems to have been an easy one. His breach with the past was no great wrench. The latently defiant poetry of his schooldays had prepared the way. Literature meant a great deal to him, and his schoolboy poems led him straight to the poets of the time, who gave expression to the vague longings for freedom that possessed him. Through them he was guided a step further. With Börne he reached the stage of development necessary for open-minded young men of the time.

His struggle with religion was infinitely harder. There is no shred of evidence to show that the young Marx had any struggle with religion whatever. But Engels only rid himself of the faith of his youth and childhood after the most harassing and agonizing torments. The doctrine of predestination was the cornerstone of the paternal faith. Whom God had chosen would be saved, whom he had damned was damned for all eternity. Man had no power in himself to do good, his fate was predetermined by God, whose grace was everything. The inhuman rigour of this doctrine repelled Engels early, but its complement, the forbidding of fatalistic resignation, the necessity of faith in one's own salvation, and of everlastingly struggling anew for assurance of it, steeped his acts and thoughts in piety. Though he rejected as fanatical exaggeration a good deal of what he had been taught to believe was essential, he was still deeply religious when he went to Bremen. The first and decisive blow that undermined his faith was Strauss's *Life of Jesus*. If the Bible contained but one single contradiction – and Strauss laid bare an abundance of contradictions – his faith in it was shattered. The very rigour with which the bigots insisted on the literal verbal inspiration of the Bible threatened the whole structure if but this one column fell. Young Engels fought with all his might against the doubts that assailed him on every side. 'I pray daily', he wrote to a friend.

I pray for the truth practically all day long. I began to do so as soon as I began to doubt, and yet I do not return to the faith that you have ... Tears come into my eyes as I write. I am moved to the depths of my being, yet I feel that I shall not be lost, that I shall come to God, for whom I yearn with my whole heart. That, surely, bears witness to the Holy Spirit, by which I live and die, even if the opposite is ten thousand times stated in the Bible.[3]

He did not return to the fold. Schleiermacher kept his religious feelings alive for some time yet. But, once entered upon the path, he trod it with characteristic firmness and unflinching honesty with himself. From religion he went to philosophy. He became an Hegelian at the age of twenty and did not stop at that. In October 1841, when he went to Berlin to serve a year as volunteer in the Artillery Guards, he was an Hegelian of the extreme left wing. A certain tendency to occupy himself with religious historical problems survived from his religious youth, besides, apparently, a spirit of intolerance that he preserved to his old age. Marx has often been reproached for obstinacy, but Engels was worse by far. He once told Eduard Bernstein that though everybody talked of Marx's intolerance when Marx presided at the General Council of the International even the most controversial questions seldom led to open conflict; when he was in the chair things were quite different.

Engels soon entered the group of Freien in Berlin,[4] with whom he took part in the controversy with Schelling, against whom he wrote two able pamphlets. He wrote for the *Rheinische Zeitung* and other radical journals. His articles were not worse and most of them were better, wittier and more lucid than those of the other Berlin Young Hegelians. When he returned to Barmen in the autumn of 1842 he could lay claim to occupying quite a respectable position in the world of letters at an age – twenty-two – at which the young Marx had not yet published a line.

Out of regard for his family he had so far written either anonymously or under the pseudonym of Friedrich Oswald. But the mentality of his 'disappointing' son was not unknown to his father, nor did the former make any attempt to conceal it. In a report on Engels's formative years which dates from 1852 an excellently informed Danish police agent states that

the family council decided to withdraw him from the enlightening atmosphere of Germany and send him to the factory in Manchester. His father told him that either he must go to England and become a decent businessman or he would entirely withdraw all paternal support. After the completion of his military service as a Prussian subject Engels found it more prudent to give in and go to Manchester. This was in the late autumn of 1842.[5]

Engels chose to travel via Cologne, in order to seize the opportunity of meeting the staff of the *Rheinische Zeitung*. His first meeting with Marx passed off coolly. Marx was just about to break with the Berlin Freien and saw in Engels one of their allies. Engels on his side had been prejudiced against Marx by Bruno Bauer. However, they agreed to the extent that it was arranged that Engels should continue to contribute to the *Rheinische Zeitung* from England. Engels sent his first dispatch, on the internal crisis in England, on 30 November, almost as soon as he arrived in London.

Engels had a special gift for rapidly finding his way about on foreign soil, and in his young years, unlike Marx, he was always quick to form a judgement. But however premature the views that he put forward might seem – a young man in a country for the first time attempting to unravel its innermost structure after two days on its soil – they were less premature than they appeared. Engels had studied English affairs 'on the quiet' in Germany, the outward reason being that he was going to Manchester. But there were other weighty reasons as well.

Engels became a communist in the autumn of 1842. In this he did not differ from other left-wing Hegelians, who, proceeding from religious criticism, had come over to Feuerbach and recognized in communism the only possibility of realizing the generic notion of man. Engels had met Moses Hess and been strongly influenced by his conception of world history, according to which the Germans were to carry out the philosophical revolution, the French the political revolution and the English the economic revolution. In a letter Hess wrote Berthold Auerbach in October 1842, he told him he had been discussing questions of the day with Engels and that Engels had left him a most enthusiastic communist.

Like Marx, Engels came to communism by way of contemporary German philosophy. But Engels's communism was fed from other than philosophical sources. The conclusions of the philosophers could only be put into practice by means of the abolition of private property, and communism alone could free mankind from barbarism. Marx reached this conclusion as the result of a process of intellectual development. Engels crossed the 't's' and dotted the 'i's' of his theory from the evidence of his senses. Engels knew the state of the proletariat at first hand – 'the status which represents the complete loss of humanity'.[6] All he needed for the whole extent of the dehumanization it involved to become plain to him was to re-tread the way to it, this time by the high road of philosophy. For him the proletariat was not just a philosophical instrument, but meant the proletariat of the Wuppertal, the workers in his father's factory. He only had to look about him to see dehumanization in its grossest form. He had known for a long time that the spinners in his father's factory in Manchester lived the same brutalized existence as their class comrades in suffering in Germany. Their brutalization was the consequence of an economic system in which he lived and which he knew from the inside. Philosophy led him, like Marx, into the field of economics. He had this advantage over Marx, that he could study economic realities while living in their midst.

Engels passed nearly two years in Manchester, and they bore rich fruit. How well he applied himself to the mastery of economics is demonstrated in his *Outlines of a Critique of Political Economy,*[7] described by Marx as a 'brilliant sketch'.[8] Engels set out to demonstrate all economic categories as aspects of private property and all contradictions of bourgeois economy as necessary consequences of private property. Expressed in philosophical language and often only by implication, the work contains the foundations of scientific socialism. The much-extolled system of free competition, it argues, leads to an ever more precipitous breach between capitalists and workers. While political economists were working out their theories about the balancing of supply and demand and the impossibility of over-production, reality answered them with trade crises which returned as regularly as comets and brought more suffering and mischief in their wake than the great plagues of old. While the reign of private enterprise lasted, crises would recur; each one more universal, therefore more severe than the last, impoverishing a greater number of small capitalists and increasing in ever greater proportion the multitude of the class living on bare work alone. Thus private property produced the revolution by itself.

The more deeply Engels penetrated the English social and economic scheme, the clearer it became to him that the English were not to be won over by the categories he had relied on up to now. However persistently he tried to drum into the heads of the 'obdurate Britons' what was taken for granted in Germany, namely that 'so-called material interests never appear in history as self-sufficient motives, but that they nevertheless, whether consciously or unconsciously, invariably provide the guiding strings of historical progress', he did not succeed. He was forced reluctantly to resign himself to the conclusion that in England only the conflict of material interests was recognized. In England interests and not principles would begin and carry out the revolution. But this applied to England only. To Germany it did not apply. 'The Germans', he tried to explain to his English friends – in English – at the end of 1843,

are a very disinterested nation; if in Germany principle comes into collision with interest, principle will almost always silence the claims of interest. The same love of abstract principle, the same disregard of reality and self-interest which have brought the Germans to a state of political nonentity, these very same qualities guarantee the success of philosophical communism in that country.[9]

But now he was in England, a country which ignored general principles, it became his task to base his communism on a foundation of material interests. Engels found a great workers' movement, that of the Chartists, in progress. Its aims were purely political, but Engels did not doubt for a moment that it was bound to become socialist, and that within a short time the Chartists would see that private property was the root of all the evils from which the working classes were suffering. After the abortive attempt at a general strike to enforce universal suffrage, they must confine themselves for the time being to propaganda. Engels was a close observer of the first great independent workers' movement to take place in a European country. It was something for which not even the preliminaries were to hand in Germany. He got into touch with the Chartists through James Leach, a Manchester workman, and in Leeds he established a friendship with George Julian Harney, editor of the Chartist paper, the *Northern Star*. [10]

He admired the practice of the Chartists, but, as a communist and an atheist, he was closer in theoretical outlook to Robert Owen. He heartily approved of Owen's struggle against the marriage tie, religion and private property, which Owen regarded as the three irrational, arch-egoistical institutions from which humanity must be freed in order that a new world founded on reason and solidarity might be built. He made contact with the Owenites, and in their paper, the *New Moral World*, he described to the English, who had scarcely heard of it, the growth and development of continental communism. [11]

Engels lived at the heart of the English cotton industry, the most modern industry in the most modern industrial country of Europe. In spite of the 'tremendous advances' made in recent years, his native Wuppertal could not compare with it. He found that just where industrialism was flourishing most exuberantly the proletariat was plunged into the greatest distress. For month after month Engels roamed through the working-class districts of Manchester, which he soon got to know better than most of its inhabitants. Though he was familiar with the plight of the German spinners and weavers, he was profoundly moved by what he saw. His book on the state of the working classes in England, based on his observations and extended researches and written in the winter of 1844–5, is the most flaming indictment of early capitalism ever written. [12]

At the end of August 1844 Engels travelled back to Germany by way of Paris, and met Marx for the second time. In the bare ten days they spent together 'they established their agreement in all theoretical fields, and their joint work dates from that time'.[13]

Engels brought Marx more than he received from him. Both had come independently to communism, both had recognized in the proletariat the class which, product and negation of private property at the same time, was to abolish private property. But Engels had an incomparably deeper insight into the economics of bourgeois society. Living in economically advanced England, he had anticipated Marx in understanding its dialectic, its inherent tendency to produce contradictions and thus its own downfall. He had come face to face with a real workers' movement, met the proletariat in its real form. In Manchester he had had his nose rubbed into the fact that

economic realities, which in history written hitherto had played either no role at all, or at best an insignificant one, were, at any rate in the modern world, a decisive historical force; that economic realities provided the foundation from which present-day class conflicts arose; that in those countries where, thanks to big industry, those conflicts had fully developed, for example in England, they were the foundation on which political parties were built and party struggles fought and thus of the whole of political history. Marx had not only come to the same conclusion but in the *Deutsch-Französische Jahrbücher* had arrived at the generalization that it was not the state that conditioned and regulated civil society but civil society that conditioned and regulated the state; and that therefore politics and their history were to be explained by economic conditions and their development and not the reverse.[14]

When Engels wrote these phrases in 1885 he represented his and Marx's insight into historical reality as more mature than it really was at the end of 1844. It was not till after their meeting and the beginning of their cooperation that these ideas were definitely formulated.[15] Engels helped Marx to make concrete his quite abstract ideas concerning the relations of state and society; and Marx helped Engels to understand that the dependence of politics on material interests, class interests, a dependence the validity of which Engels had hitherto only been willing to admit as applying to England, was in reality valid for all countries alike. But he still maintained, when he once more trod the soil of his native land, that Germany could only be won for communism by the insight of educated people.

Before the two friends parted they decided to cross swords with Bruno Bauer for the last time. Engels wrote his contribution to the planned pamphlet while still in Paris. It filled about twenty pages. Marx harried and pursued 'critical criticism' into its last lurking-place, put such enthusiasm into his attack on the jugglers with ideas that he almost appeared to be doing it for the sheer exhilaration of the thing, and to the surprise of Engels, who failed to see that their opponents' nullity merited such profusion, filled more than 300 pages. The book appeared in February 1845 under the title of *The Holy Family* [by which was meant the three brothers, Bruno, Edgar and Egbert Bauer] *or the Critique of Critical Criticism*.[16] It did not attract much attention. Bruno Bauer and his followers had reduced themselves to absurdity and nobody took any more notice of them.

Engels found the Germany he returned to very different from the Germany he had left. Increasing impoverishment of wide masses of artisans and home workers; the rapid spread of pauperization, of which hitherto people had only read in sentimental French novels and pamphlets which were not taken very seriously; the rising of the weavers, the first movements among the industrial workers, all entirely new features in the picture that educated society, leading its own life, had formed of Germany, troubled and disturbed the bourgeoisie and forced them to face the problems that had arisen. A wave of strikes passed over Germany in 1844. Workers in the calico factories in Berlin rose in insurrection, railway workers in Westphalia did the same. There were strikes in Saxony, Hamburg and elsewhere. People discovered that there was something rumbling down below, something with a menace. That something was millions of people, of whom at most the police had taken notice before. What had been discovered was the existence of the proletariat.

Pamphlets appeared giving recipes for overcoming 'the plague of the nineteenth century'. Bettina von Arnim wrote *This Book Belongs to the King*,[17] in which she ruthlessly exposed the distress in the so-called Vogtland, near Berlin. Philanthropical societies were formed, with the support of Friedrich Wilhelm IV, 'societies for the good of the working classes'. In East Prussia they remained what their founders intended them to be, but in the western provinces socialist-minded intellectuals soon gained an entry to them. At Elberfeld, Barmen, Cologne, Bielefeld, and elsewhere, these societies became socialist propaganda centres, education centres of and for the workers. It became necessary to dissolve the local Berlin society as early as the autumn of 1844.

The first German socialist papers appeared at the same time – the *Westfälisches Dampfboot* at Bielefeld, the *Gesellschaftsspiegel* at Elberfeld, the *Sprecher* at Hamm and others. The word 'socialist' should not be understood in the sense in which it is understood today. Socialism meant sympathy with the suffering masses, indignation at injustice, appeal to man's nobler instincts, and belief in a better world. The descriptions of the lives of the workers which those newspapers contained are still valuable today. They shook the conscience of all whose sensibilities had not grown blunted. A communist at that time was not much more than a resolute opponent of poverty, hunger and mass distress.

Former contributors to the *Rheinische Zeitung*, like Moses Hess and D'Ester, were prominent among these socialists-by-compassion. Engels flung himself enthusiastically into propaganda work. The way to the workers was closed to him. The authorities would not have allowed him to agitate for communism among the workers. At the best he could only have spoken to very small groups. But for the time being Engels did not believe that kind of work to be so very necessary. He still pinned all his hopes to principles to which the intellectuals must be won over first.

In the winter of 1844–5 the victory of communism seemed to him to be only a question of a few years, possibly even months. He wrote to Marx that the propaganda being carried out in Cologne was tremendous; there were marvellous fellows at Düsseldorf, there were communists at Elberfeld, and at Barmen even the commissary of police was a communist. If they could only get to work directly on the people, they would soon be on top. Everyone, from rich to poor, came to the communist meetings. Nor were their activities without success. Whichever way you turned you stumbled upon a communist. 'Communism is the sole subject of conversation, and new adherents come to us every day. In the Wuppertal communism is a reality, almost actually a power in the land.'[18] The whole unreality of the movement is revealed by the phrase: 'The proletariat is busy, we do not know what with, and we can hardly know.'[19]

Engels's position at Barmen gradually became untenable. The police started taking a very definite interest in his activities, and he had to reckon with the prospect of being arrested, possibly by the communist commissary of police himself. Life with his family was 'a real dog's life'. All his father's religious fanaticism was re-awakened and Engels's emergence as a communist stirred him to 'a glowing bourgeois fanaticism' besides. 'You have no idea of the maliciousness of the Christian heresy hunt after my soul', he wrote to Marx in Brussels. 'My father only needs to discover the existence of the *Critical Criticism* book to turn me out of the house altogether ... It is no longer to be borne.'

Marx's insistence on his friend's joining him in Brussels so that they might continue their common labours became more urgent than ever. At the beginning of April 1845 Engels went to Brussels.

[9]

Clarification

AFTER we had passed a night in Brussels, almost the first thing Marx said to me [H. Bürgers] in the morning was: 'We must go and see Freiligrath today. He is here, and I must make good the wrong the *Rheinische Zeitung* did him before he stood "on the party battlements". His confession of faith has wiped out everything.'[1]

Ferdinand Freiligrath stood out by a head from the teeming multitude of German poets. His exotic poems, in rank equal to their prototype, Victor Hugo's *Les Orientales*, glowed with passion, luxuriated in wild visions, and were technically flawless. The young people of Germany received them with enthusiasm. The effect they had on the young Engels has already been noted. About the year 1840 Freiligrath was the most popular poet in Germany. Devoted to the ideal of 'pure art', he held it to be unworthy of the poet to descend into the contemporary arena. His verses:

> Der Dichter steht auf einer höh'ren Warte
> Als auf den Zinnen der Partei*

were later quoted to satiety. He had no objection to accepting the pension of 300 thalers which Friedrich Wilhelm IV granted him in 1842 at the suggestion of Alexander von Humboldt. He wrote an open letter attacking Herwegh for wishing to bring poetry down to the level of the handmaiden of politics. His ambition seemed to be to become the court poet of Berlin.

This brought the *Rheinische Zeitung* down on him with a vengeance. It mercilessly derided the 'pensioned poet'. In Marx's opinion Freiligrath was 'an enemy of Herwegh's and of freedom'.[2]

---

* The poet stands on a higher watch-tower
Than on the party battlements.

A year later Freiligrath was in the revolutionary camp. The cry for freedom that swept across Germany like a wave awakened the dreamer. In 1844 the censor forbade the publication of his *Patriotic Fantasies*. Freiligrath, without troubling about the censor, published them under another title, *Confession of Faith*, and renounced his much-talked-of 'pension' in the preface. The book was banned. Freiligrath escaped arrest by fleeing to Belgium.

He remained in Belgium for a few months only. They sufficed for him to form a friendship with Marx, 'that nice, interesting, unassuming, resolute fellow', as he called him. Freiligrath's poetic powers reached their zenith in the revolutionary years of 1848 and 1849 and he was one of Marx's closest collaborators on the *Neue Rheinische Zeitung*. Their friendship defied all the vicissitudes of life and survived a number of temporary estrangements during the hard years of exile in London. Freiligrath was one of the few men whom Marx 'loved as friends in the highest sense of the word'.[3]

Marx met only a few German exiles in Brussels. In this 'disagreeable mongrel country' as Freiligrath called Belgium, the Germans did not feel at home, and in Brussels they were not liked. Three years later, when Marx was expelled by the anti-revolutionary government, his expulsion, to quote Engels, 'helped to mitigate Belgian hatred of the Germans'.

There were not many exiles from other countries either. But small as the colony of exiles was, it was an important one. During those years a political refugee could lead a more secure life in Belgium than in any other European country, not even excluding Switzerland. When Buonarotti, the fellow conspirator of Babeuf, had to flee from Geneva at the beginning of the Restoration, Belgium was the only country to offer him a refuge. He lived there until the revolution of 1830 and wrote his famous work on the *Conspiracy of the Equals*, the bold attempt of Babeuf and his comrades to plant the banner of socialism in Paris when the great revolution ended. The book had an influence far wider than the borders of Belgium and France. It had a strong influence on the 'physical force' Chartists. Exile set its seal upon men of Buonarotti's type. In Belgium were refugees to whom the rest of Europe was shut – French Blanquists, Polish democrats, German republicans, *émigrés* of the second and third generation.

Belgium received them all and suffered them to remain upon her soil, as long as they refrained from direct political activity. The small country had fought for and gained its independence only a few years before; it was not yet firmly in the saddle and it very intelligibly fought shy of diplomatic conflicts with its powerful neighbours. These would have been inevitable if the exiles had been allowed to carry out propaganda from Belgium, and the attempt would have cost the refugees their sanctuary. Thus, although the Press was freer than in France, there was no 'emigrant' paper or organization. This state of affairs survived until the outbreak of the February revolution, when the atmosphere changed throughout the whole of Europe, and the liberals came into power in Belgium – and then not for long.

Marx became acquainted with the peculiarities of Belgium during the first days after his arrival. The Prussian Government soon reconciled itself to the withdrawal of the expulsion of Ruge, Börnstein and the others who were to have left France with Marx, but it continued to persecute Marx. Scarcely had he arrived in Brussels when the Prussian Ambassador demanded his expulsion. Marx applied for a permit soon after his arrival. He did not obtain it. Only after many inquiries did he find out that such an application did not suffice. He had to give a written undertaking to the *sûreté publique* to print nothing in Belgium about contemporary politics. After that he obtained his permit.[4] Infuriated by the renewed persecution, tired of the struggle with 'his' officials, who wasted time he could have employed profitably, full of contempt for his reactionary fatherland, 'the backward colony of Russia', in December 1845 he renounced his Prussian nationality.

He did not find the renunciation of journalistic activity hard to bear. He had other activities in mind. In the foreword to *The Holy Family*, written in September 1844, he and Engels had announced that after completing their demolition of Bruno Bauer they would state their own constructive position to the new philosophical and social doctrines in independent works.

Marx planned to write a two-volume *Critique of Politics and Political Economy*, for which he had arranged a contract with Leske, the Darmstadt publisher, before he left Paris. As soon as he had settled down in Brussels he flung all his energy into the task. In January, Engels was urging him to complete the book quickly, even if he should be dissatisfied with it himself. Engels declared that it was essential that the work be finished before April. Men's minds were ripe for it, and they must strike while the iron was hot. This formula was to be frequently repeated during the next twenty years. Again and again Engels was to urge his friend to write 'finis' to the work in hand, stop his everlasting ploughing through books and collecting of material, and actually get down to the work of writing. Engels later confessed that while they were in Brussels together Marx taught him for the first time what hard work really meant. Marx's thoroughness, the vigour with which he grappled with a subject, not letting it go till he had mastered it in all its details, the conscientiousness with which he would read through everything that had ever been written about it, were alien to Engels's temperament. The *Critique of Politics and Political Economy* was meant to appear in the summer of 1845. The first volume, the *Critique of Political Economy*, appeared in the summer of 1859, and the first volume of *Das Kapital* in the autumn of 1867.

Once more Marx plunged into a sea of books. He read and made excerpts from the economists Buret, Sismondi, Senior, A. Blanqui, Ure, Rossi and Pecchio, to name the most important only. In the summer of 1845 he went to Manchester with Engels to study the English economists Petty, Tooke, Thompson, Cobbett and others, who were not available in Brussels. In addition to all this he planned to collaborate with Engels in publishing a whole series of important socialist books in German translations – the principal works of Fourier, Owen and others. Marx was to write introductions for the French authors and Engels for the English ones.

But in the summer of 1845 a new task intervened. Marx informed his publisher that he had to break off work on the *Critique of Politics and Political Economy*. It appeared to him to be of vital immediate importance to attack German philosophy and state his positive attitude to the present and past position of German socialism. This was necessary in order to prepare the public for a system of economics which was diametrically opposed to German preconceptions of the time.

During the lifetime of Marx and Engels this work never appeared. Excerpts from the manuscript were only published in various places years after their death. When, thanks to the tireless researches of D. B. Riazanov, it finally appeared in its complete form in 1932,[6] it was found that *German Ideology* was Marx's and Engels's first exposition of their interpretation of history – historical materialism – carried out in a detail for which they never found time or opportunity again. When Marx published his *Critique of Political Economy* in 1859, he contented himself with preparing the public for the new viewpoint with a few sentences in the foreword. A decade and a half had passed since he had arrived at it, jointly with Engels, and he had used it as a guiding thread through all his works and could well believe that it was intelligible to all who could read and only required a final and definite formulation. But if one looks back now at the endless controversies that have centred round the correct interpretation of historical materialism, one cannot help deploring that *German Ideology* found no publisher in 1846.

In his reminiscences of the origins of the Communist League[7] Engels states that Marx had developed the main outlines of his materialist interpretation of history by the time he joined him in Brussels in spring 1845. The two friends decided to elaborate jointly the antithesis between their views and the ideological background of German philosophy. This purpose was to be carried out in the form of a critique of post-Hegelian philosophy. It was impossible to carry it out otherwise at the time, not only because it was the only way in which Marx and Engels could come to terms with their previous philosophic conscience, but because in the intellectual and historical conditions of the 1840s the quintessence of their case, namely the proposition that it is not man's mind that conditions his being but, on the contrary, his social being that conditions his mind, could be stated most effectively and with the most far-reaching consequences in the field of political action in the form of a controversy with idealism and in that form only.

More than half of the two solid octavo volumes that Marx and Engels wrote between September 1845 and August 1846 is taken up with a refutation of Max Stirner, the theorist of individual anarchism.[8] Marx took up the cudgels with Stirner with real delight. He took 'the schoolmaster' sentence by sentence and harried him until nothing was left of the atheistic 'egoist' but a beer-swilling Berlin philistine.[9] He was no less pitiless in his exposure of the 'true' socialism which had recently become fashionable in Germany and deemed itself superior to 'crude' communism. He revealed it as an insipid brew of German philosophical phrases blended with half-understood propositions borrowed from French socialist and communist systems by philanthropic *littérateurs* who failed to understand the movement of which these systems were the expression. The fight against this kind of idealistic rubbish in all its forms was all the more necessary because in Germany social contradictions were not yet as developed as they were in France and England, and in that phrase-intoxicated land phrases were correspondingly dangerous. The only philosopher who deserved respect was Ludwig Feuerbach.[10]

Marx's pithiest condensation of his theory of history made at that time was in a letter to a Russian friend, Paul Annenkov. His criticism of Proudhon was in reality a criticism of historical idealism. Marx wrote:

What is society, whatever its form may be? The product of the interactions of men. Are men free to choose this or that social form? Not in the least. Take any particular stage in the development of the productive forces of man and you will find a corresponding form of trade and consumption. Take definite stages in the development of production, trade, consumption, and you have a corresponding form of social constitution, a definite organization of family, rank or classes, in a word a corresponding form of civil society. Take such a civil society and you have a definite political situation, which is only the official expression of civil society.

It remains to add that men are not free masters of their forces of production – the foundation of their whole history – because these forces are acquired, are the product of previous activity. Thus the forces of production are the result of man's practical energy, but this energy is itself conditioned by the circumstances in which men are placed by the forces of production already acquired by them, by the social forms existing before them, which they themselves have not created but are the product of the previous generation. From the simple fact that each generation finds itself confronted with forces of production acquired by the preceding one, which serves it as the raw material for new forces of production, it follows that there is a continuity in the history of mankind, and a history of mankind which is all the more his history because his forces of production and consequently his social relationships have grown in the meantime. The necessary consequence is that the social history of men is always only the history of their individual development, alike whether they are conscious of it or not. Their material relationships form the foundation of all their relationships. These material relationships are only the necessary forms in which their material and individual activity is fulfilled ... The economic forms under which men produce, consume, exchange, are *transient and historical*. With newly acquired forces of production men alter their methods of production, and with their methods of production they alter their economic conditions, which were purely and simply the necessary conditions of these definite methods of production ... Proudhon has understood very well that men make cloth, linen, silk. What Proudhon has not understood is that men produce the *social relationships* in which they produce the cloth and the linen in conformity with their capacity. Still less has Proudhon understood that men, who produce social relationships in conformity with their material productivity, also produce *ideas and categories*, that is to say, the ideal, abstract expressions of these same social relationships. Accordingly categories are just as little eternal as the conditions the expression of which they are. For Proudhon, on the contrary, it is categóries and abstractions that are the primary facts. In his opinion it is these and not men who make history ... As for him the driving forces are categories, there is no need to alter practical life to alter the categories. On the contrary, if one alters the categories, alterations in real life will follow.[11]

The last of the *Theses on Feuerbach*, which Marx wrote in his notebook says: 'The philosophers have only *interpreted* the world differently. The task is now to change it.'[12]

At the beginning of May 1846 Marx and Engels sent the greater part of the manuscript to Germany. They had found some prosperous adherents of 'true' socialism in Westphalia who had thought of publishing the work. But business difficulties, whether real or alleged can no longer be determined, intervened. Marx tried in vain to find another publisher. In spite of all his efforts and those of Joseph Weydemeyer, a former Prussian artillery lieutenant who had become a communist and visited Marx in Brussels in 1846, the book remained unpublished. In retrospect it seemed to Marx that the impossibility of publishing a work to which he had devoted a year of his life had not extraordinarily disturbed him. At the time, however, he bore the blow heavily. But it all lay a long time behind him when he wrote: 'We left the manuscript to the nibbling criticism of mice all the more willingly as we had attained our chief aim – clarification.'[13]

[10]

Face to Face with Primitive Communism

NEITHER the old communist utopias nor nebulous speculations of the type of Hess's 'theory' of the various roles of the
different countries in the revolution – which, incidentally,
Engels himself adopted for a time – could survive in the face
of the new interpretation of history. Communism in Germany
and France and Chartism in England no longer appeared
accidental events which might just as well not have happened
at all, or as ideas which could be measured against other ideas,
or as systems which could be considered and accepted or rejected from an absolute, timeless, moral or logical standpoint.
They now appeared, to use Engels's words, as movements of
the oppressed proletarian class, as forms, more developed or
less, of their historically necessary struggle against the ruling
class, the bourgeoisie. Communism no longer meant imagina-
tively concocting an if-possible complete social ideal, but an
understanding of the nature, conditions and consequent aims
of the struggle of the proletariat.

Communism was no longer a doctrine but a movement. It
no longer proceeded from principles, from the humanism of
the Young Hegelians or of Feuerbach, but from facts. Insofar
as it was theoretical, it was the theoretical expression of the
position of the proletariat in the class struggle between proletariat and bourgeoisie and the theoretical comprehension of
the conditions for attaining the freedom of the proletariat.

Marx and Engels had established their views scientifically
on the basis of German philosophical theory. It was now
equally essential for them to win over the European, and first
of all the German, working class to their point of view. 'We
set about the task as soon as we had reached clarification',

Engels relates.[1] The overthrowing of primitive communism was the first and most urgent aim.

Wilhelm Weitling came to London in September 1844.[2] The sufferings and persecution he had undergone for his communist ideals had increased his already considerable renown. He had been arrested by the Swiss authorities in the summer of 1843 and indicted for blasphemy, making attacks on the rights of property and forming a secret society for the spreading of communism. He was imprisoned for four months on remand, condemned to a further six months in gaol by the Zürich court and, at the conclusion of his sentence, was delivered over the Prussian frontier in chains. His trial and still more the official report on 'The communists in Switzerland according to the papers found in Weitling's possession' attracted attention far beyond the borders of Switzerland.[3] The wide publicity given to his case caused many people to hear of the communist movement and of communism for the first time. Where the distribution of communist literature was impossible, the official report, which everybody could buy, with its copious extracts from Weitling's writings, was not a bad substitute.

This gifted young writer – at once a poet and a philosophizing tailor's assistant – received universal sympathy. He wrote his *Gaol Poems* in prison.[4] Even the Prussian Government was aware of the prevailing mood, and although the Swiss authorities delivered him up to them as a fugitive from military service, when he was found unfit they let him go free. But after a few months he had once more made himself so unpopular with the police that he was arrested again and sent off to Hamburg, where Heine saw him. 'My legs have no aptitude to carry iron rings like those Weitling bore', he wrote. 'He showed me the marks.'[5]

From Hamburg Weitling went on to London, where his German comrades enthusiastically received him. A big celebration was held in his honour on 22 September in cooperation with the Chartists and the refugees from France. But the jubilation and the tumult died away, and before six months had passed the contradictions that had long been forming within the movement led to an open rupture.

During the years in which Weitling wrote his *Humanity as it is and as it ought to be*[6] and was developing the ideas he expressed in his most mature work, *Guarantees of Harmony and Freedom*, all the leaders of the League of the Just had been living in Paris. After the rising of 12 May 1839 they scattered. Weitling went to Switzerland, Schapper, Heinrich Bauer and Moll found refuge in England. The small communist groups in Switzerland lost themselves more and more in sentimental, primitive Christian communism and romantic plotting. Weitling, separated from his old friends, surrounded by backward artisans in a backward country, soon abandoned himself entirely to primitive utopianism and highly irrational flights of fancy. It was different with those members of the League who went westwards. They came under the influence of Chartism, at the time the most advanced workers' movement in the world. They established friendly relations with the Chartist leaders, read the Chartist Press, and contributed to it themselves. The longer they lived in England the more they shook themselves free from their primitive equalitarian communism. In 1843, when Weitling started talking of the communalization of women and concocted a hare-brained scheme for forming an army of 40,000 thieves and robbers who were to bring the exploiters to their knees by means of a pitiless guerilla warfare, they firmly protested against such folly.

Imprisonment had disordered Weitling's mind more than ever. After the Zürich trial he completely lost all sense of proportion. His outward fame seemed to confirm his own conviction that he had been chosen as the teacher, leader and saviour of mankind, to free it from all its misery and suffering. The 'Londoners' and Weitling had to part.

The dispute flared up over the London German Workers' Union. The Union had been founded in February 1840, by Schapper and six other members of the League of the Just, as a legal organization to serve as a screen for the League. The League made use of this kind of organization everywhere. The

statutes of the London German Workers' Union, printed as a
special pamphlet, became the pattern for all organizations of
the same kind founded by members of the League everywhere
where German workers lived and legal organizations of this or
a similar kind were possible. The chief purpose of these unions
was propaganda, and in addition they provided benefits for
sick comrades. It did not take long for the Union to become the
centre of the German workers' colony in London. In addition
to Germans it had among its members Scandinavians, Dutch,
Hungarians, Czechs, southern Slavs and Russians: nationalities which were of admirable service to the Germans in their
contacts with other countries. In 1847 an English grenadier
guardsman in uniform was a regular visitor. At the time the
Union reached its zenith, on the eve of the revolution of 1848,
it had between 400 and 500 members, a more than respectable
total for the time. The life of the Union was described in a
letter by Hugo Hildebrand, the political economist, who
visited it in April 1846.[7]

About half past eight we went to the Union premises in a spirit
of considerable expectancy [he wrote]. On the ground floor there
was an ordinary shop, in which porter and other beers were sold. I
did not notice any special place reserved for visitors. We went
through the shop and upstairs into a hall-like room, capable of
seating about 200 men at the tables and benches distributed about
the floor. About twenty men were sitting about in groups, eating
a simple supper or smoking one of the pipes of honour (which lay
on all the tables) with a beer-mug in front of them. Others were
standing about. Every moment the door opened to admit newcomers, so that it was clear that the meeting was only due to begin
later. One saw from their faces that most of the men belonged to
the working class, although all were thoroughly decently clothed
and an easy and unaffected but thoroughly decorous tone pre-
vailed. The language was predominantly German, but French
and English were also to be heard. At one end of the hall there was
a grand piano, with music, which in unmusical London was the
best proof that we had found the right room. As we knew no one
present we sat down at a table near the door. Very little notice
was taken of us. We ordered a glass of porter and the usual penny

packet of tobacco and awaited our host and acquaintance, Schapper. It was not long before a big, strong, healthy-looking man of about thirty-six, with a black moustache and a commanding manner, came up to Diefenbach [Hildebrand's companion]. He was promptly introduced to me as Schapper, the former Frankfurt demagogue, who later took part in campaigns, or rather revolutions, in Switzerland and Spain. He was very serious on the occasion of my meeting him, but friendly, and I could feel that he looked down at my professional status with a certain inner pride.

What Engels, looking back at the early years of the movement forty years later, said about Schapper, Heinrich Bauer and Moll, the three men who took such an important part in the birth of the Communist League, may be stated with advantage here. Engels remembered Schapper as a giant in stature, resolute and energetic, always ready to risk his life and bourgeois well-being, an ideal professional revolutionary of the type characteristic of the 1830s.[8] In spite of a certain ponderousness of thought, he was by no means inaccessible to better theoretical understanding than his own, to compensate for which he only held on the more grimly to what he had once grasped. Hence his intelligence was sometimes carried away by his revolutionary zeal. But he always saw his mistakes afterwards and candidly admitted them. Heinrich Bauer came from Franconia and was a bootmaker. He was a lively, spritely, witty little man, concealing a great deal of shrewdness and determination in his small frame. Finally Joseph Moll, a Cologne watchmaker, a middle-sized Hercules, was at least the equal of his comrades in energy and determination and was superior to them in intelligence. He was a born diplomat, besides being more accessible to theoretical understanding.

Hildebrand continues:

Schapper invited us to sit down with him at one end of the hall and showed me a notice-board on which the Union regulations were displayed. They were under the heading of 'German Workers' Educational Union'. Anyone who earned his living honestly and had nothing dishonourable against him was eligible for membership, but every application for membership had to be proposed and seconded by a member. The Union officials were a president, a secretary, a librarian and a treasurer. Members were divided into two classes: (1) those who constituted a communist club of their own, conditions for membership of which were as described and (2) other members who took part in the educational activities of the Union only. Only the first category could take part in meetings at which voting took place, elect officers and vote on the admission of new members. The others only took a passive part in the Union activities, took part in none of the communist meetings proper and only paid contributions and fines if they missed any of the educational meetings. The basic idea of the Union was that man could only attain liberty and self-knowledge by the cultivation of his mind. For this reason every evening was devoted to instruction of one kind or another. The first evening was devoted to study of the English language, the second to geography, the third to history, the fourth to drawing and physics, the fifth to singing, the sixth to dancing and the seventh to communist policy. The subjects of instruction were changed every half year...

We took our seats at the indicated place. In the meantime the hall had become crowded, and the president, of whom all I know is that he was described to me as a doctor, opened the meeting. After a solemn silence had been obtained and everyone had taken his pipe out of his mouth, the secretary, a tailor's assistant, whose descriptive powers were really enviable, read out a notice to the effect that *Citizen* Hildebrand and *Citizen* Diefenbach had been introduced as guests by *Citizen* Schapper and asked whether any citizen had any objection. After that attention was turned to current events and Citizen Schapper made a report on the events of the week. His report was very eloquent, thorough and informative. It was evident that he and the club conducted a very widespread correspondence; for he reported the contents of a letter from Madrid which contained news of the fall of the military despotism, due to Christina's hierarchist tendencies, at greater length and in far greater detail than had yet appeared in any newspaper. A strong communist colouring was naturally evident throughout, and the theme of the proletariat ran like a red thread through the entire discourse. I candidly admit that I can stand a good dose of liberalism, but in some places my hair stood on end...

The whole speech made a great impression on the audience and was followed by general and continuous applause. Next the minutes of the last communist meeting, at which the objectionableness of the Christian religion was dealt with, were read by the secretary.

After this a fresh subject came up for discussion, namely the question of what arrangements were to be made for the education of children in the communist state. During the course of the discussion I discovered to my amazement that at least half of those present were married men. Unfortunately the debate did not get much beyond the initial stages; consequently all I found out to satisfy my curiosity was that they repudiated alike the communalization of wives and the emancipation of women, and considered woman as the mental complement of man and marriage as a moral institution, in which both parties enjoyed equal rights, although the capacities, disposition and sphere of activity of man and woman were completely different. Education must be mental and physical, private and political and must actually begin before birth.

As it was past midnight by this time, further consideration of these matters was postponed to the following week. Next I had a very serious private discussion with Schapper about his hostility to liberalism, spoke to a few other members, including a Silesian joiner, inspected the Union library and bought some communist pamphlets ... The meeting dispersed in a very friendly and good-tempered spirit, so that the prevalent use of the second person singular did seem not just to spring from the club rules but to be rooted in the members' hearts.

These German workers attentively followed political events not only in England where they lived and in Germany which was their home; their view took in the whole of Europe. Weitling's realm was not of this world. The only distinction that he recognized was that between the present, which he utterly rejected, and a glittering future. All else was evil. Schapper and his friends were patiently seeking a way for themselves along the thorny path of conflicting parties and systems. Their guide was reason. Weitling followed his feelings only. He took his stand on the Bible, on Love, the Noble and the Good. In his opinion the people were long since ripe for the new social order, and the only remaining task was to free them from their oppressors for which all that was required was the determined initiative of a revolutionary organization, a small band of resolute brothers. The obsolete old world must be crushed at a blow by the dictatorship of a revolutionary minority who would act in the interests of the latently revolutionary masses and shrink at nothing to attain their ends. One almost seems to hear the voice of Bakunin, with whom Marx was forced to repeat the same struggle twenty years later, in the following phrases of Weitling, which date from 1845:

In my opinion [Weitling said], everybody is ripe for communism, even the criminals. Criminals are a product of the present order of society and under communism they would cease to be criminals. Humanity is of necessity always ripe for revolution, or it never will be. The latter is nothing but the phraseology of our opponents. If we follow them we shall have no choice but to lay our hands on our knees and wait till roasted pigeons fly into our mouths.

These words of Weitling's were spoken at a meeting of the German Workers' Union at the end of June 1845.[9] Since the beginning of the year regular weekly meetings had been held at which the fundamental questions of communism were discussed. The extent of the breach between their old comrade-in-arms and themselves had gradually become clear to the members of the Union. They found it far from easy to break with their own past. Personally attached to their leader as they were, they went on trying to reconcile the incompatible, to find a middle way. They almost apologized for their secession, but the parting could no longer be postponed. Schapper, their spokesman, said in his reply to Weitling that he himself had spoken in just the same way eight, even six years ago. But now, tempered as he was by so much bitter experience, he was compelled to express agreement with the reactionary phrase; the people were not yet ripe; for if they were ripe, such a phrase would no longer be possible. He ended his speech by saying that truth could not be knocked into people's heads with rifle-butts.

The London German workers all honoured Weitling and his candid opinions, but they decided for Schapper by an overwhelming majority. Weitling could not get over his defeat. He was unable to follow Schapper's reasoning even a little way. He left London, angered and embittered, suspecting intrigue and treachery.

Engels had met the leading members of the Union in 1843. In the summer of 1845, when he and Marx were in London, he renewed the acquaintance and introduced Schapper, Bauer and Moll, who had made a 'tremendous impression' on him two years before as the first revolutionary proletarians he had ever met, to Marx. It is impossible from the scanty material that has survived to say whether Marx attended a meeting of the Union or not, but he certainly paid great attention to the progress of the controversy with Weitling. He set the greater store by it in that it cleared the way from below for his own special task of breaking scientific socialism adrift from sentimental communism, philosophizing, and 'principles'. His most urgent practical aim was that of setting the movement on the right track and accelerating its development.

The Union had one institution which would be useful for his purpose. This was the active correspondence it kept up with members in other countries. These sent in fairly regular reports concerning political events in the countries to which they had emigrated, insofar as these events concerned the workers. It must be possible, Marx decided, to make a permanent institution of the Union's correspondence with its members, extend it to all groups and representatives of the communist and socialist movement and thereby bring it to a higher level. However desirable the sending in of reports might be, the clarifying of views was more important still. This purpose should be served by written contact maintained between individual countries and within the countries themselves.

Marx, with Brussels as his headquarters, set about founding his correspondence committees in the spring of 1846.[10] As a complement to these he planned to start a newspaper in which questions concerning the movement were to be aired from every point of view. The tasks that Marx meant the correspondence committees to fulfil – for a long time their object and nature defied the efforts of research – were indicated in a letter of Marx to Proudhon, dated 5 May 1846, which was found a few years ago. Marx wrote:

Conjointement avec deux de mes amis Frédéric Engels et Philippe Gigot (tous deux à Bruxelles) j'ai organisé avec les communistes et socialistes allemands une correspondence suivie, qui devra s'occuper et de la discussion de questions scientifiques et de la surveillance à exercer sur les écrits populaires et la propagande socialiste, qu'on peut faire en Allemagne par ce moyen. Le but principal de notre correspondence sera pourtant celui, de mettre les socialistes allemands en rapport avec les socialistes français et anglais, de tenir les étrangers au courant des mouvements socialistes qui seront opérés en Allemagne et d'informer les Allemands en Allemagne des progrès du socialisme en France et en Angleterre. De cette manière des différences d'opinion pourront se faire jour; on arrivera à un échange d'idées et à une critique impartiale. C'est là un pas, que le mouvement social aura fait dans son expression *littéraire* afin de se débarrasser des limites de la *nationalité*. Et au moment de l'action, il est certainement d'un grand interêt pour chacun, d'être instruit de l'état des affaires à l'étranger aussi bien que chez lui.

Outre les communistes en Allemagne notre correspondence comprendra aussi les socialistes allemands à Paris et à Londres. Nos rapports avec l'Angleterre sont déjà établis; quant à la France nous croyons tous que nous ne pouvons y trouver un meilleur correspondent que vous ...*

* 'Together with two of my friends, Friedrich Engels and Philippe Gigot (both of whom are in Brussels) I have organized a regular correspondence with the German communists and socialists on scientific questions and the supervision of such popular writing and socialist propaganda as one may be able to carry out in Germany by this means. The main object of our correspondence will, however, be to keep German socialists in contact with French and English socialists, and keep foreigners informed about the socialist movement in Germany and inform the Germans in Germany of the progress of socialism in France and England in turn. In this way differences of opinion will come to

Proudhon, however, declined the invitation.[11] He would very much like to give his aid when things got going, he said, but in the meantime he held it to be superfluous. Of the French socialists Louis Blanc alone seems to have got into touch with the Brussels committee. In England G. Harney declared himself willing to cooperate, though he does not seem to have been very active. Quite an animated correspondence was carried on with Schapper and his friends, and several members of the Paris section of the League of the Just, particularly Ewerbeck, cooperated. Little is known of the contacts made with communists in Germany, but there was correspondence with Silesia, with the Wuppertal, where Köttgen, a painter, was active, with Kiel, where Georg Weber, a doctor, conducted propaganda, and with Cologne. The communists of Cologne, under the leadership of Roland Daniels, a doctor and a personal friend of Marx's,[12] at first declined the invitation to found a correspondence committee as premature but later sent reports to Brussels all the same. On the whole this very loose organization of correspondence committees did not achieve very much. It failed to gain a foothold outside German communist circles, the reports came in irregularly and contributed practically nothing to the theoretical advancement of communism. But it did bring Marx into closer contact with the London German Workers' Union, which was the most important German communist organization, and in that respect achieved its purpose.

The views of Schapper and his friends came ever closer to those of Marx.

---

light; ideas will be exchanged and impartial criticism arrived at. This will be a step taken by the socialist movement on its literary side towards ridding itself of the limitations of nationality. For at the moment of action it is certainly of great interest to everyone to be informed of the state of affairs abroad as well as at home.

'Beside the communists in Germany our correspondence will include German socialists in Paris and London. Our relations with England are already established; as for France we all believe that it would be impossible to find a better correspondent than you.'

Weitling refused to have anything to do with this 'new system of propaganda'. With growing embitterment he watched the dwindling of his prestige from day to day. The free, loose form of this new organization, which aimed at attaining the cooperation of all communists upon a basis of scientific communism, ran counter to all his fundamental preconceptions, which refused to countenance anything but sentimental millenarianism and the tactics of the conspiratorial secret society. His stay in England brought him not only disappointment in the political field, but one personal failure after another. He tried a number of schemes, not one of which succeeded. His grandiose ideas, such as that for revolutionizing science by means of 'a general logical study of thought and speech', and for founding an artificial universal language, roused no interest. Obviously intriguing intellectuals were to blame. They barred his way to the publishers and to their secret 'sources of money'. Weitling had risen to fame in the role of an accuser. His first writings had been the mighty cry of resentment of the oppressed class from which he sprang, but half-educated as he was and full of mistrust for the science of 'this world', as a discoverer of systems he descended into the absurd. He was forced to look on while the London communists increasingly turned from him to follow Marx. He had had a short meeting with Marx in London in the summer of 1845, and on his way back to the Continent at the beginning of 1846 he stopped in Brussels. The Brussels correspondence committee had just been founded, and in view of the prestige Weitling still enjoyed, an invitation to collaborate with the committee could not be avoided. Marx invited him.

Two accounts are extant concerning the confrontation of Marx and Weitling on 30 March 1846. One is a letter Weitling wrote to Moses Hess and the other a detailed account of the affair by the Russian writer, Annenkov, who was very close to Marx at the time and was introduced by him to the communists of Brussels.[13] Annenkov gives the only living description of Marx dating from those years, and it reproduces incomparably the atmosphere of the movement at the time.

Thirty years later Annenkov could still call up a vivid picture of what young Marx was like on that spring evening in 1846.

Marx was a type of man formed all of energy, force of will and unshakeable conviction, a type highly remarkable in outward appearance as well. In spite of his thick, black mane of hair, his hairy hands, and his coat buttoned up all awry, he had the appearance of a man who has the right and the power to demand respect, although his looks and his manners might appear peculiar sometimes. His movements were angular, but bold and confident, his manners were contrary to all social practice. But they were proud, with a touch of disdain, and his sharp voice, which rang like metal, sounded remarkably in accordance with the radical judgements on men and things which he let fall. He spoke only in the imperative, brooking no contradiction, and this was intensified by the tone, which to me was almost painfully jarring, in which he spoke. This tone expressed the firm conviction of his mission to reign over men's minds and dictate their laws. Before my eyes stood the personification of a democratic dictator such as might appear before one in moments of fantasy.

In comparison with him Weitling appeared almost spruce – 'a handsome, fair young man in a somewhat foppishly cut coat, with a foppishly trimmed beard'. He looked more like a commercial traveller than the gloomy, embittered worker, oppressed by the burden of work and thought, whom Annenkov had imagined.

Those present at the meeting were Engels, the Belgian Gigot, Edgar von Westphalen, Marx's brother-in-law, Weydemeyer, Seiler, a German registrar who had fled from Germany, and the journalist Heilberg. These took their seats at a small green table with Marx at the head of it, 'pencil in hand, his lion's head bent over a sheet of paper'. The question for discussion was what form propaganda should take in Germany. Engels, 'tall, straight, grave and looking like a distinguished Englishman', rose and said how necessary it was to clarify opposing views and settle on a general programme, but before he had finished Marx, impatient and thirsting for battle, cut him short, with a direct question to Weitling. 'But tell us, Weitling,' he said, 'what are the arguments with which you defend your social-revolutionary agitation and on what do you intend to base it in the future?' Annenkov stresses his remembrance of the exact form of this blunt question, which opened a heated discussion in the little group round the green table.

Before this unaccustomed audience Weitling lost his usual confidence and command of speech. He spoke indistinctly and confusedly, kept on repeating himself, continually corrected what he said and only made his points with difficulty. His speeches consisted of 'commonplaces of liberal rhetoric'. He declined to create new economic theories, in his opinion the doctrines of the French were ample and sufficient. The workers must open their eyes, put faith in no promises and rest their hopes upon themselves alone.

He would probably have gone on speaking a long time yet if Marx, with angrily contracted brows, had not interrupted him and started a sarcastic reply, the essence of which was that to stir up the people without giving them firm foundations on which to base their actions was a simple act of treachery. The awakening of fantastic hopes led not to the saving of suffering people but to their downfall. Trying to influence the workers, in Germany especially, without a concrete teaching and strong, scientific ideas was hollow, unscrupulous playing with propaganda, like an enthusiastic apostle addressing a lot of open-mouthed donkeys. ' "Here," he added, pointing suddenly to me [Annenkov] with a powerful gesture, "here is a Russian among us. In his country, Weitling, perhaps there would be a place for your role, in Russia alone, perhaps, can successful unions be arranged between absurd apostles and absurd young men!" ' But in a civilized country like Germany, Marx continued, nothing could be achieved without a settled, concrete teaching, and nothing had been achieved so far but noise, harmful excitement and destruction of the very cause that had been undertaken.

In a letter Weitling wrote next day he summed up Marx's speech by saying that unsuitable people must at once be parted from the 'sources of money'. It was his old illusion of an intellectual coalition that caused him so thoroughly to mis-

understand Marx's demand for a 'sifting' of the party. He
listened to Marx without understanding him.[14] There could
be no talk of the immediate realization of communism, Marx
had said. The bourgeoisie must come to the helm first. How
could Weitling possibly understand that, Weitling who believed that he could destroy the old form of society with
40,000 bandits and build up a new society on the basis of
Christian virtue? An unbridgeable abyss separated him from
the Marxist interpretation of historical development. Marx
said on this occasion for the first time what he had to repeat
again and again in the next three years to those impatient
souls who believed that only will was needed to leap a whole
economic, and therefore political, epoch. Marx declared that
the next revolution in Europe would have to destroy the remnants of feudalism, bring the liberal and radical bourgeoisie
into the saddle and thus for the first time create the political
conditions for proletarian action. It was for this reason that
Marx demanded the sifting of the party, the struggle against
'philosophical' communism and the communism of the artisans. Weitling understood that sentiment must be hooted
from the stage. He did not understand that Marx replaced
crude sentiment by scientific understanding. When Marx
demanded that an end be put to 'secret propaganda', that
meant for Weitling the end of the movement itself. He recognized only one form of propaganda, that of the conspiratorial
secret society. Because he believed the masses to be unripe
and incapable of becoming ripe, he wanted and could want
no mass movement.

Marx's criticism had struck Weitling in his weakest spot.
With the mistrust of the self-educated, he felt once more the
feared and hated pride of the intellectual. He replied that
analysis in the study and criticism carried out far from the
suffering world and the afflictions of the people, accomplished
nothing.

At these words Marx struck the table angrily with his fist, so
powerfully that the lamp shook. He jumped to his feet and
exclaimed:

'Ignorance has never yet helped anybody!'
We followed his example and got up too. The conference was over. While Marx was striding up and down the room in unusually angry excitement I quickly said good-bye to him and the others and went home, greatly surprised by what I had seen and heard.

The definite breach between Marx and Weitling did not come till May 1848. Weitling even sent Marx an article for the paper he was going to start at the time, and he had no objection to accepting the help which the 'chief of the intellectuals', whom he alleged to be 'sitting on the funds' though he was in fact short of them, continued to give him.

But Marx insisted on the sifting of the party and the first blow fell upon Hermann Kriege, a close friend of Weitling's and a man of the same way of thinking as he. Kriege, a young, not ungifted man whom Engels had recommended to Marx only a year before as a 'splendid agitator', had emigrated to America, where he published a weekly paper, the *People's Tribune*. His never very substantial and 'emotional' communism degenerated in America into the most turgid sentimentalism. The *People's Tribune* only made communism ridiculous. On top of it Kriege applied quite indiscriminately for financial support to people who had nothing whatever to do with communism. The Brussels group felt the time had come to declare openly before the world that this activity had nothing whatever to do with them. Many of them found it hard to repudiate a man who had so recently been their comrade. But, as Marx and Engels stated in the circular letter they drafted, the cause took precedence over everything else, the party must not degenerate into a clique, and the party was more important than the persons who belonged or had belonged to it. There were long discussions, and on 11 May the group decided to make a public protest against Kriege's outpourings. Weitling alone refused to sign. On 16 May the lithographed circular was dispatched to the correspondence committees in Germany, Paris, London and New York. On the same day Weitling demanded the immediate return of his manuscript from Marx. This was the final rupture.[15]

[11]

The Communist League[1]

THE German communists, though they criticized the harsh wording of the circular, took Marx's side. The Brussels committee thereupon demanded that 'philosophical and sentimental' communism be combated outright. This hurt the feelings of Schapper and his followers, who rebelled at the 'intellectual arrogance' of the Brussels committee. They claimed to be free from sentimental aspirations themselves, but believed a milder attitude towards the 'sentimental' communists, who after all meant well, to be preferable to the violence with which Marx attacked them. Marx did not and could not give in. If the small communist élite did not have clear, definite views, any attempt to influence the broad, working masses was doomed to failure. Marx used his correspondence with the German communists in London, to which he attached supreme importance, as he later wrote,

to subject to merciless criticism in a series of partly printed, partly lithographed pamphlets the medley of English and French socialism or communism and German philosophy which then formed the secret teaching of the League, and replace it by the only tenable theoretical foundation, namely scientific insight into the economic structure of bourgeois society; and, finally, to explain in popular form that our task was not that of trying to bring any kind of utopian system into being but was that of consciously participating in a historical revolutionary process by which society was being transformed before our eyes.[2]

Where possible written propaganda was supplemented by oral propaganda. Engels was particularly active in Paris, where he settled in the middle of August 1846.

Unwilling as the members of the League of the Just, both in London and Paris, at first were to face the dilemma with which Marx confronted them, namely, that of choosing between scientific or utopian socialism, hard as it was for them to renounce what they had held dear for so many years, they nevertheless overcame their doubts and followed Marx. What they learned from him substantiated their own insight into affairs, brought sense and coherence into their own experiences, enabled them to understand the historical significance of the English workers' movement, gave them the firm standpoint that they needed. This does not imply that none of them fell back again in later years. But in the two years in question Marx won over the vanguard of the class for scientific socialism.

The central offices of the League of the Just remained in Paris – mainly out of tradition, for the preponderating majority of its members no longer lived in France – until the autumn of 1846. The real headquarters were in London. Legal organizations of workers of the kind that Schapper and his comrades had created in London were impossible in Paris, and France had no mass movement like that of the Chartists in England, not even in embryo. In Paris the old forms of the conspiratorial secret society were still kept up. They did not correspond to the needs of the rising working-class movement. The first result of the Marxian criticism was the reorganization of the League of the Just. The officers of the club were re-elected in autumn 1846. Schapper and Moll and other 'Londoners' became the leaders.[3]

They felt the approach of the revolution which, in the words of one of their circulars, 'would probably settle the fate of the world for centuries'. They realized that their immediate task must be to carry out Marx's injunctions of a year before. They must create a communist party programme and decide on their tactics. A congress was to be held in London to do these things. The proposal to hold it had been made by the London correspondence committee in the summer of 1846. In November 1846 a special circular letter was sent out, summoning the representatives of all the branches of the League to a congress to be held on 1 May 1847.

Joseph Moll was entrusted with the task of getting into

touch with Marx and inviting him to join the League. Moll arrived in Brussels at the beginning of February 1847. He was authorized to give Marx 'an oral report on the state of affairs [in the League of the Just] and receive information from him in return.' After interviewing Marx in Brussels, Moll went to Paris and interviewed Engels. He explained in his own name and that of his comrades that they were convinced of the rightness of Marx's views and agreed that they must shake off the old conspiratorial forms and traditions. Marx and Engels were to be invited to collaborate in the work of reorganization and theoretical reorientation.

To Marx the invitation to enter the League was by no means unexpected. If he hesitated to accept it it was because of his appreciation of the power of tradition and his consequently inevitable uncertainty about the genuineness of the League of the Just's determination fundamentally to reorganize itself. Marx had kept away from the secret societies in Paris. Repelled as he had been by their romanticism, which occasionally expressed itself in the most ludicrous forms, standing as he did a whole world apart from the doctrines of the insurrectionists and the utopians, now that he had recognized the historical mission of the proletariat in all its immensity he had no choice but decisively and once and for all to reject secret society conspiratorialism as the method of organizing the class movement. But Moll stated that it was essential that he and Engels should join the League if it were really to shake off all its archaic shackles, and Marx overcame his doubts and joined the League of the Just in February or March 1847.

The congress met in London on 1 June 1847 (it had been postponed for a month). Engels was the delegate of the Paris branch and Wilhelm Wolff came from Brussels. Marx stayed in Brussels. His official reason was lack of funds for the journey, and it appears from a letter that he did in fact attempt unsuccessfully to raise the necessary sum. But money cannot have been the decisive factor. If Marx had been really determined to take part in the congress it would not have been difficult for him to have persuaded the branch to send him instead of the excellent but not outstanding Wolff. No doubt the real explanation is the assumption that before associating himself definitely with the League Marx wanted to await the results of the congress.

The congress decided on a complete reorganization of the League. In place of the old name, to which any man could attach any meaning he liked – this was actually encouraged because there were only a few initiates and to lead the profane astray could not but be useful – a new name, the 'Communist League', made its appearance. The statutes of the League were entirely recast. The first sentence was: 'The aim of the League is the downfall of the bourgeoisie and the ascendancy of the proletariat, the abolition of the old society based on class conflicts and the foundation of a new society without classes and without private property.'[4] This was the language of Marx. The whole organization was built up in the Marxian spirit. It was democratic throughout. Before joining the League Marx and Engels had stipulated that 'everything conducive to superstitious authoritarianism be struck out of the rules'.[5] All the officers of the League were appointed by election and could be dismissed at any time by those who had elected them. This alone constituted an effective barrier against machinations and intrigues of the kind conducive to dictatorship, and the League was converted – at any rate for ordinary times of peace – into a straightforward propaganda organization. The statutes were drafted and sent back to the branches for discussion. They were accepted after further deliberation by the second congress in December.

Between now and the next congress a statement of the League's programme, the League's 'profession of faith', was to be worked out. Before parting the delegates also decided to publish a periodical. The 'trial number' of the *Kommunistische Zeitschrift*, the only one that ever appeared, came out in September 1847. It was edited by the German communists in London, no doubt with Engels's collaboration.[6] The old motto of the League of the Just had been 'All men are brothers.' It was changed at Engels's suggestion. Whether his reasons for regarding the change as essential were the same as Marx's is not known. Marx declared that there was a whole mass of men of whom he wished anything rather than to be their brothers. The phrase that Engels proposed and the congress of the Communist League accepted appeared for the first time on the badly printed little sheet on sale for twopence to German workers at the White Hart Inn in Drury Lane in the autumn of 1847. It was: 'Proletarians of all countries, unite!'

Marx had been trying for a long time to get hold of a legal newspaper in Germany through which he could express his views. He thought out innumerable schemes and conducted lengthy negotiations, all without success. German socialist papers competed for contributions from him and his friends, and a few articles also appeared in the *Rheinische Jahrbücher,* the *Deutsches Bürgerbuch,*[7] the *Gesellschaftsspiegel,* the *Westfälisches Dampfboot,* and others. But Marx remained only an occasional contributor, if a highly appreciated one. He had no power to dictate the policy of any paper. Next to Engels's articles and his own there appeared others favouring the 'true' socialism which Marx was combating. The sharper the division between the Marxian group and the others became, and the better organized they grew, the more essential was it to have a mouthpiece the policy of which should be determined by them and them alone.

The German censorship made it impossible to start a newspaper in Germany. It must appear abroad, nay, in the town in which Marx lived. Only in those conditions, with the control in Marx's own hands, would there be a guarantee that it would represent his views entirely. But that would require means which were not at the disposal of Marx and his friends.

Impossible as it was to found an organ of his own, the opportunity presented itself in 1847 of so influencing a paper already in existence that it would in effect be as good as his own. Since the beginning of the year the *Deutsche Brüsseler Zeitung* had been published weekly in Brussels by Adalbert von Bornstedt, who had contributed in his time to the Paris *Vorwärts.*

Bornstedt was very anxious to secure Marx as a contributor. But Bornstedt was a man with a very doubtful past and with very doubtful connections. People stated quite openly, in speech and in writing, that he was in the service of the political police. The only thing they had any doubt about was in whose pay he actually was. He was held by some to be an Austrian spy, by others to be a spy of Prussia. Others again believed that it was 'Russian roubles that seemed to smile towards him'. There is no doubt that Marx knew of these incriminating allegations, which were frequently mentioned in the letters that passed between him and Heine during the time of their friendship. Even Freiligrath, whom in the first months of his Brussels exile Marx saw practically every day, believed that Bornstedt was a spy who had come to Brussels for the special purpose of keeping watch on the 'emigrants' there.

At first Marx had no contact with the *Deutsche Brüsseler Zeitung*, if for no other reason than that politically it was completely colourless. 'So far it has no significance whatever', the Prussian Ambassador reported to Berlin on 20 January 1847. But with every number the paper became more oppositional, more revolutionary. The King of Prussia was the special subject of its attacks, and on 3 April the Ambassador reported that the paper 'attacked His Majesty's Government with revolting scurrility and savagery'. Not content with quoting the paper's 'scurrility', he made representations to the Belgian police, who should 'curb' it. At the moment, however, they were not inclined to do the Prussian's bidding. The *démarches* of the Prussian Ambassador only had the effect of causing the Belgian newspapers to take up the matter and of supplying the *Deutsche Brüsseler Zeitung* with new material. It became 'even more scurrilous and violent in its attacks on foreign governments and princes'.

In these circumstances the suspicion that had previously rested on Bornstedt necessarily diminished. Marx started writing for the *Deutsche Brüsseler Zeitung* in April 1847. Bornstedt 'had declared himself ready to do everything possible for us.' Doubtless Marx had come to the conclusion that there was no foundation for the allegations against him. Suspicion was hurled about among the German exiles at that time just as easily as it was among the Poles, among whom every political opponent, because he was an opponent, was thought capable of being a spy.

Now that the dossiers of the secret police are available it is known that there was substance in the denunciations of Bornstedt. He spied for Austria, for Prussia and perhaps for a few of the smaller German states as well. His reports, preserved among the secret state papers in Berlin, contain a wealth of material about the German exiles. But all his reports date from the 1830s and the beginning of the forties. There is, of course, no proof that he gave up his nefarious activities with the cessation of his reports, but on the other hand the possibility that he became a genuine revolutionary is not excluded. He was an adventurer. He took part in Herwegh's expedition in 1848, fought against the troops of Baden, was taken prisoner, and died mentally deranged.

As soon as Marx started writing for the *Deutsche Brüsseler Zeitung* he started trying to persuade others to do the same. He wrote to Herwegh and complained that the Germans were always finding new faults with the paper. Instead of taking advantage of it they were merely

wasting an opportunity of accomplishing something. Their attitude to my manuscripts is rather like their attitude to the *Deutsche Brüsseler Zeitung*, and at the same time the asses write to me every other day, asking me why I don't print anything, and they even try persuading me that it is better to write in French than not to write at all. One will have to atone a long time for having been born a Teuton! [8]

The advice to write in French annoyed Marx, in view of his criticism of Proudhon, which had appeared in July 1847. In his reply to the invitation to cooperate from Paris in the activities of the correspondence committees Proudhon had promised to write a book giving his own solution of the social problem. He kept his promise and wrote his *Système des*

contradictions économiques, ou la philosophie de la misère.[9]
The 'solution' turned out to be nothing but 'petty-bourgeois
reformism' wrapped up in misunderstood Hegelian dialectical
formulas. In his reply, *Misère de la philosophie*,[10] written in
French in order to be intelligible to Proudhon's readers, Marx
mercilessly cracked the 'critical whip' that Proudhon had
expected down on Proudhon's 'eternal ideas' and 'eternal
laws', his philosophical confusion, his 'moral' and 'philosophical' explanations of economic conditions. Just as Marx had
to fight all his life against pupils of Weitling – most of them
did not know who their teacher was – so also had he to struggle
against Proudhonism, in France particularly but in Germany
as well.[11]

The *Deutsche Brüsseler Zeitung* was a very useful platform
for keeping every possible kind of pseudo-socialist and pseudo-
radical in check. It very soon occupied a prominent position
in the international democratic movement. The London Chartist assembly of September 1847 hailed the *Deutsche Brüsseler
Zeitung*, the Paris *Réforme* and the *Northern Star* as 'the
three greatest and most democratic organs of Europe'. That
in spite of all obstacles it was smuggled into Germany in
fairly large numbers appears from numerous complaints in
the police reports. It was read by all the German workers in
Brussels.

Marx had already established good relations with them.
After the conversion of the Brussels correspondence committee
into a branch of the Communist League he and his friends
formed the Brussels German Workers' Educational Union.
Wherever members of the League of the Just and later of the
Communist League went, they founded legal organizations
of this kind as soon as ever it became possible. The Brussels
Union was patterned in every way, in aims, rules and constitution, on the London German Workers' Union.

Regular meetings were held twice a week. On Wednesdays
there were lectures and the speaker was usually Marx. All that
has survived of his economic lectures is what was later printed
in the *Neue Rheinische Zeitung* under the title of 'Wage-

Labour and Capital'.[12] Sundays were devoted to entertainment, previous to which Wilhelm Wolff[13] always gave 'a review of the events of the day, which were invariably masterpieces of popular description, humorous and at the same time vivid, duly castigating the individual pettiness and blackguardisms of rulers and ruled in Germany alike'.[14] Afterwards there were recitations – sometimes by Marx's wife – in addition to singing and dancing.

Police spies soon got excitedly to work on the paper and the club. A confidential report to the police authorities at Frankfurt-on-Main states:

This noxious paper must indisputably exert the most corrupting influence upon the uneducated public at whom it is directed. The alluring theory of the dividing-up of wealth is held out to factory workers and day labourers as an innate right, and a profound hatred of the rulers and the rest of the community is inculcated into them. There would be a gloomy outlook for the fatherland and for civilization if such activities succeeded in undermining religion and respect for the laws and in any great measure infected the lowest class of the people by means of the Press and these clubs ... The circumstance that the number of members [of the Workers' Union] has increased from thirty-seven to seventy within a few days is worthy of note.

The Brussels branch of the Communist League was closely allied to the left wing of the Belgian democrats, not, of course, officially, but by reason of close personal connections. The editor of the *Atelier démocratique*, a little paper published in a Brussels suburb, was L. Heilberg, a German refugee who died young. It was therefore quite natural for the Brussels branch of the League to take an active part in the formation of the International Democratic Union in Brussels.

Several attempts had been made in the 1830s and 1840s to realize the idea of linking up all the revolutionary organizations in Europe and setting up a holy alliance of peoples against the Holy Alliance of kings. French, Germans, Greeks and other nationalities gathered round the headquarters of the carbonari in Switzerland. Mazzini's *Young Europe* had national sections for Young Italians, Germans, Poles, French, etc. Public banquets, which it was difficult for the police to ban, were a favourite method of bringing representatives of revolutionary movements together. Marx took part in a banquet of this kind in Paris in the spring of 1844. Nothing is known about it except that it took place and that French, Germans and Russians used the occasion to discuss democratic propaganda.

More, however, is known about the celebrations in Weitling's honour held in London on 22 September 1844. On this occasion Karl Schapper proposed the formation of a propaganda organization with a view to uniting the democrats of all countries. There was unanimous enthusiasm for this proposal, but a year passed by before it was possible to take steps to carry it out. On 22 September 1845 more than 1,000 democrats of all nationalities gathered in London to celebrate the anniversary of the French Revolution. The initiator of the gathering was G. J. Harney, next to Ernest Jones the most zealous of the Chartist leaders who had risen above the prevalent insularity. Harney's words: 'We reject the word "foreigner". It must no longer exist in our democratic vocabulary', became a reality in the society of Fraternal Democrats, formed on 15 March 1846. At first it was quite a loose association, intended to bring foreigners living in England closer to their similarly-minded English friends. In the summer of 1847 it was organized on a more formal basis. Each nationality was given a general secretariat of its own. Harney was the English representative, the revolutionary Michelot, whose real name was Juin d'Allas, represented the French, and Karl Schapper represented the Germans. Their motto, 'All men are brothers', was that of the London German Workers' Union.

In 1847 the Fraternal Democrats were extremely active, and there was no important event in international politics to which they did not declare their attitude, either in pamphlets or in the Press. In the autumn of 1847 they published a manifesto to all nations in which they outlined a plan for the for-

mation of a widespread organization, an 'international organization eligible to people of all nationalities, with international
committees in as many towns as possible'. There was a particularly lively response to the appeal in Belgium. In July 1846
the Brussels correspondence committee had congratulated
Feargus O'Connor, the Chartist, on his victory in the Notting-
ham election. The *Northern Star* had printed an article sent
by the 'German democratic communists' and signed by Marx,
Engels and Gigot,[15] and the Fraternal Democrats greeted it as
'another proof of the advance of fraternity, and the approaching
union of the democrats of all countries in the great struggle
for political and social equality'.

On 27 September 1847 the Association démocratique, 'ayant
pour but l'union et la fraternité de tous les peuples', was
founded in Brussels. Singularly enough, it was founded originally as a counter-stroke to the local branch of the Communist
League and was intended to resist the growing influence of
Marx among the German refugee and the Belgian radicals.
Bornstedt, who was consumed by ambition but was prevented
by Marx from taking a direct part in political activity himself,
wanted in all circumstances to play a political role. In Marx's
absence from Brussels he took advantage of the opportunity
to summon a conference of democrats of various nations, at
which it was decided to form a new organization.

Marx's friends, and the nimble Engels in particular, had
no difficulty in sidetracking Bornstedt, and Engels occupied
the position of vice-president himself until Marx should return. In the middle of November Marx was formally elected
as the German representative. The veteran General François-
Aimé Mellinet, national hero of 1830, was elected honorary
president. The Belgian representative was Lucien-Leopold
Jottrand, a lawyer and editor of the Brussels *Débat social*, the
French representative was Jacques Imbert, a Blanquist with a
renowned revolutionary past, and the Polish representative
was the famous historian, Joachim Lelewel.[16]

In the months that followed Marx worked for the Association démocratique with the greatest energy. At a public meeting

in Brussels he spoke on the question of free trade, and the Association published his speech as a pamphlet.[17] He travelled to Ghent, where a meeting of more than 3,000 people, predominantly workers, decided to form a branch association. There seemed excellent foundation for the hope that the organization might grow into a strong, well-organized democratic party.

The Communist League, the Workers' Union, the Association démocratique, writing for the Brussels newspaper, an extensive correspondence with Germany, England and France, to say nothing of his literary labours, made ample claims on Marx's energy. But nothing would be more mistaken than to imagine the young Marx – at the outbreak of the revolution of 1848 he was barely thirty years old – as a gloomy ascetic and fanatic.

The letters of Marx and Engels between 1844 and 1847 are an excellent biographical source for the life of the latter. But only one letter of Marx's has come down to us from that time. All the same there are a few documents that throw light on Marx's personal life in Brussels.

His brother-in-law, Edgar von Westphalen, stayed in Brussels until the late autumn of 1847. Jenny Marx was very fond of him. 'My one, beloved brother', she called him in a letter to Frau Liebknecht. 'The ideal of my childhood and youth, my dear and only friend.'[18] He was a communist, but apparently not a very active one. He was an enemy of philistinism rather than of bourgeois society, a completely unstable and irresolute person, but good-hearted and a cheerful companion. Marx was very fond of him. Weydemeyer wrote to his fiancée in February 1846:

If I tell you what kind of life we have been leading here, you will certainly be surprised at the communists. To crown the folly, Marx, Weitling, Marx's brother-in-law and I sat up the whole night playing. Weitling got tired first. Marx and I slept a few hours on a sofa and idled away the whole of the next day in the company of his wife and his brother-in-law in the most priceless manner. We went to a tavern early in the morning, then we went by train to Villeworde, which is a little place near by, where we had lunch and then returned in the most cheerful mood by the last train.[19]

Not nearly so many Germans found their way to Brussels as to Paris. But no one who had even the most distant sympathy with communism failed to visit Marx. Stephan Born visited 'the spiritual centre of communism' at the end of October. This young printer had become a friend of Engels in Paris, turned communist and made an able defence of communism against the republican Karl Heinzen, the 'caricature of a German Jacobin' who was later known in America as the 'prince killer'.[20] In 1848 Born was one of the leaders of the Berlin workers' movement, but when he wrote his reminiscences in his old age at Basle he was a tedious social-reformist university professor. But he always retained a shy veneration for Marx. 'I found him', he wrote, writing in retrospect of the autumn of 1847,

in an extremely modest, one might almost say poorly furnished, little house in a suburb of Brussels. He received me in a friendly way, asked about the success of my propaganda journey, and paid me a compliment, with which his wife associated herself, about my pamphlet against Heinzen. She bade me a very friendly welcome. Throughout her life she took the most intense interest in everything that concerned and occupied her husband, and therefore she could not fail to be interested in me, as I was considered one of his hopeful young men ... Marx loved his wife and she shared his passion. I have never known such a happy marriage, in which joy and suffering – the latter in the richest measure – and all pain were overcome in such a spirit of mutual devotion. I have seldom known a woman, so harmoniously formed alike in outward appearance and heart and mind, make such a prepossessing impression at the first meeting. Frau Marx was fair. Her children, who were still small, were dark-haired and dark-eyed like their father.[21]

Marx's second daughter, Laura, was born in September 1845, and his son, Edgar, in December 1846. The irregular income he earned by writing did not suffice to keep the growing family, and Marx was forced to borrow. In February 1848 his material position improved, although only for a short time. For the 6,000 francs his mother, after long negotiations, at last paid him out of his father's estate, were applied to political ends, to which all personal needs had to take second place.

The second communist congress was fixed for the autumn of 1847, and by then the League's 'profession of faith' had to be ready. Schapper attempted a first draft, Moses Hess attempted another, but the Paris branch of the League rejected both. Then Engels applied himself to the task. The form he chose for it was the one that was conventional at the time for declarations of the kind by communist and other left-wing groups. It was drawn up in the form of questions and answers, like the catechism. Engels's catechism was written in straightforward, easily intelligible language and stated the fundamental ideas of scientific socialism tersely and with transparent clarity.[22] But Engels was not satisfied with it. In his opinion it was wretchedly written, and he thought it would be better to abandon the form of the catechism altogether, as it was necessary for the 'thing' to contain a certain number of descriptions of events. He suggested to Marx the title of 'Communist Manifesto'.[23]

The Paris branch appointed Engels their delegate to the congress, and this time the Brussels branch sent Marx. The two friends met at Ostend, discussed the draft and agreed that the first statement of aims of the Communist League to which they now belonged and of which they had become the leaders must not be one of the conventional popular pamphlets, however good it might be of its kind.

Marx, in addition to being the representative of the Brussels communists, had a mandate to represent the Association démocratique at the conference of the Fraternal Democrats on 29 November. The Fraternal Democrats had organized some celebrations in memory of the Polish revolt of 1830. The celebrations were typical of those held in those years of demonstrations of international solidarity in all the lands of Western Europe. The communist congress was to meet next day in the same hall, that of the London German Workers' Union, and the communist delegates took part in the celebrations in honour of the Polish revolutionaries. Marx spoke side by side with English, French, German, Belgian and Polish speakers. He spoke of the imminent revolution.

The old Poland is lost [he said], and we should be the last to wish its restoration. But it is not only old Poland that is lost, but old Germany, old France, old England, the whole of our antiquated society. But the loss of our antiquated society is no loss for those who have nothing to lose in it, and the great majority in all the countries of the present day are in that position. They have far more to win by the downfall of our antiquated society, which will bring in its train the formation of a new society, no longer resting on class conflicts.[24]

Marx announced that the Association démocratique proposed to summon an international democratic congress for the following year. It coincided with a similar proposal by the Fraternal Democrats. It was decided to hold the congress in Brussels on 25 October 1848. It was not held, for events were too fast for it.

Next day the deliberations of the communists began. They lasted for ten days, a time of strenuous activity for Marx and Engels. True, the Londoners had been won over to Marx, but much human effort and patient instruction and wary indulgence for old sensibilities were required before the last traces of mistrust of the 'intellectuals' were extinguished. The newly-organized League – the statutes were definitely fixed – was without a trace of the conspiratorial character which had been such an essential element in the League of the Just. That it must remain a secret society was obvious. Even outside Germany, in free England, the communists could not well have their organization registered with the police. But within these limits, which were set by external necessity and were not self-imposed as they were in the case of the League of the Just or the French secret societies, because the Communist League had no secret teaching for initiates only and did not plot, and because 'communists scorned to keep their views and intentions secret', within these limits it was an association for propaganda on a democratic basis.

Whether Engels laid his catechism before the congress or not is not known. The delegates decided to entrust Marx and Engels with the drafting of their programme. The head-quarters of the League remained in London, and Schapper, Heinrich Bauer and Moll remained its leaders. They were unanimous that the theoretical guidance of the League must be left to Marx.

Marx worked on the Communist Manifesto from the middle of December till the end of January. That was too slow for the German communists in London. On 24 January they admonished him to hasten. They would take disciplinary measures against Citizen Marx, they wrote rather harshly, if the manuscript were not in their hands by 1 February. But the ultimatum was superfluous, because Marx sent the manuscript to London before the prescribed day.[25]

The Communist Manifesto was the common work of Marx and Engels. It is impossible to distinguish their respective contributions. But, as Engels frequently repeated, the fundamental ideas, the groundwork, belong to Marx alone.[26] Marx gave it its form too. It is Marx's tremendous power that flows from every word, it is his fire with which the most brilliant pamphlet in world literature illuminates the times, today just as on the day on which it was completed.

The Manifesto gave an unerring lead to the proletariat in its struggle; not unerring in the narrow sense a dogmatist might attribute to the word, not unerring in the sense that every word is valid for the present day. It was written a few weeks before the outbreak of the European revolution of 1848. It proposed revolutionary measures which a quarter of a century later Marx and Engels called out-of-date because of the development of economic, social and political conditions. Unerring rather because, surveying the whole course of historical development, it enabled the workers concretely to understand their historical situation. The tremendous revolutionary pathos of the Manifesto does not dazzle but sharpens the view for the direct task ahead. Because it saw into the most distant future, it saw into the most immediate past. It was the programme for the historical epoch of the struggle for the proletarian revolution and at the same time the programme for the next day's sober, disillusioned fight.

When the last sheets of the Communist Manifesto left the printing press Marx was in the midst of revolutionary Paris.

[12]

The Revolutionary Tempest

THE first sign of revolution came from Switzerland in November 1847.

> Im Hochland fiel der erste Schuss,
> Im Hochland wider die Pfaffen.* [1]

The reactionary cantons which formed the Roman Catholic League rose against the decision of the Federal Council to expel the Jesuits. The governments of Russia, Austria, Prussia and France, always ready to step in on the side of reaction, which was the very principle of their existence, took the part of the Catholic cantons and threatened military intervention. A local Swiss conflict flared up into a question of European importance. Oxenbein, leader of the Swiss radicals, threatened that if Austria dared to intervene he would send an army of 20,000 men into Lombardy and proclaim an Italian republic. The Austrian troops gathered at the frontier but did not move and three weeks later the Catholic cantons were beaten. The arrival in London of the news of the fall of Lucerne, their capital, coincided with the opening of the communist congress.

From the Alps the revolutionary avalanche poured down into the Italian plain. In the face of the Swiss threat Austria beat a pitiful retreat. The prestige of the alien ruler was shaken. There were stormy demonstrations in Lombardy, and in some places the demonstrations developed into open fighting. In January insurrection broke out in the south, in Sicily.

> Drauf ging der Tanz in Welschland los;
> Die Scyllen und Charybden,
> Vesuv und Aetna brachen los,
> Ausbruch auf Ausbruch, Stoss auf Stoss.†

* 'The first shot was fired in the high country
  Against the priests.'
† 'The dance started in the South; Scylla and Charybdis,
  Vesuvius and Etna burst forth, outbreak on outbreak,
  blow on blow.'

The revolutionaries defeated the troops of the Bourbon Ferdinand of Naples in a five-day street-battle. Insurrection broke out in one Italian state after another. Constitutions were declared in Naples, Turin and Florence. King Ferdinand barely escaped trial by a people's court.

The industrial crisis which had made Europe ripe for revolution was particularly severe in Belgium, where economic development was relatively high. In the winter of 1847–8 unemployment in the textile areas rose from week to week, and in the workers' quarters, which were accustomed to privation, famine stalked abroad. Not a single day passed by, writes the historian of the Belgian workers' movement, without a starving worker breaking a shop-window for the sake of appeasing his hunger in prison.

The 1847 elections had brought the liberals into power. They demonstrated their incapacity to check the crisis, and the agitation of the radical democrats fell on fertile soil. The Association démocratique was the leading spirit. Branch associations sprang up one after another in Ghent, Liége, Namur and elsewhere. Members streamed in in masses. They came from the working classes, from the hard-pressed petty bourgeoisie and from intellectual circles too. Political tension grew as the economic crisis became more acute.

Events in Belgium were followed with the greatest interest abroad. 'The executioner is waiting', Engels exclaimed with joy when, in January 1848, he summed up the progress of the movement during the past year for the *Deutsche Brüsseler Zeitung*.[2] The revolutionary wave swept over all frontiers, no firm-built dam was strong enough to hold it. Engels actually anticipated by a century the collapse of the 'chequered' Austrian Empire, 'botched together of bits stolen here and inherited there'. Poland seemed to be striking a fatal blow at Europe's other gendarme, Nicholas I of Russia. Poland, as has already been observed, was the country to which the revolutionaries of all countries kept their gaze constantly riveted during the three decades of reaction. The rising of Poland must mean the rising of all Europe, the liberation of Poland would be at once a symbol and a signal for all the oppressed. In the winter of 1847–8 three great democratic demonstrations on behalf of Poland took place in Brussels. On 14 February Belgians, Poles and Germans demonstrated in honour of the heroes of the 1830 revolution and the martyrs of the rising of the Russian Dekabrists. A week later, on 22 February, Marx spoke at a meeting in memory of the Cracow rising of 1846. Marx extolled the Polish revolution and lauded the rising at Cracow for the glorious example it set Europe, 'en identifiant la cause de la nationalité à la cause de la démocratie et à l'affranchissement de la classe opprimée'.[*3] The meeting closed with a pathetic scene. Old Lelewel, the veteran of the Polish revolution, embraced Marx and kissed him.

The refugees, forced to restrain themselves for so many years, cast themselves the more passionately into political activity now. There was no meeting in which they did not participate. This applied in particular to the German exiles, who threw themselves enthusiastically into the Belgian movement, without, of course, forgetting their more particular German duties. There were innumerable contacts with the adjacent territories of Prussia, particularly with the Rhineland. After Marx and his comrades joined the Communist League they saw to it that every communist with whom they were in contact founded a branch of the League. Illegal literature published abroad was smuggled into Germany in great quantities, and the more important articles from the *Deutsche Brüsseler Zeitung* were reprinted as flysheets and fairly widely distributed.

The German communists in Belgium prepared to hurry to Germany at the first sign. Wilhelm Wolff was arrested by the Brussels police in the middle of February 1848 and stated openly that he and his friends were directing all their attention to Germany, where they were carrying out intense propaganda. 'Cologne and Aix-la-Chapelle', he is quoted as saying in a police report, 'were the places designated for the risings.'[*4]

* 'in identifying the cause of nationality with that of democracy and the emancipation of the oppressed class.'

Hitherto the Belgian police and the Belgian conservatives had not paid any particular attention to the German communists. The Prussian Ambassador never kept them out of his sight, and from time to time called the attention of the Belgian authorities to their 'criminal activities', but without result. This state of affairs altered when the situation in the country became acute and the Germans became active. Several newspapers started attacking the German exiles, and the Prussian Ambassador probably had a hand in the campaign. On 20 January he was able to inform his Government that the Belgian police now considered it necessary to keep a watch on the agitation being carried out and that they intended to take definite steps against foreigners, and against the Germans in particular. There is no doubt that the Ambassador did all he could to encourage police action. Meanwhile tension grew from day to day. But everybody knew that the revolution could only conquer after it had conquered in Paris. Everybody waited for the crowing of the Gallic cock.

Unrest was rife in France. Suffrage reforms were demanded and, in accordance with the custom of the time, a campaign of banquets was organized. But nothing pointed to an immediate revolutionary outbreak. Louis Philippe, an old cynic who had experienced many revolutions, attempted to pacify his ministers. 'The Parisians won't start a revolution in winter', he said. 'They storm things in hot weather. They stormed the Bastille in July, the Bourbon throne in June. But in January or February, no.' The stout, phlegmatic Louis Philippe forgot that salvoes fired into a crowd can cause a July temperature in February. On 23 February the military fired at a peaceful demonstration. Next morning Paris was filled with barricades. The people's cry was not for electoral reform but a republic. On the evening of 24 February the Palais Royal was in the hands of the insurrectionists. The King fled and a bonfire was made of the throne. The same evening a provisional government was formed and a republic proclaimed.

Events in Paris were known in Brussels, but even the greatest optimists had not expected things to develop so rapidly and

K.M.—6

so successfully. After the outbreak of the insurrection, connection between Paris and Brussels was interrupted.

'On the evening of 24 February 1848', writes Stephan Born, half a dozen German youths were standing on the Paris platform at Brussels station. They were practically alone. Since morning there had been no train from the French capital and no news about the unrest which had broken out. The honest inhabitants of the Belgian capital were a somewhat slow-blooded race and had to be warmed up before they got going. Curiosity about what might have happened in Paris apparently did not trouble them. We few Germans were, as I said, almost alone on the platform, and we were foreigners. But no, there were two other people, a lady and a gentleman, standing silently and anxiously in a corner. They too were waiting for the train, which, even if it did not come all the way from Paris, would at least be coming from the French frontier. Occasionally one or other of them would cast a gloomy look at us as we stood there chattering happily, expressing our conjectures and hopes concerning the news the arrival of which could not be delayed much longer now. They guessed our thoughts and advanced a few paces towards us, but suddenly a protracted whistle announced the approach of the long-awaited train. Another moment and it was in the station. Before it came to a standstill, the guard jumped down and shouted at the top of his voice: 'The red flag is flying on the tower of Valenciennes and a republic has been proclaimed.'

'Long live the republic!' we shouted as with one voice. But the lady and gentleman who had been waiting for news turned pale and beat a hurried retreat. A station official told us that they were the French Ambassador, General Rumigny, and his wife.[5]

The victory of the Paris revolution disconcerted and dismayed the Belgian Government, or at any rate so it appeared on the surface. Rogier, the Minister for Foreign Affairs, opened negotiations with his friend, Considérant, the Fourierist, who recommended a revolution from above. The Government which was in the hands of the liberals, should proclaim a republic itself. The King gave the republicans the hint that he would not oppose the people's will and was ready to abdicate if the Belgians really wanted a republic. All he wished was that everything should happen in an orderly manner and without bloodshed, and besides he hoped for a respectable pension.

Everything seemed to be developing excellently, but the whole thing was only a manoeuvre. In the meantime, the Government called up the reserves and the soldiers on furlough and marched the regiments to Brussels. So far from trying to stop the spreading of rumours to the effect that they were prepared to accede of their own accord to the most extreme demands, they rather encouraged them in order to diminish the tension and pacify the determined few.

The leadership of the movement was provided by the Association démocratique practically alone. On 27 February it summoned a mass meeting, which decided to meet again on the following day, this time outside the Town Hall, to demand the calling up of workers and artisans to supplement the National Guard and provide the necessary pressure. An appeal to arms was made at the meeting, in order not to be defenceless in case of a police attack. Late that night there were a number of minor demonstrations, which were broken up by the police and gave them the desired opportunity to forbid the meeting on the following day. The Government, now having a sufficiency of military power on which to rely, suddenly adopted an entirely different tone. When the democratic deputies said in the Chamber that the triumphal march of the revolution would advance from Paris and conquer the whole world, the Government spokesman replied that it was scarcely necessary for freedom to make a world tour of that kind before it came to Belgium.

The German exiles were in the forefront of the revolutionary movement. Marx helped to draft the address of greeting the Association démocratique sent the Provisional Government in France. The address spoke of the great tasks that still lay ahead of the revolution.[6] German *émigrés* took part in the demonstration of the night of 28 February. Wilhelm Wolff was arrested and a knife was found on him. According to the police Marx gave 5,000 of the 6,000 francs he had just received to buy weapons for the workers of Brussels. The police had their opportunity of dealing with the exiles at last. They worked in close touch with the Prussian Ambassador, who had in his possession on 29 February, only a day or two after it was drawn up, a list of those who were to be expelled. Marx's name was at the top of the list .

Marx had no intention of staying in Belgium in any case. The revolutionary centre of Europe was Paris, where his old acquaintance, Flocon, now a member of the Provisional Government, summoned him. He invited the 'dear and brave' [*cher et vaillant*] Marx to return to the land from which tyranny had banished him. 'La tyrannie vous a banni, la libre France vous ouvre les portes, à vous et à tous ceux qui luttent pour le sainte cause de la fraternité des peuples.'*[7]

The letter was sent from Paris on 1 March. Marx received it on 2 or 3 March and its arrival practically coincided with a police order giving him twenty-four hours to leave Brussels. The expulsion order was handed to Marx at five o'clock on 3 March. He had a few hours in which to settle a mass of personal and political affairs.

Almost as soon as the news of the successful Paris rising reached London, Schapper, Heinrich Bauer and others at the headquarters of the Communist League decided to hurry to Paris. The London branch of the League resolved to transfer the powers vested in it to the Brussels branch. The Brussels branch was Marx, but Marx was expelled from Brussels. On the evening of 3 March the five representatives of the branch gathered in Marx's room in the hotel in which he was living. The meeting dissolved the newly appointed League central office, invested Marx personally with full powers and entrusted him with the task of constituting a new central office in Paris. Before they had time to leave the premises, they were raided by the police. They failed to capture Marx's friends, who managed to slip away in the general confusion. But the League papers and documents fell into their hands, among them the

* 'Tyranny has banished you; free France flings wide her portals for you, and all who struggle in the sacred cause of the brotherhood of the peoples.'

minutes of the meeting which had just taken place. Thus the names of the chief officials of the League fell into their possession. As a sign and token of their new-born friendship, a copy of the minutes and other documents found in Marx's room was sent to the Prussian Ambassador.

Marx described the disgraceful behaviour of the police in a letter to the *Réforme*:

Après avoir reçu, le 3 mars, à cinq heures du soir, l'ordre de quitter le royaume belge dans le délai de vingt-quatre heures, j'étais occupé encore, dans la nuit du même jour, de faire mes préparatifs de voyage, lorsqu'un commissaire de police, accompagné de dix gardes municipaux, pénétra dans mon domicile, fouilla toute la maison, et finit par m'arrêter, sous prétexte que je n'avais pas de papiers. Sans parler des papiers très réguliers que M. Duchâtel m'avait remis en m'expulsant de la France, je tenais en mains le passeport d'expulsion que la Belgique m'avait délivré il y avait quelques heures seulement.

Je ne vous aurais pas parlé, monsieur, de mon arrestation et des brutalités que j'ai souffertes, s'il ne s'y rattachait une circonstance qu'on aura peine à comprendre, même en Autriche.

Immédiatement après mon arrestation, ma femme se fait conduire chez M. Jottrand, président de l'association démocratique de Belgique, pour l'engager à prendre les mesures nécessaires. En rentrant chez elle, elle trouve à la porte un sergent de ville qui lui dit, avec une politesse exquise, que, si elle voulait parler à M. Marx, elle n'aurait qu'à le suivre. Ma femme accepte l'offre avec empressement. On la conduit au bureau de la police, et le commissaire lui déclare d'abord que M. Marx n'y était pas; puis il lui demande brutalement qui elle était, ce qu'elle allait faire chez M. Jottrand, et si elle avait ses papiers sur elle. Un démocrate belge, M. Gigot, qui avait suivi ma femme au bureau de la police avec la garde municipal, se révoltant des questions à la fois absurdes et insolentes du commissaire, est réduit au silence par des gardes qui s'emparent de lui et le jettent en prison. Sous le prétexte de vagabondage, ma femme est amenée à la prison de l'Hôtel-de-Ville, et enfermée avec des femmes perdues, dans une salle obscure. A onze heures du matin, elle est conduite en plein jour, sous toute une escorte de gendarmerie, au cabinet du juge d'instruction. Pendant deux heures, elle est mise au secret, malgre les plus vives réclamations qui arrivent de toutes parts. Elle reste là exposée à toute la rigeur de la saison et aux propos les plus indignes des gendarmes.

Elle paraît enfin devant le juge d'instruction, qui est tout étonné que la police, dans sa sollicitude, n'a pas arrêté egalement les enfants de bas-âge. L'interrogatoire ne pouvait être que factice, et tout le crime de ma femme consiste en ce que, bien qu'appartenant à l'aristocratie prussienne, elle partage les sentiments démocratiques de son mari.

Je n'entre pas dans tous les détails de cette révoltante affaire. Je dirai seulement que, lorsque nous étions relâchés, les vingt-quatre heures étaient justement expirées, et qu'il nous fallait partir sans pouvoir seulement emporter les effets les plus indispensables.* [8]

The Belgian liberal Press made a vigorous protest against

* 'After receiving on 3 March at five o'clock in the afternoon an order to leave Belgium within twenty-four hours, on the evening of the same day, when I was still busy with preparations for my journey, a commissary of police, accompanied by ten municipal guards, entered my apartments, searched the whole house and ended by arresting me on the pretext that I had no papers. Apart from the highly regular papers which M. Duchâtel supplied me with on expelling me from France, I had in my possession the expulsion passport which Belgium had suplied me with but a few hours previously.

'I should not have spoken of my arrest and of the brutalities to which I was subjected were it not for one circumstance which would be difficult to understand, even in Austria.

'Immediately after my arrest my wife called on M. Jottrand, president of the Association démocratique of Belgium, to ask him to take the necessary steps. On her return she found a policeman at the door who told her, with exquisite politeness, that if she wished to talk to M. Marx she had only to follow him. My wife eagerly accepted the offer. She was conducted to the police station, where the commissary started by telling her that M. Marx was not there; he then rudely asked who she was, what she wanted with M. Jottrand and whether she had her papers with her. M. Gigot, a Belgian democrat who accompanied my wife and the policeman to the police station, indignant at the commissary's absurd and insolent questions, was silenced by the guards, who seized him and threw him into prison. My wife was taken to the Hôtel de Ville prison on the pretext of vagabondage and locked up in a dark room in the company of a number of prostitutes. At eleven o'clock next morning she was taken by an escort of gendarmes, in broad daylight, to the office of the examining magistrate. She was kept in a cell for two hours, in spite of violent protests which arrived from every quarter, and ex-

the ignominy with which their country was covering itself.
Engels mobilized the Chartist Press in England. The deputy
Bricourt demanded an interpellation in the Belgian Chamber.
The commissary of police who had arrested Marx and his
wife was dismissed. But by that time Marx was no longer on
Belgian soil.

He was taken to the frontier under police escort. It was a
journey with many obstacles. The trains and the stations were
packed to suffocation with soldiers on their way to the south.
The air positively hummed with rumours. It was said that the
French and Belgian legions which had been formed on French
soil intended to found a Belgian republic at the point of the
bayonet. They would be suitably received!

In France the victory of the republic was still being celebrated. The stations were beflagged, the red flag and the tricolour flew side by side and enthusiasm was still running high.
The railway lines had been torn up at Valenciennes and a
half-hour omnibus ride was imposed on the travellers before
they could resume their train journey. Here, as on the stretch
between Pontoise and Saint-Denis, coachmen and innkeepers
had taken advantage of the first days of confusion to avenge
themselves on their new competitor, the railway. They had
torn up rails, burned down stations, smashed engines and
coaches. In spite of all these hindrances Marx reached Paris
on 4 March.[9]

---

posed to all the rigours of the season and to the basest insults by the
gendarmes.

'Eventually she appeared before the examining magistrate, who was
quite astonished at the police in their solicitude not having likewise
arrested my young children. Under these circumstances the interrogation amounted to a complete farce, and my wife's only crime consists
in sharing her husband's opinions, though she is of Prussian aristocratic
origin.

'I shall not enter into all the details of this revolting business, but
merely add that when we were released the twenty-four hours' grace
had just expired and we were compelled to leave the country without
even being able to take with us even the most indispensable personal
effects.'

Paris still bore fresh marks of the fighting at the barricades. Fanny Lewald, the German writer, who arrived in Paris a few days after Marx, described the scene that confronted the newcomer.[10] The paving stones at the street corners were lying loosely instead of being cemented down. Here and there smashed bread carts and overturned omnibuses indicated the scenes of former barricades. An iron railing outside a church had been completely torn up, except for a few feet which showed where an iron railing had been. At the Palais Royal, or Palais National, as it was now called in big letters, all the windows, many window-frames and much scaffolding were broken; the Château d'Eau, the guard-house opposite the Palais Royal, in which the guards had been burned to death, lay in smoke-black ruins; other guard-houses in the neighbourhood of the Seine had been razed to the ground, and National Guards kept guard, sitting in the nearest taverns which served them as guard-room. The trees on the boulevards had been cut down and the water-pipes and pillars pulled down. Dirty white curtains fluttered from the paneless windows of the Tuileries.

The town was still at the height of its brief republican enthusiasm. 'The workers', in the words of Engels, 'ate bread and potatoes in the day-time and spent the evening planting "trees of freedom" on the boulevards, while enthusiasts ran wild and sang the *Marseillaise* and the bourgeoisie hid in their houses all day long, trying to mollify the fury of the people by exhibiting coloured lanterns.'[11] The old song of the Gironde was sung:

> Mourir pour la patrie
> C'est le sort le plus beau,
> Le plus digne d'envie.*

The tricolour flew over the Palais Royal and the Tuileries, where Marx's old friend, Imbert, was now installed as governor. Here and there the red flag of the proletarian revolution was to be seen.

Revolutionary and socialist clubs sprang up like mushrooms.

---

* 'To die for one's country is the most beautiful and enviable fate.'

Newspapers, pamphlets and fly-sheets appeared every day. Paris seethed with political life. Boundless possibilities, intoxicating perspectives suddenly opened up before the exiles' eyes. It never entered their heads for a moment that the revolution might stop at the borders of France. The revolutionary flame that had been kindled in Paris would leap the frontiers and set Germany, Austria, Poland, the whole of Europe alight.

Since the great French Revolution it had appeared self-evident that democracies and autocratic monarchies could not live peacefully side by side. If democracy were victorious it must necessarily come into collision with neighbouring states which were still in the hands of absolutism. The revolutionary war was inevitable if the revolution were not to miscarry again. During the months that followed the events of February the question of the revolutionary war was one of the most important subjects of party controversy. The Blanquists, true to the tradition of the great revolution, which with them was only too often an obstinate obsession, kept agitating for a revolutionary war with all the passion which was their best inheritance. They urged it not only on the ground that it was the only thing that could save the new France, but also because they believed that it was only by and through a war that the revolution in France could really be fulfilled.

The Provisional Government, and Lamartine, the Minister for Foreign Affairs, wanted peace. From the very first he assured all the governments of Europe that France was willing to have peaceful relations with all states, whatever their form of government might be.

But the Belgian, Italian and Polish exiles were working for war and feverishly preparing for it. Each group formed its own legion to take its place in the great army which should march against the despots, vanguard of the army of revolutionary France in the last war of all, from which a brotherly alliance of free peoples should arise. The Germans took enthusiastically to this idea.

Before Marx's arrival in Paris a huge meeting of German exiles and artisans resolved to form a German legion. The resolution had been proposed by Bornstedt, and Herwegh was elected chairman of the committee. Appeals were already plastered on the walls of Paris:

Appel aux citoyens français.
Des armes!

Pour les Allemands marchant au secours de leurs frères qui combattent en ce moment pour la liberté, qui se font égorger pour leurs droits, et qu'on veut tromper de nouveau.

Les démocrates allemands de Paris se sont formés en légion pour aller proclamer ensemble la République allemande.

Il leur faut des armes, des munitions, de l'argent, des objets d'habillement. Prêtez-leur votre assistance; vos dons seront reçus avec gratitude. Ils serviront à délivrer l'Allemagne et en même temps la Pologne.

Démocrates allemands et polonais marcheront ensemble à la conquête de la liberté.

Vive la France! Vive la Pologne! Vive l'Allemagne unie et républicaine! Vive la fraternité des Peuples!*

The first detachments of German legionaries had already started drilling on the Champ-de-Mars. They even had their anthem ready: 'We march to Germany in masses.'

The plan was to invade Germany and raise an insurrection in the Odenwald, where the people were already stirred up and memories of the German peasant wars still survived. The

---

* 'Appeal to the citizens of France
Arms!

'Arms for the Germans marching to the help of their brethren now fighting for liberty, offering their lives for their rights, whom their enemies are trying to deceive once more!

'The German democrats of Paris have formed a legion to march and proclaim the German republic.

'They need arms, ammunition, money, clothing. Help them. Your gifts will be gratefully received. They will help to deliver Germany, and Poland as well.

'German and Polish democrats will march together to the conquest of liberty.

'Long live France! Long live Poland! Long live united republican Germany! Long live the brotherhood of the peoples!'

whole of Germany, starting with the Odenwald, was to be roused to revolt. For some time, however, this plan was not nearly ambitious enough. They actually visualized an alliance with the Poles, who planned a rising in Posen and another in Galicia, to be followed by an expedition against Russia. Everything seemed possible. It was sufficient for the first revolutionary trumpets to blow for the walls of the fortress of Petropavlovsk, the citadel of European reaction, to fall of themselves. The Polish democrats, who at that time were everywhere the heroes of the day, had already started squabbling with the Russian democrats about the frontiers of free and independent Poland. Their revolutionary ardour seemed equal to the most impossible tasks. 'Oh, just for one day, dare it!' was the verse with which Herwegh spurred on the half-hearted. Only one thing was necessary: determination and again determination.

One of the few not carried away by the enthusiasm and the tumult was Marx. That France did not want war was plain enough to anyone who did not take the wish for the reality. A Blanquist government would make war, but to bring the Blanquists into power would require another revolution. If Lamartine supported and encouraged the legions it was not on revolutionary grounds but for very much more sober and mundane reasons. The Provisional Government wanted to be rid of the foreign workers, who had been a disturbing element from of old. They were actually willing to subsidize their journey to the frontier. The legion, which consisted of at most 2,000 men, had no prospects whatever if it fought alone. It could at best hope for an initial military success. To the attacked absolutist powers an inroad by the legion could only be welcome; for it would rouse national and patriotic feeling in the invaded country and willy-nilly strengthen the government.

Marx was from the first bitterly opposed to futile, nay harmful, playing at revolution. He counselled the workers not to rush headlong to destruction with the legion but to await developments in Germany, which were bound to lead to revolution in a very short time. Their place was Paris, not the Odenwald. Sebastian Seiler, then a member of the Communist League and an acquaintance of Marx, later wrote:

The socialists and communists were bitterly opposed to attempting to establish a German republic by armed intervention from without. They held public meetings in the rue Saint-Denis, which some of the later insurgents attended. Marx made a long speech at one of these meetings, and said that the February revolution was only to be regarded as the superficial beginning of the European movement. In a short time open fighting would break out in Paris between the proletariat and the bourgeoisie (as it actually did in June). On its result the victory or defeat of revolutionary Europe would depend. He therefore insisted that the German workers remain in Paris and prepare in advance to take part in the armed struggle.[12]

This was swimming against the stream. The majority of the revolutionary and democratic German exiles were opposed to Marx. They called him coward and traitor and hurled the great, fine-sounding phrases of the French Revolution at his head. In spite of his outstanding authority in the Communist League, he was opposed by some of its members. Marx did not retreat a step. The interests of the revolution and of the working class were at stake.

At the beginning of March the Fraternal Democrats had sent a workers' deputation to Paris with an address to the Provisional Government. M'Grath represented the Chartist national executive committee, Jones the London section of the party, Harney the Fraternal Democrats, and Schapper and Moll the London German Workers' Union. They were given a friendly reception by Garnier-Pagès and Ledru-Rollin. The London and Brussels branches of the Communist League, assembled now in Paris, were able to constitute the new central office in all due form. Marx was elected president, Schapper secretary, and the members were Engels, Moll, Bauer, Wilhelm Wolff and Wallau. Marx was now able on the League's behalf to break with the organizations which acknowledged Herwegh and his legion. Bornstedt, who had been elected to the League in Brussels, was expelled. The decision and the reasons for it were published and some newspapers in Germany actually reprinted the news, including the *Trierer Zeitung*, published in Marx's native town. Marx and his adherents withdrew from the democratic organization and founded an organization of their own, the German Workers' Union, which met at the Café de la Picarde in the rue Saint-Denis. This club consisted almost exclusively of workers, especially tailors and bootmakers, men whom Alphonse Lucas, the reactionary chronicler of the clubs of this period, sneered at for arrogating to themselves the right 'd'indiquer à la France la manière dont elle devait se gouverner', of showing France how she ought to be governed.[13] Marx, however, was successful. As early as 20 March the Ambassador of Baden reported to his government that Marx's adherents were 'very numerous'. At the beginning of April the Union numbered 400 members.

Soon after his arrival in Paris, Marx revived his contacts with French revolutionary circles that he knew from 1844 and 1845. On the evening of the day on which he left Brussels he spoke at the *club central* of the Société des Droits de l'Homme et du Citoyen, the leader of which was Barbès, a right-wing Blanquist.[14] Marx's relations with the groups which were represented in the Provisional Government by Ledru-Rollin and Flocon were particularly good. Both these ministers were praised in the letters Engels wrote his brother-in-law, Emil Blank. Engels said the workers would hear of no one but Ledru-Rollin, and they were quite right, because he was more resolute than any of the others; the men round Ledru-Rollin and Flocon were communists without knowing it. Marx and Engels were on terms of personal friendship with Flocon, whom they frequently visited. Flocon offered them money to start a newspaper in Germany, but they did not accept it.[15] Marx's relations with Ledru-Rollin and Flocon later changed, but to the end he criticized them comparatively mildly.

The European movement advanced with a giant's stride. 'Marvellous' news arrived daily.

A complete revolution in Nassau; in Munich students, artists and workers in full insurrection; at Cassel revolution is at the gate; in Berlin there is unbounded fear and trepidation; freedom of the Press and a national guard proclaimed throughout the west of Germany. That is enough for a beginning. If only Friedrich Wilhelm IV remains stubborn! If he does, everything is won and in a few months we shall have the German revolution. If only he clings to his feudal ways! But the devil alone knows what that moody, crazy individual will do next.

Thus wrote Engels in Brussels to Marx in Paris on 8 March.[16]

On 19 March there was a parade of Herwegh's democrats at the Butte de Monceau, with sabre-rattling, fixing of bayonets, rifle practice, marching and counter-marching. At the final rally Herwegh read a German address to the Polish democrats. At about four o'clock some thousand men marched back to Paris in military formation. When they reached it they learned the news that had just come to Paris: a revolution in Vienna, Metternich deposed, the Emperor forced to yield to all the demands of the fighters at the barricades. Tens of thousands of Frenchmen exuberantly fraternized with the Germans. Next day there came the news of victory in Berlin. The boldest dreams were more than fulfilled. Rumours spread beyond all bounds. The King of Prussia was said to have been arrested by the insurgents and thrown into prison, Warsaw had risen and the Russians had been put to flight, and the garrison of St Petersburg had hoisted the flag of insurrection.

The legion was no longer to be restrained. It left Paris on 1 April. It was given a magnificent send-off. The son of Marshal Ney, the Prince of Moscow, made an eloquent speech in which he referred to the great revolutionary traditions and spoke of the revolution's struggle against the bulwark of absolutism in the north, and then the adventure which was to end so quickly and so pitifully began. The leaders of the legion had not yet even decided what they wanted; whether to kindle a peasant war or march peacefully through Germany, their weapons in their hands, to attack Russia, or fight a civil war in Germany until the French advance began. When Ledru-

Rollin tried to find out what the exact aims of Herwegh's movement were, he is said to have brought a long conversation to a close with the words: 'Ah, now I understand, you want to take a corps of barricade professors to Germany.'

The 'barricade professors' were stopped at Strasbourg. That they carried with them the heartiest good wishes of the Blanquists helped them not at all. Lamartine had very guilefully and diplomatically done everything in his power to give the German Government time to prepare their troops for the legion's reception. The forces the legion met when it crossed the Rhine were so infinitely superior and it was so inadequately armed that it was overwhelmed and beaten at the first encounter.

This outcome had been foreseen by Marx. He had opposed the blind, desperate enthusiasm, the reckless, plunging spirit of the insurgents without heeding the mockery and scorn heaped upon him as a doctrinaire.[17] In his view it was infinitely more important for the revolutionaries to make themselves acquainted with the programme dictated to them by the precipitous course of events. The outcry against Marx among the hyper-revolutionaries had reached its zenith at a moment when, they believed, all true revolutionaries ought to be teaching the workers the use of arms, while he spent his time lecturing them on political economy, damping down their enthusiasm and turning them into doctrinaires.

The outbreak of revolution in Germany gave the communists new tasks. Their place was no longer in Paris, but in the country in which they and they only could show the working class the way. That country was Germany. Marx advised the exiles to return to Germany individually and start building up proletarian organizations.

By a coincidence the leaders of the Communist League left Paris on the same day as Herwegh's legion; but without music and without a speech by the Prince of Moscow. A young member of Herwegh's expedition sent a report about it to some German newspapers. 'The German communists left Paris too', he wrote. 'Unlike the German democrats, they did not depart fraternally and sociably, in closed ranks, but each man went to a different point on his own initiative – travellers each carrying the salvation of the world in his own breast.' The writer of those lines soon saw how misguided was the contempt with which he wrote. He was Wilhelm Liebknecht, then aged twenty-two.

The communists left Paris. Four and a half years before, Marx had transplanted himself from the Prussia of Friedrich Wilhelm IV to the Paris of Louis Philippe. Since then there had been the breach with the left-wing Hegelians, the arrival at clarification, the rejection of semi-demi, muddle-headed, sentimental socialism, the Communist Manifesto, the Communist League. When Marx left Paris the flag of the republic was flying from the Palais Royal and Germany was in flames.

[13]

The 'Mad Year' in Cologne

IN Germany the members of the Communist League scattered in all directions. Most of them went to their native town or to the place where they had lived before going into exile. Engels spent April and May in the Wuppertal, Wilhelm Wolff went to Breslau, Schapper to Wiesbaden, Born to Berlin, Wallau to Mainz. In practically every place where workers' unions arose in the months that followed the lead was taken by members of the League or of organizations affiliated to it.

The immediate task was to bring together the workers' organizations that had been founded before the outbreak of the revolution. The first appeal for unity came from the Mainz Workers' Educational Union. Marx, who stopped for two days at Mainz on the way from Paris to Cologne, helped to draft it.

Marx went to Cologne because he had connections with that city which had never been entirely broken off during his years of exile and because Cologne, the biggest city in the most highly industrialized part of Germany, was the obvious place for the headquarters of the Communist League. He arrived on 10 April, accompanied by Engels and Ernst Dronke, a gifted young political writer who had earned himself a good reputation by his books and stories and been made famous by his big trial for *lèse-majesté*, when he was condemned to two years' imprisonment. His daring escape from the fortress of Wesel made him still more famous.

A branch of the Communist League had existed in Cologne since the autumn of 1847. Its leaders were Andreas Gottschalk, a physician, and August von Willich, a former artillery lieutenant. Both these highly distinctive personalities, each in his own way characteristic of the 'mad year' of 1848, will be re-

Karl Marx: Man and Fighter

peatedly mentioned in the pages that follow, and a few words about their careers will not be out of place.

Gottschalk, son of a Jewish butcher, was born at Düsseldorf in 1815. He studied medicine and philosophy at Bonn – he was at Bonn at the same time as Marx – and passed his finals with distinction in 1839. In 1840 he started a medical and surgical practice in Cologne. From the first he worked almost exclusively in the working-class quarters of the city, as healer, helper and friend of the poorest workers. 'It is intelligible', states a pamphlet written in his memory in 1849,

that the man who had the most abundant opportunity of observing poverty, misery and distress at close quarters and was also a warm sympathizer with the sufferings of the proletariat, who were almost on the brink of utter destitution – it is readily intelligible, I say, that such a man should reflect upon the ways and means of most rapidly and effectively redressing pauperization and distress.[1]

Gottschalk made the workers' cause his own. The Cologne workers idolized their warm-hearted doctor and friend. He was their undisputed leader.

August von Willich was a man of entirely different type. He was descended from an ancient, aristocratic, military Prussian family, attended the military academy at Potsdam, and at the beginning of the 1840s was a captain in an artillery brigade stationed in Westphalia. The ideas of the time – democracy, socialism, revolutionary substitution of a new world for the old – found their way even into the stuffy atmosphere of a Prussian barracks. Willich belonged to the not so very small group of officers to whom these ideas appealed. When Lieutenant Fritz Anneke, later Gottschalk's closest friend and colleague, was deprived of his officer's status because of his courageous avowal of socialism, Willich wrote an open letter to the King on his behalf. For this he was placed before a court of honour and deprived of his rank.[2] He went to Cologne and joined the local branch of the Communist League. He earned his living as a carpenter. When the former Prussian army captain made his way across the Cologne parade ground, as he did deliberately every morning on his way to work, walking very slowly past the drilling squads, wearing his leather apron and with his tools on his back, it had a very provocative effect. This was just what Willich intended. He wanted to get himself – and consequently democracy and socialism – talked about. The Cologne communist group attached great importance to propaganda in the army.[3]

Its members met twice a week, discussed 'communism and history', and carried on 'retail propaganda', to employ an expression Gottschalk used in a letter to Hess.[4] The branch did not yet number twenty members. Its influence on the working-class population of Cologne was effectively demonstrated when things started to happen.

The revolution in Paris made a great impression throughout Germany, but nowhere was its effect so great as in the Rhineland. In every Rhineland town petitions to the Government were drafted, demanding radical reforms in an altogether unprecedented manner. They were promptly covered with thousands and tens of thousands of signatures. The initiative for all this activity came from Cologne, and in Cologne itself the initiative came from the branch of the Communist League. On 3 March it organized a mass meeting outside the town hall. A deputation led by Gottschalk and Willich appeared in the council chamber and announced their demands to the startled city fathers. The 4,000 people outside lent emphasis to what they said. Soldiers were brought to the scene, there were collisions between them and the demonstrators, the soldiers fired, there were dead and wounded, and Gottschalk, Willich and Anneke were put under arrest. Three weeks later they were freed by the victory of the revolution in Berlin. The demonstration had attained its purpose of setting the movement on the Rhine under way.

At the end of March, when Gottschalk and his friends were set at liberty, the situation had completely altered. As Marx had foreseen, the news that a republican legion was coming from France to invade Germany had visibly helped the forces of conservatism. A panic fear of the French seized the south and west of Germany. The French were visualized going through the land, looting and burning. The governments of Germany diligently fostered the general alarm. 'You have no idea of how our bourgeoisie fear the word "republic"', Gottschalk wrote on 26 March to his friend Hess. 'For them it is synonymous with robbery, murder, or a Russian invasion, and your legions would be so execrated as bands of murderous incendiaries that but few proletarians would come to your aid.'[5] Georg Weerth wrote to Marx on 25 March almost in the same terms, also from Cologne.[6] Communism, he added, was a word people shuddered at, and anyone who came out openly as a communist would be stoned. And when the legion crossed the frontier and on top of it the rapidly suppressed republican rising took place in Baden, the word 'republic' took on the most evil connotations, at any rate for the time being, in people's minds. Another thing that added strength to the counter-revolution was that the newspapers printed lies about letters of Marx said to have been found on captured leaders of the legion, so that republican, communist and national enemy became synonymous.

A furious hue and cry for the ringleaders of the dispersed demonstration started in Cologne, a 'veritable *battue*', as one newspaper put it, and Willich felt the place had become too hot to hold him. He went to Baden and took part in the insurrection there, and Cologne saw him no more. Gottschalk remained to defy the storm. Finding himself defended by the moderate democrats either faint-heartedly or not at all, he did not mince matters but turned his face from them and confined the whole of his agitation to the workers. On 6 April, four days before Marx's arrival in Cologne, he issued an appeal for the foundation of a 'democratic socialist union'.

Three hundred people were present at the inaugural meeting on 13 April. The overwhelming majority were workers. For this reason they promptly adopted the additional title of 'Workers' Union'. The success of the new organization was astonishing. At the beginning of May the newspapers estimated its membership at between 3–4,000. By the end of June the membership had risen to nearly 8,000. Every one of its meetings at the Gürzenich Haus was packed to overflowing. The workers in their blouses sat before a platform adorned with the red flag, wearing red sashes across their breasts, some of them with red Jacobin caps on their heads. Many of the audience were women, and many were illiterate workers, porters and boatmen, who were particularly hard hit by the prevailing unemployment.

Popular as Gottschalk was among the workers of Cologne, his name alone would not have sufficed to hold this great mass of people together had he not skilfully and effectively represented their most immediate interests. The Workers' Union was at one and the same time an educational association, a political club, and also a breeding-ground of trade unionism. Gottschalk divided the union into occupational sections, and what with the prevalent trade crisis – for the employers, hampered by no law, lowered wages, lengthened hours, gave their apprentices worse victuals – these sections had enough and more than enough to do. They worked out wage rates, tried to establish standards for the working day, busied themselves with conditions of labour. The workers brought their troubles and needs to the Union as though it were omnipotent.

It was hated by the employers in proportion. Not only the employers but the whole propertied class regarded the Workers' Union as a nefarious assault upon humanity. The most incredible rumours gathered round the Union and its president, Gottschalk, 'the communist apostle'. One reactionary journal stated that the demagogue was putting the craziest ideas into the workers' heads. The workers no longer worked but spent all their evenings at the political clubs, from which they went home drunk and beat their wives and children, whom they left to starve. Gottschalk was credited with hatching the most infamous plots. It was said at the end of April that Gottschalk nightly had 'terrible troops of workers drilling with the 11,000 flints that Abd-el-Kadr had sent him'.

However absurd it may sound, all this was taken perfectly seriously by a great many people. The more sinister the

Workers' Union came to appear in the eyes of the property-owners, the more willingly did they listen to the voice of re-action. But dislike of the Workers' Union was widespread even among the most democratically-minded artisans of Cologne. The Association of Employers and Employed, the leader of which was Hermann Becker, a democrat, who be-came active in the Communist League in 1850 and 1851, though later he underwent a complete change of view and eventually became burgomaster of Cologne, was mainly an association of small master-craftsmen and educated artisans. It took its stand on the basis of class peace.

Such was the situation when Marx arrived in Cologne. At first he naturally enough adhered to the party of Gottschalk. He took part in the first meetings of the Workers' Union. But in a very short time differences of opinion concerning the policy of the Union arose between Gottschalk and him. A contemporary record has survived of a meeting which took place shortly after Marx's arrival between the leaders of the Communist League on the one side and the members of the Cologne branch on the other. The discussion became 'very violent' and Dr Gottschalk was harshly criticized in regard to the organization of the Workers' Union.[7] Further infor-mation is not available, but from the subsequent develop-ment of the dispute it is safe to conclude that as soon as he had surveyed the situation in the first few days after his arrival Marx resolutely opposed Gottschalk's policy. The situation in Germany being what it was, Gottschalk's programme could not result in anything but parting the proletariat from the democratic movement and completely isolating it.

The revolution had created, for the first time in German history, a parliament for the whole of Germany, including Austria. The National Assembly was to meet in Frankfurt. In Prussia a chamber was to be elected by a secret and univer-sal indirect ballot. Gottschalk demanded a boycott of the elections both for the Frankfurt and the Berlin assemblies. He claimed that indirect voting was objectionable in itself, and besides there was not sufficient time for the necessary preliminary campaign. The majority of the workers who supported Gottschalk followed him in this, and other extreme left-wing groups also proclaimed an election boycott, in which they may have been influenced by the example of the Blanquists in France. There is no doubt that the Blanquist example influenced Gottschalk. Blanqui was not Gottschalk's model in this alone. Gottschalk may well have had some contact with Blanqui as early as 1848. Herwegh bears witness to his having visited Blanqui in prison when in Paris at the beginning of 1849.

Marx condemned the extreme left's boycott of the elections as an idle and futile demonstration, ultra-revolutionary in form, reactionary in content. By it the left cleared the political battlefield for the forces of reaction and the lukewarm centre. Marx's dispute with Gottschalk became intensified.

Gottschalk's standing out for a boycott was merely the consequence of his general attitude. He utterly rejected all and every compromise and would not hear of even the most temporary coalition with non-proletarian democratic groups. The probable effects of his demands and slogans on others than his own followers did not trouble him at all. He conducted his propaganda openly under the republican banner, and not just the republican banner, but the socialist banner too – the banner of the republic of labour. Gottschalk simply shut his eyes to the whole political backwardness of Germany.

The democrats were not themselves agreed as to how the three dozen fatherlands of Germany were to be united. There were advocates of constitutional monarchy upon the broadest democratic basis, there were advocates of a 'republic with hereditary royal officials', there were those who wanted the several states to be republics subject to an all-German monarchy, while others again wanted their own state to be a constitutional monarchy subject to a German federal republic. Between the advocates of extreme federalism and extreme centralization there were advocates of every conceivable form of compromise. Even among the democrats, to say nothing of the liberals, there were but few who favoured the 'one and indivisible republic' which was the first of the seventeen demands which the Communist League formulated and distributed in the form of a leaflet.[8] Marx was convinced of this by letters sent him by friends and sympathizers from all over Germany. Engels wrote from Barmen: 'If a single copy of our seventeen points were distributed here, as far as we were concerned all would be lost.' Marx issued warnings against illusory hopes in the *Neue Rheinische Zeitung* not long afterwards.

> We do not at the outset make the utopian demand for a single and indivisible German republic [he wrote], but we demand of the so-called Radical-Democratic Party that it do not confound the point of departure of the struggle and of the revolutionary movement with its final aims. It is not now a matter of realizing this or that point of view, this or that political idea, but of insight into the course of development. The National Assembly (in Frankfurt) has only to perform the immediate and practically possible steps.

In these circumstances, Gottschalk's line of action meant parting the advanced workers not only from the liberal and democratic bourgeoisie but also from the great mass of the workers themselves. It meant destroying the coalition of proletariat and revolutionary bourgeoisie in the struggle against absolutism, a coalition that the Communist Manifesto had proclaimed as inevitable but temporary.

Marx's attitude was clearly defined in the very first months of revolution. He was opposed to coming out prematurely and independently with the seventeen points. 'When we founded a great newspaper in Germany', Engels wrote in 1884,

> the banner for us to take our stand under presented itself. It could only be the banner of democracy, but the banner of a democracy which emphasized its specifically proletarian character in details only, since it was not yet possible to proclaim its proletarian character once and for all. Had we been unwilling to do this ... we should have had no choice but to content ourselves with teaching the doctrines of communism in an obscure local paper and founding a small sect instead of a great party of action. The time had passed for us to be preachers in the wilderness. We had

studied the utopians too well not to know that. We had not drafted our programme for that.[9]

In the middle of April Marx and his friends participated in the formation of the Democratic Union in Cologne. It did not at first stand out in any particular way, but took the line that the form of government of the future united Germany should be left to be decided by the National Assembly at Frankfurt and that the relations between throne and people in Prussia should be left to the Chamber in Berlin. This evasion of a clear answer to the most elementary questions left the members of the Democratic Union more than dissatisfied. Someone at the meeting asked what the members of the Democratic Union wanted themselves. Seven eighths of them were in favour of a republic, as the discussion showed, but no resolution in favour of a republic was made. The few who had not yet made up their minds should not be antagonized and driven over to the moderates.

The Democratic Union's first definite action was taking part in the elections for Frankfurt and Berlin. Marx's critics maintained that thanks to his tactics not so much as a single democrat was sent to Parliament, but only a fortuitous left-winger of the type of Franz Raveaux, whom Marx himself was very soon forced to criticize in the *Neue Rheinische Zeitung*. But there is no doubt that but for the Democratic Union Cologne would have been represented by the right and moderates only.

The Communist League was not equal to the situation the revolution had created. It was inadequate in every way. It very soon demonstrated itself to be incomparably weaker in Germany than the central office had supposed. All the emissaries of the League, who were dispersed in every direction, were unanimous to that effect. In Berlin there was no organization whatsoever, and the handful of approximately twenty sympathizers had practically no contact with each other. In Breslau the League was entirely unrepresented. In Mainz the organization was on the point of collapse, and in other centres the story was the same. The League's emissaries were certainly not lacking in energy and enthusiasm, but the branches, in the places where they did manage to found them, very soon demonstrated that they had no real life in them. All the really active members devoted themselves to legal work in the workers' unions, on newspapers and so forth. Marx refused to keep the Communist League alive artificially and go on leading a movement because it had once existed. Besides, there were difficulties Marx had to contend with within the League itself.

In Marx's opinion the appearance of the *Neue Rheinische Zeitung* did away with the excuse even for the appearance of the Communist League's existence. A secret organization had become entirely superfluous, and all that Marx had to say, all the general guidance he had to offer, could be made public through the Press. Because of the infinite variety of conditions in Germany, which varied from state to state and from province to province, it was not possible to give more than general guidance. Marx therefore proposed to the central office that the League be dissolved. Schapper and the other members of the London group put up some opposition to this course. Though they agreed with him on general political questions and sided with him in the struggle with Gottschalk, they had lived in the League and with the League and for the League and it had been dear to them too long for them to be able to consent to its dissolution. So Marx, in the words of a contemporary,[10] 'made use of his discretionary powers and dissolved the League'.[11]

Gottschalk had agreed with Marx with regard to the dissolution of the League. In the Workers' Union he had an incomparably more powerful weapon than the small local branch of the Communist League, so he was able to watch it die with a light heart. Another motive may also have influenced him. He wanted to sever all party connection with Marx in order to be able to attack him with the less restraint. Even before the appearance of the *Neue Rheinische Zeitung* sharp collisions arose between Marx's and Gottschalk's followers. After the collapse of the republican rising in Baden, Willich fled to France and gathered the fugitives at Besançon. Most of them were workers, and their state was so piteous that Willich appealed to the democrats in Germany to assist them. Anneke had joined the Democratic Union in spite of his friendship with Gottschalk. At a meeting of the Union he rose, read Willich's letter of appeal, and proposed that the Union collect money for the republican refugees at Besançon. A lively discussion ended in a vote heavily turning down the proposal. Anneke was the only one to vote for it. According to the newspapers the democrats, in spite of their sympathy for the hungering and exiled worker-refugees, declined to help them because doing so might be interpreted as approval of the policy by which they had been guided. Anneke resigned from the Democratic Union. At his and Gottschalk's suggestion the Workers' Union started a collection which raised quite a respectable sum. That made it perfectly clear, of course, that Marx and his democrats were cowardly and inhuman, while Gottschalk and the Workers' Union were noble and courageous republicans.

Marx's name had not yet been mentioned and the second attack was not directed openly at him, either, but at the *Neue Rheinische Zeitung*, the first number of which had recently appeared. The printer did not pay the wages which the Workers' Union was trying to establish as the minimum for the trade. No other printer in Cologne paid the minimum wage either, but Gottschalk had no need to mention that. The editorial staff of the *Neue Rheinische Zeitung*, i.e. Marx, had nothing whatever to do with the printer and the wages he paid his staff. Gottschalk's newspaper [12] started a violent campaign against the *Neue Rheinische Zeitung*, which described itself as an organ of democracy but was in the hands of a group of inveterate aristocrats – indeed the most dangerous kind, money-aristocrats. They were 'trampling on the proletariat and betraying the people'.

Marx had just obtained an organ in which he could state his position clearly. His task was by no means confined to defending himself against the agitation carried on against him by the ultra-left in Cologne. The paper was to be a substitute for the Communist League throughout Germany and, over and above that, the organ of the 'great party of action' of the German revolution. A few radicals, in particular Georg Weerth and Heinrich Bürgers, both friends of Marx from earlier years, had busied themselves with the project of founding a newspaper before Marx's arrival in Cologne. Bürgers was no communist, and the paper was not originally intended to be more than a local Cologne newspaper, and Marx had not been intended to work on it. When he arrived he was advised to go to Berlin. He declined. 'We knew the Berlin of that time only too well from personal observation', Engels wrote later. 'Berlin with its barely arisen bourgeoisie, its loquacious but timid and obsequious lower middle class, its completely undeveloped workers, its teeming bureaucracy, its swarms of obsequious nobles and courtiers.'[13] The decisive factor, however, was that the Code Napoléon was in force in Cologne, involving freedom of the Press, which was not even remotely conceivable in Berlin even after the events of March.

Marx succeeded in gaining control of the paper within a very short time. For this purpose it was necessary to secure the consent of the Cologne democrats. The newspaper had to be

edited from the German democratic viewpoint, which regarded the question of whether Germany should have a monarchy or a republic as an open one, though it gave the advantage to the republican idea both from the practical and the theoretical point of view.[14]

This was how Bürgers formulated the conditions on which the editorship would be given to Marx. Bürgers was himself on the editorial board. Marx naturally accepted these terms.

There was greater difficulty in raising the money for the paper than its backers had expected. The upper bourgeoisie would have nothing whatever to do with the democrats, particularly with those suspected of having anything whatever to do with communism. Marx appealed to Engels to try to

place some of the shares in the Wuppertal. His success was
meagre. According to his son, old Engels would rather send
him a thousand bullets than a thousand thalers.[15] Marx did
not fare much better in Cologne. Meanwhile events were pressing. The National Assembly met at Frankfurt and from the
first day showed itself so timid, so undecided, so conscience-
stricken that the future of this half-revolution seemed to
promise the worst. It was essential that the paper should
appear as soon as possible. Marx plunged his hand in his own
pocket and produced every penny he possessed. All the money
available, such as it was, was laid down, and the first number of the *Neue Rheinische Zeitung* appeared on 1 June
1848.

With the exception of Bürgers, the editorial board consisted
entirely of ex-members of the Communist League: Dronke,
Weerth, Ferdinand Wolff, Wilhelm Wolff. Marx was the
editor. The organization of the editorial staff, in the words of
Engels, was

a simple dictatorship by Marx. A great daily which had to be
ready by a definite time could not maintain a consistent attitude
in any other way. Marx's dictatorship was accepted as a matter of
course. It was undisputed and gladly acknowledged by us all. It
was above all his clear views and firm principles that made it the
most famous newspaper of the revolutionary years.[16]

Marx's editorship was distinguished by the fact that he did
not publish any general theoretical articles of the kind that
filled the other democratic newspapers of the time to a surfeit.[17]
Facts were the language of the *Neue Rheinische Zeitung*.
While democrat professors explained the advantages of the
republican form of government at interminable length – to
which they were particularly prone in the South German Press
– lectures of this kind were completely absent from the *Neue
Rheinische Zeitung*. The reason for this was not alone because
of the agreement with Bürgers. Marx's task was to give his
readers an 'insight into the course of development'. The way
in which Marx presented his facts, made them demonstrate

the inevitability of a republican solution, was the most effective possible propaganda for republicanism, though the word
was never mentioned.

The paper's policy was determined by Marx and Marx
alone. Marx edited it as he had edited the *Rheinische Zeitung*
five years before. Just as behind every word of the *Rheinische
Zeitung* there had been the voice of Marx, so did he now make
every word of the *Neue Rheinische Zeitung* his own. The
paper called itself the 'organ of democracy' and in speaking of
the battle-front against the forces of feudal absolutism it used
the phrase 'we democrats'. During the first months it avoided
anything that might possibly disturb the united front. Not
a word was spoken of the antagonism between proletarian and
non-proletarian, bourgeois, or petty-bourgeois democracy.
There was not a word about the special interests of the working
classes, of the workers' special tasks in the German revolution.
Neither Engels nor Marx wrote a word about the position of
the workers until the end of 1848.[18] Engels, writing to Marx
from Barmen before the appearance of the paper, expressed
himself very strongly on this question of the policy of the
united front at any price. 'The workers are beginning to stir
a little, still very crudely, but in a mass. That, however, does
not suit us,' he wrote.[19] The proletariat must march in the
great democratic battle-line, always at the extreme left wing,
always taking care not to lose connection with the rest of the
army. It must be at its most impetuous in attack, its fighting
spirit must animate the host in the storming of the Bastille.
For the Bastille is not yet taken, Marx cried to those who
threatened to tire, absolutism is not defeated yet. As long as
the Bastille is still standing the democrats must remain united.
The proletariat must not isolate itself; however difficult the
task may be, it must reject everything tending to divide it
from the rest.[20]

The Communist Manifesto had allotted the Communist
Party a twofold task, not only that of taking part in the common struggle of the bourgeoisie against the reactionary classes,
but of

instilling into the workers the clearest possible recognition of the antagonism between bourgeoisie and proletariat, so that the German workers may straightway use, against the bourgeoisie, as so many weapons, the social and political conditions which the bourgeoisie must necessarily introduce with their supremacy, and in order that the fight against the bourgeoisie may immediately begin after the downfall of the reactionary classes.[21]

First the bourgeoisie must come into power, but really into power. The proletariat must support it in this, urge it forward, pitilessly scourge every weakness, every hesitation, every compromise the bourgeoisie might want to make with the forces of reaction. But so long as the revolutionary advance of the bourgeoisie continued it must maintain a united front with it. After the victory the united front must be destroyed. Once the bourgeoisie had in all essentials got the power, the struggle against it would begin. In Germany it could not, must not begin yet. In France and England it was different.

The *Neue Rheinische Zeitung* gave more space to events abroad than any other German paper. What had already come to pass in France and England must come to pass in Germany tomorrow. There could be no better way of creating the 'clearest possible awareness of the antagonism between bourgeoisie and proletariat' than by constantly drawing the workers' attention to events abroad. But in Germany the Bastille must first be stormed. In Germany compromise was inevitable. In Germany 'we democrats' must fight shoulder to shoulder until victory was gained. In France the time for compromise had passed. Strenuously as Marx avoided anything that might have weakened the joint democratic forces in Germany, he sided just as resolutely with the insurrectionary Paris workers in those days of June.[22]

Consideration for his allies in the struggles did not mean that he spared their weaknesses. The *Neue Rheinische Zeitung* treated its contemptible opponents, the monarchy, the military camarilla, the whole of the forces of reaction, with the greatest contempt. That goes without saying. It poured just as much scorn and contempt upon the irresolution and pusillanimity of the left. The revolution had not yet been accomplished. It was an illusion to suppose that nothing was left now but to gather in its fruits. The Assembly at Frankfurt was only a timid beginning, and if it stood still it must be whipped forward. 'The very first number began with an article which ridiculed the ineffectiveness of the Frankfurt Parliament, the uselessness of its long-winded speeches, the vanity of its timid resolutions. It cost us half our shareholders.' [23] Engels still remembered that with pleasure nearly forty years later.

War with Russia would drive the revolution forward, cut off every possibility of a bourgeois retreat, destroy half-slain feudalism with a single mighty blow. The *Neue Rheinische Zeitung* demanded it from the very first day. There was no other way of freeing Poland than by war. Russia was the mainstay of European reaction; it must be overthrown in war. With every month it became clearer that only war with Russia could save the German revolution. The German revolution had got stuck in 'a tedious philistine farce', as Marx complained in September 1848.[24] It failed to overcome the old impediment of its division into innumerable petty states. Prussia, though it had sustained some heavy blows, was fundamentally intact, and remained the single serious internal opponent. Austria stood firm in spite of all shocks and threatened to become strong once more. The only possibility of uniting Germany was for Germany to make a united war on Russia. 'If Germany could be brought to war with Russia, it would be all up with Habsburgs and Hohenzollerns, and the revolution would be victorious all along the line.'[25] Marx scarcely expected the war to revolutionize Russia. The liberation of Poland, though a desired aim, was nevertheless a by-product. The war must be fought for the salvation and completion of the German revolutionary will. The Tsar would be the saviour of the German revolution, because he would centralize it. That was how Marx regarded the question of war.

But the Tsar hesitated and did not attack the revolution, and the revolution in its turn was too feeble, too little centralized, to take the offensive itself.

A perceptible change took place in Cologne after Marx started addressing the workers directly. The *Neue Rheinische Zeitung* found its way to the workers and to the members of Gottschalk's Union, who obviously started by mistrusting it. The Workers' Union published a pitiful little sheet which contained practically nothing but minutes of Union meetings and short paragrahps about the workers' everyday life. It did not satisfy even the most modest demands. Complaints about it were made at meetings, but Gottschalk, a good speaker and organizer, was a less than mediocre journalist.

Marx's field of activity also extended in another direction. The various democratic unions, which were distributed all over Germany, sent their representatives to a congress which took place in Frankfurt-on-Main on 14 and 15 June. The Workers' Union in Cologne also took part in it. If Gottschalk had been consistent he would have boycotted the democratic congress just as he had boycotted the two Parliaments. He did not do so. The Workers' Union sent him to Frankfurt as their only delegate, because 'Gottschalk alone was completely competent to represent the Workers' Union of Cologne.' He was to demand an open avowal of a republic and an open disavowal of the Frankfurt and Berlin Parliaments.

Gottschalk played an important role at the democratic congress. One delegate described him as a man 'born to be a dictator, possessing indefatigable energy and intelligence as sharp as a guillotine, an image of Robespierre'. Of the two resolutions that he proposed, the anti-parliamentary one was rejected and the other accepted with a highly significant alteration. A democratic republic was declared to be not, as Gottschalk demanded, the 'only possible' system of government but as the 'only tenable' one. He did not leave the congress on this account but actually gave his vote in favour of the resolutions which determined the constitution of the Union itself. These declared the *Neue Rheinische Zeitung* to be one of the three official organs of the Democratic Party, and appealed to all democratic associations existing at any one place to unite.

Three organizations had sent their representatives to the

K.M.—7

congress from Cologne: the Workers' Union, the Democratic
Union and the Association of Employers and Employed.
These ought now to have united. Gottschalk wanted a complete fusion of the three, which, in view of the great numerical
preponderance of the Workers' Union, would have meant the
complete submergence of the other two organizations in his.
The Democratic Union declined to be submerged and proposed that a bureau of cooperation be created instead.
Negotiations were still in progress when events occurred which
fundamentally altered the situation of the Cologne democrats.

The bourgeoisie were not alone in their hatred of Gottschalk. The police had had an eye on him for a long time,
and they stepped in now. According to the police report
Gottschalk and Anneke were said to have proposed to the
Workers' Union 'the foundation of a republic by violent
means'. Gottschalk and Anneke were arrested on 3 July. The
prison gates closed behind them for six months.

An interregnum in the Workers' Union now began. Not
one of Gottschalk's adherents was capable of replacing him.
Joseph Moll was elected temporary president. Although he
was an opponent of Gottschalk's, his energy, courage, and
knowledge had earned him general respect. He and Schapper
now became the leaders of the Union, and both of them were
political partisans of Marx. An attempt to attack Marx from
another quarter miscarried. Marx's old opponent, Wilhelm
Weitling, came to Cologne in the middle of July. On 21 July
at the Democratic Union he made 'an exciting speech in
which he proclaimed the necessity of a complete reorganization of our political and social institutions', in the words of a
newspaper favourably disposed towards him. This speech was
reported in full in the official organ of the Democratic Union.
In America, Weitling had learned nothing whatever. He still
preached government by the 'judicious'[26] because neither in
Germany nor in America nor even in the Democratic Union,
as he not very politely added, was the mob capable of recog-
nizing where its real interests lay. Marx answered him at a

meeting on 4 August.[27] In their social development, he said, the Germans were now where the French had been in 1789. To set up a dictatorship to realize any one man's ideas would be absurd. The sovereign power, as in the case of the Provisional Government in Paris, must be formed of the most heterogeneous elements, which then, by the exchange of ideas, must decide on the most effective method of government.[28] The drafting of the report cannot be said to be very clear, but Marx's line of argument can be detected through the muddled statement. He demanded that the German revolution be completed, the bourgeois revolution, the German 1789, representing the coalition of all the forces of democracy, all 'the highly heterogeneous elements'.

In the meantime a joint committee of Cologne democrats had been formed. Marx and Schneider, a lawyer, represented the Democratic Union, Schapper and Moll the Workers' Union, and two others represented the Association of Employers and Employed. This combination assured the leadership of Marx. The committee displayed tremendous activity. In the middle of August it organized the first Rhineland democratic congress, at which forty delegates represented sixteen organizations. Marx was the life and soul of the congress. Karl Schurz, the German-American statesman, who was a young student at Bonn at the time, described forty years later the impression that Marx made upon him.

Marx was thirty years old and already the recognized head of a school of socialism. A thick-set, powerful man, with his high forehead, his pitch-black hair and beard and his dark, flashing eyes, he immediately attracted general attention. He had the reputation of great learning in his subject, and what he said was in fact solid, logical and clear.

People with unclear minds were always repelled by Marx's clarity and logic. Schurz was of the opinion that he had never met a man of such wounding and intolerable arrogance of manner. He never forgot the tone of biting contempt with which he uttered, almost spat the word 'bourgeois'. Albert

Brisbane, correspondent of the *New York Tribune*, who was staying in Cologne at the time, also saw Marx but saw him through different eyes. 'His features gave one the impression of great energy, and behind his sober-minded reserve one could see the passionate fire of a courageous spirit.'[29]

The more outspoken the *Neue Rheinische Zeitung* became, the more energetically it denounced the left for an irresolution bordering on cowardice, if not positive treason, to the revolution; the more plainly it hinted that the cooperation of bourgeoisie and proletariat couuld only be temporary, however necessary it might be in Germany at the moment; the more alarmed the shareholders became. Half of them were lost as soon as the newspaper appeared, and articles about the June fighting cost Marx the other half. The paper was brought sharply up against serious practical difficulties. The printer refused to extend credit any further, and one issue of the paper failed to appear. Fortunately another printer was found, but the position became so threatening that at the end of August Marx had to undertake a journey through Germany and Austria to raise the funds necessary to continue. His travels took him to Berlin, to Vienna, then to Berlin again. In Vienna Marx addressed the local Democratic Union and he lectured on wage-labour and capital at the First Vienna Workers' Union. In both cities he negotiated with the leaders of left-wing organizations. Whether he obtained the assistance he required is not known. All that is known is that the *Neue Rheinische Zeitung* received very generous support from the Polish democrats. On 18 September Vladislav Koscielsky sent the *Neue Rheinische Zeitung* 2,000 thalers in their name.[30]

Marx returned to Cologne just when the events of September, the stormiest period of the 'mad year' in Cologne, were beginning. Their outbreak coincided with the resignation of the Prussian ministry of Auerswald-Hansemann. Marx had castigated it for the cowardice with which it retreated step by step before the forces of reaction, which were growing bolder every day. Incompetent a government as it had been, it had by no means been reactionary in intent, and all the key positions in it had been occupied by members of the bourgeoisie. Its resignation was an indication of the impending crash. Marx summoned the democrats to mass action. In the midst of this critical situation a number of clashes which had been brewing for a long time and had no connection, at least no direct connection, with the political change of scene, broke out in Cologne. In Cologne, as everywhere else along the Rhine, feelings between townsmen and soldiery were very strained. The garrisons consisted predominantly of troops from east of the Elbe and were systematically incited against the people by their officers. There had been serious collisions between military and civilians in Mainz and Aachen during the past spring. Cologne's turn came now. Soldiers attacked and beat civilians without any cause whatever. There was general indignation at this, and it was by no means confined to the democrats. It was widespread among the otherwise entirely 'loyal' population. The editorial staff of the *Neue Rheinische Zeitung* took the protest in hand. Wilhelm Wolff and Engels summoned an open-air mass meeting at which the brutality of the soldiery was denounced and a committee of public safety, thirty strong, was elected to prevent a repetition of such attacks. Marx was a member of the committee.[31]

To the excitement caused by these events in Cologne there was now added indignation at the advance of reaction in Prussia and at the Prussian armistice with Denmark. This indignation swept through the whole of Germany and created a situation which caused many to believe that the outbreak of a second revolution was at hand. To the democrats and liberals, even the most moderate of them, the war with Denmark was an affair of the whole of the German people. Schleswig-Holstein was German territory subject to the Danish throne; to liberate it from its Danish overlords was one of the foremost tasks of the United Germany movement. When the war broke out students and workers who had just been fighting at the barricades in Berlin hurried to volunteer for the army. The struggle for Schleswig-Holstein had become a symbol of German unity. And now Prussia signed an armistice with

Denmark. That meant its abandonment of the United German front and its return to the old, purely Prussian and purely dynastic policy. The armistice at Malmö was felt as a deliberate challenge, an insolent slap in the nation's face. As for the National Assembly, it vacillated, swung unworthily this way and that, and on 16 September expressed its consent to the armistice.

On 17 September a huge mass meeting gathered at Worringen, near Cologne. It was attended by delegations from innumerable Rhineland towns and many peasants from the surrounding district. It resolved, on Engels's proposal, that should Prussia and the National Assembly at Frankfurt come into conflict they would stand by Germany 'through thick and thin'.[32] That the National Assembly had capitulated to Prussia in the meantime was not yet known at Cologne. When the news arrived anger knew no bounds. Indignation was widespread throughout Germany. There was serious fighting in Frankfurt on 18 September, and two of the most hated reactionary deputies were lynched. The Democratic Union and the Workers' Union at Cologne declared their solidarity with the fighters at the Frankfurt barricades and the *Neue Rheinische Zeitung* started a subscription fund for the insurrectionaries and their families. Next day the King appointed General Pfuel Prime Minister of Prussia. Pfuel was hated by the democrats as the oppressor of the Poles. His nomination only served to pour oil on the flames.

The military had made their preparations, the troops in the fortresses were ready for action and guns were directed on the town. The second Rhineland democratic congress was intended to meet on 25 September. On that day, at seven o'clock in the morning, Hermann Becker and Karl Schapper were arrested. Moll escaped arrest because a crowd quickly gathered and prevented the police from seizing him. The city militia refused to help the police. The whole city was in an uproar. Marx hurried to the Workers' Union. He and Bürgers, who were informed of the situation in full, 'declared in the name of the congress that in no circumstances, least of all at the present moment, did they want a rising.'[33] The workers, exasperated at the loss of their leaders, listened 'with gloomy looks'. Other meetings took place, here and there people actually started putting up barricades, but no actual fighting took place. The preponderance of the military was so great that the city militia, who in any case were not so very determined to carry matters to extremes, held back, and the workers, unarmed or badly armed, could not fight alone. The outbreak must not be confined to Cologne and could not start yet. The crisis must first become even more acute. Marx declined to consent to a local riot. Germany was not ready for a general rising yet.

Not a single shot had been fired in Cologne, but the military wished to savour their triumph to the full. Martial law was proclaimed, all political associations were dissolved, all meetings were forbidden, and the radical papers, starting with the *Neue Rheinische Zeitung*, were suspended. The reactionary Press could scarcely contain itself with joy at the end of its hated enemies. 'The entire editorial staffs have had to take flight', it exulted. This was an exaggeration. Warrants were issued for the arrest of Engels, Dronke and the two Wolffs. Marx not having spoken at any public meeting, the police had no excuse for taking proceedings against him. But the position of the newspaper was more than difficult. Besides Marx, only Georg Weerth, who was in charge of the feuilleton, remained. All the rest of the staff had been forced to fly.

If the reaction thought the time had come for rejoicing, they rejoiced a little too soon. Marx had no intention of laying down his arms. In spite of the paper's financial position, which was now, of course, more desperate than ever, he promptly opened negotiations to continue publication at Düsseldorf should the state of martial law be prolonged.

The negotiations turned out to be superfluous. The unnecessary declaration of martial law roused even the tamest citizens of Cologne against the military command. The city council unanimously demanded its withdrawal. There were debates about it in the Berlin Chamber, and they were very embarrassing to the Government. On 3 October the military authorities withdrew martial law very reluctantly, but under orders from Berlin. The *Neue Rheinische Zeitung* appeared again a week later. Marx prominently announced that the editorial staff remained unchanged, but with the addition of Ferdinand Freiligrath, who had just been acquitted of a charge of high treason. Before the period of martial law the newspaper had had 6,000 subscribers, which placed it in the front rank of German newspapers, in circulation as well as in influence. In a short time it reached its old position and even surpassed it.

Marx's influence on the Workers' Union had grown stronger and stronger. It was only natural that the Union should now invite him to become its leader. It had lost its president for the second time since Gottschalk's arrest. Moll was a fugitive and Schapper in prison. A delegation approached Marx, but it was only after a good deal of hesitation that he agreed to accept the position. He explained his reasons at a meeting on 16 October. His position in Cologne was precarious. He was no longer a Prussian subject, and although the Cologne council had granted him a permit to stay in the city, the state authorities would not hear of his nationality being restored.[34] Besides, he would shortly have to appear before a jury because of an alleged offence against the Press laws, to say nothing of his being overwhelmed with work on account of the temporary dispersal of the editorial committee of the *Neue Rheinische Zeitung*. 'Nevertheless', according to the minutes of the meeting, 'he was prepared temporarily to comply with the wish of the workers until Dr Gottschalk should be released. Government and bourgeoisie must be convinced that despite all persecution there are always people ready to place themselves at the workers' disposal.'[35]

Marx, who had in effect been president of the Workers' Union ever since the temporary election of Moll to that position, now became its president in name as well. It was the outward sign of his victory in the struggle he had been carrying on for six months in the ranks of the workers' organizations and the Communist League in Cologne.

[14]

Defeat with Honour

THE reactionary Press poured scorn on the workers for their 'cowardice' in retreating when things grew difficult. Marx denied that it was cowardice. It merely meant that they were not reckless. The moment for a general rising would only come when great questions and mighty events urged the united population into battle.

The October rising should have been such a moment. The revolutionaries of Vienna rose once more, in alliance with Kossuth's Hungary, to fight the decisive battle with the re-habilitated forces of Habsburg absolutism. On its outcome depended not the victory or defeat of the revolution in Austria alone. The fate of the whole German revolution would be decided in Vienna. If the Habsburgs conquered, so would the Hohenzollerns, and March would have been in vain. For Germany's sake they must not win.

The *Neue Rheinische Zeitung* issued impassioned appeals to the democrats of Germany, employed its most powerful arguments, used the glowing verses of Freiligrath, urging them to make Vienna's cause their own:

> Wenn wir noch knien könnten, wir lägen auf den Knien,
> Wenn wir noch beten könnten, wir beteten für Wien.*

The left produced their usual resounding rhetorical phrases in praise of the Viennese. But they failed to understand, would not listen, no longer had the strength to carry out the task of the moment: that of defending Vienna in Berlin, Dresden and Frankfurt. Germany's calamitous division into minor states meant that every general question assumed a variety of local forms – a Prussian form, a Saxon form, a Badenese

* 'If we could only kneel, we should go down on our knees,
   If we could only pray, we should pray for Vienna.'

form, a Bavarian form and so on. As local questions they were incapable of solution. There could be only one German revolution. The alternative was the German counter-revolution.

The second democratic congress met in Berlin at the end of October. There were debates and more debates, and the time was frittered away with eloquent but empty speeches. In its appeal for the Viennese, 'pulpit pathos' was substituted for 'revolutionary energy', in the words of Marx. Germany did not rise, and Vienna was left to its fate. The imperial troops entered the Austrian capital on 1 November.

Prussia's turn, quite logically, came next. On 2 November Pfuel's cabinet resigned in Berlin. It was not reactionary enough for the King, who felt himself strong enough now. The new Prime Minister he appointed was Count Brandenburg, an illegitimate son of Friedrich Wilhelm II. Brandenburg ordered the Berlin Parliament out of Berlin. It was unwilling to go, so a regiment of guards quite easily dispersed it. In March the King had said that soldiers were the only thing of any use against democrats.

The Assembly opposed force not with force but with phrases. It had spent its whole time retreating step by step. Now, when its members should have organized armed resistance, acted like revolutionaries, ready to face every peril, even a sanguinary defeat, which would have been a thousand times better guarantee of a resurrection than a timid capitulation, the Chamber ceremoniously 'took its stand on the law'. The soldiers, of course, took their stand on the more solid ground of Berlin. The Chamber offered passive resistance, which meant in effect no resistance at all. The utmost to which they roused themselves was to issue an appeal to the country not to pay taxes to an unconstitutional government.

That was only the first and most obvious answer to the reactionary onslaught. Marx had proclaimed a tax boycott in the Rhineland before the Chamber made its decision. Now blow after blow must inevitably follow. Cologne waited for the signs of battle from the capital. News was spread that the Berlin city militia had refused to hand over their arms. This was the moment that Marx had been waiting for. Now the hour had struck. He appealed to the west of Germany to go to the assistance of Berlin, 'with men and arms'.[1]

But the news was false. The people of Berlin remained quiet. The city militia handed over their arms. *Junker* officers promenaded up and down Unter den Linden as of yore, full of contempt for the civilian rabble. Even the forcible dispersal of the Prussian National Assembly failed to enliven the feeble glow of the German revolution.

Cologne was swarming with soldiers. The military were thirsting for an opportunity to shoot and stab to right and left to their heart's content. It would have been madness to have stood up to be butchered by them. Marx issued warnings against false heroism. At the same time he did everything possible to extend the movement. To open an attack in Cologne alone would merely have resulted in the riot he had condemned as hopeless in September. Berlin did not stir. But at all costs something must be done. The German revolution must not be allowed to go down to defeat so ignominiously.

On 18 November, Marx, jointly with Schapper and the lawyer Schneider, issued an appeal for a tax boycott in the name of the Rhineland district democratic committee. Passive resistance presupposed active resistance, the *Neue Rheinische Zeitung* proclaimed, otherwise it would be equivalent to the struggles of a calf in the slaughter-house. Marx therefore appealed for a general levy of the people, of all men of military age, for the distribution of weapons, for the forming of committees of public safety and for the removal of officials who remained loyal to the Government.[2]

The Prussian National Assembly might still, perhaps, have been able to carry the people with it, although the most favourable moment had passed. But it grew afraid of its own courage. It had been banished by the King to the reactionary little country town of Brandenburg.

It spent two weeks raging and fuming and then, with plaintive whines and ineffectual murmurs, went to Brandenburg. Once there it was promptly dissolved.

On 5 December 1848 Prussia was granted a new constitution.

A rising for such a Chamber, a popular revolution for the benefit of a bourgeoisie such as this would have been senseless. Marx explained to a Cologne jury a few weeks later what the struggle was about. 'What confronted us', he told them, 'was the struggle between ancient feudal bureaucracy and modern bourgeois society, the fight between the society of landed property and industrial society, between the society of faith and the society of knowledge.'[3] Between these two forms of societies there could only be a struggle to the death. But the bourgeoisie, who should have fought for their own interests, their class interests, cried off, shirked, evaded their task. They wanted the revolution, they could not help wanting it, but they shrank from the cost. They cast fearful glances at the masses whom they had set in motion because they themselves were too weak to face feudalism alone, the masses whom they also feared. For behind their own revolution they could already perceive the second revolution lurking, the revolution that would be against them. Lacking initiative, lacking faith in the people and faith in themselves, they failed to exert the strength to seize the power as they might have seized it. They did not even go halfway. They allowed the whole of the old state apparatus to remain intact, in the ingenuous hope of establishing their supremacy and preserving it with its help. The nobility, the army, the bureaucracy allowed them to hold sway as long as the elementary popular movement threatened to sweep everything away. The bourgeoisie were good enough as a screen to shelter behind, while danger threatened. As soon as they were no longer necessary for this purpose the feudal classes dispensed with their services.[4]

The experiences of the past nine months had made one thing plain beyond all doubt. Vienna and Berlin, the Prussian Chamber and the National Assembly at Frankfurt, the speech-making and still more the behaviour of the parties, all pointed to one thing. The revolution could only be accomplished *against* the bourgeoisie. In a series of articles in which he summed up the progress of events Marx concluded that the alternative before Germany now was the counter-revolution of feudal absolutism or the 'social-republican revolution'.[5]

'Social-republican' was the term he used, not 'socialist' or 'proletarian'. The seventeen points of the programme of the Communist League had demanded a republic with socialist institutions, a republic with equal suffrage for all, which should free the peasants of all feudal burdens, assure the workers a livelihood by national workshops, the breaking of the power of the aristocracy of finance for the benefit of industry and the petty bourgeoisie, a state bank to replace the private banks and control credit. Social republicanism involved neither the abolition of private ownership of the means of production nor the abolition of class conflicts. It meant capitalism still, but capitalism in a state in which workers, petty bourgeoisie and peasants had maximum concessions. The social-republican revolution did not emancipate the proletariat; it merely prepared the ground for the struggle for its emancipation. If the bourgeoisie failed, if they did not manage to attain what was expected of them, i.e. a constitutional monarchy in theory but their own supremacy in fact, the other anti-feudal classes must part from them and workers, petty bourgeoisie, and peasants must advance for the social republic.

From the autumn of 1848 onwards the *Neue Rheinische Zeitung* started changing its tone. If previously it had only paid slight attention to specifically working-class questions, wishing to avoid anything tending to disturb harmonious co-operation between bourgeoisie and proletariat against the forces of absolutism, it now set itself to demonstrating the full extent of the antagonism between proletariat and bourgeoisie. It gave publicity to the work-book that the municipal authorities of Cologne imposed on its workers, a shameless document demonstrating the workers' lack of rights. The *Neue Rheinische Zeitung* declared that this was evidence of what kind of constitution the German bourgeoisie would give the people if it came into power.

The weakness of the German revolution was now manifest. Its most deep-seated cause lay in Germany's defective econ-

omic development. All the negative factors which had come
to light, the splitting up of the revolutionary movement in the
separate states, the weakness of the bourgeoisie, the inertia of
the petty bourgeoisie, the uncertainty of the workers, all had
their deepest roots in it. After the collapse of Vienna and
Berlin, in the face of the growing apathy and paralysis which
seemed to be extending its grip from day to day, all hope that
the German revolution might once more find sufficient
strength within itself seemed to disappear. Towards the end
of 1848 Marx rested all his hopes upon a blow from without.
The Gallic cock must grow again. The revolution in its course
through Europe had started out from Paris, in Paris the
counter-revolution had gained its first victories, in Paris likewise it would suffer its next defeat. Not a country in Europe
now lived its own life alone; the same battle-front ran through
them all. The revolution could not conquer in any country unless the counter-revolution were overthrown in France. The article with which the *Neue Rheinische Zeitung* greeted the
New Year ended with the words: 'Revolutionary rising of the
French working class, world war, that is the programme for
1849.'[6]

In the revolution's period of decline the respective social
forces stood out far more plainly than during its period of
advance. The strength and weakness of the various classes
were now apparent. The ultra-left chose just this moment to
lose all sense of proportion. They clung the more fanatically
to their wish-picture the farther reality departed from it. At
the beginning of 1849 a fresh attack on Marx was hatched
in the Workers' Union.

In spite of the unrelenting efforts of the public prosecutor,
supported by the partisan president of the court, to secure a
conviction of Gottschalk, 'who appealed to the crude masses,
the lowest section of society, the most incapable of all of forming an opinion', the jury had acquitted him. Marx's acceptance
of the presidency of the Workers' Union had only been provisional. Now that Gottschalk was free once more, he was able
to resume it. But in the meantime a great deal had changed in

the Union, and Gottschalk's long imprisonment had not been without its effect on him. The school through which the Union had passed in those stormy days under the leadership of Marx and his friends had not been in vain. It had evolved, its understanding of the course of development had become infinitely clearer, it no longer only differentiated between black and white, between heaven and hell, as it had done in the past; it had learned to differentiate both in the camp of the counter-revolution and in its own, it no longer stood for all or nothing.

Gottschalk was bitterly disappointed. 'His' Union, which he regarded so tenderly as his own creation and believed he could sway this way and that as if it were his own property, had been stolen from him. He decided that it needed reorganization, and proposed that full powers be vested in the president – that, of course, meant Gottschalk himself – to appoint his own officers, for he alone possessed the necessary knowledge, understanding and authority. The Union declined to submit to a dictatorship of this sort, and Gottschalk was enraged at its 'ingratitude'. His vanity was so wounded that at the beginning of January 1849 he left Cologne without saying anything to anybody and went to Brussels. But before leaving he gained control of the Union newspaper, and the new editor whom he put in charge was his unconditional adherent, as he was destined soon to show by what he wrote about the forthcoming elections.

Gottschalk may have asked the members of the Workers' Union to put him up as candidate for the Prussian National Assembly and they may have refused. This was later believed to have been the chief reason for his departure from Cologne. Gottschalk denied it, however, and recalled his attitude to the elections of 1848, to participation in which he had been so strongly opposed. But that had been in 1848. In 1849 Gottschalk became a candidate, though not in Cologne. He stood in Bonn and also in a peasant constituency near Bonn, on both occasions without success.

The elections, under the new constitution granted by the

King, were due to take place on 22 February 1849. The Workers' Union spent weeks discussing whether to participate in them or not. Anneke, who was a friend of Gottschalk, though he did not remain a partisan of his to the end, was in favour of the Workers' Union putting up their own candidate. Marx opposed this, in the first place for the practical reason that the time till the election was too short to make the necessary preparations. In principle, of course, he was in favour of putting up workers' candidates, but for the moment it was not a question of 'doing something on grounds of principle but of creating opposition to the Government, to absolutism and to feudal domination'. He was far from agreeing on matters of principle with Raveaux, whom he had relentlessly criticized, and with Schneider, both of whom were standing as candidates. But it was not a question of a struggle between 'red' and 'pink' democrats now. 'In view of the impossibility of putting one's own principles into effect it was necessary to unite with the other opposition party in order not to leave the victory to absolute monarchism.'[7]

This was another attempt to go part of the way with the radical bourgeoisie. It was an attempt undertaken without much hope of rallying the ranks in a battle that was almost lost. Yet it was the only course open in Germany as long as a blow did not come to clear the stifling atmosphere from without. In this situation, with the forces distributed as they were, anything else would have amounted to so much empty verbiage.

The second Prussian National Assembly was also elected by indirect voting. The primary voters elected the electors who elected the actual deputies. The left-wing bloc were successful in Cologne. Of the 344 electors 200 were democrats and opponents of the constitution the King had granted. They sent two deputies to Berlin: Kyll, and Schneider the lawyer, with whom Marx had worked for months in the Democratic Union.

The majority of the members of the Workers' Union were followers of Marx. Gottschalk's closest followers, utterly opposed to compromise as of old, clinging to their principles all the more obstinately because they were utterly incapable of practical political thinking, wrong even when an error in their calculations accidentally produced the right result, now threw all discretion to the winds and used their paper to attack Marx more and more violently. Gottschalk still retained his control of the Union paper, and the Union failed to regain it. Consequently it was forced to start a new paper of its own. From February onwards there were two workers' newspapers in Cologne, fighting each other hammer and tongs. Gottschalk's paper[8] declared relentless warfare on 'all parties, from that of the *Neue Preussische Zeitung* [the mouthpiece of the extreme right] to that of the *Neue Rheinische Zeitung*'. In the issue of 25 February 1849 there appeared an open letter 'to Herr Karl Marx', which laid plain the substance of the dispute between Gottschalk and him. It was not signed but was written by Gottschalk, who remained behind the scenes but took a very lively part in the sectional squabble as before. Wounded pride was not the smallest of his motives. At the Frankfurt Democrats' Day Schapper had said that Marx was destined to play a great role, and this had hurt him. He consoled himself with the thought that this Goliath must meet his David too.

The 'open letter' seized on an article of Marx's in the *Neue Rheinische Zeitung* of 21 January. Gottschalk chose well. Never before and never again in the *Neue Rheinische Zeitung* did Marx express with such clarity his interpretation of the tasks of the revolution and the role played in it by the various classes.[9]

The elections for the second Prussian National Assembly were at hand. The bourgeoisie were prepared to put up with the new constitution. Marx laid bare once more – in words that were crystal-clear and were this time entirely lacking in that scorn which he seldom spared usually – how inseparably their interests were interwoven with this constitution. It was not a question now of a republic or even of a red republic, but simply of the old absolutism with its hierarchy on the one hand and the representative system of the bourgeoisie on the other. Prussia must either attain the political organization corresponding to the social conditions of the century or retain

a political constitution corresponding to the social conditions
of the past. The struggle against the bourgeois system of
private property could not yet be. It confronted England and
was on the order of the day in France. In Germany the struggle
was rather against a poltitical system which threatened bourgeois private property because it left the helm of the ship of
state to the representatives of feudal private property, to the
king by the grace of God, the army, the bureaucracy, the provincial *Junkers*, and a number of finance barons who were
their allies.

Marx then proceeded to demonstrate in detail how Prussian
feudalism had injured and was continuing to injure the bourgeoisie, how it was restricting the development of modern big
industry, hampering foreign trade, delivering German industry helpless into the hands of English competition. He
demonstrated how Prussian fiscal policy and the Prussian
bureaucratic machine had cut everything, great and small, to
the measure of the feudal classes. The class interest of the bourgeoisie was to destroy the feudal state themselves. That was
their historical task, and this revolution was their revolution.

What of the workers and the petty bourgeoisie?

We say to the workers and the petty bourgeoisie: rather suffer in
modern bourgeois society, which by the development of industry
creates the material means for the foundation of a new society
which will free you all, than step backwards into an obsolete form
of society, which, under the pretext of saving your class, will
plunge the whole nation back into medieval barbarism.

In these words Marx expressed, brutally and without the
slightest regard for fondly nourished illusions, the fact that
the revolution, on whomsoever's shoulders it might be borne,
must be the bourgeois revolution first and could be no other,
because it was necessary to free bourgeois conditions of property, i.e., in later language, capitalist economy, from all the
fetters that hampered its development. The proletarian revolution would only be possible after capitalist economy had
created the conditions that presupposed it.[10]

Gottschalk's reply to Marx was:

What is the purpose of such a revolution? Why should we, men of the proletariat, spill our blood for this? Must we really plunge voluntarily into the purgatory of a decrepit capitalist domination to avoid a medieval hell, as you, sir preacher, proclaim to us, in order to attain from there the nebulous heaven of your communist creed? [11]

It was the question that Weitling put, it was the question that Willich and his supporters were to put a year later, it was the question that Bakunin's followers put in the 1870s. Every time the bourgeois revolution was the order of the day this question was put to scientific socialism, expressing the same impatience as that to which the London communists gave its classic formula in 1850 – 'We must come into power at once or lay ourselves down to sleep.'

Gottschalk's open letter also contained the reproach that such ideas could only come from an intellectual. 'They are not in earnest about the salvation of the oppressed. The distress of the workers, the hunger of the poor have only a scientific, doctrinaire interest for them. They are not touched by that which stirs the heart of men.' Thus did Gottschalk, himself an intellectual in the guise of a proletarian, make play with the mistrust of intellectuals felt by many workers; as if the threatened relapse into barbarism held terrors for Marx, i.e. for aesthetes and cultivated minds, but not for the workers. No, said Gottschalk, the party of the revolutionary proletariat knew no fear. He derided Marx for making the outbreak of revolution in Germany dependent on an outbreak in France and an outbreak in France dependent on an outbreak in England. He maintained that the proletariat must carry out its revolution here and now, without hesitations or misgivings. The revolution must be permanent and must continue until the victory of the proletariat. It was obvious that, holding views like these, Gottschalk was bound to reject cooperation with the bourgeois democrats even if they were not (and this was another dig at Marx) such 'weaklings and nobodies' as the Cologne deputies whom Marx had recommended for election.

If Gottschalk expected Marx to continue the controversy he was sadly disappointed. Marx ignored the attack. He had succeeded in keeping his controversy with Weitling behind the scenes and he did not engage in polemics 'towards the left' this time either. Instead of indulging in a theoretical battle with Gottschalk in a situation which demanded the concentration of all forces against the right, instead of engaging in a controversy that might easily be miscontrued and was in any case inopportune, he preferred setting forth his own positive point of view. Later, in a situation that was in many respects similar, on the occasion of Lassalle's agitation against the Prussian Progressive Party, Marx adopted the same attitude. But it was impossible for his comrades in the Workers' Union to keep silence. The breach between them and Gottschalk's followers was so great that the Union ended by splitting into two. Gottschalk's adherents resigned and formed their own organization. It only survived for a few months. A year later the old Union also expired, shattered by the blows of the reaction.

After Gottschalk's return to Cologne in the summer of 1849, he took practically no more part in political activity. He resumed his medical practice as a faithful and selfless helper of the poor. Cholera broke out in the autumn, and Gottschalk, actuated by the sympathy for the poor which was the whole reason of his being, was the first and for a long time the only doctor to work in the infected slum districts. He caught the disease himself and died, after a day's illness, on 8 September 1849. Many hundreds of workers followed their dead friend to his grave.

In the struggle against the majority of the Workers' Union, a substantial proportion of Gottschalk's adherents had been actuated by personal motives and emotional attachment to their leader. Gottschalk had expressed, in however distorted and mutilated a fashion, an undercurrent of feeling in the revolutionary movement that grew stronger and stronger as time went on and affected even those who had hitherto followed Marx in his policy of coalition with bourgeois democracy. The same aspiration, to liberate the workers' movement from all burdensome and oppressive ties, called the Communist League into being once more.

Its old leaders, with Schapper and Moll at their head, had never been entirely reconciled to the dissolution of the League, although they had not been able to resist Marx's arguments for its dissolution. The branches of the League abroad had never acknowledged its dissolution. At the second democratic congress in Berlin, Ewerbeck, leader of the Paris branch, had conversations with former League members, with whom he arranged to summon a general League congress in Berlin for December 1848. The congress was to appoint new executive officers in place of those previously appointed by Marx. The victory of reaction in Berlin prevented the congress from taking place, but the will to revive the League was there. Moll, who settled in London after fleeing from Cologne, was particularly active in the matter. Members of the London branch cooperated with him in drafting new League statutes. Moll, Heinrich Bauer and George Eccarius were to be the leaders of the resuscitated League.

At the beginning of 1849 Schapper was informed by Moll of the London decision and invited to found a branch in Cologne. Schapper summoned the old members of the League and a few of the most active members of the Workers' Union and established a branch. Marx, Engels and the rest of the editorial staff of the *Neue Rheinische Zeitung* seem to have been invited to join it in vain. A short time afterwards Moll appeared surreptitiously in Cologne as the representative of the new central office. He travelled all over Germany establishing contacts on behalf of the organization. His chief aim was to persuade Marx and Engels to rejoin the League.

A meeting took place at the editorial offices of the *Neue Rheinische Zeitung*. Marx, Engels and Wilhelm Wolff were present, besides Moll and members of the Cologne branch. 'The discussion centred on whether the League ought to be re-established or not', one of those present at the meeting later wrote.

Those who took part in the debate were chiefly Marx, Engels and Wolff on the one side and Schapper and Moll on the other. Marx declared once again that under existing conditions, with freedom of speech and freedom of the Press, the League was superfluous. Schapper and Moll, on the other hand, insisted that the League was absolutely essential. Marx and his colleagues also objected to the statutes that Moll proposed.[12]

Marx's objections were based on the League's proposed programme – its aims, as set forth in the statutes, were not those of the communists – as well as on its proposed organization, which 'tended towards the conspiratorial'. Marx was supported by Engels and Wolff, besides a few members of the Cologne branch, and Moll left Cologne without attaining his object.

The freedom of speech and of the Press, which in Marx's opinion made the re-establishment of the League superfluous, still existed, certainly, but they were increasingly menaced every day. The *Neue Rheinische Zeitung* had to defend itself against more and more violent attacks. The officials whom it so pitilessly criticized had harassed it with complaints ever since the first day of its existence. They felt themselves 'slandered' every other minute. Among those who complained were the Prussian general Drigalski, a high official named Zweiffel, a policeman, and Hecker, the attorney-general. Some of their objections were so absurd that they had obviously been inspired from above. For instance, after Marx printed a republican appeal by the notorious Gustav Hecker, Hecker, the attorney-general, protested at his not having pointed out that Gustav Hecker was not the same man. He claimed that this omission might possibly have led the reader to suppose that he, an official of royal Prussia, was making a republican appeal. Far more serious was an accusation against Marx and his comrades based on his appeal to the people to refuse to pay taxes.[13]

At first the officials persecuted Marx with accusations which they knew to be baseless obviously for the sole purpose of temporarily silencing him by a longer or shorter period in prison on remand. The democrats of Cologne became alarmed at the persecutory zeal of the courts. The workers had already lost two presidents of their Union, and they were not minded to permit a third to be incarcerated. In the middle of November, when Marx was asked to appear before the examining magistrate on account of some trivial libel allegation, a large crowd of workers gathered outside the court and refused to disperse until Marx reappeared. They received him with jubilation and he was forced to make a short speech, the only one he ever made in the streets of Cologne.[14] But there was even greater indignation, to say nothing of very justified anxiety, a week later, when Marx and the other members of the comittee of the Democratic Union were ordered before the court once more, this time for accusing the Government of high treason and of violating the constitution. Before the accused appeared before the examining magistrate, a special delegation insisted on a high administrative official assuring them that they would not be arrested.

The civil officials preserved at least the outward appearance of legal forms. The military took more solid measures. The *Neue Rheinische Zeitung* had by no means soft-pedalled its exposures of the excesses committed by the soldiery at the instigation of their officers, particularly during the period of martial law. The officers, naturally enough, loathed the paper and plied the War Ministry with appeals for the suppression of the 'pernicious rag'. Threatening letters poured in by every post. One day two non-commissioned officers presented themselves at Marx's private address and, announcing that the newspaper had insulted the rank of non-commissioned officer, made threats of violence against the editorial staff. 'Marx received them in his dressing-gown, with the butt of an unloaded revolver protruding from one of the pockets', Engels relates. 'This sight was sufficient to cause the gentlemen to refrain from further parleying, and they withdrew meekly, in spite of the fact that they were carrying their side-arms.'[15]

These crude attempts at intimidation had no effect whatever. The civil authorities had no better success. In February

1849 Marx twice appeared before a jury to answer their accusations. On the first occasion he was accused of insulting officials; on the second occasion the charge arose out of his November tax-boycott appeals.[16] The first charge was easy to rebut, and the jury acquitted him after very short deliberation. Marx took advantage of his second trial to make a brilliant speech showing up the whole hypocrisy of the reaction, who themselves tore the law to shreds and then, when men denounced them and called for violence against them, they, the lawbreakers, accused them of violating the law. 'When the Crown makes a counter-revolution the people rightly reply with a revolution.' They could rid themselves of him as a conquered enemy but they could not condemn him as a criminal. The jury acquitted Marx once more, and the foreman thanked him on behalf of his colleagues for his 'extremely informative speech'.

The courts having failed them, the now completely infuriated officials were compelled to resort to other measures. A favourable opportunity appeared to present itself in March. Though Joseph Moll had failed by a long way in attaining the objective of his journey in Germany, he had succeeded in establishing some connections and he had managed to found a branch in Berlin. The police were very soon on its track, for there appear to have been spies among its members. They did not know a great deal, but they did know some things; the rest they guessed or invented. At the end of March 1849 the police conducted a number of house searches, in the course of which some papers fell into their hands, including the statistics drafted by Moll. They also secured a clue which led them to suppose that the headquarters of the secret organization were in Cologne. The police decided that the leaders must necessarily be Engels, Gottschalk, Moll and Marx, who in turn took their orders from a Paris committee of three, consisting of Herwegh, Heinzen and Ewerbeck. Thus truth and falsehood were inextricably mingled, partly in sheer defiance of common sense, partly as a consequence of sheer ignorance. But a sinister conspiracy had been discovered, the fatherland was in danger, and it was possible to act at last. A special commissioner travelled from Berlin to Cologne, entrusted with the task of searching the houses of those implicated, confiscating their papers and issuing warrants for their arrest in accordance with the result of his investigations. In addition the correspondence of the conspirators was to be watched. The police visualized their hated enemies as already in prison. They were bitterly disappointed. The Cologne authorities were anxious 'in all friendliness and willingness' to oblige the police, but, in view of the mood of the city and the complete unreliability of the assize courts, they were unwilling to risk another fiasco. They would not even agree to a house search being undertaken without specific instructions from the higher authorities in Berlin. So this step misfired as well.

The Rhineland was not Berlin, and the sympathies of the overwhelming majority of the population on the Rhine were to the left. Steps the reaction were able to take with impunity elsewhere in Prussia had to be pondered well here. The political situation became more strained every day. The new Prussian National Assembly was far more radical than its predecessor and its left wing was stronger and more active. The Democratic Party, under the leadership of D'Ester of Cologne, prepared an armed rising. During the Easter holidays deputies from various parts of Germany discussed common action should that eventuality occur.

A 'live' section of the bourgeoisie, especially the petty bourgeoisie, had roused themselves once more at the eleventh hour. But it was a section only. The vast majority of the bourgeois democrats befuddled themselves with talk and nothing but talk. The experiences of the past year had taught Marx that when things grew serious they would cower by their firesides just as timidly as they had done in September and November. The republican question was discussed by the Cologne Democratic Union. There were two long meetings at which the question whether it should continue to call itself 'democratic' or 'democratic-republican' was debated. It remained faithful to the democratic title. But what had been good and right in

April 1848 no longer sufficed in April 1849. According to the
Neue Kölnische Zeitung, which was edited by Anneke, the
Union was thus determined 'to plunge deeper into the wide
waters of democracy, which nowadays has quite taken the
place of liberalism'. On 14 April, Marx, Schapper, Wilhelm
Wolff and Anneke resigned from the Rhineland sectional
committee of the Democratic Union.[17] Their reasons were that
the 'present organization of the Democratic Union included
too many heterogeneous elements to permit of activity beneficial to the cause.' Three days later the Workers' Union
decided to summon a congress of all the workers' unions of the
Rhine province and Westphalia and all other organizations
which acknowledged social democracy, at Cologne on 6 May.

Thus was the separation between bourgeois and proletarian
democracy finally achieved. In August 1848 Marx had been
in favour of a coalition of the 'most heterogeneous' elements.
In April 1849 he parted from the democrats because they embraced too many heterogeneous elements. In 1848 he had been
in favour of a united front of all the anti-feudal classes; now
he directed that the alliance be dissolved. A cleavage had become inevitable. The differences in equipment, tempo, *élan*,
fighting spirit, between the various columns of the great army
which should have marched as a united front and with a
single objective against the forces of absolutism and compelled
the victory, had become too great. A close connection with
bourgeois democracy had been maintained as long as possible,
but it no longer worked, and it was necessary to abandon it.
That did not exclude the possibility of future coalitions between the workers' unions and democracy if circumstances
should demand it. In February Marx supported the candidature of the democrats, in April he parted from them, in June
he went to Paris as a representative of a democratic committee.

Marx may have had an additional reason for deciding on a
public separation from the democrats at that particular
moment. In the spring of 1849 the resurrected Communist
League was to all appearances still very weak. But it existed
nevertheless, and it was to be anticipated that it would soon

be of greater importance. The closer the counter-revolution approached the greater would be the justification for its existence. The workers had been only reluctant adherents of the necessary but disagreeable alliance with the democrats, and the pick of them were obviously disposed to join the League and thus sever all connection with the democratic unions. Marx may well have foreseen the danger that, if he postponed parting from the democrats too long, it might result in isolating himself and his colleagues from the impatient workers. When Marx rejoined the Communist League is not known. It may have been at the time when he resigned from the democratic committee. The journey he started in the middle of April may possibly have been a tour of organization. The immediate reason for it was, of course, the increasing financial difficulties of the *Neue Rheinische Zeitung*.

Its circulation increased from month to month, and it was read all over Germany. But its difficulties were increased by its very success. Printers, compositors, paper-makers, dispatch clerks had to be paid in cash, and subscriptions flowed in irregularly and belatedly. After the desertion of practically all the shareholders no capital was left. The newspaper swallowed up the remnants of Marx's legacy and all his wife's capital. This staved off things for a short time, but in the spring of 1849 the paper was once more on the brink of ruin. Marx tried to raise money in Westphalia and the north-west of Germany, but with little success. When he returned to Cologne on 9 May he brought only 300 thalers with him.

Cologne was quiet, but in other Rhineland towns fighting had begun. In May 1849 the German revolution flared up for the last time. Dresden rose and fierce fighting raged in the streets for four days. The revolutionaries – among whom was the director of the Royal Saxon Orchestra, Richard Wagner[18] – were defeated, for the Prussian forces were overwhelming. The Bavarian Palatinate was in wild insurrection. Baden was in the hands of a revolutionary democratic government. In Rhenish Prussia the workers rose at Elberfeld, Iserlohn, and elsewhere. The Government's military supremacy was so great and the few fighters were so pitifully left in the lurch by the petty bourgeoisie that the isolated outbreaks in the Rhineland collapsed in a few days. This was also the fate of the *Neue Rheinische Zeitung.*

Even now the Government did not dare to ban the paper outright. They still feared an open rising, though Cologne teemed with soldiers. True to their nature, they adopted crafty bureaucratic measures. They took no steps against the paper, they 'only' banished Marx. Marx having become an 'alien' by reason of his loss of Prussian nationality, they had the formal right to do so. He was a disturber of peace and order,[19] so he was desired to leave Prussia at short notice. Marx received the expulsion order on 16 May. On 18 May the last number of the *Neue Rhenische Zeitung* appeared, printed in red.[20]

A prominent position was given to Freiligrath's powerful valedictory poem:

> ... Auf der Lippe den Trotz und den zuckenden Hohn,
> In der Hand den blitzenden Degen,
> Noch im Sterben rufend: Die Rebellion!
> So bin ich in Ehren erlegen...
> Nun Ade, nun Ade, du kämpfende Welt,
> Nun Ade, ihr ringenden Heere!
> Nun Ade, du pulvergeschwärztes Feld,
> Nun Ade, ihr Schwerter und Speere!
> Nun Ade, doch nicht für immer Ade!
> Denn sie töten den Geist nicht, ihr Brüder!
> Bald richt'ich mich rasselnd in die Höh.
> Bald kehr, ich reisiger wieder! *

The last issue of the *Neue Rheinische Zeitung* warned the workers against any sort of rising. In view of the military

* 'Defiance and scorn quivering on my lips, the gleaming dagger in my hand, still exclaiming: rebellion! in death, thus am I honourably defeated. Now farewell, farewell, you world of battle, farewell, you struggling hosts; farewell, you powder-blackened fields, farewell, you swords and spears. Farewell, but not for ever; for they cannot kill the spirit. Soon I shall once more be on high; soon I shall return on a steed!'

situation in Cologne they would have been irretrievably lost. 'The Prussians will be infuriated by your quiet. In taking their farewell the editors of the *Neue Rheinische Zeitung* thank you for the sympathy shown them. Their last word will always and everywhere be: "The emancipation of the working class!"' [21]

The reaction were highly gratified at the disappearance of the paper 'with which the *Moniteur* of 1793 paled in comparison'.[22] 'Its surviving friends will be incapable of rivalling their Rhenish master in scurrility and desecration of the holiest in mankind.' The attitude of the people of Cologne to its disappearance is demonstrated by the words of a correspondent who was anything but sympathetic:

No number of the *Neue Rheinische Zeitung* caused a greater sensation than the last. It was printed in red from beginning to end. The rush at the editorial offices and the demand for this number were really extraordinary. About 20,000 copies must have been printed, and some of them are already fetching a thaler a piece. Real idolatry was roused by the issue of 18 May. One hears again and again of instances of the paper being expensively framed.

Marx liquidated the affairs of the newspaper with all speed. He devoted the cash in hand, the proceeds of the sale of the printing press (which belonged to him), etc., to pay the paper's debts. His own and his wife's fortune had been swallowed up to the last penny. Frau Marx had to pawn her silver to pay for immediate necessities. The staff distributed themselves among those parts of Germany where risings had, or had not yet, taken place. Marx and Engels went south, to the area of insurrection in the Palatinate and Baden.

Not that they expected a great deal from it. They had got to know the nature of the petty bourgeoisie, even the best and most upright revolutionaries among them, and of the German lower middle class in particular, too well to be able to have great expectations. But even their most moderate expectations were disappointed. Marx travelled by way of Frankfurt and tried to persuade the left-wing representatives at the German

National Assembly to summon the revolutionary troops from Baden and the Palatinate to Frankfurt by parliamentary decree. But that might perhaps have been falsely construed, they held. No, no, even the left intended to keep itself 'within the framework of the law'. It was no better in areas where risings had taken place. Marx represented to the leaders that if anything at all could save them it could only be the most resolute offensive. They must promptly occupy Frankfurt, place the National Assembly under their protection, even if the Assembly did not explicitly ask for it, and so turn the struggle into an all-German one, i.e. one of the National Assembly against the reactionary governments. But the men of Baden and the Palatinate did not look beyond Baden and the Palatinate. They stayed where they were and there they were crushed. The last rising of the German revolution, like all the others, foundered on its local limitations.

In Germany there was no more work that Marx could do. He was no soldier, and his place was not in the army. He went to Paris as the representative of the Palatinate democratic committee to get as much help for the insurrection as he could from the French democrats. Engels was unwilling to miss an opportunity of gaining a little practical experience of war. 'As after all it was necessary *honoris causa* that the *Neue Rheinische Zeitung* be represented in the army of Baden and the Palatinate, I girded on a sword to my side and went to Willich.'[23]

Gottschalk's followers warned the workers against taking up arms. Their ultra-radicalism ended in a passivity which was in fact counter-revolutionary. Their paper claimed that the workers should quietly wait until the absolutists and the constitutionalists had exhausted each other. The communists, faithful to the words of the Manifesto which urged them to support every revolutionary movement aimed at existing social and political conditions, stepped without a moment's hesitation into the ranks of the insurrectionary army.

[15]

The End of the Communist League

THE more desperate the situation in Germany became the greater hopes did the revolutionaries entertain of France. 'In France the battle will start again in the spring', Marx wrote at the beginning of 1849.[1] The 'revolutionary volcano' in France seemed on the eve of an eruption, and it seemed to him that its flames must inevitably overflow into Germany, Austria and Hungary. The German counter-revolution could only be, must only be an incident in the European revolution. What did Baden and the Palatinate matter? If Paris rose the whole of Europe would be in flames.

Marx went to Paris. But Paris viewed from within was different from Paris viewed from without. Cholera was rampant in the city. 'The air was sultry', wrote Alexander Herzen, the Russian revolutionary, who was in Paris at the time. 'A sunless heat oppressed mankind. Victims of the contagion fell one after another. The terrified population, and the procession of hearses dashing to the cemeteries as if they were racing, seemed in keeping with events' – i.e. the political events of June 1849. The irony of history had once more placed revolutionary warfare upon the order of the day, but it was very different from what it had been a year before. At the end of May an expeditionary force of the French Republican Army, sent to Italy for the official purpose of defending Italy's freedom and independence, had stormed Rome, the last stronghold of Italian liberty, and delivered its republican defenders into the hands of the Papal Inquisition. The French constitution still contained the fine phrase: 'La République française n'emploie jamais ses forces contre la liberté d'aucun peuple.'*

On 11 June, only a few days after Marx's arrival in Paris,

* 'The republic never employs its forces against the liberty of any people.'

Ledru-Rollin, leader of the Montagnards, proposed in the Chamber that the President, Louis Bonaparte, and the cabinet be arraigned for violation of the constitution. To quote Marx in his *Class Struggles in France*, his words were 'plain, blunt, unpretentious, matter-of-fact, pithy and powerful'. The Chamber postponed the debate on this proposal, but its fate was not destined to be settled in the Chamber.

In the evening a meeting took place between the leaders of the Montagnards and the delegates of the workers' secret societies. Marx's account of the meeting indicates that he either was present himself or was given detailed information by one of the principals at the meeting. He very successfully fulfilled the task entrusted to him by the German democrats, namely that of making contact with the French revolutionaries. There is some evidence that would seem to indicate that he actually became a member of one of the secret communist organizations in Paris. As he wrote to Engels, he came into contact with the whole of the revolutionary party and had good grounds for hoping that within a few days he would have every revolutionary journal in Paris at his disposal.[2] But a week later no revolutionary journals were left.

The Montagnards were not one whit behind the German parliamentarians of the 'left' in indecision. They rejected the proposal of the workers' delegates that they should strike that very night. True, the chances of a successful rising were no longer very great, but the refusal to act cost the Montagnards their last chance. For when they summoned a demonstration to the streets on 13 June the Government had long completed its preparations. It was a simple matter for their dragoons and riflemen to drive the unarmed masses from the streets. Some of the Montagnard deputies were arrested, others escaped. From that day on the National Assembly was 'nothing but a committee of public safety of the Party of Order'.[3]

The last resistance of the revolutionaries in Central Europe collapsed at the same time. In the Danube basin the army of independent Hungary capitulated to the Russian troops, which were far superior in numbers and equipment. Those of

its leaders who fell into the hands of the counter-revolution
were hanged. Those who managed to escape to Turkey lived
in fear of being handed over to the Austrian hangmen by the
Sublime Porte. In dismembered Germany the revolution died
piecemeal. Even to the very last everything was done to make
the victory of the counter-revolution as easy as possible. The
risings in the spring of 1849 broke out one after another, each
outbreak coinciding with the suppression of its predecessor.
There was brave fighting in Dresden and on the Rhine, and
many hundreds, most of them workers, left their lives on the
barricades. The words 'artisan', 'miner', day labourer', etc.,
constantly recur in the lists of dead.

Many of them were members of the Communist League.
Only the extreme left wing of the workers' movement, the
group that followed Gottschalk and Weitling, opposed the
rising. The organ of Gottschalk's followers warned the workers
against participation in a movement which was not the immediate concern of the proletariate but of the bourgeoisie.
This was but a consequence of an attitude which started out
from extreme revolutionism and necessarily ended in complete passivity. Whatever their position may have been in
1848 and 1849, the overwhelming majority of the members of
the League flung themselves headlong into the struggle and
fought to the bitter end. Joseph Moll, who was unable to
return to London after his German journey, helped in the
preparations for the rising in Baden. With characteristic
courage he even managed to enlist in the insurrectionary
army under the fire of the Prussian guns. Then he went to
Baden, where he fought bravely and fell in the fighting on the
Murg, shot in the head by a Prussian bullet.

Engels took part in the campaign, first as a simple infantry-
man, later as an adjutant to Willich, who was in command of
a corps of volunteers. His was one of the best units of the
revolutionary army and consisted almost entirely of workers.
The sober, clear-thinking, sceptically-inclined Engels entered
the struggle without any great expectations, for the weak sides
– and it had practically nothing but weak sides – of the whole

enterprise did not escape his keen intelligence; but he could not deny himself the pleasure of heartily and unceremoniously laughing at the mixture of excitement and alarm manifested by the petty-bourgeois revolutionary statesmen. During the course of the expedition he drew nearer to Willich, the 'one practical officer' who took part in it, and he praised him as bold in action, cool-headed, clever and quick in decision. Engels took part in four engagements, two of which were fairly important. 'I have discovered', he wrote to Frau Marx soon afterwards, 'that the much-lauded quality of impetuous courage is one of the most ordinary properties that man can have.'[4] He fought to the very end and marched into Swiss territory with his corps, which was one of the very last units of the revolutionary army to survive.[5]

That was the end of the revolution of 1848, the beginning of which had been so full of promise; moreover, it was the end of the period of European history which culminated in it. But those who had been in the thick of the fray did not believe it, could not and would not believe it. The more fervently they identified themselves with the world that had departed, that world in comparison with which the new and greater world which it had engendered dwindled practically into non-existence in their eyes, the greater was their difficulty in acknowledging the existence of the new. The whole thing could not be over. Tomorrow or the day after it would all break out again and everything would be altered. He who in such a situation thought anything else would have been no revolutionary. But he who remained subject to this mood too long, unable to shake it off and reconcile himself sternly to the fact that a new historical epoch had begun, was no true revolutionary either.

Marx had battled so ardently that for a time he too was subject to these inevitable illusions. He was dominated by them for a whole year. A letter he wrote to Weydemeyer on 1 August 1849 gives some clue to the extent to which his analytical intelligence, generally so accurate, could err. Disagreeable as the situation was at the moment, he belonged nevertheless to those who were *satisfaits*. 'Les choses marchent trés bien, and the Waterloo of official democracy is to be regarded as a victory. The governments by the grace of God have taken over the task of revenging us on the bourgeoisie and are chastising them for us.'[6]

Marx searched for the weakest point in the enemy's front. England attracted his particular attention, and he began to hope that the next blow might come from there, and that England would be the scene of the 'beginning of the next dance'. England seemed to him to be on the eve of a tremendous economic crisis, and not long afterwards he confidently predicted its outbreak for August 1850.[7]

In spite of the hopes he had of England in the immediate future he had no intention of going there. At the beginning of July 1849 his wife and children came to Paris. Marx rented a small flat and settled down as if for a long stay. He was an optimist. From 13 June the reaction was the undisputed master of Paris; and it was not to be expected that the police would allow a man like Marx to remain completely unmolested for long.

The police devoted great attention to refugees from Germany, who were said to be playing the leading part in an 'international revolutionary committee' which did not exist outside the police imagination. One prominent *émigré* after another was arrested and expelled. Marx's turn was not long postponed. His expulsion order was signed on 19 July. Quite possibly the police learnt of his presence in Paris from the German Press, which was indulging at the time in 'sketches from emigrant life'. The police were not very well informed, and some weeks passed before they discovered his address.

'We stayed one month in Paris', Frau Marx wrote in her diary, 'but we were not allowed to stay there long either. One fine morning the familiar figure of a police sergeant appeared, to inform us that Karl *et sa dame* must leave Paris within twenty-four hours. They were kind enough to offer us permission to stay at Vannes, in Morbihan.'[8]

Frau Marx was expecting her fourth child and Marx was in

desperate financial straits. Morbihan was considered one of the unhealthiest departments of France, the 'Pontic Marshes' of Brittany. Banishment to such a place was 'equivalent to a disguised attempt at murder', as Marx wrote to Engels.[9] Marx did not accept it. He tried hard to have the expulsion order revoked, but in vain. He stated in an open letter to the Press that he was staying in Paris purely for purposes of scientific research. The only concession he obtained was a respite for his wife. He had no choice but to leave France. If he attempted to return to Belgium he was certain to be turned back at the frontier. In Switzerland a regular hue and cry after the German *émigrés* was beginning, and England alone remained. Marx crossed the Channel on 24 August 1849 and his wife followed on 15 September. Fate cast him into the land in which he believed the 'next dance was going to begin', perhaps to cure him of his illusions the more quickly.

When Marx came to England for the third time in his life in the summer of 1849, he did not believe his visit would be much longer than the two previous ones. It might last a few weeks, possibly months, at the very most a year; but instead of the short visit he anticipated, he spent the second half of his life in England, which became his second home.

A great deal had changed in England since his last visit to London two years before. The Chartist movement had not recovered from its serious defeat in April 1848,[10] and the whole political landscape had undergone a profound alteration. Marx nevertheless met some old acquaintances. The Fraternal Democrats, at whose meeting on 29 November 1847 he had hailed the approaching revolution, still existed, and so did the German Communist Workers' Educational Union, with whose leaders Marx had discussed the programme and statutes of the Communist League. Not a few of the old members had answered the call of the revolution in their native land, but many were too deeply rooted in England to be able to tear themselves away. They had shared Germany's hopes, exhilarations and disappointments. The Union was the obvious centre for the new refugees to gather in.

When Marx came to London very few of them had yet arrived. But every Channel boat brought a fresh influx. At first they were almost exclusively workers and artisans. The 'great men of the emigration',[11] with whom Marx was destined to have such unpleasant experiences, made their appearance gradually. The refugees arrived in a state of pitiful distress. Many had not a penny in their pockets. The continuation of the crisis meant that even the most highly-skilled workers had difficulty in finding work, and often had to be content if the pittance they could pick up as day labourers sufficed to enable them to stave off the pangs of hunger with a loaf of bread.

Many of these unfortunates [a newspaper recorded] consider themselves fortunate in finding a job the nature of which makes one recoil. The work is stamping raw pelts at a German fur factory in East London. Imagine a big barrel in a very warm room, filled to the very top with ermine and sable skins. A man climbs into the barrel stark-naked and stamps and works with his hands and feet from morning till night. The perspiration pours from his body in streams. This soaks into the skins and gives them their suppleness and durability, without which they would be useless for more elegant purposes. Thus our rich ladies, with their boas and muffs, though they do not suspect it, are literally clothed in the sweat of the democrats.

Most of them, however, could not even find work of this kind.

To help the hungry was the first and most important task. Marx was among the founders of the London Assistance Committee. Similar relief societies came into being wherever German refugees were gathered. The difference between the London committee and the rest was that it was controlled by communists from the start. Of the five leading members three were communists, with Marx at their head. This was in accordance with the social composition of the London refugees. It was a period of wearing and exhausting work, involving dozens of interviews every day, dashing from one end of London to the other, collecting money and distributing it. Marx had an enormous amount of work to do. He succeeded in inducing the Fraternal Democrats to cooperate in the work of relief, but the results were meagre. The total receipts of a fund the Fraternal Democrats kept open for three months amounted only to £1 14s.[12]

Marx's active participation in the relief work was a matter of course, but however urgent and necessary the work of relief might be, to him political work in the Communist League was incomparably more urgent.

The London branch, which Moll had used in his efforts to resuscitate the League at the beginning of the year, had survived the revolution. The central office Marx found in London was the only one that had any sort of contacts, though not very close ones, with Germany and other refugee centres abroad. Marx at once got in touch with the branch and soon joined it. The central office was reorganized and completed in the months that followed. Willich, who had come to London with a recommendation from Engels, was at once elected to the central office. Although Engels considered him 'a "true" socialist and a more or less tedious ideologist',[13] he was of the opinion that he would be useful at the central office. Engels soon appeared on the scene himself. Three of the members – Heinrich Bauer, Eccarius and Pfänder – survived from the committee of November 1847. A fourth, Schapper, arrived in the summer of 1850, and a number of new members were elected as well. There were altogether ten members of the central office in the summer of 1850, more than had ever been known in the history of the League.

The election of Willich was the event that had the most lasting consequences. He was a personal friend of Gottschalk and shared many of his views, though he had not gone so far as Gottschalk and Weitling in refusing to take part in the democratic insurrections. Willich was the representative of the 'left' wing of the communist movement. Willich's presence at the central office was an indication of Marx's and his friends' political compromise with the 'left'. This compromise was the natural consequence of Marx's new estimate of the European situation, of which mention has been made above. It found its expression in the so-called first circular of the central office of March 1850, which was drafted by Marx and Engels. Whether the document in all its details really represents Marx's ideas is difficult to decide. There is a good deal that points to the fact that at this period Marx once more considered it necessary to warn his followers against extreme maximalism. But in any case Marx believed that he could achieve a compromise with the 'left' on the basis of this circular.[14]

The document criticized Marx's own tactics of 1848 and 1849, and in particular the decision to dissolve the League and not put up workers' candidates of their own.

A large number of members who took part in the revolutionary movement believed that the time for secret societies was past and that activity in the open was adequate by itself ... While the organization of the Democratic Party in Germany, the party of the petty bourgeosie, constantly improved, the working class lost its one firm hold, remained at best organized for purely local aims in single localities and thus came completely under the domination and leadership of the petty-bourgeois democrats in the general movement.[15]

In these phrases Marx and Engels criticized themselves and admitted to the 'left' that they had been wrong on a very definite issue.

But the point of the document lay not in its liquidation of the past but in its statement of the movement's future tasks.

The fundamental assumption, on which all the rest depended, was the firm expectation of a new revolutionary outbreak in the immediate future. Marx, while engaged in drafting this document, was also busy writing the article in which he prophesied that there would be a crisis in England in August 1850, a crisis with which the renewal of the revolution would coincide. He assured Engels that the English would take it up just at the point at which the February revolution had interrupted it. And in France and Germany it could not

be otherwise. In England and France the proletariat would
be engaged in the direct struggle for the state power. In Germany the revolution had suffered a defeat. The bourgeoisie
had been forced once more to relinquish the power to the party
of feudal absolutism, but

all the same they had assured the conditions which meant in the
long run that, because of the Government's financial embarrass-
ments, the power would fall into their hands and all their interests
would be safeguarded; it was possible that from now on the revolutionary movement might assume a so-called peaceful development.

The bourgeoisie had ceased to play a revolutionary role.
Only two revolutionary classes were now left in Germany:
the petty bourgeoisie and the proletariat. There was not the
least doubt that there would be a moment in the further development of the revolution when petty-bourgeois democracy
would have the predominant influence in Germany. It was
therefore imperative that the relations of the proletariat with
this petty-bourgeois democracy be accurately determined.
They must strive for a democratic state, whether it be constitutional or republican, which would give them and their
allies, the peasants, the majority. They must fight for a change
in social conditions which would render the existing state of
society as tolerable and as comfortable as possible for the petty
bourgeoisie. But democracy was far from being disposed to
revolutionize the whole of society for the benefit of the revolutionary proletariat. Therefore the proletariat must rise together with the petty bourgeoisie, but it must not for one
moment forget the treacherous role which democracy would
continue to play in the future.

While the democratic petty bourgeoisie will be inclined towards
bringing the revolution to as speedy a conclusion as possible, it is
our interest and our duty to make the revolution permanent,
until all the more or less possessing classes are forced from power,
the state power is seized by the proletariat and the partnership of
the proletarians of the world has advanced to such an extent that

competition between the proletariats has ceased, not just in one country but in all the principal countries of the world, and at least the vital forces of production are concentrated in the hands of the proletariat.

In the forthcoming German revolution the proletariat must in all circumstances preserve the independence of their organizations.

Next to the new official government they must set up their own revolutionary workers' governments, whether in the form of local committees, branch councils, workers' clubs or workers' committees, so that the bourgeois democratic government not only be promptly deprived of the workers' support but also be supervised and threatened from the very outset by organizations which have the whole mass of workers behind them.

The immediate consequence of the downfall of existing governments would be the election of a national assembly. The proletariat – here once more the criticism of Marx's own activities in 1848 and 1849 is particularly significant – must see to it that

workers' candidates are put up everywhere beside the democratic candidates, even where they have no prospect whatever of being elected. The progress which the proletarian party is bound to make by coming forward independently in this way is infinitely more important than the disadvantage of a few reactionaries being elected.

Henceforward the necessity of establishing contacts with related revolutionary parties in England and France was urgent. The Fraternal Democrats were an open propaganda society, they were capable of doing something in the way of putting workers' educational unions in touch with one another, but they were not adequate to the tasks of the times. It was necessary to create an associatin of secret societies for simultaneous action in the revolution which might break out any day. The circular was issued to the branches of the League in March 1850, and an international militant alliance was formed in April. It was called the Société Universelle des

Communistes Révolutionnaires. Its statutes bore the signatures of Vidil and Adam, representing the London Blanquist 'emigrant' organizations, Marx, Engels and Willich representing the Communist League and Harney representing the Chartists.[16] Thse six men also constituted the central committee of the new society.

Their programme and organizational structure are of great interest. 'Le but de l'association', the first paragraph of the statutes reads, 'est la déchéance de toutes les classes privilégiées, de soumettre ces classes à la dictature des prolétaires en maintenant la révolution en permanance jusqu'à la réalisation du communisme, qui doit être la dernière forme de constitution de la famille humaine.'*

This goal, to which the members of the association swore an oath of loyalty, was to be attained by 'des liens de solidarité entre toutes les fractions du parti communiste révolutionnaire en faisant disparaître, conformément au principe de la fraternité républicaine, les divisions de nationalité'.†

The rank and file of the secret societies did not themselves become members of this secret society, which was restricted to their leaders. Thus it was a secret society of higher degree. An essential feature of this organization was that it should not come out into the open. What appears to be an allusion to it is the statement in the second circular, issued by the central office in June 1850,[17] to the effect that delegates of the secret Blanquist societies were in permanent contact with the delegates of the League and that the League delegates had been entrusted by the Blanquists with important preparatory work in connection with the next French revolution. Who these delegates were and the nature of their duties is unknown.

---

* 'The aim of the association is to make an end of the privileged classes, to submit these classes to the dictatorship of the proletariat by maintaining a permanent revolution until the realization of communism, which shall be the last form of constitution of the human family.'

† 'bonds of solidarity between all sections of the revolutionary Communist Party by breaking down the barriers of nationality, in conformity with the principle of republican fraternity'.

But what the Blanquists were occupied with during the years 1850 and 1851 is known. They were engaged in preparations for an armed rising, just as they had been. before 1848 and just as they continued to be afterwards. They were engaged in plotting, devising schemes to gain the political power by simple surprise attacks. Their confident assumption was that a comparatively small number of resolute, well-organized men, given a favourable moment, would be capable not only of seizing the rudder of the ship of state, but, by the exercise of great and unflinching energy, of maintaining their position until such time as they had brought over the whole of the people to the revolution and caused them to adhere to the small leading group. The fact that Marx accepted this kind of revolutionism, which he condemned so violently both before and afterwards, and was so utterly foreign in every way to the essential nature of the proletarian revolution, the fact that he formed an alliance with the Blanquists, proves better than anything else the extent to which his judgement had been affected by the breakdown of his immeasurable hopes. In later years Marx by no means excluded cooperation with the Blanquists as a matter of principle to be adhered to rigidly in all circumstances. However violently he was opposed to their methods, he valued their determination highly.[18] But after 1851 it would have been inconceivable for him to have encouraged the members of any organization which he led to join a Blanquist group. It should be observed, however, that the rules of the super-secret society assured the existence of the Communist League and – a highly important consideration in Marx's eyes – preserved it from the danger of being outvoted by the other organizations. A two-thirds majority was needed to pass a resolution and new members could only be elected unanimously.

However greatly Marx's outlook as indicated in the first circular differed from his attitude in 1848 and 1849, the same fundamental ideas were at the heart of both. Sooner or later these ideas were bound to part him from the ultra-left again. Marx was in the first place convinced that the development of the revolution in one country was closely bound up with its development in all other countries; in the second place he was convinced that all revolution had quite definite phases to go through and that the various classes must necessarily come into power in a definite order conditioned by economic facts. It was at these points in the Marxian doctrine that Gottschalk had directed the spearhead of his attack. Gottschalk had criticized Marx for the 'heartlessness' with which he asked the workers to 'wait', for his 'deviation' from action in his own country by referring to the coming revolution in France, England, etc. Marx still firmly maintained that the democratic petty bourgeoisie must become the ruling class before the proletariat could follow in its shoes. He yielded to his former opponents, now his colleagues, in their estimate of the time that must intervene. In Cologne he had talked of decades, but now the process of development seemed concentrated into an incomparably briefer period, though he still avoided defining it more closely than that.

Marx was in error. He had impatiently anticipated a process of development. He leapt across the years – and who at that time would not have wished to have done so? But in his fundamental attitude to the revolutionary process he took back nothing of what he had maintained in 1848 and 1849.

If the new revolution was at hand the Communist League must do everything in its power to be forearmed. Marx was intensely active in the spring and summer of 1850. Heinrich Bauer was sent to Germany as an emissary and had a successful journey through North Germany, Saxony, Württemberg and the Rhineland. Bauer was a skilful organizer and an excellent judge of men, and he was able to bring once more into the League organization ex-members who had either lapsed into inactivity or started working independently on their own. In the summer of 1850 the League had as many as thirty branches. Karl Schurz, the subsequent American statesman, who was travelling in Germany at the time on behalf of a democratic organization founded in Switzerland for the purpose of reviving broken contacts, was forced to admit that 'all the usable forces were already in the hands of the Communist League'.[19]

The League was far bigger, stronger and better organized than at the time of the revolution of 1848. The revolution had come too soon for it, but the next revolution, contrary to expectations, seemed to be tarrying. Marx was convinced that an economic crisis was due in the autumn of 1850. But summer passed and autumn came and the crisis failed to appear. There was not even the slightest indication of its approach. In June, Marx obtained admission to the reading-room of the British Museum and made an intense study of the economic history of the past decade, and the economic history of England in particular. His notebooks of this period are full of long columns of figures, tables, statistical information of every kind. The more Marx mastered his material, the more plainly did he see the vanity of his hopes. Europe was not on the verge of a crisis but on the threshold of a new era of prosperity. 'To him who had eyes to see and used them', Engels wrote later, 'it was obvious that the revolutionary storm of 1848 was gradually dying away.'

At the beginning of 1850 Marx once more had his own paper. He had a great deal of difficulty in raising the money for it, in spite of the help of Engels and friends in Germany. 'The *Neue Rheinische Zeitung,* a politico-economic review, edited by Karl Marx',[20] appeared in Hamburg in February 1850. It started as a monthly, but was intended to develop as soon as possible into a fortnightly or if possible a weekly, so that as soon as conditions permitted a return to Germany, it could promptly emerge as a daily again.

The first three numbers contained Engels's description of the rising in the Palatinate and Baden,[21] as well as Marx's analysis of the revolution in France from February 1848 to November 1849. Marx ended his survey with an estimate of the prospects of the imminent revolution:

The result [of Bonaparte's fight with the Party of Order] is postponed, the *status quo* is upheld, one section of the Party of Order is compromised, weakened, made impossible by the other, and repression of the common enemy, the great mass of the nation, is extended and stretched to the breaking-point at which economic conditions will once more have reached the point of development when a new explosion will blow the whole of these quarrelsome parties into the air, together with their constitutional republic.[22]

The last double number of the review appeared at the end of November. Marx summarized the results of his studies as follows:

In view of this general prosperity, in which the productive forces of bourgeois society are flourishing as exuberantly as they possibly can under bourgeois conditions, there can be no talk of a real revolution. Such a revolution is only possible at periods when the two factors, modern forces of production and bourgeois forms of production, come into conflict. The incessant squabbles in which the representatives of the individual factions of the continental Party of Order are now indulging and compromising one another are remote from providing an opportunity for a new revolution. On the contrary, they are only possible because conditions for the time being are so secure and – what the reaction does not know – so bourgeois. All attempts of the reaction to put a stop to bourgeois development will recoil upon themselves as certainly as all the moral indignation and enthusiastic proclamations of the democrats. A new revolution is only possible as the result of a new crisis. But it is just as inevitable as a new crisis.[23]

To have clung any longer to a policy which had been correct as long as a crisis and with it a revolution had seemed imminent would have meant being guided by 'sheer wish' instead of by 'real circumstances'. At first it was by no means easy for Marx to reconcile himself to acknowledging that the years that followed would belong to the bourgeoisie. Willich and his supporters simply ignored the altered situation. In their view real circumstances might be what they would. If they were adverse, all that was required was the will to change them.

Willich's immediate reaction to Marx's analysis of the class struggle, of the position of the classes in the revolution, and of the necessary phases of the revolution was that it was nothing but a lot of intellectual theorizing. He felt Marx's view of historical development was false. That the classes – capitalists, middle class and proletariat – that is to say the victory of their class interests – must necessarily follow one another in succession seemed to him entirely absurd. He hated the middle classes and shrank from the thought that the petty bourgeoisie would ever rule in Germany. They would smash all the big factories and there would be 'a hue and cry after the loot and a demoralization that would be all the greater the more proletarians managed to grab a share of it for themselves.' Willich only admitted the existence of two social classes. One was opposed to oppression of every kind, whether on ideal or practical grounds. The other was the class of the selfish oppressors. With men of the first class he was convinced the proletariat could work together towards bringing about the downfall of the political powers-that-be. By these men the proletariat would not be betrayed.[24]

From this simplified view of society he deduced practical consequences. Just as at night all cats are grey, political exiles are always inclined completely to deny the very power which has driven them abroad. The German exiles of the 1850s were no exception. Practically all of them accused their enemies of 'every kind of oppression' and were, at least according to their words, determined to struggle relentlessly against their oppressors. Willich found in them the colleagues he sought, not just as companions for a portion of the way, as the democrats had been for Marx in 1848 and 1849, but as comrades in the activity he was pining for. The only form this activity could take was that of conspiracy. He hatched every conceivable kind of plot with every conceivable clique of exiles. As Marx later wrote, Willich and his friends demanded, 'if not real conspiracies, at least the appearance of conspiracies, and hence direct alliance with the democratic heroes of the day.'[25] The more such alliances with other groups of exiles led to adventurous conspiracies the more violently Marx repudiated them.

Marx had become associated with some conspirators himself, the Blanquists. But in France conspiracy had a historical tradition. It had become an essential part of the revolutionary movement and it had to be reckoned with. Marx knew its negative sides only too well. He signed an agreement with the Blanquists in April and the *Neue Rheinische Zeitung-Revue* appeared in the same month, with reviews of books by A. Chenu and Lucien de la Hodde. Marx's judgement of the professional conspirators was annihilating. 'To begin with, their social position conditions their social character', he wrote.

Proletarian conspiracy, of course, offers them only a very limited and uncertain means of existence. They are therefore perpetually forced to lay their hands on the conspiratorial purse-strings. Many of them, of course, fall foul of bourgeois society and make more or less of a good show in the police courts... It goes without saying that these conspirators by no means confine themselves to organizing the revolutionary proletariat. Their business consists in forestalling the process of revolutionary development, spurring it on to artificial crises, making revolutions extempore without the conditions for revolution. For them the only condition required for the revolution is a sufficient organization of their own conspiracy. They are the alchemists of the revolution, and they share in every way the limitations and fixed ideas of the alchemists of old... The police tolerate the conspiracies, not merely as a necessary evil. They tolerate them as centres, easy to keep under supervision, uniting the most powerful revolutionary social elements, as workshops of insurrection, which in France have become just as necessary a means of government as the police itself, and finally as recruiting grounds for their own political spies... Espionage is one of the chief occupations of the conspirator. No wonder, therefore, that the small jump from routine conspirator to paid police spy is made so frequently, encouraged as it is by distress and imprisonment, threats and promises. Hence the huge ramifications of suspicion within these organizations, suspicion which so blinds its members that they end by taking the best among their colleagues for spies and accept the real spies as reliable men.[26]

The conspirator, Marx continues, busy with his scheming and plotting and having no other aim before his eyes but that of the immediate downfall of the existing régime, has the most profound contempt for the theoretical enlightenment of the workers concerning their class interests. At a moment when, in their opinion, it behoved every revolutionary to act, i.e. plot and prepare risings, Willich and his followers certainly regarded the lectures Marx delivered to the workers as a senseless waste of time. Wilhelm Liebknecht, who had come to London in the summer of 1850 and attached himself to Marx, writes vividly of Marx's lectures in his memoirs:

In 1850 and 1851 Marx gave a course of lectures on political economy. He had been very unwilling to give them, but after addressing a small circle of friends a few times he allowed himself to be persuaded by us to address a larger audience. In this course ... Marx laid bare all the broad outlines of the system which lies before us in *Das Kapital*. In the hall of the Communist Workers' Educational Union, which was full to overflowing ... Marx manifested a remarkable talent for popularization. No one hated the vulgarizing, the devitalizing, the falsifying, the watering-down of science more than he, but no one possessed in a higher degree the capacity for clear exposition. Clarity of speech is the result of clarity of thought. Clear thought demands a clear form of expression.

Marx's method was methodical. He would lay down a proposition as briefly as possible, and then elucidate it at greater length, taking extreme care to avoid using expressions unintelligible to the workers. Then he would invite questions from his audience. Should there be none, he would subject them to an examination, exhibiting such pedagogic skill that no loopholes or misunderstandings escaped... Marx had the qualifications of a first-class teacher.[27]

Liebknecht only heard the lectures on economics. Marx also dealt with other questions, more concrete ones, dealing with the situation as it had developed in the Communist League. In a letter he wrote in July 1850 to P. G. Röser, a member of the League in Cologne, Marx mentions that he lectured on the Communist Manifesto at the London Workers'

Union in the winter of 1849–50. Röser remembered the details of this letter four years later. In the course of an interrogation by the police, Röser said that Marx demonstrated in these lectures that communism could not be attained for a good many years yet, that communism itself would have to go through a number of phases and that it could not be attained at all except by the way of education and gradual development. But Willich opposed him violently with his 'rubbish', as Marx called it, and said that communism must be introduced by the next revolution, if necessary by the power of the guillotine. Marx was afraid that the idea of advancing at the head of his bold Palatinate troops and imposing communism by force, if necessary against the will of the whole of Germany, had become so firmly rooted in 'General' Willich's head that it would lead to a split in the Communist League.[28]

Every word of this letter, which Röser repeated from memory, need not be weighed too carefully in the balance. But it throws light once more on the conflict between Marx and Willich. Marx assigned the Communist League one task, the task of propaganda. He repudiated conspiracy, rash adventure, insurrection. All Willich's mediations and aspirations were concentrated on insurrection. Marx saw in revolution a historical process as the result of which the proletariat could only seize the power after passing through quite definite phases, which could not possibly be skipped. Willich's attitude was: now or never. In all essentials Marx returned to his views of 1848 and 1849. One thing he stood out for, now and in the future – the absolute necessity of an independent party.

Willich regarded the theoretical discussions in the Communist League with contempt. He considered himself 'a man of action', and when he started to act Marx was forced to break with him. The danger that Willich might involve the Communist League in his insurrectionary adventures had become too great.

The situation in the League was a complicated one. Marx had a majority at the central office. Of the four members who had been elected at the communist congress of November

1847, three, Heinrich Bauer, Pfänder and Eccarius, supported Marx. The minority supported Willich, Schapper alone of the 'old' members of the central office among them. But Willich had a majority in the London branch, as well as in the London Workers' Educational Union. There were several reasons for this. Willich's crude revolutionism was bound to appeal to the hungry, desperate workers assembled in both organizations. Moreover, Willich was closer to them as a man. While Marx, 'scholar' and 'theorist', lived his own life and only came to the Union to lecture, Willich, who had no family, shared in the joys and sorrows of the exiled proletarians. He had created a cooperative society and lived with the workers, ate with them and addressed them all in the familiar second person singular; Marx was respected but Willich was popular.

Marx proposed to the members of the central office that the headquarters of the League be transferred to Germany and that the central office transfer its authority to the central office at Cologne, the headquarters of the most important branch of the League, both by reason of its activity and its numerical strength. Marx's majority at the central office accepted his proposal, which was viewed with favour at Cologne. Willich's minority declared it to be contrary to the statutes and founded a new central office of its own. Part of Marx's speech is recorded in the minutes of the meeting at which the decision was made.

In place of a critical attitude the minority set up a dogmatic one, in place of a materialistic attitude an idealistic one. They make sheer will instead of real conditions the driving-wheel of the revolution. While we say to the workers: you have fifteen or twenty or fifty years of bourgeois and national wars to go through, not just to alter conditions but to alter yourselves and qualify for political power – you on the contrary say: we must obtain the power at once or we might as well lay ourselves down to sleep. While we specifically draw the German workers' attention to the undeveloped state of the German proletariat, you outrageously flatter the national sentiment and social prejudices of the German artisan, a course which, of course, is far more popular. Just as the democrats make a sacred entity of the word 'people' so do you do the same with the word 'proletariat'.[29]

The meeting took place on 15 September 1850. Willich believed that the revolution would break out at any moment, and went on believing it even when the crisis, and with it the basis for the revolution, came to an end. On 6 September the Bank of England met banknotes with gold for the first time for a long period. The crisis was over.

The split in the League took place just in time, for Willich plunged into activities that were henceforward entirely quixotic. He was positive that things were going to happen quite soon, and sent off letter after letter to Germany. He had high hopes of the Cologne branch, whom he believed to be on his side, or at least hoped to bring over to his side. A conflict between Prussia and Austria was threatening, and the reserves had been called up. Willich believed the communists should take advantage of the opportunity too seize Cologne, confiscate all private property, ban all newspapers but one, and establish a dictatorship. Thereupon he, Willich, would arrive and march to Paris at the head of the revolutionary troops, turn Louis Napoleon out, and promptly return to Germany to proclaim a one and indivisible republic, etc. He circulated his crack-brained appeals to his followers, but fortunately no one took any notice of them. The Cologne branch did everything in its power to counteract all such wildcat schemes.

Three weeks after severing connection with Willich, Marx liquidated the Société Universelle. Nothing is known of the activities of this organization, and it is doubtful if it was ever really active at all. The Blanquists had set up a fencing and shooting establishment in London, obviously intended for training and preparing plotters for a rising. Liebknecht relates that Marx went there to practise shooting and fencing, not so much with the aim of leading an attack on the Paris Hôtel de Ville within the next few weeks as in memory of his year at the University of Bonn. When the Blanquists invited Marx and Engels to a joint discussion with Willich of questions arising out of the Société Universelle, the answer given them was that Marx and his friends regarded the society as long since dead.[30] From that time onwards the London Blanquists had the most intense hatred for Marx, and one of them, the adventurous Barthélemy, described Marx as a traitor, and 'traitors deserved death'. But the quarrel did not go farther than words.

The London communists who stood by Marx after the split in the League were fairly regular at first in their attendance at the weekly meetings, but gradually started dropping out. Marx's own attendances became more and more infrequent. 'The public isolation in which you and I now find ourselves pleases me very much', Marx wrote to Engels in February 1854.

It is entirely in accordance with our position and our principles. The system of mutual concessions and compromises, which one had to put up with for decency's sake, and the duty of bearing one's share of ridicule in common with all the other asses of the party has now ceased.[31]

Marx had joined the revived Communist League on the assumption of the imminence of a new revolutionary outbreak, which made the League, with its secret organizations, its branches, emissaries and circulars, necessary, as it had been before 1848. The assumption had turned out to be false, and the League had lost the reason for its existence. There was no longer any necessity to make concessions to the Blanquists, compromises had become superfluous, the League itself had become superfluous. Soon after the rupture with Willich, and as soon as the danger of Willich's stirring up the branches in Germany to senseless insurrection had been eliminated, or at any rate notably diminished, Marx 'postponed' his further activities in the League 'indefinitely'. He only had occasion to busy himself with League affairs once more, but the occasion was a highly important one. It arose out of the trial of the leaders of the Cologne branch.

The communists in Cologne, which was now the centre of

the movement in Germany, had little experience of illegal work, and they worked with incredible carelessness, sometimes to the point of naïveté. The Prussian police were not very clever either. They themselves did not get on to the track of the 'conspirators', but had to be given a fillip from outside. In May 1851 the Saxon police arrested an emissary of the League, a tailor named Nothjung, in Leipzig, and discovered from his papers the existence of the organization in Cologne and the names of its most important members. The Prussian police took no steps whatever until practically the whole of the essential facts had been communicated to them. What they lacked in professional skill they made up for by brutal treatment of prisoners under arrest and shameless provocation.

The genuine documents which came to light in the course of the house searches in Cologne were quite sufficient to bring the members of the Cologne branch before a court of justice. But under the Code Napoléon, which was in force in the Rhineland, the accused would have to appear before a jury, and police and public prosecutor, not without reason in view of past experience, feared that the accused, charged as they were with activity as part of an organization which stood for Marx's point of view and was concerned with propaganda, might be acquitted. Therefore more substantial material must be produced. If there were none, it was necessary to create it. The authorities were aware of the existence of Willich's crack-brained letters to the Cologne communists, and although the Cologne branch had specifically repudiated his plans for an insurrection, their repudiation made no difference. According to the police, they and Willich were all the same, and no distinctions were recognized. In the eyes of the police no such things as a rupture because of fundamental political differences existed. Willich and Marx were the same, and the quarrel between them was a purely personal one, arising out of rivalry for the leadership of the secret society. The police made promises to all sorts of people, including convicts and prisoners on remand. They promised them every sort of favour – withdrawal of proceedings against them, quashing of their convictions – if they would agree to give suitable evidence. Not content with that, they sought for documents – evidence in writing that would compromise Marx and implicate him personally.

The Cologne police even spread their net to London, where most of the better-known refugees, above all the leaders of the 'Marx Party' [32] and the 'Willich-Schapper Party', were living. An army of spies was set to watch the political refugees. The Germans were trailed not only by the police agents of Austria, Prussia and other German states but also by French spies, Belgian spies, Dutch spies and Danish spies. A regular trade in information about the German refugees sprang up, with a veritable market at which information was bartered or paid for in cash. Information was anxiously sought by diplomats, who used it to curry favour with the German potentates, and the agents formed rings or engaged in fierce competition with each other. It was a dirty and lucrative business.

In many reports Marx appeared as a desperate terrorist who used London as a base for organizing attempts on the crowned heads of Europe. The Prussian Ambassador in Brussels reported in December 1848 that there were rumours in Belgium that Marx was preparing an attempt on the King of Prussia. Consequently, when a good royalist non-commissioned officer made an attempt on the life of Friedrich Wilhelm IV in the spring of 1850, special agents were sent to London who naturally confirmed the fact that Marx was the organizer of the outrage. The chief of the Belgian police passed on to the Prussians his own agents' report that Marx forgathered every evening at a tavern with a group of desperadoes, to whom he made inflammatory speeches – 'il endoctrine ses séides qu'il compte lâcher un jour individuellement en Allemagne avec une mission déterminée facile à deviner.' *[33]

The police also discovered that Marx, not satisfied with the assassination of German princes, had aims on the lives of

---

* 'he indoctrinates his henchmen, whom he counts on one day sending individually to Germany on missions the nature of which may easily be guessed.'

Queen Victoria and the Prince Regent. The Prussian policeman who sent this sensational report to Berlin asked whether
it might not be advisable, in view of the tremendous importance of the matter, to seek a personal audience of the Queen.
The audience was not granted, but on 24 May 1850, Manteuffel, the Prussian Prime Minister, sent copies of the report
to the British Foreign Office. Verbal representations seem also
to have been made to the British authorities, for in the summer of 1850 Marx feared he was going to be expelled from
England. The English police were more intelligent than the
Prussians believed them to be, for they soon discovered what
lay behind the Prussian denunciations.

During the preparations for the Cologne trials police activities were redoubled. Their agents, having unlimited resources
at their disposal, got busy among the starving refugees and
succeeded in buying several of them. One of the most important refugee-spies was the Hungarian, Colonel Bangya, who
was in the confidence of Kossuth and in the pay of the French,
Austrian, and Prussian police at the same time. The police
dossiers of the time are full of reports of his having attended
a refugee meeting yesterday, of having read certain letters
the day before, and having gained the friendship of this leader
or the other. These bought ex-revolutionaries were able to give
information about Marx, and sometimes their reports were
very well-informed. Bangya supplied particularly detailed reports, for he enjoyed Marx's friendships for several months
and was a frequent visitor at his house.[34]

The reports of the properly informed agents did not help
the police, for they tended rather to vindicate than incrimin-
ate the Cologne accused. They were unanimous in stating
that Marx repudiated armed risings and plots. So the police
had recourse to other methods. They had the house of one of
Willich's followers broken into, and the records of the 'Willich-
Schapper Party' fell into their hands almost complete. They
rounded these off with letters they forged themselves. The
'Marx Party' documents were in the possession of Marx and
Engels and were better looked after, but the police managed

to get at them too. They manufactured a minute book with forged reports of meetings that never took place. And now the case was ready to begin.

For months Marx did practically nothing but work for the accused, to whose defence he devoted all his energies, both before and during the trial, which lasted for weeks. At the end of October 1852 Frau Marx wrote to a friend in America:

You will have followed the communist monster trial in the *Kölnische Zeitung.* On 23 October the whole thing took such a splendid and interesting turn, and one so favourable to the accused, that our spirits began to revive a little again. You can imagine that the 'Marx Party' is active day and night, and is working with head, hands and feet.

The whole of the police case is lies. They steal, they forge, they break desks open, they commit perjury and give false evidence, and consider they have a perfect right to do so in the case of the communists, who are beyond the pale. This and the blackguardly way the police have of taking over all the functions of the public prosecutor and producing as proof, as legally proved fact, unverified documents, sheer rumours, reports and hearsay evidence is really hair-raising. My husband has to work all day and far into the night, for all the proofs of forgery have to be elaborated in London. Whole documents have to be copied six or eight times over and sent to Germany by the most various routes, via Frankfurt, Paris, etc., for all letters addressed to my husband, and all letters from here to Cologne are intercepted and opened. The whole thing is now a struggle between the police on the one side and my husband on the other, for everything, the whole revolution and now the whole conduct of the defence, has been thrust upon his shoulders.

Forgive my confused writing, but I have been somewhat immersed in the plot myself, and I have been copying so much that my fingers ache. Hence the confusion. Whole masses of business addresses and fake business letters have just arrived from Weerth and Engels to enable us to dispatch documents, etc., safely. A regular office has been established here. Two or three of us write, others run messages, still others scrape pennies together to enable the writers to keep themselves alive and furnish proofs of the scandalous behaviour of the official world. At the same time my three merry children sing and whistle and their papa keeps on losing patience with them. Such a hustling and bustling.[35]

Marx's efforts resulted in the unmasking of some of the chief forgeries and four of the eleven accused were acquitted, but the pressure of the police and the Government on the jury was so great that the other seven were convicted. They were sentenced to from three to six years' imprisonment in a fortress.

That was the end of the Communist League. After the arrests in Cologne in 1851 it ceased to exist. In England it only continued as an organization to help the accused. Sentence was pronounced in Cologne on 12 November 1852. Five days later, the League, at Marx's proposal, was declared dissolved. Marx's reason for this decision was that the League was 'no longer opportune'.

Marx never again belonged to a secret organization. General political grounds and private grounds united in causing him to refrain. Some American communists proposed to reorganize the League at the end of the 1850s, but he would have nothing to do with it. He told them he was convinced he could do more good to the working classes by his theoretical labours than by participation in organizations, the time for which had gone by. He refused to join any secret organizations, 'if only on the ground that such organizations might endanger human beings in Germany'. [36] The conviction of his Cologne comrades was a terrible blow to him. Roland Daniels, the man for whom Marx had more affection than for any other, succumbed early to illness contracted in prison. 'His was a delicate, finely organized, thoroughly noble nature', Marx wrote in his letter of condolence to Frau Daniels. 'In him character, talents and aesthetic vision were in unusual harmony. Daniels stood out among the people of Cologne like a Greek statue thrust by some whimsical mischance among a lot of Hottentots.'[37] Marx never got over the fact of men like Daniels dying a sacrifice to Prussian police infamy. He was convinced that the time for the workers' movement in Western Europe to organize itself into secret societies had gone.

Marx wrote his pamphlet, 'Revelations of the Communist Trial in Cologne', in November and December 1852. He exposed all the abominable practices of the police, produced documentary evidence of their forgeries, utterly demolished the web of lies that they had spun. But the pamphlet did not reach Germany. A fairly large edition of 2,000 copies was printed in Switzerland, but was confiscated when an attempt was made to smuggle it over the frontier.[38]

Another of Marx's works had not fared much better shortly before. Joseph Weydemeyer had founded a weekly paper in America, where he emigrated in the autumn of 1850. It was the only German paper at Marx's disposal after the death of the *Neue Rheinische Zeitung-Revue*. Marx started writing for the *Revolution*, as it was called, an essay on 'The 18th Brumaire of Louis Bonaparte', referring to the Bonapartist *coup d'état* of 2 December 1850. But Weydemeyer was not able to proceed with his first number, and the most brilliant of Marx's shorter historical works, in which, as Engels said, he gives a magnificent example of how the materialist interpretation of history can explain an event which remains baffling from all other viewpoints, might have remained unpublished had a German worker not given Weydemeyer forty dollars, the whole of his savings, to enable him to print it. 'The 18th Brumaire' appeared as the first number of the monthly the *Revolution*. Although several hundred copies found their way to Germany not a single one appeared in any bookshop.[39]

After the dispersal of the Communist League Marx resigned from the Workers' Education Union and the refugees' assistance committee. He shared in none of the busy inactivity with which the more or less well-known democratic leaders in London, 'the great men of the emigration' as Marx called them, filled their time waiting for the outbreak of the revolution which they believed to be imminent. He had nothing but bitter sarcasm and contempt for their empty pathos, their cliques and their factions, the whole of the hollow motions through which they went. They regarded him as a mischief-maker, a proud, unsociable man who went his own way alone.

They hated him for being an obstinate communist. An example will suffice to show of what excesses the bourgeois 'emigrants' were capable when they wanted to make Marx appear contemptible.

In the summer of 1851 a rumour was spread in London that Marx had become a contributor to the *Neue Preussische Zeitung*, the paper of extreme reaction. It was partly under the control of Ferdinand von Westphalen, the Minister of the Interior, of whom Marx had said to his wife in jest in 1848 that her brother was so stupid that he was sure to become a Prussian minister one day. Neither Marx nor his wife had had the slightest contact with him for many years. An obscure German paper published in London eagerly took up the slander and surpassed itself in innuendoes about the excellent relations existing between the red revolutionary and the minister of state. At that Marx, who granted the Press the right to insult politicians, comedians and other public figures, but not to slander them, lost patience and challenged the editor to a duel. The editor was frightened out of his life and printed in his next issue the apology that was dictated to him and thus the incident was closed.

Since Engels had gone to live in Manchester, Marx was practically alone in London. Material needs became more and more pressing. In 1848, when the German revolution began to peter out, Engels looked back with a smile of regret to the 'sleepless night of exile'[40] during the years that led up to the revolution. The real and dreadful 'sleepless night of exile' started now.

[16]

The Sleepless Night of Exile

BONAPARTE'S *coup d'état* put the finishing external touch to
the European counter-revolution, which now held the whole
Continent in its grip. In Hungary, where the defence had
been heroic, the hangman now held sway. Austria was ruled
as it had been in the time of Metternich. In Prussia nothing
was left of the triumphant achievements of March but a pitiful mock-constitutionalism which served as an admirable
prop of military despotism. The inner enemy was everywhere
defeated. The way was once more clear for an active foreign
policy.

The revolution had not succeeded in solving a single one of
the numerous European national problems. Germany remained carved into little pieces, Poland remained divided,
Italy was still rent asunder and Hungary enslaved. In the last
resort Austria and Prussia had been saved by Russia. Russian
troops had kept down the Poles and suppressed the Hungarian
revolution; and now the Tsar proceeded to claim his recom-
pense for saving Central Europe from 'chaos'. The opportunity
of coming a step nearer to the capture of Holy Byzantium, the
principal aim of Russian foreign policy, was more favourable
that it had ever been before. Austria, just saved by Russia from
Kossuth and practically bankrupt in any case, was bound to remain inactive, and Prussia was a vassal state. No danger threatened from the West. France, or so they believed in St Petersburg, was not yet strong enough to resist Russia alone, and the
Tory Government in England could not well defend the
Crescent against the Cross.

The calculation was erroneous. France and England, much
as they wished to avoid war, were forced to come to the assistance of Turkey. It was impossible for them to tolerate Russia,
even in the guise of a champion of Christianity, gaining a

foothold on the Dardanelles. In the spring of 1854 Russia found herself at war with England, France and Turkey.

This was not the war Marx had longed for in 1848 and 1849. This was no war against the stronghold of counter-revolution, but a war of the three most important counter-revolutionary powers among themselves. Marx welcomed it, for he who fought Russia was working for the revolution, though he knew it not and willed it not. Recent experience had shown once more that the overthrow of Russia was an essential preliminary to the victory of the proletariat. In the 1890s Engels summarized Marx's reasons in two sentences:

> In the first place the Russian Empire constitutes the great stronghold, reserve position and reserve army of European reaction. The mere fact of its existence is itself a danger and a threat to us. In the second place it constantly interferes in European affairs with the object of securing geographical points of vantage, all with the aim of obtaining an ascendancy over Europe, and in so doing interferes with our normal development and thus makes the liberation of the European proletariat impossible.[1]

Being anti-Russian meant anything but being pro-English or pro-French or even pro-Turkish. In France the most arbitrary despotism held sway, in spite of, or rather because of, the universal suffrage which under the Empire had become a gigantic instrument of popular betrayal. Freedom of assembly was as good as abolished, the workers' right to combine was taken away, the increase in the severity of the conditions of the work-books made them the slaves of every minor police official, and the whole country was given over a helpless prey to the rapacity of the December bands, who did not hesitate to take advantage of their opportunity. As for England, it pretended to be waging 'a war of civilization against barbarism', but in defending Turkey it was really defending the flanks of the route to India, where in Marx's words, 'the real hypocrisy and the barbarism native to bourgeois civilization appears in all its nakedness'. England treated the Irish with even greater inhumanity, if such a thing were possible, than that with which the Russian proprietor treated his serfs; England was the country whose fate was determined by its aristocracy and heartless middle class alone, who were roused to indignation at the maltreatment of Christians in Turkey today, and at the suppression by the Russians of the noble peoples of the Caucasus tomorrow, but had no objection to eleven-year-old children slaving for ten or eleven hours a day in the textile factories.[2]

Europe was on the move again, but Marx was entirely cut off from any possibility of direct political activity. After the dissolution of the Communist League, which in any case would not have been a suitable instrument for political action, no other organization existed. The German Press was closed to Marx. He started writing for an unimportant paper in Breslau, but that was not till the beginning of 1855, and in any case it was sheer hack-work and after a year the paper was discontinued.[3] Marx's connections in France were even more tenuous; an occasional letter from a refugee in Paris, and that was all. In England things were slightly better.

The Chartist movement never succeeded in recovering from its defeat in the spring of 1848.[4] A few groups survived here and there, practically without contact with one another. Many leaders had deserted it, and with the end of the crisis the great English workers' movement seemed to be at an end too. Of the two men whom Marx knew from earlier days, G. J. Harney was undoubtedly as well-meaning and as devoted to the workers' cause as anyone could be, but he was quite obviously incapable of resurrecting the expiring movement. He was always full of enthusiasm, for Kossuth and Mazzini, for Marx and for Willich. They were all such excellent men, and he made heroes of them all. Marx and Engels had a private name for him – 'Citizen Hip-Hip-Hurrah!'[5] They soon parted from him.

The one Chartist leader with whom Marx remained in contact for long was Ernest Jones.[6] Jones, energetic, pertinacious, clever, if sometimes over-clever, educated and an excellent speaker, well-tried in struggle – he spent two years in prison because of his part in the stormy demonstration of 1848 – had all the qualities of a great agitator. His fiery spirit breathed new life into the movement. In March 1854, he actually succeeded in causing an all-English workers' parliament to meet in Manchester. Marx, who was invited as an honorary delegate, sent an address in which he defined the task of the parliament as 'organization of its united forces, organization of the working class on a national scale'.[7] But the Chartists lacked the strength to overcome their defeat and the movement increasingly disintegrated. Some of its old adherents merged into petty-bourgeois reformist groups, others lost interest, and Jones himself ended by joining John Bright's radicals.

Marx found it exceedingly difficult to reconcile himself to the idea of a powerful movement, which but a few years before had been the champion of the European proletariat, ending in this way. He went on hoping that it would flare up again, be rekindled by some spontaneous act. When 200,000 workers, artisans and small tradesmen demonstrated against the Sunday Trading Bill in Hyde Park in June 1855, Marx believed the affair to be no less than 'the beginning of the English revolution'.[8] He and other German exiles took an active part in it. Liebknecht writes in his memoirs that Marx, who was liable to become very excited on such occasions, was 'within a hair's breadth of being seized by the collar by a policeman and hauled before a magistrate, had not a warm appeal to the thirst of the brave guardian of the law eventually met with success'.[9] After a second demonstration the Bill was withdrawn and the flickering flame extinguished.

The whole weakness of the Chartist movement in the first half of the 1850s was demonstrated, among other things, by its newspapers. Harney's paper, the *Red Republican*, which published the first English translation of the Communist Manifesto, ceased to appear after a short time and its successor, the *Friend of the People*, had no better fate. From February 1852 onwards Jones produced a weekly, the *People's Paper*, but had the greatest difficulty in keeping the 'poor sheet' (as Marx called it) alive. Marx helped to edit it for a time. From the autumn onwards he occasionally wrote articles for Jones and allowed him to reprint articles which had appeared elsewhere. But even the *People's Paper* had only a very limited circulation. It was several times on the verge of bankruptcy and ended by passing into the hands of a bourgeois radical group.[10]

Apart from the Chartist Press, which was insignificant, the only papers in England at Marx's disposal were the Urquhartite papers. When the Oriental Question cropped up once more in the spring of 1853 Marx at first paid very little attention to it. In March he was still convinced that 'in spite of all the dirty work and the ranting in the newspapers it would never be the cause of a European war'. Six months later Russia and Turkey were at war, and when France and England entered the fray a local dispute flared up into a European war. Marx flung himself into the *détestable question orientale*, and for a time even thought of learning Arabic and Turkish. He read everything on the Near East he could lay his hands on,[11] and found particular interest in the writings of David Urquhart, to which Engels had drawn his attention.

I am now reading Urquhart, the crazy M.P., who declares that Palmerston is sold to Russia. The explanation is simple; the fellow is a Highland Scot of Lowland education, by nature a romantic and by training a free trader. The fellow went to Greece a philhellene and, after being at daggers drawn with the Turks for three long years, he went to Turkey and became an enthusiast for the very Turks he had just been quarrelling with. He goes into raptures over Islam, and his motto is: if I were not a Calvinist I should be a Mohammedan. In his opinion Turks, particularly those of the Golden Age of the Osmanli Empire, are the most perfect nation on earth, without any exception whatever. The Turkish language is the most perfect and melodious in the world. The Turkish constitution in its 'purity' is as fine as any there could be, and is almost superior to the British. In short, only the Turk is a gentleman and freedom exists only in Turkey.[12]

Urquhart went into raptures over Turkey because it was barbaric. He went into raptures about the Middle Ages and

K.M.—9

the Catholic Church for the same reason. He hated modern industry, the bourgeoisie, universal suffrage, the Chartists and revolutionaries of every kind. He was profoundly convinced that all these were nothing but the tools of Russian diplomacy, which made use of them to cause unrest in the West and deliver it a helpless prey to Russian plans of world conquest. Marx soon saw that Urquhart was a complete monomaniac, but his hatred of Russia might make him a useful ally.

Marx frequently praised the writings of Urquhart in the articles on the Oriental Question he wrote for the *New York Tribune* from the summer of 1853 onwards.[13] Whatever else the Scot might be, he certainly knew the Near East better than most of his contemporaries. The fact that there was no infamy of which he did not think Russia capable only served to make Marx more favourably inclined towards him. Moreover, there seemed to be an element of truth in his exaggerations. In spite of Marx's original scepticism, the more closely he studied the recent history of Anglo-Russian relations the better-founded did Urquhart's imputations against British statesmen, and Palmerston in particular, appear. Marx made an exhaustive study of Hansard and subjected the diplomatic Blue Books from 1807 to 1850 to an assiduous analysis. In November 1853 he communicated the result of his researches to Engels: 'Curious as it may seem to you, as a result of closely following the footprints of the noble viscount for the past twenty years, I have come to the same conclusion as the monomaniac Urquhart, namely that Palmerston has been sold to Russia for several decades.'[14]

The irresolute, vacillating manner in which England and France waged the war and their complaints of the Tsar's intransigence, which made the compromise they desired so difficult to obtain, only served to intensify Marx's conviction that Palmerston did not mean the war seriously and that the war was a sham. Marx became a monomaniac like Urquhart. He examined hundreds of diplomatic documents in the British Museum, and in his opinion they revealed a secret connivance between the cabinets of London and St Petersburg dating from the time of Peter the Great. Marx now attacked Palmerston with great vehemence. He did not directly accuse him of being corrupted by Russia, but demonstrated 'Palmerston's connivance with the St Petersburg cabinet from his transactions with Poland, Turkey, Circassia, etc.'

Urquhart was delighted at Marx's articles on Lord Palmerston, which were published in the *New York Tribune* and the *People's Paper*. E. Tucker, a publisher and a friend of Urquhart's, printed 15,000 copies of one of these articles in pamphlet form, and not long afterwards he reproduced two more articles in the same form.[15] In the summer of 1854 the Urquhartites, this time with the support of the Chartists, started a campaign against secret diplomacy. The campaign was chiefly directed against Palmerston. Their organs, the *Free Press* in London and the *Sheffield Free Press*, reprinted many of Marx's articles.[16] Marx maintained his contact with them until the middle of the 1860s. Marx shrank at nothing when it came to striking a blow at Russian Tsarism. Later he actually wrote anti-Russian articles for conservative papers.

Apart from the Chartist movement and the Urquhartite committees, some unimportant weeklies, and two or three pamphlets, Marx's voice in England was echoing in the void. For ten whole years Marx had only one big newspaper through which to speak, though his voice did not reach the English, French and German proletariat for whom his words were meant. From the summer of 1852 onwards Marx was a regular correspondent of the *New York Tribune*, which in the middle of the 1850s had the largest circulation in the world.[17]

The *New York Tribune* was founded in April 1841 as an organ of the advanced bourgeois intelligentsia by Horace Greeley, a former compositor who became a journalist. Greeley was a friend of Albert Brisbane and the Rev. George Ripley, two zealous disciples of the socialist teaching of Fourier. In the spring of 1842 he put his paper at the disposal of Fourierist propaganda. Fourierism had many followers among the educated classes in America at the time. Its colony at Brook Farm, near Boston, was visited and encouraged by

Nathaniel Hawthorne, Emerson, Channing and Margaret
Fuller. It was destroyed by fire in 1846 and financial difficulties
prevented its reconstruction. Many of the colonists went to
New York, where Charles A. Dana became city editor and
Ripley critic of the *New York Tribune*. It had a roll of contributors unequalled by any other American paper, an uncom-
monly high literary and political standard, and excellent European correspondents, but was only moderately successful
prior to 1848, when, as the best-informed paper in America, its
circulation increased as a consequence of the outbreak of the
revolution. Dana was sent to Europe as a special correspondent. He was in Paris during the June rising, went to Berlin
in the autumn and in November went to Cologne. It may have
been Brisbane, who was in Berlin at the time and had met
Marx in Paris, who drew Dana's attention to him.[18] Dana paid
Marx a visit and spent a 'delightful' evening with him, as he
was fond of recalling in later years, and took away with him
an abiding impression that in Marx he had met the most
acute and far-seeing of the revolutionaries. In July 1850 he
wrote to Marx from New York that he always kept himself
informed of Marx's activities and whereabouts and asked him
whether he would not like to come to America. Marx's answer
is unknown. At the time Marx certainly had plans to emigrate
to America, as will be mentioned later.

After the collapse of the German revolution a great stream
of emigrants poured into the new, the free world. Half a million Germans landed in New York in the years 1852 to 1854
alone. They took with them a lively interest in the affairs of
their native land. Even the native Americans, who did not
generally pay much attention to Europe, took much more
notice of it now than formerly. The *New York Tribune*, with
its excellent connections among the democrats of the emigration, advanced in circulation by leaps and bounds. At the beginning of August 1851 Dana invited Marx to contribute.

Between August 1851 and September 1852 eighteen articles
on the revolution and counter-revolution in Germany appeared in the *New York Tribune*. They appeared over Marx's

signature, though not one of them was written by him.[19] Marx was so fully occupied on the great economic work which he was anxious to complete as quickly as possible that he asked Engels to write them in his stead, and Engels wrote them, as he later wrote many more articles for Marx, either entirely or in part. In May 1852 Dana asked Marx to send him articles on 'current events which throw light on the brewing revolutionary crisis'. Marx submitted the first article in August. As his English was not yet adequate, he wrote in German, which Engels translated. From February 1853 onwards Marx wrote his English articles himself. From then onwards Marx worked very hard for the *New York Tribune*. During the first year he sent no fewer than sixty articles to New York.

The work Marx did for the *New York Tribune* was not that of an ordinary foreign correspondent. He contributed articles which were comprehensive evaluations of recent events. Sometimes he wrote regular essays. They were composed hurriedly, because the steamer sailed twice a week, and if Marx missed the mail an article was lost and he was £2 the poorer. But every line he wrote was based on careful study. Marx lacked both inclination and ability for the work of a newspaper correspondent proper. He had little contact with political circles, still less with bourgeois circles, he avoided journalists and could not dance attendance on the latest sensations. From ten in the morning till seven at night he sat in the reading-room of the British Museum. Before writing an article on British rule in India he studied dozens of books on the subject,[20] and before his series on the Spanish revolution he went through the whole of ancient and modern literature relevant to the subject.[21] Engels cooperated valiantly in his own departments, i.e. military matters and geography. The *New York Tribune* was more than pleased with the work of its contributor. Sometimes Marx's contributions were printed as leading articles, and Dana did not shrink from inserting sentences here and there and altering the beginning and end to make it appear that the articles had been written in the office. Engels's military articles on the Turko-Russian War[22] attracted so much attention that their author was taken to be the prominent General Winfield Scott, who was friendly with Greeley and stood as a candidate for the presidency.[23]

The *New York Tribune*, which was not so anxious to let its readers see how much of the work was not its own, started omitting Marx's name more and more frequently. Marx eventually insisted that either all his articles be signed or none, and from the spring of 1855 they all appeared unsigned. At first other Germans had contributed to the *New York Tribune*, including Freiligrath, Ruge, and even Bruno Bauer, but from the mid 1850s Marx was its only diplomatic correspondent in Europe.

The fees paid Marx for his articles were hardly in accordance with the *New York Tribune*'s appreciation of him as 'its most highly-valued contributor'. For the first article Marx was paid £1, and the fee was then raised to £2. Marx was not paid for all the articles he submitted but only for those that were printed. The greatest concession that Marx ever obtained was in the spring of 1857, when the *Tribune* agreed to pay him for one dispatch a week, whether it were used or not. The remainder were only to be paid for if they actually appeared. The number of articles paid for rose and fell in accordance with American interest in events in Europe, whether because they directly affected the United States or whether such things as wars, risings or crises were 'sensational' enough for them.

It is really disgusting [Marx wrote to Engels in January 1857] to be condemned to take it as a favour that such a rag admits you to its company. To pound and grind dry bones and make soup of them, as paupers do in the workhouse, that is the sum total of the political work to which one is generously condemned in such society. Although I am only an ass, I am conscious of having given these rascals, I will not say recently, but in former years, too much for their money.[24]

Irregular and uncertain as Marx's income from the *New York Tribune* was for nearly ten years, it was all he earned. In spite of Engels's unlimited sacrifices he would have been lost without it.

When Marx arrived in London he was not in the least worried about his immediate monetary prospects. He was convinced that he would soon succeed in putting the *Neue Rheinische Zeitung* on its feet again in the form of a review. But negotiations with the publishers dragged on for month after month, and then Marx was taken ill. The contributions were not ready in time and the first number appeared at the beginning of March 1850 instead of on 1 January. The money Marx brought with him – his wife had sold the furniture in Cologne and she had pawned the silver in France – quickly vanished. Other exiles, poverty-stricken themselves, were unable to help. Marx had to provide for his wife, four young children (Guido, his second son, was born in October 1849) and Lenchen Demuth, the faithful housekeeper. The household was reduced to an appalling state of destitution. At the end of March 1850 they were evicted. About this time Frau Marx wrote to Weydemeyer:

I shall describe one day of this life as it really was, and you will see that perhaps few other refugees have had to suffer so much. Since the cost of a wet-nurse is prohibitive here, I decided, in spite of continual and terrible pains in the breasts and the back, to nurse the child myself. But the poor little angel drank in so much sorrow with the milk that he was continually fretting, and in violent pain day and night. He has not slept a whole night through since he was born, but sleeps at most two or three hours. Recently he has been subject to violent cramps, so that he is continually hovering on the brink of life and death. When he was suffering in this way he sucked so violently that my nipple became sore and bled. Often the blood streamed into his little mouth. As I was sitting like this one day our landlady suddenly appeared. In the course of the winter we had paid her more than 250 thalers, and we had arranged with her that in future we were not to pay her but the landlord, who had put in an execution. Now she denied this agreement and demanded the £5 we still owed her. As we could not pay this sum at once two brokers entered the house and took possession of all my belongings; bedding, linen, clothes, everything, even the poor baby's cradle and the better toys belonging to the girls, who stood by, weeping bitterly. They threatened to take everything away in two hours' time, when I should have had to lie on the bare floor with my freezing children and my aching breast. Our friend Schramm hurried into the town to seek help. He got into a cab, but the horses ran away. He jumped out and was brought back bleeding to the house, where I was in despair with my poor shivering children.

We had to leave the house next day. It was cold and rainy and dreary. My husband tried to find a lodging for us, but no one was willing to have us when he mentioned the four children. At last a friend helped us and we paid what was owing. I quickly sold all my beds in order to settle with the chemist, the baker, the butcher and the milkman, who were all filled with alarm when they heard the broker's men were in and rushed to send in their bills. The beds I sold were taken to the street door and loaded on to a handcart – and what do you think happened? By this time it had grown late and it was long after sunset, after which moving furniture in this way is illegal by English law. The landlord appeared with a number of constables, and said that some of his property might be on the cart, we might be escaping to a foreign country. In less than five minutes a crowd of two or three hundred people had gathered outside our front door – the whole Chelsea mob. The beds were brought in again, and could not be sent to the purchaser until next morning. Now that the sale of our goods and chattels had enabled us to pay our debts to the last penny, I moved with my little darlings to two tiny rooms at our present address, the German Hotel, 1 Leicester Street, Leicester Square, where we found a human reception for £5 10s. a week.

Do not imagine that these petty sufferings have bent me. I know only too well that our struggle is no isolated one, that I belong to the favoured and the fortunate, since my dear husband, the mainstay of my life, is still at my side. The only thing that really crushes me and makes my heart bleed is all the pettinesses that he has to suffer, the fact that so few have come to his aid, and that he, who has so willingly and gladly helped so many, should be helpless here. But you are not to think, my dear Herr Weydemeyer, that we are making claims on anyone. The only thing that my husband might have expected of those who have had so many ideas, so much encouragement, so much support from him was that they might have devoted more practical energy to his *Review*, might have taken a greater interest in it. I am proud and bold enough to suggest this. That little I think they owed him. But my husband thinks otherwise. Never, even at the most terrible times, has he lost his confidence in the future, or even his cheerful humour.[25]

In the middle of May, Marx and his family moved to Soho, the quarter where the most poverty-stricken refugees lived. He rented two small rooms in Dean Street, and there he lived for six years, in a noisy, dirty street, in a neighbourhood where epidemic after epidemic raged. In 1854 the cholera was worse in Soho than anywhere else. Three of his children died there. Those were unspeakably dreadful years.

The *Neue Rheinische Zeitung-Revue* brought Marx in less than thirty thalers in all, and it was impossible to go on with it. Marx sold his library, which he had left in Cologne, got into debt, pawned everything that was not nailed fast. After the miscarriage of their literary plans Engels could no longer remain in London. He returned to 'fiendish commerce' in the autumn of 1853 and went to Manchester, to his father's cotton-mill, where he worked at a moderate salary as an ordinary employee. Engels's conviction that the revolution would soon free him from his 'Egyptian bondage' enabled him to tolerate a life he hated. But his chief aim was to help Marx. Marx, the brains of the revolutionary party, the genius, in comparison with whom he felt his own gifts to be merely talents, must not be allowed to perish in poverty-stricken refugeedom. For twenty long years Engels worked at a job he hated, abandoning his own scientific work in order to make possible the work of his friend. He wrote newspaper articles for him and gave him as much money as he could. During the early years this was not a great deal. Engels's salary increased only gradually, and he had considerable social responsibilities of his own. He had to maintain a 'respectable' household, and another in which he lived with an Irish daughter of the people named Mary Burns, and he kept Mary's relatives as well, but every pound he could possibly spare was sent to Marx, whose position became more and more desperate every month.[26] In the autumn of 1850 Marx seriously considered the idea of emigrating to America, where he hoped to be able to found a German paper. Rothacker, who had taken part in the rising in Baden, was asked to prepare the ground among friends and acquaintances in New York. He wrote to Marx in November, saying that the prospects were as bad as they could possibly be. The immediate prospects in London, whatever they were, were better than they were in New York. Little Guido died, 'a sacrifice to bourgeois misery', as Marx said to Engels.[27] A daughter, Franziska, was born in March 1851. When she died, barely one year old, Marx was forced to borrow money from a French *émigré* to pay for the coffin.

Marx wished to continue the review as a quarterly, but the publisher refused. Marx devoted all his energy to his book on economics. He and his friends in Germany spent months negotiating with every conceivable publisher, but not one of them was willing to have anything to do with him. Marx's name alone was sufficient to put them into a panic. Hermann Becker tried to get Marx's *Collected Essays* published in Cologne.[28] One volume appeared and that was all. Marx offered the publishers a pamphlet on Proudhon, then a translation of *Misère de la philosophie*; he offered to contribute to periodicals and was willing to write 'completely innocuous' articles. But all his suggestions were declined. Had friends – notably the excellent Daniels – not helped him, he would have starved in 1851. 'You can well imagine that the situation is very gloomy,' Marx wrote to Weydemeyer.

It will be the end of my wife if it goes on much longer. The never-ending worries of the petty, paltry, bourgeois struggle are a terrible strain on her. To add to it there are all the infamies of my opponents, who never dared attack me but avenge themselves for their impotence by spreading the most unspeakable infamies about me and making me socially suspect. I should, of course, only laugh at the filth. I do not let them disturb me for one moment in my work. But you will understand that my wife, who is ailing, and has to endure the most dismal poverty from morning till night, and whose nervous system is upset, is none the better for having to listen to stupid go-betweens who daily report to her the out-pourings of the democratic cesspools. The tactlessness of some of these people is often amazing.[29]

Naturally Marx did not receive a single penny for his '18th Brumaire'. That was work for the party. His battle for the defendants at the Cologne trial and his unmasking of the police in his *Revelations* was party work too. During the second half of 1852 these activities occupied all his time. All this work was carried out under the most unspeakable difficulties. In February he reached the 'pleasant point' when he could not go out because his coat was in pawn and he could no longer eat meat because he could not get any more credit. His wife, little Jenny and Lenchen Demuth were taken ill. 'I could not and cannot fetch the doctor', Marx wrote to Engels, 'because I have no money for medicine. For the last eight to ten days I have fed my family on bread and potatoes, and today it is still doubtful whether I shall be able to obtain even these.'[30] To-wards the end of the year the situation at last began to im-prove. Engels was able to send more money and the first pay-ments arrived from the *New York Tribune*. But up to 1858 there were always times, even in the 'good' years, when Marx scarcely had a penny in his pocket. The children learned to resist the siege of creditors – the butcher, the milkman, and the baker – by saying: 'Mr Marx ain't upstairs.'[31] Once Marx was forced to fly to Manchester because of a doctor who threa-tened to sue him for a £26 debt, and the gas and water were going to be cut off.[32] The following description of Marx's household, written by a Prussian spy who managed to ingra-tiate his way into it, is not without malice and is not to be credited word for word, but gives a pretty good idea of the general atmosphere of the life Marx led in 1853.

The chief leader of this party [i.e. the communists] is Karl Marx; the minor leaders are Friedrich Engels in Manchester, Freiligrath and Wolff (called 'Lupus') in London, Heine in Paris, Weydemeyer and Cluss in America. Bürgers and Daniels were the leaders in Cologne and Weerth in Hamburg. All the rest are simple members. The moving and active spirit, the real soul of the party, is Marx, for which reason I propose to give you a personal description of the man.

Marx is of medium stature, and is thirty-four years of age. Although he is still in the prime of life, his hair is turning grey. His frame is powerful, his features bring Szemere [a Hungarian revolutionary] to mind very strongly, but his complexion is darker and his hair and beard quite black. Lately he does not shave at all. His big, piercing, fiery eyes have something demoniacally sinister about them. The first impression one receives is that of a man of genius and energy; his intellectual superiority exercises an irresistible power on his surroundings.

In private life he is an extremely untidy and cynical human being. He is a bad host and leads a regular Bohemian existence. Washing and combing himself and changing his linen are rarities with him, and he likes getting drunk. He often idles away for days on end, but when he has a great deal to do he works day and night with tireless endurance. He has no fixed times for going to bed or for getting up. He often stays up for whole nights, then lies down fully clothed on the couch at midday and sleeps till evening, untroubled by people coming in or going out, for everyone has a free *entrée* to his house.

His wife is the sister of von Westphalen, the Prussian minister, and is a cultured and charming woman, who has accustomed herself to this Bohemian existence out of love for her husband, and she now feels quite at home in poverty. She has two daughters and a son, and all three children are really handsome and have their father's intelligent eyes.

As husband and father, Marx, in spite of his restless and wild character, is the gentlest and mildest of men. He lives in one of the worst, therefore one of the cheapest neighbourhoods in London. He occupies two rooms. The room looking out on the street is the parlour, and the bedroom is at the back. There is not one clean or decent piece of furniture in either room, but everything is broken, tattered and torn, with thick dust over everything and the greatest untidiness everywhere. In the middle of the parlour there is a large old-fashioned table, covered with oil-cloth. On it there lie manuscripts, books and newspapers, besides the children's toys, bits and pieces from his wife's sewing basket, and cups with broken rims, dirty spoons, knives, forks, lamps, an ink-pot, tumblers, some Dutch clay-pipes, tobacco ash – all in a pile on the same table.

On entering Marx's room smoke and tobacco fumes make your eyes water to such an extent that for the first moment you seem to be groping about in a cavern, until you get used to it and manage to pick out certain objects in the haze. Everything is dirty, and covered with dust, and sitting down is quite a dangerous business. Here is a chair with only three legs, there another, which happens to be whole, on which the children are playing at cooking. That is the one that is offered to the visitor, but the children's cooking is not removed and if you sit down you risk a pair of trousers. But all these things do not in the least embarrass either Marx or his wife. You are received in the most friendly way and are cordially offered pipes, tobacco and whatever else there may happen to be. Eventually a clever and interesting conversation arises to make amends for all the domestic deficiencies, and this makes the discomfort bearable. You actually get used to the company, and find it interesting and original. That is a faithful picture of the family life of Marx, the communist chief.[33]

However bad things were with Marx, he always kept up the outward appearance of an orderly bourgeois life. He was unwilling to allow the 'asses of democrats' a cheap triumph and his pride brooked no sympathy. Only his most intimate friends knew of his distressed condition. He did not bow under the burden of want, but reacted to it only with anger at its compelling him to put aside the work which alone meant anything to him and which, as he well knew, he alone could do, and forcing him to postpone it again and again for the revolting slavery of working for his daily bread. Unshakeable belief in his mission kept up Jenny's courage as well as his own. Even in their most difficult years Jenny and and Marx remained happy people. Unfortunately there are very few documents that throw light on this period. There are Wilhelm Liebknecht's memoirs, a few pages from a diary of a friend of Jenny's youth, and a few letters written by other exiles. The following passage from Liebknecht's memoirs is characteristic of Marx and his friends :

Our outings to Hampstead Heath! If I live to be a thousand I shall never forget them. A Sunday spent on Hampstead Heath was our greatest treat. The children would talk of nothing else during the whole week and even we grown-ups looked forward to it, old and young alike. Even the journey there was a treat. The girls were excellent walkers, as nimble and tireless as cats. When we got there the first thing we would do was to find a place to pitch our tent, so that the tea and beer arrangements might be thoroughly looked after. After a meal, the company would search for a comfortable place to sit or lie down, and when this had been done everybody would pull a Sunday paper, bought on the way, from his pocket, and – assuming a snooze was not preferred – would start reading or talking politics, while the children, who would quickly find playmates, would play hide-and-seek in the bushes.

But this placidity sometimes demanded a change, and we would run races, to say nothing of indulging in wrestling, stone-throwing and similar forms of sport. The greatest treat was a general donkey-ride. What laughter and jubilation a general donkey-ride caused! And what comic scenes! And how Marx enjoyed himself and amused us too. He amused us doubly; in the first place by his more than primitive horsemanship and secondly by the fanaticism with which he asserted his virtuosity in the art. The virtuosity was based on the fact that he once took riding lessons during his student years, but Engels maintained that he never had more than three lessons, and that when he visited him in Manchester once in a blue moon he would go for one ride on a venerable Rosinante. On the way home we would usually sing. We seldom sang political songs, but mostly popular songs, especially sentimental ballads and 'patriotic' songs from the 'fatherland', especially *O Strassburg, O Strassburg, du wunderschöne Stadt*, which enjoyed universal popularity. Or the children would sing nigger songs and dance to them. On the way there and back politics or the plight of the refugees were banned as subjects of conversation. But to make up for it we would talk a lot about literature and art, and Marx had the opportunity of displaying his astonishing memory. He would declaim long passages from the *Divina Commedia* and scenes from Shakespeare, in which his wife, who was also an excellent Shakespearian scholar, often relieved him.[34]

Among the Marxes Shakespeare was a regular family cult.

Frau Marx once wrote to Frau Liebknecht, telling her with great satisfaction that her youngest daughter had made a Shakespeare museum of her little room. When Marx wanted to perfect his English, at a time when he could read but not speak it, he sought out and listed all Shakespeare's own expressions. In later years the whole Marx family would often walk all the way from Haverstock Hill to the Sadlers Wells Theatre, to see Phelps, the Shakespearian actor. They used to stand, for they could not afford seats. The children knew whole scenes of Shakespeare by heart before they could read properly.

In January 1855, Frau Marx, who was then forty-one years old, had a daughter. 'The "bona fide traveller" is, I regret to say, of the sex *par excellence*', Marx wrote to Engels. He had wanted a son to replace the dead Guido, who had been called 'Foxie', after the popular Fawkes of the Gunpowder Plot. Everyone was given a nickname in Marx's house. Marx himself was called 'the Moor', as he had been called ever since his student days on account of his dark complexion and black hair, and his wife and children and all his acquaintances called him that too. The children varied 'Moor' mostly with 'Devil' or 'Old Nick'. Frau Marx was never called anything but 'Möhme'. The eldest daughter, Jenny, was called 'Qui-qui', 'Di' and even the 'Emperor of China'. The next daughter, Laura, was called 'Hottentot' and 'Kakadu', the son, Edgar, was called 'Musch' or, more respectfully,'Colonel Musch', and the youngest daughter, who was named Eleanor, was at first called 'Quo-quo' then 'Dwarf Alberich' and finally 'Tussy'. Tussy described some of the incidents of her childhood in 'A Few Stray Notes', published in 1895. She remembered how Marx carried her on his shoulders, and put anemones in her hair.

Moor was certainly a magnificent horse. I was told that my elder sisters and brother used to harness Moor to an armchair, seat themselves in it and make him pull it. Indeed he wrote several chapters of 'The 18th Brumaire' in his role as 'gee-up neddy' to his three children, who sat behind him on chairs and whipped him.[35]

Everyone intimate with Marx – Liebknecht, Lessner, Lafargue, and even only occasional visitors to his house – spoke of Marx's unbounded love for his children.[36] Marx often remarked that what he liked best about Jesus was his love of children, and his daughter had heard him say that he could forgive Christianity a great deal for teaching the love of children. A year before his death Marx wrote to his daughter, Laura, that he was coming to Paris to find peace there. 'By peace I mean family life, children's voices, the whole of that "microscopic little world" which is so much more interesting than the "macroscopic" world.'

The voice of his favourite child was extinguished on 6 April 1855, when little Musch died. Marx generally hid his feelings, even from his closest friends. He was by nature so shy that he, a German, behaved with English reserve when it came to expressing his feelings. But in the letters he wrote during the days that followed the child's death his grief broke through the barriers. The beginning of a letter to Engels written on 30 March is quite matter-of-fact. He said that he had put off sending a daily health bulletin, because the course of the illness was so up and down that one's opinion changed almost hourly. Finally the illness had turned into abdominal tuberculosis, and even the doctor had seemed to give up hope. For the last week his wife had been suffering from a nervous breakdown more severe than she had ever had before. Marx's next words were: 'As for me, my heart bleeds and my head burns, though of course I have to keep control of myself.' The next sentence sounds as if Marx were making an apology. That a father should so far forget himself as to talk of his heart bleeding over the death of his favourite child seems to him to demand an explanation. 'During his illness the child did not for a moment act out of harmony with his original, kind and independent character.'[37] On 6 April he wrote: 'Poor Musch is no more. He fell asleep (literally) in my arms between five and six o'clock today. I shall never forget how your friendship helped us through this terrible time. You understand my grief for the child.'[38] A week later he wrote:

The house is naturally utterly desolate and forlorn since the death of the dear child who was its living soul. It is impossible to describe how we miss him at every turn. I have suffered every kind of misfortune, but I have only just learned what real unhappiness is ... In the midst of all the suffering which I have gone through in these days, the thought of you and your friendship, and the hope that we may still have something reasonable to do in this world together, has kept me upright.

At the end of July Marx answered a letter of condolence as follows: 'Bacon says that really important people have so many contacts with nature and the world, have so much to interest them, that they easily get over any loss. I am not one of those important people. My child's death has affected me so greatly that I feel the loss as keenly as on the first day. My wife is also completely broken.'[39] The wound never completely healed. Even after ten years and more Jenny Marx had not overcome her grief. 'The longer I live without the child, the more I think of him and with the greater grief', she wrote to a friend.

In the summer of 1856 Frau Marx went to Trier with her daughter to visit her mother. She found her dying. An uncle of hers had died not long before, but he was an old man of eighty-seven whom she barely knew, and his death, as Marx put it, 'was a very happy event'. The bequest from the two relatives made it possible for them to pay their old debts. In the autumn of 1856 they were at last able to change their two-room dwelling in Soho for a comfortable little house on the outskirts of the city at 9 Grafton Terrace, Maitland Park, Haverstock Hill. But the improvement did not last for long. The *New York Tribune* accepted fewer and fewer of Marx's articles. They needed practically all their space for American politics and articles on the presidential elections, which had to be given preference to events in Europe, and then the approaching crisis began to cast its shadows before.

Marx and Engels had expected the crisis even sooner. As early as January 1855, England, in Marx's opinion, was in the midst of a great trade crisis. Yet the *dies irae*, which, Engels

hoped, would 'ruin the whole of European industry, glut all
the markets, involve all the possessing classes, and cause the
complete bankruptcy of the bourgeoisie',[40] did not arrive until
the autumn of 1857, and then not nearly so dramatically as
Engels expected, though assuredly it was terrible enough.

The first great crisis of the capitalist world started in
America and embraced the leading countries of Europe; England as well as Germany and France. Marx and Engels
thought their time had come. Marx wrote to his friend that,
in spite of his own 'financial distress', since 1849 he had never
felt so 'cosy' as after this outbreak,[41] and Engels himself felt
'enormously cheered'.[42] The time had come to finish his economic work. On 8 December 1857 he wrote to Engels that he
was working 'like mad' right through the night summing up
his economic studies, in order to have at least the outlines in
his head before the deluge.[43]

In the winter of 1850–51 Marx had resumed work on the
economic study he had started in Brussels and had had neither
the time nor the inclination to complete during the years of
revolution.[44] In his thorough way he collected all the available
material, made his way once more through the works of the
great economists, and in April 1851 believed that after the
five more weeks he intended to devote to 'tout ce fatras économique (ça commence à m'ennuyer)',[45] he would be able to sit
down and start to write his book. Two months later he set
himself a new date. The material, he remarked to Weydemeyer, had so many damned ramifications that in spite of all
his exertions he would not be ready for another six or eight
weeks. All the same, in spite of all outward disturbances, the
thing was hurrying to a conclusion. 'The democrat simpletons,
to whom enlightenment comes from above, naturally do not
need to make such exertions. Why should they, born as they
are under a lucky star, trouble themselves with economic and
historical material? The whole thing is so simple, as the valiant
Willich used to tell me.'[46] But even this respite expired. First
more political work intervened, and from 1853 to 1856 his
theoretical economic labours lanquished altogether. Though

Marx gave a great deal of attention to economic events, his own economic work had to give way to the task of trying to earn a living. Occasionally Marx looked through his old note-books and read fragments here and there, but it was the crisis that first compelled him to take up the work at the point at which he had broken off more than six years before.[47]

The crisis affected Marx personally very severely. In October the *New York Tribune* informed him that it had dismissed all its European correspondents except B. Taylor and himself, and that in future he was only to send one article a week. Distress once more entered the household from which it had only just been banished. Marx's wife was ill and the first signs of the serious liver trouble which was to attack Marx repeat-edly in years to come made their appearance in the summer. Marx's financial distress increased rapidly during the winter, and at the beginning of 1858 he had reached a pitch when he wished himself a hundred fathoms deep under the earth rather than go on living in the same way. He wrote to Engels that he himself was able to escape from the wretchedness by concentrating hard on all sorts of general questions, but his wife did not have this resource.[48] A few weeks later he wrote that it was fortunate so many cheering things were happening in the outside world, because personally he was leading 'the most troubled life that can be imagined'.[49] There could be nothing more stupid for people of universal aspirations than to marry and give themselves up to the 'petites misères de la vie domestique et privée', he said. But even if the house tumbled about his head he was determined to finish his book. Marx worked so hard that in April 1858 he collapsed. He complained to Engels that if he so much as sat down and wrote for a few hours it meant that he had to lie down and do nothing for a few days.[50] In the summer the situation had become 'absolutely intolerable'.[51] On 15 July 1858 he wrote to Engels that as a direct result of the position he was in he was completely in-capable of work, partly because he lost the best part of his time vainly running about trying to raise money, partly be-cause his powers of concentration could no longer hold out against his domestic troubles, 'perhaps in consequence of physical deterioration . . . The inevitable final catastrophe cannot be averted much longer.'[52] A loan of £40 which Freiligrath arranged for him and on which Marx had to pay 20 per cent interest, helped him over the worst for a few weeks.

Marx's manuscript was finished at the end of January 1859. It was not *Das Kapital*, the great work that Marx had planned. The first volume, an edition of 1,000 copies of which now appeared in Berlin – it had been very difficult to find a publisher – was called *Critique of Political Economy* and consisted of only two chapters, on goods and money.[53] It had appeared, as Marx hoped it would, 'before the deluge', but that was because the deluge did not occur. In 1859 the crisis had passed, the old world had not collapsed, the revolution had not come. The effects of the crisis continued.

New political life awoke in Germany, though very faint-heartedly. In Italy the movement for national liberation flared up anew. France's industry had been hard hit by the crisis, the state finances were disorganized, the price of corn fell, the peasants, who constituted Bonaparte's strongest support, were grumbling, opposition reared its head among the petty bourgeoisie, the workers were gradually shaking off the paralysis which had held them in its grip since June 1848. In this threatening situation the Emperor took the way out that lay nearest to his hand and went to war – not a general European war, the consequences of which could not be foreseen, but a localized war in which he had the maximum chances of victory. A victory over Austria and the expulsion of the Austrians from Italy was bound to strengthen his position, bind the army to him once more and confirm the false Napoleon as the legitimate successor of the true.[54]

Marx's attitude to the Franco-Austrian War of 1859 was determined, like his attitude to the Crimean War, by the interests of the revolution only. The revolutionary party, weak as it might be, must do everything in its power to prevent Bonaparte's victory. The Austrian hangman's yoke in Italy must certainly be broken, but he who assumed the task of delivering the people of Italy was the enslaver of the people of France, and victory would only confirm his power. The defeat of Austria, which since the middle of the eighteenth century had opposed the advance of Russia in Eastern Europe, though its opposition was 'helpless, inconsequent, cowardly but stubborn', could only be advantageous to Russian Tsarism. The enemy was Napoleon III and Russia. Even if victory should liberate the Italians – as in fact it did not – the interests of the European revolution came before those of Italian national liberation.

In their attitude on this occasion Marx and Engels were practically alone in the revolutionary camp. To the German radicals the Russian danger seemed remote, but reactionary Austria was close at hand. It was difficult to be anti-Austrian without being Bonapartist. Lassalle achieved this *tour de force*.[55] Some of the German democratic *émigrés* were noticeably edging towards Badinguet (which was what Marx called Napoleon. He either called him Badinguet or Boustrapa or Barnum, or at most Louis Bonaparte, but Napoleon never). The German *émigrés* had political reasons for their attitude. But there were also those who proclaimed the Emperor's European and more specifically German mission in a torrent of tyrannicidal words because they were paid to do so. Among them was Karl Vogt, a former left-wing leader in the Frankfurt Parliament, and now a professor in Switzerland and the ideal of the 'enlightened' philistines.

A small German newspaper in London which was more or less on good terms with Marx accused Vogt of being a bought agent of Napoleon. The accusations were reproduced in a leading reactionary paper in Germany. Vogt well knew that his patron would not betray him and brought an action against the newspaper. When it came into court the people in London who had hitherto acted as if they had the clearest proofs of Vogt's venality suddenly assumed the attitude of knowing nothing whatever about it, and Vogt, though his case was dismissed on technical grounds, left the court in the triumphant role of injured innocent. He published the report of the trial, at the same time attacking Marx as the ringleader of those who had slandered him, in spite of the fact that Marx had nothing whatever to do with the whole affair. Vogt alleged that Marx was the leader of a gang of *émigrés* who made a good living by blackmailing revolutionaries, threatening to denounce them to the police, and by forging banknotes.

Vogt's allegations were woven into such a highly ingenious web of lies, with truth and known fact so skilfully blended with half-truths and impudent fabrications, that some of the insinuations were bound to stick in the minds of those not fully acquainted with the facts of 'emigrant' history. Marx tried in vain to bring an action against Vogt and his friends. It was impossible to allow the slander to go unchallenged. Distasteful though it was for him to reply, and hating as he did the necessity of replying to personal accusations and thus of talking about himself, which, as he said with truth, he generally scrupulously avoided, he decided that the measure of success likely to be obtained by Vogt's tissue of lies compelled him to speak. His polemical *Herr Vogt*, a book of 190 pages, appeared at the end of November.[56] Marx transferred the accusation of lying to its author, and his analysis of Vogt's writings made practically a certainty of the suspicion that he was in the pay of Napoleon. Papers published by the Republican Government in 1871 supplied the documentary proof. In August 1859 40,000 francs had been paid Vogt out of the Emperor's private fund.

Marx's fight against the attempt to secure his political annihilation by means of these denunciations occupied more than a year of his life. He was not able to resume his economic work until the middle of 1861. The years 1860 to 1863 were among the gloomiest of Marx's life. At the end of November 1861 his wife went down with smallpox. She had barely recovered when Marx was taken ill himself. For years he suffered from carbuncles and boils, which were apt to break out again as soon as they had healed, and often made him unable to work for weeks. He was 'plagued like Job, though not so godfearing', as he wrote to Engels. The doctors gave him excellent advice. 'Everything the gentlemen say boil down to the fact that one ought to be a prosperous *rentier* and not a poor devil like me, as poor as a church mouse.'[57] When Marx said that in 1868 he was much better off than he was at the beginning of the 1860s. In January 1860 the *New York Tribune* asked him to send nothing for six weeks. After this interval his work was only accepted intermittently. A connection with the Vienna *Presse* seemed to offer a substitute, but after three months' hard work Marx only received £6 in all. His connection with the *New York Tribune* finally ended in April 1862. He was told that all its space was needed for American affairs, and therefore his correspondence must cease. This dried up Marx's only source of income. Engels, whose position in the firm of Ermen and Engels had gone on improving, sent Marx what he could and preserved the numerous family from the worst.

Once more everything that could be spared, and many things that could not be spared, including the children's shoes and clothes, resumed the trail to the pawnshop. In the spring of 1861 Marx went to Holland to see his uncle, Lion Philips, who gave him an advance of £160 on his mother's estate.[58] Most of this sum went to repay old debts, and in November Marx was once more forced to write to Engels, telling him that his wife was suffering from such a serious nervous breakdown that he was afraid that if the struggle went on much longer, there would be a disaster. 'Take all in all', he wrote in February 1862, 'a lousy life like this is not worth living.'[59] In the summer of 1862 Marx tried once more to persuade his mother to help him, but she would not give him a penny. 'My wife says she wishes she were with her children in her grave', he wrote to Engels at the time, 'and I really cannot blame her, for the humiliations, sufferings and horrors which we have had to go through are really indescribable.'[60]

Marx was determined to pursue his aim through thick and thin. In 1859 he wrote to a friend that he would not allow bourgeois society to turn him into a 'money-making machine'. But he had now reached such a pitch of distress that he wanted to become a money-making machine. In 1862 he applied for a job in a railway office, but his application was rejected on account of his bad handwriting. Jenny, the eldest daughter, unknown to her parents, wanted to go on the stage, not because she had any special inclination towards it, but for the sake of earning some money. Marx considered whether he should not break up his home, find posts as governesses for his two elder daughters and move with his wife and youngest child into a lodging house in the poorest district in London. Engels sent a five-pound note, and then another and another, and nearly lost his temper when Marx apologized for 'pressing' him.

In January 1863 their friendship survived the first and only strain to which it was submitted. Engels lost his wife. 'I simply cannot tell you how I feel', he wrote to Marx in a short note telling him the news. 'The poor girl loved me with all her heart.' [61] Marx wrote back: 'The news of Mary's death has both astonished and dismayed me. She was extremely good-natured, witty and very attached to you.' He then went straight on to describe his own desperate attempts to raise money. His letter ended with:

It is revoltingly egoistical of me to retail all these horrors to you at such a moment. But the thing is homeopathic. One evil cancels out another. At the end of my tether as I am, what am I to do? There is not a single human being in all London to whom I can speak freely, and at home I play the silent stoic, to counter-poise the outbreaks from the other side. Work under such circumstances is absolutely impossible. Instead of Mary should it not have been my mother, who is full of bodily infirmities and has lived her life? You see what strange notions we 'civilized' people get under the stress of certain circumstances. [62]

Engels was deeply hurt. He wrote to Marx that all his friends had shown him more sympathy and friendship than he could have expected on this occasion, which affected him deeply, and 'to you it seemed a suitable moment for the display of the superiority of your frigid way of thinking. So be it!' [63]

Marx allowed some time to elapse before replying. 'It was

very wrong of me to write that letter, and I regretted it as soon as it was sent', he wrote.

It was not prompted by heartlessness. My wife and children will confirm me when I say that your letter, which arrived early in the morning, affected me as much as the death of one of my own nearest and dearest. When I wrote to you the same evening it was under the stress of very desperate circumstances. The brokers had been put in by the landlord; I had a summons from the butcher; there was neither coal nor food in the house and little Jenny was ill in bed. The only way out of such circumstances that I know is, generally speaking, cynicism.[64]

Engels thanked his friend for his frankness. 'You will understand the impression your first letter made on me. I could not get it out of my head for a whole week. I could not forget it. Never mind, your last letter has made up for it, and I am glad that in losing Mary I have not at the same time lost my oldest and best friend.'[65]

During the course of the year Engels gave Marx £350, which was a great deal considering how bad his business was as a consequence of the cotton crisis. Marx's mother died at the end of November, and the legacy was not a large one. It mitigated at least the worst of Marx's distress. In May 1864 the faithful Wilhelm Wolff died in Manchester and left Marx £800. From September Engels, who had become a partner in his firm, was able to give him greater financial aid. From 1864 onwards Marx's financial position was tolerable and his freedom from petty cares enabled him to devote himself to his work. But his anxieties only really ended in 1869, when Engels sold his share in the cotton mill and was able to make Marx a definite, if moderate, yearly allowance.[66]

Das Kapital was born in the years of illness and poverty, when Marx was sometimes reduced to the point of starvation. He wrote it while harassed with cares, agonized by his children's distress, tormented by thoughts of the next day. But nothing could completely overwhelm him. From time to time Engels urged him to finish the work at last. He knew Marx's over-conscientiousness. But Marx went on pruning and filing, and keeping up to date with the latest literature on the subject. 'I cannot bring myself to send anything off until I have the whole before me', he wrote to Engels. 'My writings, whatever shortcomings they may have, have one characteristic: they form an artistic whole. In my opinion that is only obtainable by never letting anything be printed before I see the whole before my eyes.'[67]

The fair copy of the first volume was completed in March 1867. Marx, as he wrote to Becker, 'could throw it at the head of the bourgeoisie' at last.[68] Marx read the final proofs on 16 August. At two o'clock in the morning he wrote to Engels as follows: 'So this volume is finished. Thanks are due to no one but you for making it possible. Without your sacrifice for me it would be impossible to carry out the three volumes of this tremendous work. I embrace you, full of thanks. I greet you, my dear and faithful friend!'[69]

An edition of 1,000 copies of *Das Kapital* appeared in Hamburg at the beginning of September.[70]

In 1867 Marx wrote to Siegfried Meyer:

You must think very badly of me, the more so when I tell you that your letters not only gave me great pleasure but were also a real comfort to me during the painful period during which they came. Why did I not answer you? Because I was perpetually hovering at the brink of the grave. I therefore had to use every available moment to work, in order to finish my book, to which I sacrificed health, happiness and family. I hope this explanation will be sufficient. I laugh at the so-called 'practical' men and their wisdom. If one wants to be an ox, one can easily turn one's back on human suffering and look after one's own skin. But I should have regarded myself as really impractical had I died without finishing my book, at least in manuscript.[71]

Paul Lafargue says that Marx's favourite motto was 'travailler pour l'humanité', to work for humanity.

The twelve years from 1852 to 1864, from the dissolution of the Communist League to the foundation of the International, were filled with journalistic hack-work performed to keep body and soul together, and with poverty endured for the sake of his life-work.

Apart from his contacts with Chartists and Urquhartites, which were so slight that they hardly counted, Marx, who had been at the very centre of the furious political *mêlée* of the year of revolution, kept entirely aloof from political activity. His interests were devoted to foreign politics, the war, the Indian Mutiny, the Anglo–French campaign in China, the trade crisis, the internal state of France, the anti-slavery movement in America – events which he could only observe.[72] In the articles Marx wrote and the correspondence he conducted with Engels there is little reference to Germany, the land to which the communists had paid chief attention in 1847 and in which the Communist League had worked under Marx's leadership. Marx certainly did not ignore developments in Germany, but he followed them only incidentally. The revival of the German workers' movement was not his work. It happened without him. It happened against him, through Ferdinand Lassalle.

Lassalle was born in Breslau in 1825. He was the son of a Jewish businessman. He studied Hegelian philosophy in Berlin and adhered to it in its orthodox, idealistic form throughout his life. His political position after the middle of the 1840s was at the extreme left wing of democratic radicalism. He made friends with Marx and became a communist during his few weeks of freedom in 1848 – he was in prison until the middle of August and was re-arrested at the end of October for inciting to arms against the Crown. When he came out of prison the *Neue Rheinische Zeitung* was on its last legs. Marx and Lassalle did not meet again until the spring of 1861.[73]

They wrote to each other in the meantime. Lassalle was the more industrious correspondent of the two. He kept Marx informed of his literary labours – he wrote a portly philosophical tome as well as a play – consulted him on political questions, offered and gladly gave Marx financial help. It was thanks to his mediation that the *Critique* was able to appear. He was the only man in Germany who was loyal to Marx.

Marx had a high opinion of the younger man's energy and talents, though from the first he was repelled by his consuming ambition and his unbounded vanity. If no line remained of all Lassalle's writings except a letter of his dating from September 1845, it would suffice to explain the human gulf that parted him from Marx. At the age of twenty Lassalle wrote:

So far as I have power over human nature, I will use it unsparingly . . . I am the servant and master of ideas, priest of the god who is myself. I would be a player, a plastic artist, my whole being is the presence of my will, the expression of the meaning I put into it. The vibrant tone of my voice and the flashing light of my eye, every line of my face must reflect the imprint which I put upon it.[74]

Lassalle loved theatrical attitudinizing, which Marx detested from the bottom of his heart. He naïvely placed personalities as far before causes as Marx did the reverse, and was utterly careless about what means he chose to achieve his ends. He was a man who was ready to sacrifice everything for immediate success. From the first Marx did not completely trust him. The Cologne communists refused to admit Lassalle to the League. But Marx regarded Lassalle as a front-rank politician and agitator even after personal contact with him in 1861 and 1862 had enabled him to form a better opinion of the negative sides of his character than was possible from letters.

Marx visited Lassalle in Berlin in the spring of 1861. The Prince Regent of Prussia, the subsequent Emperor Wilhelm I, issued an amnesty which made it possible for exiles to return on certain conditions. Marx, who did not believe he would be able to hold out much longer in London, was thinking of returning to Germany. Lassalle proposed that Marx should collaborate with him in publishing a paper. Marx said to Engels that Lassalle might be very useful under strict supervision as a member of an editorial staff; otherwise he could only be harmful.[75] The plan, however, came to nothing. Marx's

attempt to re-acquire Prussian nationality, an essential preliminary to assure his being able to remain in Prussia, came
to nothing too. The police suspected him of republican or at
any rate of non-royalist views.

After the passing of the economic crisis in Germany a period
of prosperity set in. The consequence in the political field was
a revival of liberalism. The Progressive Party in the Chamber
opposed the Government more or less violently, and outside
it tried to win over the 'fourth estate' (the tactical resources
of the bourgeois revolution are very limited and always repeat
themselves). Workers' educational associations, founded by
democratic intellectuals, sprang up on every side. Life revived
in the workers' movement. Lassalle went to London in the
summer of 1862 and proposed to Marx that the two of them
together place themselves at the head of the new movement.

Marx refused, both on personal and political grounds. He
could not interrupt his work on economics. His personal dis-
taste for Lassalle had developed into a violent aversion. 'Lassalle is now set up not only as the greatest scholar, the most
profound thinker, the most brilliant of investigators, etc., but
also as a Don Juan and a revolutionary Cardinal Richelieu,
with his everlasting chatter, unnatural falsetto voice, his un-
beautiful demonstrative gestures and his didactic tone on top
of it all.' [76] That was how Marx wrote to Engels while Lassalle
was in London, and it was one of the mildest of his utterances.
The political and economic theoretical foundations that
Lassalle proposed for the new workers' party were completely
unacceptable to Marx. Lassalle's party was to start by demanding that the state should put capital at the disposal of
the workers to found cooperative societies. [77] Lassalle knew
very well that even if these cooperative societies materialized,
which was more than doubtful, they would at best create a
few enclaves within capitalist economy. Concentrating on the
cooperative movement meant weakening at the outset the
proletarian struggle which had only just begun. Marx foresaw
that Lassalle, 'like every man who believes he has a panacea
for the sufferings of the masses in his pocket, will give his

agitation the character of a religious sect'.[78] Lassalle put the Chartist demand for universal suffrage on his programme side by side with the demand for state aid. 'He overlooked the fact that conditions in Germany and England were entirely different', Marx later wrote. 'He overlooked the lessons of the *bas empire* concerning universal suffrage.'[79] In London Lassalle did not mention the over-cunning tactics he had prepared for leading the workers' movement and started to apply as soon as he returned to Germany.

Lassalle conducted his propaganda in speech and writing from 1862 until his early death in the late summer of 1864. His speeches were brilliant, his pamphlets magnificently written. He did in fact create a German workers' party. The General Union of German Workers was founded in May 1863. But before it started its existence Lassalle had started to negotiate with Bismarck.

The conflict between the Prime Minister of Prussia and the Progressive majority in the Chamber was becoming more and more acute. Anything or anybody likely to damage them was welcome to Bismark, even a socialist and Jewish agitator like Lassalle, for whom the Prussian *Junker* would otherwise not have had much use. Most of the workers who were at all politically awake adhered to the Progressives. Lassalle's first task was necessarily to part them from the bourgeoisie. That the liberal opposition would be temporarily weakened as a result was not of great importance. For once the workers' party was formed it would have to fight not only the liberal bourgeoisie but the incomparably more resolute militaristic monarchists. Bismark was aware of this. In making a compact with Lassalle he acted like a power coming to terms with a party which might be a power in the future, but for the time being was only a pawn on the chessboard next to other and more powerful pieces. Bismarck did not betray his class, but Lassalle nearly betrayed the workers' movement to Bismarck. How far Lassalle went with Bismarck Marx never knew as long as Lassalle lived, and even after his death he never learned the whole truth. It did not come to light until an old cupboard in the room of the Prime Minister of Prussia was opened in 1927. It contained the letters exchanged between Bismarck and Lassalle.[80] The Workers' Union was so organized that its president, who of course was Lassalle himself, ruled over it like a dictator. Lassalle was justified in calling it his 'kingdom'. He was able to show Bismarck how gladly the workers subjected themselves to a dictatorship when they saw that it was working in their interests, and even how readily they would be to honour the King as the socialist dictator. Lassalle believed in *Realpolitik*, which meant, in Marx's words, that he only admitted as real what was immediately in front of his nose. In this case what was in front of his nose was the goodwill of the Government in its fight with the Progressives about the independent workers' party. The workers were to start establishing their independence by renouncing it to the party of reaction. Lassalle was on the point of turning the General Union of German Workers into a small auxiliary corps of feudal reaction against the bourgeoisie. Even his state aid slogan prompted him to seek Bismarck's friendship. Lassalle told the workers that if only the state helped, the cooperative societies could be formed at once. That state was the existing state, the Prussian monarchy. Lassalle, by limiting the proletarian struggle to one small aim, was bound to compromise with the rulers of Prussia, for it was they and not some power in the dim and distant future who were to help.

It was impossible for Marx in London to know how deeply Lassalle was involved with Bismarck. Lassalle believed he could outmanoeuvre Bismarck, but was in fact outmanoeuvred by him. Lassalle sought Bismarck's help – only temporarily, of course, for as long as he should need it against the Progressives, after which, when it was no more needed, he would free himself from this powerful patron. But in fact his strange alliance only resulted in his increasingly becoming Bismarck's tool. Marx could not possibly know the full extent of Lassalle's deviation. Nevertheless he followed Lassalle's agitation with the most extreme suspicion. It became clear that he would have to oppose the fatal tendencies of the new movement. Marx broke off personal relations with Lassalle in 1862. Lassalle still sent Marx his pamphlets, but without a line of greeting. Marx found nothing in them but unskilful plagiarism of the Communist Manifesto and his later works, which Lassalle knew very well.[81] Marx never replied.

In spite of all his deficiencies and mistakes, his compromises and his manoeuvres, in spite of his dictatorial attitude, which was fundamentally inimical to the workers' movement, in spite of the limitations of his economic insight, Lassalle has the immortal merit of having revived the workers' movement in Germany.[82] The creed of Lassalle remained that of a sect. After some vacillations and hesitations the German proletariat followed another route than that which Lassalle showed them.

On 30 August 1864 Lassalle was killed in a non-political duel. Four weeks later the International Working Men's Association was founded in London.

[17]

The International Working Men's Association[1]

IN the long years of exile Marx had so consistently declined to associate himself with any sort of political organization that he felt that the change of attitude indicated by the appearance of his name on the list of founders of a new international workers' organization in the autumn of 1864 required an explanation to his friends and sympathizers. On 29 November 1864 he wrote to his old friend Weydemeyer that he had consented 'because it is an affair in which it is possible to do important work'.[2] The initiative for the formation of the new organization had come from men who were leaders of really active mass organizations. That was the factor that distinguished it from its predecessors, and it was the decisive factor in causing Marx to abandon his customary aloofness. He saw its negative sides plainly enough. He was only too well aware of its heterogeneous nature and the wavering and unclear political views of many of those who were at the back of it. Nevertheless he joined it. 'I knew that this time real "forces" were at work both on the London and the Paris sides', he explained to Engels on 4 November, 'and that was the reason why I decided to depart from my otherwise inflexible rule to decline any such invitations.'[3] Engels approved of both Marx's decision and Marx's reasons. It was necessary, he said, to be guided by the 'real circumstances'. To accept contact with the active leaders of a real movement was their duty. 'It is good that we should once more be coming into contact with people who at least represent their class. After all, that is the main thing in the end', he wrote.[4]

It was indeed the main thing. The immediate future demonstrated what a huge sphere of activity the new organization opened up for Marx. The new organization was the 'International Working Men's Association', which was so soon destined to become famous and is known today as the First International. A new epoch in the history of the workers' movement and in Marx's life began with its foundation. The 'sleepless night of exile' was over, and with it the loneliness and isolation from active, practical life. Marx became once more, for the second time in his life, the organizer of the political struggle of the working class.

At the beginning of the 1860s there was an upsurge of the workers' movement not only in Germany, as has already been mentioned, but also in England and in France, the two countries which took the chief part in the formation of the International Working Men's Association. After a decade of apathy and paralysis, in which the active struggle of the proletariat was practically at a standstill, the workers once more took up the weapon of the strike and showed a new tendency to organize. The workers in France had different traditions and fought under different conditions from those of the workers in England, and their principles and practice necessarily differed, but on both sides of the Channel they sooner or later realized that without independent organizations of their own they must necessarily remain impotent. Even if theoretical clarity were sometimes wanting, experience in the end compelled it.

French and English very soon saw that it would be necessary to get together. There were two outstanding reasons for this. The strike movement, which assumed particularly large dimensions in England, demanded a close *entente cordiale* with the workers of the other country, from which the employers attempted to import strike breakers. In addition there arose at this time a whole series of international questions in which French and English workers must make common cause.

The first contacts between English and French workers were made in 1862. The great World Exhibition took place in London in that year. It was visited by a delegation of French workers. The idea of this visit arose in Bonapartist circles which nourished a 'Caesarian socialism' of their own and aimed at propitiating the workers with the Empire. They had the support of the Emperor's cousin, Prince Napoleon, the so-called 'Plon-Plon', who saw to it that the workers were allowed to form their own organizations in the factories to elect their delegates and raise funds to finance the journey. Such a 'legal opportunity' had of course to be exploited. Among those who took part in the electoral campaign and were elected to the delegation were men who had inaugurated an independent workers' movement in France. Many other delegates were inevitably Bonapartists to a greater or less degree, but the representatives of the most active English workers' associations were not represented on the London committee formed to welcome the French delegation. The London committee owed its formation to moderate Liberal Members of Parliament and equally moderate men of the cooperative movement – people who represented the extreme right wing of the workers' movement and took their stand on the principle of class peace, with which the speeches made at the meeting of welcome on 5 August 1862 were in entire conformity. The English speakers declared that 'good understanding between our employers and ourselves is the only way to smooth out the difficulties by which we are at present surrounded'.[5]

The meeting was really tame, with unctuous speeches and love, friendship and fraternal kisses. Festival of harmony though it was, with it the history of the 'Red International' begins. Apart from the beautiful ceremonies, the independent French delegates met the young English trade union leaders, entirely unfêted, and sowed the first seeds of the Anglo–French workers' alliance, the fruits of which manifested themselves in the following year.

The old sympathy for Poland and the old hatred of Russian absolutism were still alive in England and France. Both drew fresh strength from the Polish rising of 1863. The workers in both countries demanded intervention on Poland's behalf. Petitions to Napoleon bore hundreds of signatures, and a huge workers' meeting in England sent a deputation to the Prime Mnister. The French Emperor declined to receive the workers, but Prince Napoleon gave them to understand that France would like to intervene, in fact it would prefer to do so today rather than tomorrow, but unfortunately action was hampered by English sabotage. On the English side Palmerston deplored the impossibility of stepping in on Poland's behalf, however much he would have liked to have done so, because France, unfortunately, insisted on standing aside. Then there arose a plan for a joint Anglo–French pro-Polish demonstration. It took place in London on 22 July 1863. A special delegation came from Paris, and this time it consisted exclusively of adherents of the independent workers' movement. The demonstration failed in its purpose, if for no other reason than that by this time the Polish rising was on the verge of collapse. But before the French delegates left England a decision had been made which was destined to be of great historical importance. They and the representatives of the English workers agreed in principle to the foundation of an international association of workers and elected a committee to do the work preparatory to an inaugural meeting. The preliminaries dragged on for more than a year, 'addresses' were exchanged about the duties of the future association, manifestoes were drafted, and finally the inaugural meeting took place in St Martin's Hall, Long Acre, on 28 September 1864.

Marx took no part in the preliminary work. He read about the meeting of 22 July 1863 in the newspapers, followed the course of the Polish rising with passionate interest, became indignant at the attitude of British diplomacy, and was considering writing a pamphlet on the Polish question.[6] The Anglo–French workers' demonstration could not possibly have escaped his notice. But he had no direct contact with the organizers of the meeting and knew nothing of the preparatory work that was quietly going on. He only heard of the organizers' plans a week before the inaugural meeting. A young French exile, Le Lubez, a republican, was the contact man between the French workers and the English trade unionists, and he told Marx who were at the back of the movement and what their intentions were and invited him to take part in the meeting as the representative of the German workers. Marx recognized that this was a serious undertaking and accepted the invitation. Marx suggested his friend Eccarius, an old member of the Communist League, as spokesman for the Germans and he himself 'assisted as a silent figure on the platform'.

The meeting was a complete success. The big hall was filled to the point of suffocation. Speeches were made by Frenchmen, Englishmen, Italians and Irish. A unanimous resolution was passed to found an International Working Men's Association, with headquarters in London, and a committee was elected to draft the programme and statutes. Marx was elected a member of this committee.

The committee was far too big. It had fifty-five members, of whom twenty-seven were English. These were mainly trade union leaders. Of the rest the French and Germans had nine representatives each, and the Italians, the Swiss and the Poles two each. The majority of the non-English members were *émigrés*. Politically the committee was heterogeneous, including old Chartists and Owenites, Blanquists and followers of Proudhon, Polish democrats and adherents of Mazzini. Its social composition, however, was far more uniform. Workers formed the preponderating majority.

In these circumstances it was not very easy to agree on the fundamental aims of the association, its programme and its statutes.[7] Marx was unable to take part in the committee meetings during the first few weeks, partly because he was ill, partly for the simple reason that the invitations never reached him. In the meantime the committee asked Weston, an old Owenite, to draw up a draft programme, a task to which he devoted himself with the most righteous zeal, pondering over each sentence for weeks at a time. The task of translating the statutes of the Italian workers' association, which it was intended to make the basis of the associations' own statutes, devolved upon Major Wolff, Mazzini's secretary. When the two finally laid the fruit of their labours before the committee, its inadequacy was patent even to the least exacting. Weston's exposition, in Marx's opinion and everybody else's too, was 'full of the most extreme confusion and unspeakably verbose'. His suggested statutes were more impossible still. Mazzini repudiated the class struggle and believed in solving the problems of modern industrial society with sentimental phrases of the kind that had been the fashion in the 1830s. The old carbonaro, who had been the leader of the movement for national liberation in Italy for generations, placed the national question above all else and could conceive of no method of organization other than that of the carbonari. The Italian workers' organizations which adhered to him were nothing but benefit societies founded to help in the national struggle. Apart from its other shortcomings, the Italian draft was rendered impossible by the fact that, in Marx's words, 'it aimed at something quite impossible, a kind of central government of the European working class (of course with Mazzini in the background)'. The committee gave both drafts to Le Lubez to revise. The result was, if possible, worse than ever. Le Lubez presented his text at a committee meeting on 18 October, the first that Marx attended. Marx, as he wrote to Engels, 'was really shocked as he listened to good Le Lubez's frightfully phrased, badly written and entirely ill-considered preamble, pretending to be a declaration of principles, with Mazzini peeping out through every word, and encrusted as it was with vague scraps of French socialism'. Marx made 'gentle' opposition and succeeded in having Le Lubez's draft passed to a sub-committee to be revised again.

Marx now got to work himself. He summed up the sub-committee's duties in his own characteristic way. It was decided 'if possible not to leave a single line of the thing standing'. The sub-committee left him a free hand. In place of the declaration of principles Marx wrote an 'Address to the Working Classes'.[8] The only thing it had in common with the draft was the title of 'statutes'. 'It is very difficult', he wrote to Engels, 'to manage the thing in such a way as to make our views appear in a form which make them acceptable to the workers' movement at its present standpoint. Time is required to give the re-awakened movement its old boldness of speech. *Fortiter in re, suaviter in modo* is what is required.'

The sub-committee accepted Marx's proposals, and only added a few moralizing phrases. These were so placed 'that they could not do any harm'. The 'inaugural address' was unanimously and enthusiastically accepted at a meeting of the general committee. The 'International' had its constitution, and now it started its work.

The fundamental idea of the inaugural address and of the statutes was expressed in the phrase: 'The emancipation of the working class must be the work of the working class itself.' The International served this aim by founding proletarian mass organizations and uniting them in joint activity. Point 1 of the statutes said: 'This association was founded in order to create a central means of unity and cooperation between the associations of workers which already exist in the various countries and aim at the same goal, namely, the protection, the rise and the complete emancipation of the working class.' The International left complete freedom to its various national sections as to the form their organization might take, and refrained from prescribing any definite methods of conducting the struggle. Only one thing did it rigorously insist on. That was the absolute independence of the member organizations. The inaugural address also demonstrated from the experience of the English workers that the 'capture of political power has become the great duty of the working class'.

The inaugural address and the statutes are typical of the work Marx did for the International in the five following years. Marx saw it to be his duty to educate the masses, and gradually and carefully, but firmly and surely lead them towards a definite goal. The groundwork of all his labour was a profound belief in the sound instinct of the proletarian mass movement. Bitter experience in the years of revolution and still more in the years of exile had convinced him that it was necessary to keep aloof from all intermediary groups, especially organizations of exiles. He had also become convinced that great workers' organizations, able to develop freely within their own country, associated with the class movement as a whole, would find the right way in the end, however much they might vacillate and go astray. The inaugural address and the statutes and Marx's work in the International were founded on the sound instinct of the proletarian movement. The task that Marx set before his eyes was to help it, bring it to awareness and theoretical comprehension of that which it must do and of the experiences through which it must pass.

As Marx said, his old ultra-left-wing opponents in the 1840s had made the same error as Proudhon, the error into which Lassalle also fell. They did not seek, in Marx's words, 'the right basis for agitation in real conditions, but wanted to prescribe the course of the letter by certain doctrinal recipes'.[9] Marx sought its basis in the forms of the movement which life itself created. He avoided giving prescriptions. That does not of course mean that he let things take their own course. What he did rather was to help every movement to get clear about itself, to come to an understanding of the connections between its particular interests and the whole, of how its special aims could only be realized by the realization of the demands of the whole class, by the complete emancipation of the proletariat. An excellent example of Marx's tactics in the International was the way the inaugural address dealt with the cooperative societies. The cooperative movement was important at the time, and its influence was not always to the advantage of the workers' movement as a whole. The idea of independent cooperation was not seldom substituted for the idea of the class struggle. Protection of the workers, the trade-union struggle, and even the downfall of capitalist society seemed superfluous, if not actually noxious to many, who believed the cooperative movement capable of emancipating the working class. Marx did not attack the cooperative societies outright. By so doing he would have alienated from the International the groups of workers who adhered to the cooperative ideal. He said that the value of the great social experiment represented by the cooperative movement could not be overestimated. The cooperatives, particularly the cooperative factories, had demonstrated that large-scale production, production in harmony with modern scientific developments, was possible without the existence of a class of entrepreneurs employing a class of 'hands'. The cooperative societies represented a victory of the political economy of the working class over the political economy of ownership. But experience had also demonstrated that, in spite of the excellence of their principles and their usefulness in practice, the cooperative societies were confronted with limits which they could not overstep. The cooperative movement, to save the working masses, must be developed on a national scale and consequently be promoted by national measures. Thus the adherent of the cooperative ideal was forced to the conclusion that he who wanted cooperative enterprise must necessarily desire the capture of political power by the working class.

The fundamental idea of the inaugural address and of the whole of Marx's activity in the International was that the workers, acting on the basis of 'real conditions', which of course differed in every single country, must create independent parties, take part in the political and social life of their country and so make the proletariat ripe for the capture of political power.

In the General Council, as the committee elected at the inaugural meeting soon came to be called, Marx was the acknowledged leader. The work to be done was more than ample. The magnitude of the need that the International fulfilled and the timeliness of its foundation were proved by its extraordinarily rapid growth. On 23 February 1865 Marx wrote to Kugelmann that the success of the International in London, Paris, Belgium, Switzerland and Italy had exceeded all expectations.[10] On 4 March he wrote to Engels[11] that the organization was in touch with twenty-five towns in France, and on 15 April – six months after the meeting in St Martin's Hall – he wrote to one of the leaders of the Belgian section that there were more than 12,000 members in England.[12] Inquiries, suggestions, requests showered in upon the General Council from all sides. News of new sections being formed poured in. All sorts of questions concerning matters of organization, inevitable in the case of any big new body, continually cropped up. 'The French, particularly the Paris workers, regard the London Council as a regular workers' government for foreign affairs', Marx wrote to Engels at the beginning of March 1865.[13] The General Council, and in most cases that meant Marx, had to give instructions and advice and answer inquiries and incessantly take up positions towards political and economic events. Marx complained to Engels in the middle of March 1865 that the International took up an enormous amount of his time, because he was in effect the head of the whole affair.[14] He gave an example of how he had recently been occupied. On 28 February he had had a meeting with the Frenchmen, Tolain and Fribourg, who had come from Paris. The meeting, which lasted till twelve o'clock at night, was in conjunction with an evening meeting, at which he had to sign 200 membership cards. On 1 March there was a Polish meeting. On 4 March a meeting of the sub-committee dealing with the French question lasted till one o'clock in the morning; on 6 March another meeting also lasted till one o'clock in the morning; on 7 March a meeting of the General Council lasted till midnight. 'Well, *mon cher, que faire?*' Marx wrote. 'If you have said "A" it follows that you go on and say "B".'[15] Marx often grumbled, but never missed a meeting of the General Council. If at first it had seemed that the pressure of work was only going to be so great at the beginning, the belief soon turned out to be illusory. It very soon became clear that the demands the International made on Marx were going to increase with every month. One question gave rise to two others. It was inevitable and right that it should be so. The International developed, not according to a system, but according to the inner logic of the movement, according to the 'real conditions'.

In the case of internal questions within the organization Marx declined to exercise pressure, and he insisted that the General Council adopt a strictly above-party attitude in all disputes between the various groups. 'Whom they have for a leader is their business and not mine,' he said on the occasion of an internal German dispute in 1868.[16] At the beginning of 1865, when violent disputes arose between a group of workers led by Tolain and Fribourg, who took their stand by Proudhon, and another led by Lefort and Le Lubez, who were republicans and socialists, Marx made every effort to compose the dispute and keep both parties in the International.[17]

The International had no programme if by 'programme' is meant a single, concrete, detailed system. Marx had intentionally made the statutes so wide as to make it possible for all socialist groups to join. An announcement in the spring of 1870 declared that it was not the duty of the General Council to express a theoretical opinion on the programme of individual sections. Its only duty was to see that they contained nothing inconsistent with the letter and the spirit of the statutes.[18] Marx, in his pamphlet on the apparent rifts in the International written in 1872, again emphasized that the International admitted to its organs and its congresses all of socialist views without any exceptions whatever.[19]

It must not be concluded that Marx's toleration of all the political lines of thought represented in the International meant that he abandoned his own critical attitude. His letters, especially those to Engels, contain the severest judgements on the confused mentalities with whom he had to deal. The illness from which he suffered during the first few years that followed the foundation of the International did nothing to make his mood milder; and in fact a good many of the things the sections did were more than a little trying. What is remarkable is not that Marx grumbled to his friends about the Proudhonists and the rest but the consistency and pertinacity with which he maintained his attitude and the restraint with which he tolerated all the conflicts that were bound to arise in the young movement. It was not infrequent for him actually to defend a group on some internal matter whose programme, if what they stood for can be dignified with such an expression, he contemptuously dismissed in private letters.

Tolerant as Marx was towards the various undercurrents

within the workers' movement, he resolutely fought all attempts to anchor the International to the programme of any single group or take away its character as a class movement. It was on the latter question that the first conflict arose. Mazzini's followers demanded the deletion from the inaugural address and the statutes of certain passages which emphasized the class character of the International. The General Council emphatically refused. The Italian Workers' Union in London, which had been founded and set going by followers of Mazzini, broke with its 'fathers'. This was the first victory of the 'Internationalists' in their long struggle with Mazzini. An echo of it is the judgement of Marx made by Mazzini years later. 'Marx', he said, 'a German, a man of penetrating but corrupting intelligence, imperious, jealous of the influence of others, lacking strong philosophic or religious convictions, has, I fear, more hatred, if righteous hatred, in his heart than love.'[20]

The struggle with the followers of Mazzini was but a small prelude to the far more important struggle between Proudhonists and collectivists which filled the whole first period of the International up to 1869.

During the first years of the International its main support came from English and French workers' organizations. There was a fundamental difference in the nature and political outlook of the two.

England was economically the most advanced country in the world. Big industry had developed more rapidly in England than anywhere else, and for this reason class contradictions were pronounced and the workers' movement on a relatively high level. The workers were able users of the weapon of the strike. Just at the time when the International arose one wave of strikes after another swept across the country. At the beginning of the 1860s flourishing trade unions developed from the benefit societies they had hitherto mainly been into fighting organizations raising their own strike funds. They constituted the most important group within the International. The number of organizations formally associated with the International was not large. Even the London Trades Council, one of the most resolute bodies in the trade union movement, did not accept the International's invitation to join. But some trade unions did join the International and were on its membership list. From the beginning British trade union leaders had an important voice on the General Council. Interested in immediate, practical results, they were utterly indifferent to theoretical questions and the ultimate aims of the International as Marx conceived them. They understood very well the importance of working-class legislation, upon which, under Marx's influence, the International laid great stress. But they preferred conducting the struggle for it, like the struggle for electoral reform, through the channel of Liberal and Radical Members of Parliament rather than as an independent party. Among them there were always a few who insisted that the movement must not assume an explicit class character. But so far as the day-to-day struggle of the proletariat was concerned the young English trade union leaders had incomparably more experience than all the workers' leaders of the Continent combined. The main thing that interested them in the International was the possibility of using it for gaining victories in strikes. They were attracted by the possibility of making the International use its connections with countries abroad to prevent the introduction of foreign strike breakers, which was a favourite expedient of the employers at the time. Fribourg, one of the founders of the International, said that the English regarded the International purely as an organization from which the strike movement could receive great assistance.[21]

France was far behind England in the industrial respect. In France the handicraftsman was still supreme, particularly in Paris, with its art and luxury trades. It was natural enough that many of the leaders of the movement in France should be followers of Proudhon, whose teaching expressed the interests of the small independent artisan or trader, the small businessman and the peasant. The 'mutualists', as the followers of Proudhon described themselves at the time, demanded cheap credit, assured markets, cooperative societies, and the same measures that hard-pressed master-craftsmen have always demanded everywhere. To most of them the slogan of the collectivization of the means of production sounded absurd, unjust and evil. Hence also they were in favour of peaceful, gradual development, and they flatly repudiated revolutionary methods. From his point of view Fribourg regarded the International as an instrument 'for aiding the proletariat in legally, pacifically and morally gaining the place in the sun of civilization to which it is entitled'.[22] They had very little trust in legislation or state measures for the working classes, and they regarded strikes as extremely dangerous, though sometimes inevitable; in any case as always undesirable. Varlin, one of the leaders of the International in Paris who fell in the bloody week of May 1871, declared as late as 1868 that the International repudiated strikes as an anti-economic weapon.[23] The mutualists wanted an International which should occupy itself with investigating the position of the workers, cause alterations in the labour market and thrash out these problems theoretically.

Marx saw the weaknesses of the mutualists and of the English trade unions alike.[24] He did not have a particularly high opinion of the trade union leaders. He said later that he regarded some of them with suspicion from the first, as careerists in whose devotion to the working-class cause he found it difficult to believe. But in relation to the immediate tasks of the International, the tactics of the day-to-day struggle, he stood far nearer the Englishmen than the Proudhonists. 'The gentlemen in Paris', he wrote to Kugelmann in 1866, 'had their heads full of Proudhon's emptiest phrases. They chatter of science, knowing nothing of it. They scorn all revolutionary action, i.e. which springs from the class struggle itself, all concentrated social movement, that is to say movement realizable by political means (for example, the legal shortening of the working day).'[25]

In spite of all his dislike of Proudhonist phraseology, Marx stuck to his tactics. In drafting the agenda for the first congress of the International in 1866[26] he took pains to avoid anything that might have given rise to general theoretical discussions, and he confined the programme 'to points which permitted of immediate accord and immediate concerted action of the workers, corresponded directly to the needs of the class struggle and the class organization of the workers, and at the same time spurred the workers on.'[27] The strike question was certainly a question of the moment, but Marx did not put it upon the agenda as such but in the form of 'international assistance for the struggle of Labour with Capital'.[28] He wished to avoid alienating the Proudhonists. He instructed the London delegates not to discuss the usefulness or the reverse of strikes but to put in the foreground the struggle with the strike breakers, which the Proudhonists could not repudiate.

It was not Marx and his followers but the Proudhonists who opened the fray. The Proudhonists wanted to anchor the International to their own system. The most important thing to them was not those things on which all were agreed but their own particular hobby-horse, their 'mutualism'. The first congresses took place in Latin Switzerland, for which reason the majority of the delegates came from western Switzerland and adjacent France, i.e. from the areas where the Proudhonists predominated. At the Lausanne congress of 1867 they were fairly successful.[29] The representatives of the General Council were not sufficiently prepared – Marx was busy at the time with the publication of *Das Kapital* and was not present. But their success was their own downfall. At a time when the strike movement was constantly extending and affecting even France and western Switzerland, the rejection of the strike weapon was going too far even for many of the Proudhonists. There was a rift, which soon spread to other questions too.

The Proudhonists were the first to bring up for discussion the fundamental question of the socialization of the means of production. At the congress of 1867 they raised the question of the socialization of the means of transport. At the time the railways were using their monopoly to favour big industry at the expense of the small producer. So the principal opponents of collectivization decided that an exception must be made in the case of the railways, which must be collectivized. Very well, their opponents replied, why stop at collectivization of the means of transport? To their horror and alarm the Proudhonists saw opponents rising within their own ranks. Young heretics, led by César de Paepe, a Belgian, arose among the orthodox and tried hard to reconcile their mutualist doctrines with the ideal of collectivization. This breakdown on the part of the Proudhonists assured the success of the collectivist idea in the International. The young Proudhonists became more enthusiastic about collectivization than anyone, and it was thanks to them that the International came out for collectivism in its official resolutions. In 1868 Marx was still opposed to declarations of principle on such critical questions. 'It is better not to make any general resolutions', he wrote to his closest colleagues, Eccarius and Lessner, who represented the General Council at the congress of 1868.[30] It was only in the last stages of the debates on collectivization that Marx intervened. He drafted the resolutions on the nationalization of the soil which were accepted by the Basle congress of 1869.[31]

Marx, who in other respects demonstrated the most extreme tolerance, only abandoned his restraint when the problem of political struggle arose acutely within the International and he began to feel that, unknown to it, something had formed behind the scenes, something that aimed quite systematically at forcing the International in a direction which was completely unacceptable to him and, after the experiences he had had, he was convinced would be injurious to the workers' movement.

Everybody in the International had been agreed from the start that the workers must take an active part in the political struggle. The English trade unionists naturally supported the movement for the extension of the franchise in every way they could. Those Proudhonists who had cooperated in the foundation of the International were all in favour of taking part in the political struggle, and would have regarded any discussion of the advisability of doing so as a sheer waste of time. Their leading Paris group had originated out of an attempt to set up an independent workers' candidate in 1864, and Proudhon himself had given his enthusiastic consent to this step in his work, written shortly before his death, *De la capacité politique des classes ouvrières.*[32] The German workers' movement – though it had played no great role in the inner life of the International it had a notable influence upon the development of its ideas – fought, as Lassalle had taught it, for universal suffrage. Even the Swiss 'Internationalists' took part in the elections as a matter of course. The Lausanne congress of 1867 passed a resolution – the minority was only two – to the effect that the conquest of political power was an absolute necessity for the working class. This was the congress at which the Proudhonists were in a majority, and among those who voted for the resolution were many who were later among the most resolute opponents of any political activity whatever.

The situation altered pretty quickly. In 1867 and 1868 the International made extraordinary progress. The economic crisis which was setting in intensified social antagonisms, and one strike after another broke out in the countries of Western Europe. The International very soon proved a useful instrument in the direct economic struggle of the proletariat. It succeeded in many cases in preventing the introduction of strike breakers from abroad, and, in cases where foreign workers did strike-breaking work without knowing it, succeeded in causing them to practise solidarity. In other cases it organized the raising of funds for the relief of strikers. This not only gave the latter moral support but caused real panic among the employers, who no longer had to deal with 'their own' workers alone but with a new and sinister power, an international organization which apparently had resources at its disposal with which the individual employer could not compete. Often the mere rumour that the International was going to intervene in a strike was sufficient to cause the employers to grant all the workers' demands. In its panic the reactionary Press exaggerated the power of the International beyond all bounds, but this only resulted in enhancing the respect in which it was held by the working class. Every strike, whether it succeeded or not, resulted in all the strikers joining the International, the Conservative, E. Villetard, wrote in 1872 in his *History of the International*. In those years it often happened that the whole of the workers at a factory would join the International together. No government repressive measures, arrests or trials succeeded in stemming the movement's advance; they merely served to drive the workers into the revolutionary camp and strengthen the International thereby. Its sections seemed to spring up like mushrooms. At the 1866 congress only four countries were represented – England, France, Germany and Switzerland – but at the congress of 1869 there were nine, America, Austria, Belgium, Spain and Italy being the newcomers. Individual sections had arisen in Hungary, Holland, Algiers, South America and elsewhere. Because of big fluctuations and the weak development on the organizational side it is difficult to establish how many members the International really had. 800,000 workers were formally associated with the International in any case. At the International trial in Paris the public prosecutor, who had access to the papers of the French section, stated that there were 443,000 members in France alone. At the Basle congress of 1869 the English claimed 230 sections with 95,000 members. In Belgium in the summer of that year there were more than 200 sections with 64,000 members.[33] The membership of the workers' organizations which declared their solidarity with the International was greater by far. The International was recognized in 1869 by the English Trades Union Congress, in 1869 by the Nuremberg congress of German Workers' Educational Unions, in 1868 by the Association of German Workers' Unions in Austria, in the same year by the Neuchâtel congress of German Workers' Educational Unions in Switzerland, in 1869 by the American Labour Union, etc.[34] Testut, who wrote his history of the International on the basis of police reports, estimated its number of members as five million, and the newspapers of the International actually put the figure as high as seven million. These figures are, of course, utterly fantastic. But the élite of the European proletariat adhered to the International.

In the last third of the 1860s it had become a power to be reckoned with.

At the same time political questions developed from theoretical propositions to be discussed at congresses into practical questions requiring a practical answer. The two groups within the German workers' movement, the followers of Lassalle and the 'Eisenacher', were the first to take part, in 1867, in the North German parliamentary elections. In 1867 and 1868, after the extension of the suffrage to workers having a house of their own, the English labour movement prepared to enter the electoral fray. In 1869 the French workers set up their own candidates in many places. The International now had to decide what attitude to take up to other parties, and to elections. The weak organization of the sections and the political inexperience of their leaders made mistakes and differences of opinion inevitable as soon as the question of voting became an actual one, and this lead to a reaction. A section arose who opposed participating in elections and 'politics' as a whole.

In Latin Switzerland the Internationalists made particularly grave mistakes. The pioneer of the International there was Dr P. Coullery, an old democrat who had long been interested in social problems. He was an official of the Radical Party, had a high reputation, and represented it as deputy to the cantonal legislative council. Dr Coullery founded the first section of the International in Latin Switzerland in 1865, and worked for the extension of the International in the western cantons, and in 1867 his paper, *La Voix de l'Avenir*, became the chief organ of the section of that area. His activity on behalf of the International led to a rupture with the radicals. When he became a candidate for the office of *juge de paix* in La Chaux des Fonds the radicals opposed him. That induced the conservatives to vote for Coullery, and it was due to their aid that he was elected. By the election of 1868 Coullery's *rapprochement* to the conservatives had proceeded so far that he actually made a regular pact with them. The local Press called it 'la coalition aristo-socialiste'. The list of candidates went under the name of the International, but on it the names of

members of the International were next to those of extreme
conservatives. Other sections of the International in western
Switzerland protested violently against this policy, particularly the section at Locle. Its founder and leader was a young
schoolmaster, James Guillaume, who was later a very prominent member of the anti-Marxist group in the International.[35]
He was a former member of the Radical Party, and he and his
group, which had started as the 'Jeunesse radicale', continued
to support the radicals in local questions. The slogan in the
fight against Coullery was: 'The International keeps out of
political strife'; which in this case was equivalent to support of
the radicals. Gradually the Locle group generalized their views
and ended by absolutely repudiating the policy of participating
in elections. Coullery, it maintained, was bound to err, to compromise the International, as was anybody who participated
in elections. Coullery's tactics had, of course, nothing whatever in common with the tactical line of Marx. Marx always
vigorously opposed any coalition of the revolutionary proletariat with the reactionaries against the bourgeois democrats.
When Lassalle's followers started openly practising this
policy, which Lassalle himself initiated, Marx publicly and
ruthlessly broke with them. What Marx demanded of the
workers' parties was that they should criticize the Government and the reactionaries no less severely than they did the
bourgeois democrats.

The Locle group of 'Internationalists' formed the kernel of
the later anti-authoritative faction, whose struggle against the
General Council led to the split and the downfall of the International. Its leader was Michael Alexandrovich Bakunin.

[18]

Michael Bakunin[1]

BAKUNIN was born in 1814 in the Government of Tver. He was the son of a prosperous and noble landed proprietor. He became an officer but soon left the Army and in 1840, being an enthusiastic Hegelian, went to Germany to study philosophy at Berlin University. His teachers were partly the same as Marx's. Bakunin entered the left-wing Hegelian group and it was not long before he was in the thick of the revolutionary movement. His bold and open opposition to Russian absolutism attracted universal attention, and Europe heard the voice of a Russian revolutionary for the first time. In 1848 Bakunin was a close associate of Herwegh's and he shared the poet's visionary dream of a European revolutionary army which should set forth against the realm of the Tsars. During the years of revolution he went from place to place in Germany, always on the look-out for an opportunity of carrying the agitation into Russia and the other Slavonic countries. He was in contact with the leaders of the German democratic movement, founded a Russian–Polish revolutionary committee, and prepared a rising in Bohemia. But not one of his numerous plans bore fruit. He participated in the rising in Dresden in May 1849 more in a mood of desperation than of faith in victory. He was arrested and sentenced to death by a Saxon court. The Austrians, to whom he was handed over, sentenced him to death a second time, and he spent months in chains in the condemned cell. Then the Austrian hangmen handed him over to the gaolers of Russia, who kept him for five years in solitary confinement, first in the fortress of Petropavlovsk, then in the Schlüsselburg. His treatment was unspeakably dreadful. He contracted scurvy, lost all his teeth, and was only amnestied and banished to Siberia after writing a humiliating petition to the Tsar. At last, after five years, there came an opportunity to escape, and he returned to Western Europe by way of Japan and America.

His first meeting with Marx was at an international democratic banquet in Paris in March 1844, but the two had heard of each other before.[2] They had a good deal in common. Both had become revolutionaries by way of Hegelian philosophy and both had trodden the path from theory to revolutionary practice. But they differed entirely in their idea of revolutionary practice; in fact in their whole conception of the revolution they were poles asunder. In Marx's eyes the revolution was the midwife of the new society which had formed in the womb of the old. The new society would be the outcome of the old, and a new and higher culture would be the heir of the old culture, preserving and developing all the past attainments of humanity. For Bakunin the revolution meant a radical annihilation of existing society. What were all its so-called attainments but a chain by which free humanity was held in bondage? For him the revolution, if it did not mean making a clean sweep of the whole of this accursed civilization, meant nothing at all. Not one stone of it should remain upon another. Bakunin dreamed of a 'gigantic bonfire of London, Paris and Berlin'. His was the same hatred as that which drove insurrectionary peasants to burn down castles and cities – not just the hated prison and tax office but everything without exception, including schools and libraries and museums. Mankind must return, not just to the Middle Ages, but to the very beginning, and from there the history of man must start again. Weitling and Willich, with whom Bakunin was acquainted, had similar ideas, but compared to the master of complete and absolute negation they were but pitiful and harmless pupils.

It was evident that in these circumstances it was impossible for Marx and Bakunin to come very close to one another. Bakunin appreciated Marx's clear and penetrating intellect, but flatly repudiated his political activity. At the beginning of 1848, when he met Marx in Brussels, he said to a friend that Marx was spoiling the workers by turning them into *raisonneurs*. Marx was giving his lectures on wage-labour and capital at the time, summarizing the results of his investigations into the structure of capitalist society. Bakunin was convinced that this could have but one consequence; theorizing was bound to paralyse the workers' revolutionary will, their 'spirit of destruction', which for him was the only 'creative spirit'.[3] Marx never had the slightest sympathy for such incendiary fantasies. He had a fundamental mistrust of preaching such as his, and he could not help mistrusting Bakunin personally. Marx printed a letter in the *Neue Rheinische Zeitung* which accused Bakunin of being in the pay of the Russian Government. The letter had been sent him by Polish democrats, and when the groundlessness of the accusation was demonstrated Marx apologized and explained that he had necessarily believed that the Poles must be well-informed about Russian affairs. At that time the whole of revolutionary Europe looked at Russia through Polish spectacles, and in this Marx differed in no way from everybody else. He admitted having been hasty and did what he could to make good the wrong to Bakunin. Marx publicly defended Bakunin when a similar rumour was spread about him during his imprisonment in Russia. But Bakunin could not forgive Marx the mistake of 1848, which went on rankling for a long time.[4] To make matters worse Bakunin was persuaded by evil-tongued go-betweens, who did not mention Marx's defence of him during his compulsory silence, that Marx actually repeated the old slander.

Bakunin visited Marx in London at the end of October 1864, when he was writing the inaugural address for the International. The meeting passed off in an entirely amicable manner. Marx wrote to Engels that Bakunin was one of the very few people who after sixteen years had not receded but had gone on developing. What Bakunin said to cause Marx to pass this favourable judgement on him is not known.[5] In his long years of imprisonment Bakunin had suffered greatly and thought much. He had altered, and no longer wanted to make giant bonfires of capital cities. In Siberia he had almost got to the point of repudiating his revolutionary way of thinking altogether,[6] and when he was free once more he spent a considerable time hesitating whether to adhere to the bourgeois radicals or to the socialists. He then started returning step by step to his original negative anarchism. In his conversation with Marx he asserted that henceforward he would devote himself to the socialist movement alone, and said that in Italy, where he was just going, he proposed working for the International.

Marx did not know Bakunin well enough to realize how little these words were to be credited. There was a streak of naïve slyness in Bakunin's character, and he was skilful at adapting his speech to his company. Bakunin would by no means say all he thought; indeed, he would quite often say the reverse. A story of how he tried to make a revolutionary of the Bishop Polykarp, an adherent of the old faith, provides a pretty instance of Bakunin's way of tackling people he wanted to win over. According to the story Bakunin entered the Bishop's room singing a sacred song and requested an explanation of the difference between the persecuted old faith and the prevalent orthodoxy. He said he was willing to become an old believer himself if the Bishop could convince him. After listening humbly to the Bishop he drew a magnificent picture of the revolution, by which the true old faith would be allowed to triumph over the orthodox Church and cause the Tsar himself to be converted, and much more of the same kind. This story need not be credited entirely, but it illustrates in all essentials how far Bakunin could occasionally go.[7]

Bakunin had no intention of keeping his promise to work for the International in Italy. Even before starting on his journey he set about the formation of his own secret society, which had nothing whatever to do with the International, either in programme or organization. In respect of organization Bakunin was a revolutionary of the old school. He belonged entirely to the epoch of the illuminati and the carbonari. In his opinion the one thing necessary to prepare the way for the revolution and consolidate it after victory was a highly conspiratorial band of determined men, a band of professional revolutionaries and plotters, who lived for nothing but the revolution. 'In the midst of the popular anarchy that will create the very life and energy of the revolution, the unity of revolutionary thought and revolutionary action must find an organ. That organ must be a secret and universal association of revolutionary brothers.'[8] That is Bakunin's own summary of his revolutionary creed. Bakunin was continually engaged in founding organizations of one kind or another, and sometimes he was engaged on several at the same time. They all had secret statutes and programmes that varied with the degree of initiation of the members, and ceremonial oaths, if possible sworn on a dagger or some similar theatrical requisite, were usual. Bakunin formed a secret society of this kind in 1865 – the Fraternité Internationale. It never entered his head for a moment to do anything for the International, and he barely answered the letters that Marx wrote him.

In the autumn of 1867 Bakunin travelled from Italy to take part in the first congress of the League of Peace and Freedom. This organization represented the last attempt of the democratic celebrities of 1848 and 1849, who for two decades had been the 'great men of the emigration', to venture once more into the realm of high politics. The reawakening of political life throughout Europe seemed to proffer this organization some prospect of success, and there were some famous names upon its list of founders: Victor Hugo, Louis Blanc, John Stuart Mill, Guiseppe Garibaldi. The League's programme was a nebulous mixture of democracy, anti-clericalism and pacifism, intended to mean as much to as many people as possible. In practice it did nothing for anybody.

The League, having practically no solid popular backing of its own, was very anxious to be on good terms with the International. An attempt was made to have it incorporated as a kind of subsidiary organization within the International, to enable it to propagate its own special aims among the proletariat. Marx was necessarily opposed to any such plan. The development of the young workers' movement could only be hampered by connection with these generals without an army, for the important men had only lent their names to the League at its inception and in reality the movement was in the hands of democratic leaders of the second and third rank. To involve the International with the League would mean burdening it with a swarm of ambitious, wrangling and clique-forming political intriguers.

Marx was not able to convince the International of all this until 1868. The Brussels congress of that year unanimously carried a resolution embodying Marx's attitude to the League.[9] A year before not a few members of the International had sympathized with the idea of the League and had been only too pleased to take part in its congress. The League had counted on this and held its inaugural congress at the same time and place as the second congress of the International, and a number of delegates remained and took part in the League congress after the International had concluded its deliberations. At the League congress they made the acquaintance of Bakunin.

His appearance was an event of first-rate importance for the League. Many of the older generation knew him from earlier years, from his life of wandering before the revolution or from the exciting days of Paris, Berlin, Dresden or Prague. Everyone had heard of the man who had been dragged through the prisons of Europe and had been twice sentenced to death, and his escape from the grim horror of Siberia had already become legendary. 'I well remember his impressive bearing at the first session of the congress', a Russian journalist wrote in his memoirs,

As he walked up the steps that led to the platform, with his heavy, peasant gait – he was, as usual, negligently dressed in his grey blouse, out of which there peeped not a shirt but a flannel vest – a great cry of 'Bakunin!' arose. Garibaldi, who was in the chair, rose and went forward to embrace him. Many of Bakunin's opponents were present, but the whole hall rose to its feet and the applause was interminable. Bakunin was no speaker if by that word is meant a man who can satisfy a literary or educated public, who is a master of language and whose speeches have a beginning, a middle and an end, as Aristotle teaches. But he was a superb popular orator, and he knew how to talk to the masses, and the most remarkable feature of his oratory was that it was multi-lingual. His huge form, the power of his gesticulations, the sincerity and conviction in his voice, his short, hatchet-like phrases all contributed to making a profound impression.[10]

To quote another Russian writer who heard Bakunin at another meeting:

I no longer remember what Bakunin said, and in any case it would scarcely be possible to reproduce it. His speech had neither logical sequence nor richness in ideas, but consisted of thrilling phrases and rousing appeals. His speech was something elemental and incandescent – a raging storm with lightning flashes and thunderclaps, and a roaring as of lions. The man was a born speaker, made for the revolution. The revolution was his natural being. His speech made a tremendous impression. If he had asked his hearers to cut each other's throats, they would have cheerfully obeyed.

That was how Bakunin's speech echoed sixty years later in the ears of a man who was no revolutionary at the time and was certainly no revolutionary when he wrote his memoirs. His name was Baron Wrangel, and he was the father of the well-known General Wrangel, who fought against the Bolshe-viks in South Russia in 1919 and 1920.[11]

Bakunin's forceful personality gained him devoted followers in the League and among the members of the International. As was his invariable habit he hastened to confirm his first success by enrolling new initiates into one of his secret socie-ties. The Fraternité Internationale appears to have been some-what reorganized on this occasion, and it may well have received a new name. (The history of Bakunin's secret societies is still in many respects uncertain. They were so often re-organized that even Bakunin himself could not remember all their ramifications and vicissitudes.) At any rate the Frater-nité was transplanted from Italy to Central Europe.

At the same time Bakunin became a member of the League central committee. He did all he could to make the League accept a revolutionary programme and bring it into line with the International. His undoubted aim was to bring the two organizations together and, by means of his secret organization, become the unseen leader of both. In this he failed. The majority of the League's members were by no means revolutionary-minded, and all Bakunin's proposals were voted down. He became increasingly convinced of the possibility of converting the League into a suitable instrument for his revolutionary work, and he awoke to the fact that there was far greater scope for his activity in the International. He met many of its members and became acquainted with the development of its ideas. He had hitherto refrained from joining it himself, but in July 1868 he joined the Geneva branch. In the autumn, after the International had definitely broken with the League, he broke with it himself. At the second League congress, held at the end of September 1868, he proposed that it make a public avowal of socialism. His resolution was obviously unacceptable, and when the League turned it down he and his followers left the congress and resigned from membership.

He promptly summoned his followers, most of whom were adherents of the Fraternité Internationale, and proposed that they join the International in a body. This was intended to keep his followers together. Joining the International in this way would intensify rather than weaken their corporate sense. His followers approved his plan, with a few unimportant alterations. An open association, L'Alliance internationale de la Démocratie sociale, was founded to exist side by side with the secret society.[12] The Alliance was intended to include members outside the secret society, and thus act as a screen for the secret society. It was to have its own programme and statutes, its own leaders, its own sections in various countries, its own international congresses to be held at the same time and place as those of the International. The plan was to form a state within a state within the International. Officially the object of the Alliance was the unpretentious one of 'investigating social and philosophical questions'. Its real purpose was to gain control of the International and lead it whither Bakunin wanted, for behind it there would be his secret organization. There was to be a three-storey pyramid, with the International as the base, the Alliance on top of it and on top of the Alliance the secret society, with Bakunin the 'invisible dictator' at the pinnacle.

The plan was too clever and consequently too clumsy to succeed. It failed to get farther than the initial stages. The Alliance was successfully founded and quite a number of respectable and deserving members of the Swiss sections of the International joined it. The statutes were duly drawn up and signed and dispatched for confirmation by the General Council. Bakunin's name was among the signatures, tucked in inconspicuously among the rest.

Marx had no means of divining the details of Bakunin's plan, but promptly discerned Bakunin's object. This was no new turn of the working-class movement, no new organization of workers demanding admission to the ranks of the united international proletariat. This was an organization created by a plotter of the old school who aimed at gaining control of the great new movement represented by the International, which under Marx's leadership was striving to guide the struggle of the proletariat in the only way it ought to be guided, in all openness, as a mass organization. Marx had not spent twenty years fighting the methods of the carbonari, and all the poison-and-dagger nonsense, to let it creep into the International by the back door now.

When the statutes of the Alliance came up for consideration by the General Council, its members, of course with Marx's concurrence, expressed a wish that the International should publicly repudiate it. Marx wrote to Engels late that night after the meeting. The thing of which he had heard previously and had regarded as still-born, he said, and had wanted to let quietly die had turned out to be more serious than he had expected. 'Herr Bakunin – who is at the back of this affair – is kind enough to want to take the workers' movement under *Russian* control.'[13] Marx was particularly incensed at such a thing having been perpetrated by a Russian, citizen of a country that had no workers' movement of its own and was therefore less fit than anybody to grapple with the difficulties confronting the European movement. Engels pacified Marx a little. He said it was as clear as daylight that the International would not allow itself to be taken in by a swindle such as this state within a state, this organization which had nothing whatever behind it. 'I, like you, consider it to be a still-born, purely local, Geneva affair. Its only chance of survival would be for you to attack it violently and give it importance thereby. In my opinion it would be best firmly but quietly to dismiss these people with their pretensions to insinuate themselves into the International.'[14] Marx agreed with Engels, and the General Council declined to confirm the statutes of the Alliance as an organization within the International.[15] After protracted negotiations the Alliance as such was eventually dissolved. Individual groups of its members were permitted to enter the International under the usual conditions and to form local sections. No mention of the secret society was made throughout, and the General Council did not know of its existence. The secret society disintegrated once more and was once more reconstructed. Bakunin quarrelled with the majority of the *directoire centrale* of the Fraternité Internationale, resigned from the Fraternité and dissolved it, only to found it anew promptly afterwards with his most devoted followers. His first *rapprochement* with Nechaiev, of whom more will be said later, occurred during these months.

Bakunin had not answered Marx from Italy, and he gave no sign of life from Switzerland. Marx sent him a copy of *Das Kapital*, but Bakunin remained silent and did not even write a line of thanks. But a few days after the Alliance had submitted its statutes to the General Council, Bakunin wrote. It was a long letter, overflowing with friendliness. 'Ma patrie

maintenant, c'est l'Internationale, dont tu es l'un des principaux fondateurs. Tu vois donc, cher ami, que je suis ton
disciple, et je suis fier de l' être.' * [16]

This sounded genuine, upright and sincere, but it was anything but what it seemed. The letter was a calculated part of
the web of intrigue that Bakunin was spinning round Marx.
Bakunin certainly had a high opinion of Marx and considered
Das Kapital to be a scientific achievement of supreme importance. He even wanted to translate it into Russian. But that
did not affect Bakunin's conviction that Marx was his arch-
enemy, whose main purpose was to lay snares and traps for
him; and he believed himself to be thoroughly justified in
fighting Marx. Some three months after this declaration of
love Bakunin wrote to his old friend, Gustav Vogt, one of the
founders of the League, of the 'distrust or even ill-will of a
certain coterie the centre of which you no doubt have guessed
as well as I'.[17] That coterie was the General Council of the
International which had been against amalgamation with the
League of Peace and Freedom, and its centre was Marx,
Bakunin's *cher ami*.

In a letter he wrote Alexander Herzen on 28 October 1869,
Bakunin explained in all clarity the methods he proposed to
use in his campaign against Marx. Herzen had remonstrated
with Bakunin for daring to attack some of Marx's followers
in the Press without daring to attack Marx himself. Bakunin
replied that he had two reasons for refraining from attacking
Marx. The first was the real service that Marx had done by
laying the foundations of scientific socialism.

> The second reason is policy and tactics . . . I praised and honour-
> ed Marx for tactical reasons and on grounds of personal policy.
> Don't you see what all these gentlemen are? Our enemies form a
> phalanx, and to be able to defeat it the more easily it is necessary to
> divide it and break it up. You are more learned than I, and there-
> fore know better than I who first said: *Divide et impera*. If I

* 'My country is now the International, of which you are one of the
principal founders. You see, therefore, my dear friend, that I am your
disciple, and I am proud of it.'

started an open war against Marx now, three quarters of the International would turn against me, and I should find myself slipping down an inclined plane, and I should lose the only ground on which I wish to stand.[18]

To weaken the Marxian phalanx Bakunin chose to attack Marx's little-known followers, and in the meantime he stressed his friendship for Marx.

Marx was not for a moment deceived as to what his expression of friendship was really worth. He did not answer Bakunin's love letter. Marx had not a few defects. He was not always easy and pleasant to get on with, but he was incapable of simulating friendship for a person while he was busy laying a trap for him.

Bakunin worked very hard to build up and extend his secret society, and it was important to be on good terms with the group of young 'Internationalists' at Locle, who have already been mentioned. Bakunin made the acquaintance of Guillaume, their leader, in January 1869. Guillaume invited him to Locle. He accepted the invitation and was received like a hero. Guillaume's account of the events of that day [19] deserve to be repeated, for he paints such a characteristic picture of Bakunin, illustrating not only Bakunin as seen through his followers' eyes, but how Bakunin presented himself to them.

La nouvelle de la venue du célèbre révolutionnaire russe avait mis le Locle en émoi; et dans les ateliers, dans les cercles, dans les salons, on ne parlait que de lui ... On se disait que la présence, dans les rangs de l'Internationale, d'un homme aussi énergique, ne pouvait manquer de lui apporter une grande force.*

Locle was an obscure provincial township and for a celebrity to visit it was an epoch-making event; and now a rare and

---

* 'The news of the arrival of the celebrated Russian revolutionary had put Locle into a state of high excitement. He was the sole subject of conversation in workshops, clubs and drawing-rooms ... Everyone said that the presence in the ranks of the International of a man as energetic as he could not fail to be a source of great strength.'

exotic celebrity was actually on the spot. The big watch-making village could scarcely contain itself with excitement. 'J'étais allé l'attendre à la gare avec le père Meuron, et nous le conduisîmes au Cercle International, où nous passâmes le reste de l'après-midi à causer avec quelques amis qui s'y étaient réunis.'* The local branch, the *Cercle International*, was just celebrating the sixty-fifth birthday of 'Father' Meuron, a French *émigré*, who had been a carbonaro in the days of the July Monarchy and perhaps in the days of the Restoration too. The 'Internationalists' of Locle, all hungry for experience, surrounded Bakunin. 'Si l'imposante stature de Bakounine frappait les imaginations, la familiarité de son accueil lui gagnait les cœurs; il fit immèdiatement la conquête de tout le monde.'† Bakunin showed himself a blithe and sociable human being, a good raconteur, homely and simple. 'Dans les conversations, Bakounine racontait volontiers des historiettes, des souvenirs de sa jeunesse, des choses qu'il avait dit ou entendu dire. Il avait tout un répertoire d'anecdotes, de proverbes, des mots favorits qu'il aimait à répéter.'‡ Guillaume particularly remembered one story which Bakunin told. 'Une fois, à la fin d'un dîner, en Allemagne, il avait, nous dit-il en riant, porté ce toast, accueilli par un tonnerre d'applaudissements : "Je bois à la destruction de l'ordre public et au déchainement des mauvaises passions." ' § Bakunin described the seven stages of happiness as follows : 'En premier lieu, comme

* 'I went to meet him at the station with Father Meuron, and we took him to the International Club, where we spent the rest of the afternoon talking with some friends who had gathered there.'

† 'If Bakunin's imposing stature struck the imagination, the familiarity of his greeting gained men's hearts. He promptly made a conquest of everybody.'

‡ 'In conversation Bakunin willingly related anecdotes, gave reminiscences of his youth, told us things he had said or heard. He had a whole repertoire of anecdotes, proverbs and favourite sayings that he liked to repeat.'

§ 'Once, at the end of a dinner in Germany, he had proposed a toast, he told us laughing, saying: "I drink to the destruction of public order and the unleashing of evil passions." '

bonheur suprême mourir en combattant pour la liberté; en second lieu, l'amour et l'amitié; en troisième lieu, la science et l'art; quatrièmement, fumer; cinquièmement, boire; sixièmement, manger; septièmement, dormir.' *

Twenty years before, Bakunin had defined the seven stages of happiness in the same way, and he had spoken of the unleashing of the passions then too. Only in the meantime the sentiments had grown somewhat faded. Richard Wagner had heard Bakunin say all these things in 1849, only in Wagner's memoirs they sound like extracts from some dim northern saga. But retailed by Guillaume they remind one of a provincial schoolmaster describing the bounty of some brilliant talker to an admiring audience.

Bakunin accepted Guillaume into his secret society. Bakunin no longer attached importance to swearing oaths upon a dagger. He explained the object of the society as 'Le libre rapprochement d'hommes qui s'unissaient pour l'action collective, sans formalité, sans solennité, sans rites mystérieux, simplement parce qu'ils avaient confiance les uns dans les autres et que l'entente leur paraissait préférable à l'action isolée.' † Guillaume is no objective witness, but he must have been pretty faithful to the facts in this. However much Bakunin wanted to assimiliate his organization to the International, it remained a secret society within the International, keeping its existence secret from it and aiming at gaining control of it. Guillaume bears witness to this, for he describes how Meuron, the old carbonaro, who joined the secret society at the same time, rejoiced. 'Il réjouissait à la pensée que l'Internationale serait doublée d'une organisation secrète qui la préserverait du

---

* 'In the first place, the supreme happiness was to die fighting for liberty; in the second place, love and friendship; in the third place, science and art; in the fourth place, smoking; in the fifth place, drinking; in the sixth place, eating; and in the seventh place, sleeping.'

† 'A free association of men who united for collective action, without formality, without solemnity, without mysterious rites, simply because they felt confidence in one another and deemed unity preferable to isolated action.'

danger que pouvaient lui faire courir les intrigants et les ambitieux.' *

The contrast between the ideas of the old illuminati, carbonari and the rest and those whose aim was to use the International to lead the workers into forming great mass organizations could not have been better expressed than it was by *père* Meuron. He had spent his whole life as a member of one or other small band of conspirators, and he could not conceive that a mass organization in which there was such a thing as an open struggle of ideas could be anything but a cockpit for the intriguing and ambitious. It seemed obvious to him that the unrestricted life of a large, public organization, open to all the world, must be supervised by groups of the type familiar to him. These groups, set up behind the back of the mass organization, must obviously refrain from openly proclaiming their programmes, and even their existence must not be known of. It was these groups that must be the real controllers of the movement. Meuron and those who thought like him regarded all this as entirely open and above board. So far from regarding it as partaking of the nature of intrigue, they actually regarded it as a sure defence and shield against the ambitious and intriguing.

Bakunin managed to extend his secret society pretty quickly, in spite of obstacles. He and his friends had great hopes of the next International congress, to be held at Basle in September 1869. They made every effort to be as well represented at it as possible. The secret Alliance sent instructions to its adherents in every corner of Europe, directing them whom to choose as delegates and to whom to give a mandate if they could not send one of their own men. In many areas members were very surprsed indeed to find that for the first time in the history of the International the selection of delegates was not being carried out in a straightforward, open, matter-of-fact

* 'He rejoiced at the thought that the International would be doubled by a secret organization which should preserve it from the dangers to which the intriguing and ambitious might subject it.'

way, and letters reached the General Council asking what was in the wind.

Bakunin and his followers had not worked badly, and they were represented at the congress in pretty respectable numbers.[20] Nevertheless their expectations were not entirely fulfilled, though they had one or two successes. The most important was in the debate on the inheritance question. The congress rejected the resolution of the General Council, which was drafted by Marx, and accepted Bakunin's resolution instead. But they did not succeed in their principal aim, which was to have the headquarters of the General Council transferred from London to Geneva, where Bakunin would have been its lord and master.[21]

The Basle congress marks an important stage in the struggle between Marxists and Bakuninists. The fundamental differences were not mentioned, the root problem was not debated, and the real dispute was only hinted at. But anyone who followed the progress of the congress attentively and had a certain experience of the history of the movement could plainly detect the call to battle. Moses Hess, the 'communist rabbi',[22] had a practised ear. He had been present at Marx's struggle with Weitling and had known the cause of dissension between Marx and Gottschalk and had followed Marx's struggle with Willich and his followers in the Communist League. He attended the congress and heard the unspoken words: 'The collectivists of the International believe that the political revolution must precede the social and democratic revolution.' Bakunin and his followers made the political revolution coincide with the social revolution. They made no concealment of their opinion. The organ of Bakunin's followers in Switzerland wrote as answer to Hess's utterance, 'We shall persist in refusing to associate ourselves with any political movement *the immediate and direct aim of which is not the immediate and direct emancipation of the workers.*'[23] The qualifying relative clause is emphasized in the original. The Bakuninists did not reject political struggle of any kind, as was later supposed. If its object was the direct realization of their ultimate aim, 'the revolution and social democracy', they were ready to participate. They were even capable of making quite big concessions and deviating widely from their usual tactics. But they insisted that any political movement in which they took part must lead directly to the social revolution. That was the condition from which they would not depart. The emphasis was on the definition of *direct and immediate*.

About this time, at the end of 1869, the Bakuninists started proclaiming the principle of not taking part in elections for any kind of parliament, and with this their struggle with the Marxists in Switzerland began. Taking part in the Swiss elections, i.e. in the political movement, meant embarking on a long period of patient work of enlightenment among the workers, and only those who believed that the political and social revolution could not be one, could undertake it. On the other hand, in lands where the revolution was ripening quickly, the Bakuninists by no means declined to participate in elections, granted that the elections were the first step to the social revolution. But the elections had to be the first step. The second step must be the social revolution itself. Those were the tactics of Bakunin's followers in Paris, the leader of whom was Varlin, the best-known representative of the Paris section of the International at the time. He proclaimed himself, in the Press and in court, an adherent of 'anti-authoritarian communism', which was the name by which the Bakuninists started calling themselves.

Varlin had joined Bakunin's secret society at the Basle congress, and was Bakunin's closest confidant in Paris. Nevertheless at the end of 1869 he joined the staff of *La Marseillaise*, which was edited by Rochefort and was the most influential radical paper in Paris. It was actually the organ of the General Council of the International and of Marx personally and it stood for participation in the elections. Its policy was that the electoral movement and parliament must be used for the revolution. Varlin explained his motives in a letter to his Swiss associates. He said that the existing situation in France did not permit the socialist party to remain aloof from politics.

At the moment the question of the imminent fall of the Empire took precedence of everything else, and it was necessary for the socialists to be at the head of the movement, under pain of abdication. If they held aloof from politics, they would be nothing in France today, while as it was they were on the eve of being everything.[24] Neither the Swiss nor Bakunin himself had any objection to this policy, which in their eyes was justified if it led to the revolution and was the most direct way to the social revolution.

Whatever criticism may be made of Bakunin, he was not a man to be satisfied with empty formulas. He acted in accordance with the demands of his ideas, and he acted very energetically. Immediately after the conclusion of the Basle congress, at which he strengthened and extended his secret society, he set about preparing for a revolutionary rising. What his plans were, the exact details of what he was preparing for, are not known, but it is known that in December 1869 and January 1870 he was conducting a lively correspondence with members of his organization in various French towns, for the revolution was to break out first in France. His people worked devotedly and successfully.

A large number of the most active members of the International, revolutionary-minded young men like Varlin and Pindy in Paris, Richard in Lyon, Bastelica in Marseilles, entered Bakunin's organization and prepared for an insurrection. The situation seemed more favourable than ever. The prestige of the Empire was severely shaken and everyone felt that its days were numbered. The revolution, the downfall of Louis Bonaparte, might perhaps be delayed a little longer, but it was inevitable nevertheless. The policy of the General Council, led by Marx, was based on the imminence of a revolution in France. But it differed fundamentally, in general and in particular, down to even the most insignificant details, from that of Bakunin. Bakunin's societies, unknown to the working masses, with a programme that they carefully concealed, worked outside society, worked deliberately outside society, planning and plotting violence.

The General Council strove to lead the workers as a whole, as a mass movement, towards a political and economic struggle with the Empire that should be above board and patent to everybody, and they strove to teach the workers the incompatibility in practice of their interests and those of their rulers. In May 1870 the French Imperial Government started a hue and cry after the International, dissolving its sections and arresting a number of its leaders. To Marx this declaration of war was welcome. 'The French Government', he wrote to Engels on 18 May, 'has at last done what we have so long wanted – turned the political question of empire or republic into a question of life and death for the working class.'[25] The International, suppressed by Napoleon, must promptly re-arise and openly defy the ban, exploiting in every one of its utterances every opportunity, however meagre, of proclaiming to rulers and workers alike its determination not to allow itself to be suppressed and its resolution to continue with its mass propaganda. 'Our French members are demonstrating beneath the eyes of the French Government the difference between a secret political society and a real workers' movement', Marx wrote in the same letter. 'Scarcely had the committee members in Paris, Lyon, Rouen, Marseilles, etc., been locked up (some of them succeeded in escaping to Switzerland) when twice the number of new committees immediately proclaimed themselves their successors with the most impudent and defiant announcements in the newspapers, even giving their private addresses.'

The Bakuninists went on plotting in the dark. Marx heard of their existence for the first time in the spring of 1871, and for some time all he knew about them was the fact of their existence. When material dealing with the Bakuninist organizations fell into the hands of the Paris police as a result of the arrests in May 1871, and the public prosecutor announced in the Press that a secret society of conspirators existed besides the official International, Marx believed it to be one of the usual police discoveries. 'It's the old tomfoolery,' he wrote to

Engels. 'In the end the police won't even believe each other any more. This is too good.'

Marx did not yet know how wide the ramifications of Bakunin's organization were. The abyss that separated his conception of programme, tactics and method from that of Bakunin at the beginning of 1870 had become so wide that it was unbridgeable. Marx had to engage once more in the struggle in which he had been engaged for the greater part of his life in constantly changing forms. Meanwhile war had become inevitable. European events postponed it, complicated it, blurred the issues. That it was bound to break out was clear to everyone in the winter of 1869.

[19]

The Franco–Prussian War[1]

In the year of the foundation of the International Prussia and
Austria were at war with Denmark. Two years later there was
war in Lombardy for the unification of Italy and in Bohemia
for the hegemony of Germany. After 1866 war – *revanche pour
Sadowa* – had become inevitable between the France of Louis
Napoleon and Bismarck's Prussia. The International, from
the first day of its existence, had had to take a stand towards
war and foreign politics. The inaugural address had proclaimed
the necessity of the proletariat's having its own foreign
policy, based on the solidarity of the workers of all countries.
The workers' International must answer ruling-class policy
with its own. This principle was accepted as a matter of course
by all groups within the International, even those of the most
divergent views. But as soon as it came to putting principle
into practice acute differences arose.

The Polish question was the first. Sympathy for the fate of
the unfortunate people of Poland was universal among revolutionaries and mere radicals too, and this widespread feeling
had contributed substantially to the foundation of the International. The International had helped to organize the meeting
of 22 July 1863, summoned to consider ways and means of
assisting the Polish rising. Poland enjoyed the sympathy of
all. But there were not a few who shrank from the inevitable
political implications of a more or less sentimental mood.
Marx's phrases about Russia in the inaugural address had
roused a good deal of opposition, for he maintained, just as in
1848, that Russia was still the mainstay of European reaction
and that Russia must therefore be vanquished first. Marx was
pro-Polish because he was anti-Russian. Poland's resuscitation
would involve the break-up of the Holy Alliance, which was
always re-arising from its ashes in spite of the celebrations over

its decease, and the end of the Russian nightmare which lay oppressively over Europe, stifling every revolutionary movement.

There were many in Germany and still more in England who thought as Marx did. In the Latin countries it was otherwise. The Proudhonists were the chief of those who repudiated Marx's 'Russophobia'. They did not deny that it had been justified in the 1840s, but they claimed that it was superfluous, actually harmful now. They held that however obnoxious Russian despotism might be in principle, from the working-class point of view it differed not at all from the governments of Napoleon III or Bismarck or even of Queen Victoria's cabinet. All were bourgeois governments alike. The Proudhonists declined to recognize the alleged excessive influence of Russia on the destiny of Europe. They rejected the notion of directing the whole weight of International policy primarily against Russia, and at the Geneva congress of 1866 declined to vote for a foreign policy resolution demanding the 'annihilation of Russia's despotic influence on Europe' on the ground that the resolution should have been worded 'the annihilation of all despotism'.[2]

In the dispute between Marx and the Proudhonists concerning the attitude to be adopted towards Russia and Poland, the differences in their estimates of the historical period through which Europe was passing and the tasks that confronted the International in it emerged for the first time. They were soon to assume a more manifest form.

During the revolutionary period of 1848 and 1849 in Central Europe the demand for national unity had been intimately associated with the demand for political freedom. It was an axiom at that time that the way to national unity lay only through the overthrow of the princes. Only freedom created unity and only in unity was there freedom. This article of faith was adhered to even by the German bourgeois democrats, though their consciences were mightily plagued by their inherited petty-bourgeois respect for every crowned head; and it remained part of the creed of the Italian democrats. But the wars of the 1860s seemed to confute it utterly. For Italy was not united by Mazzini but by Cavour, a royal minister of state, and the German people were not united by themselves, but by Bismarck, with blood and iron, under the spiked Prussian helmet.

To the Proudhonists national movements were simply incomprehensible, and nations themselves were 'obsolete prejudices'.[3] They could not understand how 'the social question' could be mixed up with antiquated 'superstitious ideas' about national unity and independence at a time when 'the social question' overshadowed everything else, and was indeed the only question that mattered at all. In their eyes anyone who connected 'the national question' with 'the social question' was a reactionary. That a man like Bismarck was able to assume the leadership of a national movement only confirmed them in their entirely negative judgement of what they regarded as belonging to long-obsolete historical phases. In their eyes every single state, without any exception whatever, was founded on 'centralism and despotism', the contradictions of which, as long as the world had not found its 'economic equilibrium', would continue to be fought out in wars. In these ever-recurring conflicts they did not regard it as the business of the proletariat to try and find out which side was objectively serving the cause of human progress, and then to support that side. No, the proletariat had only one duty. This, as de Paepe stated at the International congress of 1868, consisted in the fundamental reconstruction of social and political institutions; because that was the only way a permanent end could be made of ever-recurring international disputes. The Proudhonists stood for energetic anti-military propaganda, demanded the abolition of standing armies, and were the first to raise the question of the general strike as the weapon of the proletariat against war.

For these radical-sounding phrases Marx had little use. Ever since 1848 he had been preaching war with Russia, for he believed such a war would be a most powerful engine of the revolution. As in the past, he regarded war as a factor in historical growth and in some circumstances a factor of historical advance. Whether a particular war were really the latter or not and what attitude the proletariat should adopt towards it were questions to be decided on the merits of the particular case. In foreign just as in domestic politics Marx rejected the idea of anything being in itself 'reactionary' (J. B. von Schweitzer's expression). Which of two warring nations gained the victory could not possibly be a matter of complete indifference to the proletarian movement, the attitude of which should not be one of rigid adherence to a comfortable position of apparent extreme radicalism, but should be supple and pliant, ready to change in accordance with the changing situation.[4]

In spite of Proudhonist criticism Marx remained convinced, as he had been in 1848, that national movements had a progressive function, at any rate among great peoples such as the Germans, the Italians, the Poles, and the Hungarians. In a letter to Karl Kutsky written many years later Engels neatly summarized the reasons for Marx's belief. 'It is historically impossible for a great people to be in a position even to discuss any internal question seriously as long as national independence is lacking', he wrote. 'An international movement of the proletariat is only possible among independent nations, between equals.'[5] In this national nihilism of the Proudhonists Marx discerned not only a remarkable form of French nationalism but the lurking assumption that the French were the chosen nation.

After a meeting of the General Council in June 1866, at which there was a lengthy discussion of national questions, Marx described their attitude in a letter to Engels as 'Proudhonized Stirnerianism'.

They want to reduce everything to small 'groups' or 'communes', and then build up a 'union' but no state. And this 'individualizing' of humanity with its accompanying 'mutualism' is to be brought about while history in other countries stands still and the whole world waits until the French are ripe for the social revolution. They will then demonstrate the experiment before our eyes and the rest of the world, overcome by their example, will follow it . . . It is exactly what Fourier expected from his *phalanstères*.[6]

At the meeting in question Marx remarked that the French 'while denying all nationality appeared quite unconsciously to reconcile it with their own absorption into the model nation which was France'. True, Napoleon's hypocritical concern for the destinies of nations that had not yet achieved unity drove his opponents to the opposite extreme; and the petty-bourgeois socialists' dislike of national concentration, i.e. economic concentration, came out in their dislike of the economic developments that led to it.

Just because he regarded the movement towards national unity as a historical advance over the period of national subdivision into minor and petty states, Marx regarded Bismarck's policy with the greatest suspicion. For a long time he had mistrusted Bismarck's policy as an exclusively Prussian one, and held Bismarck to be the tool now of Napoleon, now of Russia. To Marx the idea that Germany could be united by being Prussianized seemed absurd. He and Engels were certainly not pro-Austrian during the Prusso–Austrian war, but still less were they pro-Prussian. Engels hoped the Prussians would 'get a good hiding' and Marx was convinced that they would 'pay for their boasting'. Marx expected that the defeat of Prussia would lead to a revolution in Berlin. 'Unless there is a revolution', he wrote to Engels on 6 April 1866, 'the Hohenzollern and Habsburg dogs will throw our country fifty or a hundred years back by civil (dynastic) wars.'[7] Unless there were a revolution, he repeated in a letter he wrote on the same day to his friend Kugelmann in Hanover, Germany would be on the threshold of another Thirty Years' War, and that would mean a divided Germany once more.[8]

To Marx, Prussia's rapid and brilliant victory was entirely unexpected. Prussian hegemony in Germany became a fact. The unpleasant prospect of Germany being merged into Prussia became a possibility to be reckoned with. That Bismarck's ambitions were not German ambitions but 'dynastic Hohenzollern' ambitions was plain enough. But his blunt refusal to entertain the French demand for 'compensation' for having remained neutral in the Austrian war and the harshness with which he asserted Prussian demands in the dispute about Luxembourg immediately afterwards finally destroyed the suspicion that he was only a tool of Napoleon.[9] The reactionary *Junker* Bismarck introduced universal suffrage into the North German Reichstag, though for reasons that differed profoundly from those for which Lassalle had agitated for it only a few years previously. The irresistible progress of the Prussianization of Germany became clearer every day, and those in the workers' movement could afford to ignore it less than anybody. It had to adapt itself to the new situation, be as pliable and resilient as its opponent, Bismarck. Universal suffrage created a vast new field of action for it. The two socialist parties were represented in the North German Reichstag, the followers of Lassalle and the 'Eisenacher', the latter led by Liebknecht and young August Bebel.

In the Paris Chamber the opposition parties, consisting of more or less determined republicans and Orleanists, were represented plentifully enough. But there was not a single socialist. Germany's greater social maturity was demonstrated by that alone. German industry had already surpassed the French. New, scientifically equipped factories were rising in the Rhineland, in Saxony, in Silesia, every year, and genuine proletarian centres were forming round them, and class differences were making their appearance more rapidly and more acutely than in any other country, including France.

The traditional idea of the leading role played by France in social development grew less and less justified as the years went by. In the 1840s Marx had held up France as a model to the Germans and measured Germany's level by that of its neighbour. From the beginning of the sixties Marx gradually began to doubt the old, familiar idea. Engels had started doubting it even earlier; and as German economic developments became more and more impressive and as the process of the unification of the state, albeit in crooked, incomplete and half-feudal forms, became more manifest, Marx gradually became convinced that it was to the German workers' movement that the future belonged. In 1870, before the outbreak of the Franco-Prussian war, he wrote to Engels:

It is my firm conviction that, though the first impulse will come from France, Germany is far riper for a social movement and will outdistance France by far. The French are guilty of great error and self-deception if they still believe themselves to be the 'chosen people'.[10]

In the middle of February 1870 he wrote to Kugelmann that he expected more for the social movement from Germany than from France.[11] The unification of Germany had become the preliminary to and the guarantee of a proletarian movement in the heart of Europe.

In the summer of 1870, when the Franco-Prussian war broke out, Marx did not hesitate for a moment. For the patriotic excesses of the German upper class and petty bourgeoisie he had nothing but contempt, reserving particular scorn for the dithyrambic outbursts of those who had recently been his comrades and even friends. After reading Freiligrath's war poems he wrote to Engels that he would rather be a miaowing cat than a ballad-monger of that kind. He was indignant at the leaders of the Lassalle faction, who gave unconditional support to the Prussian Government in making war on France, but approved of Bebel and Liebknecht, who voted against war credits, though he did not agree with their reasons. It seemed obvious to Marx that in the struggle with Bismarck there could be no truce, even in war.[12]

Germany's cause was not the Hohenzollerns' cause. Germany was attacked and not Prussia, and Germany must defend herself. But a German victory was essential above all in the interests of the workers' movement. Marx held that there were two reasons why it would be fatal for Louis Napoleon to win. In France the Bonapartist régime would be consolidated for many years and Central Europe would be thrown back whole decades, and the process of the unification of Germany would be interrupted. And then, as he wrote to Engels on 15 August

1870, there could be no more talk of an independent German
workers' movement and everything would be absorbed in the
struggle for the re-establishment of the national existence. On
the other hand a German victory would mean the end of
Bonapartism, and whatever government followed the French
would have a freer field.[13] 'If the Prussians win', Marx wrote
to Engels immediately after the outbreak of war,

> the centralization of the state power will be useful for the centrali-
> zation of the German working class. Moreover, German prepon-
> derance will cause the centre of gravity of the workers' movement
> in Western Europe to be still more definitely shifted from France
> to Germany, and it is only necessary to compare the movement in
> the two countries from 1866 till now to see that the German work-
> ing class is superior both theoretically and in organization to the
> French.[14]

On 23 July 1870 the General Council issued a manifesto on
the war. It was written by Marx. Addressed as it was to the
workers of the whole world, it was obviously impossible for it
to contain all the arguments that determined Marx's position.
It stated that 'on the German side the war was a war of defence', which immediately raised the question of who had
placed Germany in the position of having to defend herself.
In Bismarck Marx no longer saw a servant but rather a pupil
and imitator of Napoleon. The manifesto, which was issued
when the war had only just begun, stressed the fact that the
defence of Germany might degenerate into a war upon the
French people. But if the German working class permitted
that, victory or defeat would be equally evil. 'All the evils that
Germany had to suffer after the so-called wars of liberation
would be revived and redoubled', the manifesto concluded.
'The alliance of the workers of all countries will finally exterminate war.'[15]

In a letter to Wilhelm Liebknecht Marx gave his German
comrades still more specific advice. This letter has not survived, but Engels's letter to Marx, dated 15 August 1870, in
which he laid down the tactical line to be adopted in a manner

with which Marx entirely agreed, has been preserved. He wrote:

In my view, what our people can do is (1) associate themselves with the national movement as long as it is confined to the defence of Germany (in some circumstances an offensive persisting right up to conclusion of peace might not be inconsistent with this); (2) at the same time emphasize the distinction between the national interests of Germany and the dynastic interests of Prussia; (3) oppose the annexation of Alsace-Lorraine – Bismarck's intention of annexing Alsace-Lorraine to Bavaria and Baden has already transpired; (4) as soon as a republican, non-chauvinist government is at the helm in Paris, work for an honourable peace with it; (5) continually stress the unity of interests of the workers of France and Germany, who did not want the war and are not at war with each other; (6) Russia, as in the International manifesto.[16]

There had been only one sentence in the manifesto about Russia, pointing out that its 'sinister form' was 'lurking in the background of this suicidal struggle'.

The manifesto commended the French workers for declaring themselves against the war and against Napoleon. But that was all. Neither in the manifesto nor in the correspondence between Marx and Engels is there a word about the duties of the French proletariat during those pregnant weeks. Marx, in all the years during which a stupefied world hailed Napoleon III as a genuine heir of the Corsican, clung to his opinion that he was but 'commonplace *canaille*',[17] and long before the rottenness of the Bonaparte régime had become manifest to all beholders Marx held that its fate was already sealed. 'Whatever the result of Louis Napoleon's war with Prussia may be', the manifesto stated, 'the death knell of the Second Empire has already sounded in Paris.' From the first day of hostilities Engels, as a student of war, was convinced that Germany would win. His articles on the campaign in the *Pall Mall Gazette*[18] attracted a great deal of attention, and the accuracy with which he predicted the catastrophe of Sedan, even to the very date, confirmed his reputation as the 'General', which was the nickname by which his friends henceforward invariably called him. Napoleon's defeat was certain, and Napoleon's defeat would mean a revolution in France. But in what a situation! 'If a revolution breaks out in Paris', Marx wrote to Engels on 8 August, 'the question arises: have they the resources and the leaders to put up serious opposition to the Prussians? It is impossible to deny that the twenty-year-long Bonapartist farce has caused enormous demoralization. One is scarcely justified in counting on revolutionary heroism.'[19] In the middle of August Engels still believed that the position of a revolutionary government, if it came soon, need not be desperate; but it would have to abandon Paris to its fate and continue the war from the south. It might still be possible to hold out until fresh munitions had been procured and new armies organized with which the enemy might gradually be forced back towards the frontier. But five days later Engels believed that even that possibility had vanished. 'If a revolutionary government had been formed in Paris as late as last week,' he wrote to Marx, 'something might still have been done. Now it is too late, and a revolutionary government can only make itself ridiculous, as a miserable parody of the Convention.'[20]

The revolution was bound to come. That was certain. But Marx was just as certain that its victory in Paris could only follow defeat at the front. His certainty on this point explains the silence of the manifesto.

The French sections of the International did not allow themselves to be carried away by the wave of patriotic enthusiasm that swept the country upon the outbreak of war. Their hatred of Napoleon alone was sufficient to preserve them from that. For them to have wanted the Emperor to win the war and thus consolidate Bonapartism would have been inconceivable; and they did not believe he would win, for the weaknesses of his system were too familiar to them. The police, as usual unremitting in the invention of falsehood, alleged that cheers for Prussia had been called for at peace meetings just before the outbreak of war. Such meetings were held in places, and it became necessary to forbid patriotic demonstrations in the suburbs of Paris, because they occasionally developed into demonstrations the very reverse of patriotic. It is quite possible that some crank, conceiving himself to be a revolutionary, may actually have called for a cheer for the Prussians, but it is certain that the workers who adhered to the International had no love for Bismarck, however much they despised Napoleon. Disunited as the French socialists were – the Internationaux de la dernière heure', as the 'old' Internationalists remarked, only served to bring more differences into the ranks – they certainly did not want a Prussian victory at the expense of France. Enslaved, humiliated and oppressed as their country might be at the hands of an iniquitous government, it nevertheless remained the country of the revolution, the heart of Europe, now and for the future. They did not believe in Napoleon, but they believed in France and France's mission.

Bakunin, who at this time was held in high regard by the members of the International in France, thought as they did. Nay more, he was an almost ideal embodiment of French revolutionary patriotism. Like Marx, he considered that indifference in international conflicts was pseudo-radical and could only be harmful to the revolution. Like Marx, he demanded the intervention of the proletariat to the full limit of its strength. But, unlike Marx, he regarded Germany and not Russia as the enemy and the chief bulwark of reaction; and Bakunin did not just mean contemporary Germany; in his eyes Germany had been the hub and pattern of despotism for centuries, ever since the Reformation and the suppression of the peasant risings in the first third of the sixteenth century. Though there were other despotic governments even more brutal than the German, that fundamental truth was not affected in his eyes, because 'Germany had made a system, a religious cult, of what in other countries was only a fact.'[21] It was a feature of the German national character. Bakunin liked quoting the saying of Ludwig Börne that 'other people are often slaves, but we Germans always lackeys'.[22] He called the servility of the Germans a natural characteristic which they had elevated into a system, thus making of it an incurable disease. If the Germans, condemned to slavery themselves and spreading the plague of depotism wherever they went, were to conquer France, the cause of socialism would be lost and all hope of a revolution in Germany – a hope that in any case could only be justified by a spirit of optimism that ran counter to all experience – would have to be buried for at least half a century, and France would be threatened with the fate of Poland.

Even before the war had properly begun he believed, as Marx did, that Napoleon's defeat was inevitable; but he did not regard the defeat of France as inevitable, that is, assuming she bethought herself and a revolution broke out in time. A revolution and a revolution alone could save France, Europe, and socialism. The French, above all the workers, must rise, trample Bonapartism in the dust and hurl themselves at the enemy of France and of civilization with the all-compelling enthusiasm of a revolutionary nation. In converting the imperialist war into a revolutionary one lay their only hope.

Bakunin became intensely active as soon as war broke out. His new activity was essentially a continuation of the old; it consisted in organizing militant groups and preparing armed risings. The war had put immediate insurrection upon the order of the day. During the last days of July and the first week of August Bakunin overwhelmed his friends in France with letters, counselling them, encouraging them, urging them to immediate action. On 11 August he mentions that he had written twenty-three detailed letters to France that day. 'I have my plan ready', he said.[23] The details of his plan are unknown, but what they were it is not difficult to guess. On 8 August revolutionaries led by Bakuninists seized the town hall of Marseilles, and a rising in Paris was planned for 9 August. The 'committee of action' there consisted chiefly of Bakuninists, and its leader, Pindy, was a prominent member of Bakunin's secret organization. But the result was a fiasco, for on the morning of the ninth Pindy and his fellow conspirators were arrested.

Bakunin was not discouraged by these abortive attempts. What did not succeed in one place must succeed in another –

must succeed. For time was racing by and the German army was relentlessly advancing into France. 'If there is no popular rising in France within ten days, France is lost,' he wrote to his friends, almost in desperation. 'Oh, if I were young, I should not be writing letters but should be among you.'[24] Danton's words were constantly upon his lips: 'Avant de marcher contre l'ennemi, il faut le détruire, le paralyser derrière soi.'*

On 14 August Blanqui and some of his followers carried out an attack on the police barracks in the Grande Rue de La Villette. Their cry: 'Vive la République! Mort aux Prussiens! Aux armes!' was greeted with silence by a gaping throng. The rising collapsed pitifully.

News of the disaster of Sedan reached Paris on 4 September; 125,000 men had been taken prisoner, 600 guns had been captured and the Emperor had surrendered to the Prussians. The Empire collapsed without raising a finger in its own defence. A republic was proclaimed in Paris, and the provinces, insofar as they had not anticipated Paris, followed suit.

Napoleon left the republic a fearful heritage. The enemy was in the land, the armies were in disorder, the exchequer was bare. Marx's anxious query about the future was destined soon to have an answer.

On the night of 5 September Marx received a telegram from Longuet: 'Republic proclaimed.' The names of the members of the Provisional Government followed, with the words: 'Influence your friends in Germany immediately.'[25] He need not have added this injunction. The manifesto of the Paris sections of the International, which Marx received next day, was not calculated to make him hurry. On the contrary, it merely repelled him as being 'ridiculously chauvinistic',[26] with its demand that the Germans promptly withdraw across the Rhine – as if the Rhine could possibly be the frontier. But it was not a question of criticizing inept phraseology or the style of a well- or ill-written manifesto now. This was no time for

* 'Before marching against the enemy, it is necessary to destroy, to paralyse the enemy behind one.'

historical analyses. On 6 September Marx addressed the General Council on the fundamental alteration in the European situation brought about by the downfall of Napoleon in France. Thanks to the tremendous authority he exercised on the General Council, he succeeded in persuading it to acknowledge the young French republic, in spite of the hesitation and vacillation of some of its English members. It was decided that the new situation merited the issue of a second manifesto. This was also written by Marx, with the assistance of Engels in those passages which dealt with military matters. It was published on 9 September.[27]

The main theme of the manifesto, on which all the rest depended, was this: after Sedan, Germany was no longer waging a war of defence. 'The war of defence ended with the surrender of Louis Napoleon, the capitulation of Sedan and the proclamation of the republic in Paris. But long before these events occurred, at the very moment when the whole rottenness of the Bonapartist armies was revealed, the Prussian military camarilla set its heart on conquest.' To refute the alleged necessity of the annexation of Alsace-Lorraine for the defence of Germany Marx used arguments with which Engels supplied him. These were convincing, but they were only calculated to make an impression on military experts. The chief emphasis lay in the political argument, which made the General Council's manifesto the most significant document of the time.

With the victory and the consequences that threatened to follow in its wake Russia, from being a shadowy figure lurking in the background, came to the fore in a fashion that grew ever plainer and ever more menacing. Marx saw it, and did all that was in his power to make it visible to the world. But in Germany he was talking to men who were dazzled and blinded. Russia was far away, but Strasbourg was near, near enough to seize, and they seized it.

Did the Teuton patriots really believe [the manifesto said] that Germany's independence, freedom and peace would be assured if they forced France into the arms of Russia? If the success of

German arms, the arrogance of victory and dynastic intrigues drive Germany to rob France of French soil, only two ways remain open to Germany. She must either become a conscious vassal of Russia's plans for self-aggrandizement, with all the risks that that involves – a policy that corresponds to Hohenzollern traditions – or, after a short rest, arm for a new 'defensive' war, not one of these new-fashioned 'localized' wars, but a war against the allied Slav and Latin races.

A week after Sedan, Marx clearly delineated the main lines that German foreign policy was to follow up to the outbreak of the First World War; first the 'friendship' with Russia that Bismarck fostered, followed by preparations for war against the Franco–Russian *entente* that began as soon as that friendship was dissolved. A few sentences Marx wrote to his friend Sorge on 1 September 1870 bear brilliant witness to his foresight.

What the Prussian donkeys don't see [he wrote] is that the present war leads just as necessarily to war between Germany and Russia as the war of 1866 led to war between Prussia and France. That is the *best* result that I expect of it for Germany. 'Prussianism' as such has never existed and cannot exist other than in alliance and in subservience to Russia. And this War No. 2 will act as the mid-wife of the inevitable revolution in Russia.[28]

Forty-four years later Germany went to war with Russia and France, in 1917 revolution, unleashed by the war, broke out in Russia, and in 1918 the semi-feudal military might of Prussia collapsed.

Marx was not deceived as to the weakness of the German workers' movement and its inability to prevent the approaching catastrophe. 'If the French workers were unable to check the aggressors in the midst of peace, have the German workers a better prospect of checking the victor in the midst of the clash of arms?' he wrote. Nevertheless, however difficult the position of the German proletariat might be, he believed 'it would do its duty'.

The fall of Louis Bonaparte opened up new and tremendous prospects to the French working classes. The General Council sent its greetings to the young republic – to the republic and not to the Provisional Government of National Defence. The mistrust felt for the latter in revolutionary circles was not misplaced. It consisted partly of avowed Orleanists, partly of 'middle-class republicans, on some of whom the insurrection of June 1848 had left an indelible mark'. Suspicion of the Orleanists, who occupied all the most important positions and regarded the republic as but a bridge to the Restoration, was well-founded. Nevertheless, or rather for that very reason, Marx decided that the most pressing duty of the French workers was to support and defend the young republic in spite of all its defects. The situation was full of dangers and full of temptation, requiring the most extreme caution and the most courageous initiative, iron self-control and all-daring heroism.

The struggle was no longer between Louis Napoleon, that 'commonplace *canaille*', and a Germany which was on the defensive; republican France was now defending herself against rapacious German militarism. The manifesto called on the workers of France to do their duty as citizens. Their duty was to defend the French republic against the invading Germans. 'Any attempt to overthrow the new Government with the enemy at the gates of Paris would be a desperate act of folly.' But at the same time it was obvious that the French working class must not forget its own class duties, and the General Council bade it exploit the favourable opportunity of forwarding its own interest to the extreme. Eugène Dupont, the representative of the French sections on the General Council, wrote to the Internationalists at Lyons:

The bourgeoisie still have the power. In these circumstances the role of the workers, or rather their duty, is to let the bourgeois vermin make peace with the Prussians (for the shame of doing so will adhere to them always), not to indulge in outbreaks which would only consolidate their power, but to take advantage of the liberty which circumstances will provide to organize all the forces of the working class ... The duty of our association is to activate and spread our organization everywhere.[29]

Six weeks later he wrote once more to Chavret at Lyons: 'The role [of the International] is to take advantage of every opportunity and every occasion to spread the organization of the working class.'

'Restraint on the part of the International in France until after the conclusion of peace', as Engels put it, was far from meaning that the French workers were to go on quietly and calmly organizing as if they were living, say, in Belgium or in England or as if the date were still 1869. Their role was a wider one than mere active participation in the struggle against the invaders and continuing to build up their organization. Marx praised highly what the members of the International did at Lyons before Bakunin ruined everything there. On 19 October 1870 he wrote to Beesly, saying that under pressure of the local section of the International a republic had been set up before Paris took that step, and a revolutionary government immediately established; a commune, consisting partly of workers belonging to the International, partly of middle-class radical republicans. The *octroi* had been immediately abolished, and rightly so. The Bonapartist and clerical intriguers had been intimidated and energetic steps taken to arm the whole population.[30] Activity of this kind was far more than mere work of organization; it meant that working-class organizations were actively cooperating in introducing and consolidating the republican régime; and this was the only way the working-class movement could grow, by cooperating in shaping the country's destiny. Independent action of the working class must be postponed till later, until after the war was over and the necessary work of preparatory organization had been done. Engels went so far as to stress the fact that the working class 'would need time to organize'[31] even after the conclusion of peace. Hence it was impossible to decide in advance what form its future action might take. 'After the conclusion of peace', Engels wrote in a letter to Marx on 12 September, 'the workers' prospects in every direction will be brighter than ever before.' A remark in the same letter that 'not much fear need be entertained of the army returning from internment from the point of view of internal conflicts' indicates that he reckoned on the possibility – not the probability and definitely not the inevitability – of an armed struggle. In the same letter he warned the workers against any action during the war. 'If one could do anything in Paris', Engels wrote,

the thing to do would be to prevent the workers from striking until after the peace. Should they succeed in establishing themselves under the banner of national defence, they would take over the inheritance of Bonaparte and the present wretched republic, and would be vainly defeated by the German armies and thrown back again for twenty years... But if they do not let themselves be carried away under the pressure of foreign attacks but proclaim the social republic on the eve of the storming of Paris? It would be dreadful if the German army's last act of war were a battle with the workers at the Paris barricades. It would throw us back fifty years, put everyone and everything into a false position, and the national hatred and the demagogy that would take hold of the French workers! In this war France's active power of resistance is broken and with it goes the prospect of expelling the invaders by a revolution.[32]

For France the war was lost. He who continued it would be beaten and must humble himself before the victor. All other considerations must recede before that one decisive fact. The military situation alone forced the workers to hold back at least until the conclusion of peace. The manifesto warned them 'not to let themselves be swayed by national memories of 1792 as the French peasants had let themselves be deceived by national memories of the First Empire. Theirs was not to repeat the past but to build the future.' The argument sounded well, but if it had any validity it was but a secondary one. In the middle of August Engels had said that any government that tried to repeat the Convention would be but a sorry parody of it.[33] After the Battle of Sedan a revolutionary war in the manner of 1792 seemed completely impossible. A letter of Marx's to Kugelmann, written on 14 February 1871, makes it clear that his attitude was determined by this estimate of the war situation. 'If France holds out, uses the armistice to reorganize her army and gives the war a real revolutionary

character – and the crafty Bismarck is doing his utmost to this
end – the great new German Borussian Empire may still receive the baptism of a wholly unexpected thrashing.'[34] To give
the war a revolutionary character would be to repeat the Convention. In September 1870 it would only have been a miserable parody of the Convention. 'To sacrifice the workers now',
Engels wrote to Marx on 7 September, 'would be strategy *à la*
Bonaparte and MacMahon.'[35]

While Marx did all he could to prevent the workers from
attempting to overthrow the Provisional Government while
the war lasted, Bakunin and the 'Jacobins' held the overthrow
of the Provisional Government to be their most pressing task.
The 'Jacobins', students, intellectuals, and *déclassés* of all sorts,
seized on the traditions of the French Revolution – not so
much those of the Jacobin clubs, for many of them considered
Robespierre to be an irresolute weakling, as to those of the
Hébertists. Many of them had vague socialist ideas, and all of
them every day went politically a step farther left than the
day before. They were conspirators by tradition and inclination, completely unorganized as a group or even as a party;
but they were united by that mental kink exhibited in its
purest form by the Bohemians of the Left Bank, who were in
revolt against absolutely everything.

In the history of London's political exiles in the 1860s the
'Jacobins' did not play a very honourable role. Such of them
as had formed a special 'French branch' of the International
soon came into violent conflict with the General Council. Anyone who worked for the International in France was immediately suspect in their eyes. Such a person was bound to have
inclinations towards Bonapartism, if he were not actually an
agent of Napoleon. Félix Pyat, Vésinier, and others of their
leaders outdid each other in radicalism. Tyrannicide was their
ideal. Pyat constantly drank toasts to 'the bullet that will slay
a tyrant', and he opened a subscription to buy a 'revolver of
honour' for Beresovsky, the Pole who made an attempt on the
life of Alexander II in Paris in 1867, and indulged in many
similar pranks. Though not himself a member of the 'French

branch', he used it as his platform and behaved as though he were the living embodiment of the International itself. The behaviour of this irresponsible would-be politician, which in other circumstances would have been nothing but a bad joke, became a matter of occasionally serious embarrassment for the International. The General Council had repeatedly to announce that Pyat and his friends had nothing to do with them. It could not allow legal organizations on the Continent to be jeopardized by Pyat's ranting. Marx had bitter contempt for 'these heroes of the revolutionary phrase, who, from a safe distance of course, kill kings and emperors and Louis Napoleon in particular', and for Pyat, 'the pre-1845 mountebank'.[36]

The news of the fall of the Empire turned these people's heads completely. 'The whole French branch has set off for Paris today', Marx wrote to Engels on 6 September 1870, 'to commit imbecilities in the name of the International. They wish to overthrow the Provisional Government, proclaim the Paris Commune, appoint Pyat French ambassador in London, etc.'[37] As Marx considered this an extremely dangerous enterprise he sent Serraillier to Paris after the Jacobins to warn people of the danger of insurrectionary action.

Bakunin did not lag behind them in zeal. The seed he had sown so carefully seemed to have ripened now. The moment had come to strike. All the old powers had collapsed; and there was only one way to save France now, Bakunin's way, anarchism. An uprising of popular passion would achieve both victory over the external enemy and the complete reorganization of society. The two were inseparably united in his eyes. Bakunin left Switzerland on 14 September. The difficulty he had in raising money for the fare cost him several valuable days, or so he feared. With a Pole and a former Russian officer as his travelling companions he went to Lyons, where his most devoted followers lived. At first there were only a very few who were willing to follow him, but he succeeded in winning over the hesitators and the doubters. Two days after his arrival he wrote to Ogarev: 'The real revolution has not yet broken ou

here, but that will come. Everything is being done to prepare
it. I am playing for high stakes. I hope to see the triumph
soon.'[38] A week later he was as good as certain of the victory
of his cause: 'Tonight we shall arrest our principal enemies;
tomorrow there will be the last battle and, we hope, victory.'[38]
On 28 September Bakunin and his followers seized the town
hall of Lyons and proclaimed a revolutionary commune. Paragraph 1 of the first decree stated: 'The administrative and
governmental machinery of the state, having become powerless, has been abolished.' But with this the revolutionary
energy of the Lyons Bakuninists was exhausted. The venture
collapsed pitifully after a few hours, and Bakunin only just
managed to escape. In other towns, as in Marseilles, where
Bakunin tried again, and in Brest, where his followers went
to work, things did not even get as far as that.

When Marx learnt of Bakunin's adventures in Lyons he
was indignant. 'Those asses have ruined everything', he wrote
to Beesly. Since they belonged to the International, the
Bakuninists, Marx stated, unfortunately had sufficient influence to cause his followers to deviate. Beesly would understand,
Marx added, that the very fact that a Russian – represented
as an agent of Bismarck by the middle-class newspapers – had
he presumption to impose himself as the leader of a French
committee of public safety was quite sufficient to sway the
balance of public opinion.[39] It would have been difficult indeed
to have saved France by decreeing the abolition of the state
at a moment when she was engaged in a life-and-death struggle
with a terrible enemy whose demands were increasing from
day to day.

The fair words spoken by the King of Prussia at the beginning of the war – as usual, he had invoked God as his witness
and declared that he was fighting Napoleon but not the people
of France – were now completely forgotten. Anyone who dared
remember them was denounced as a traitor. When the 'Eisenacher' party committee issued a proclamation to the workers
protesting against the Prussian plans of conquest and demanding an honourable peace with the French republic, a general

had them arrested and led away in chains. The Government Press described the demand that a King of Prussia should keep his promises as 'ingenuous'.

France defended herself desperately. All revolutionary elements everywhere were on her side. Old Garibaldi hurried to the assistance of the French republic with a legion of volunteers. It was necessary to help her from without.

Immediately after the proclamation of the republic in Paris the General Council set itself at the head of the movement that demanded that Great Britain should recognize it. On 10 September a great workers' meeting in St James's Hall demanded recognition of the French republic and the conclusion of an honourable peace. The latter demand was closely associated with and indeed followed from it. Demonstrations increased during the winter months and at the turn of the year a large number of bourgeois politicians joined the pro-French front. Not satisfied with diplomatic intervention, they actually claimed that the time had come for British military intervention as well. Marx, as a foreigner, could not come forward publicly himself, so the campaign of meetings was led by Odger, an English member of the General Council. But Marx seized every opportunity of action that came his way. In January 1871 he learned of the difficulties of the German army in France from an informed source, namely Johannes Miquel, a high Prussian official who had been a member of the Communist League. Marx saw to it that the news was transmitted to the Government of National Defence through Lafargue. For, as Marx once more stated in an open letter to Bismarck in the *Daily News* of 19 January 1871, 'France was now fighting not only for her own independence but for the liberty of Germany and of Europe.'[40] The General Council of the International was behind a mass demonstration in Trafalgar Square on 23 January, to which the workers marched carrying the tricolour.

Engels energetically pleaded France's cause in articles in the *Pall Mall Gazette*. He denounced the brutal retaliatory

measures the Prussians took against the *francs-tireurs*. There
was an answer to these methods, he said.

Wherever a people allowed itself to be subdued merely because
its armies had become incapable of resistance it has been held up
to universal contempt as a nation of cowards [he wrote], and where-
ever a people did energetically carry out this irregular resistance,
the invaders very soon found it impossible to carry out the old-
fashioned code of blood and fire. The English in America, the
French under Napoleon in Spain, the Austrians in 1848 in Italy
and Hungary, were very soon compelled to treat popular resistance
as perfectly legitimate, from fear of reprisals on their own
prisoners.

Engels tried to convince the British that military intervention need only be on a very small scale to succeed. 'If thirty
thousand British soldiers landed at Cherbourg or Brest and
were attached to the army of the Loire, they would give it a
resolution unknown before.'[41] He followed the heroic resistance
of the raw French armies with great sympathy, and with more
than sympathy.

Engels sent to Gambetta's secretary, through Lafargue, a
memorandum containing a carefully thought-out plan for
raising the siege to Paris. The original document has never
been discovered and may have perished in those agitated times.
But Engels's executors, Bebel and Bernstein, found the preliminary draft after his death and destroyed it, fearing the
possibility of its being used as evidence of 'treason' against
the German social democrats. Bernstein refused to discuss the
matter during the whole of his lifetime, and that was the reason why that very remarkable document has practically never
been mentioned in print before. However, hints in memoirs,
taken in conjunction with Engels's own statements in the articles he wrote on the war, enable one to form a pretty accurate
idea of what he proposed. His underlying idea must have corresponded exactly with the plan that Bourbaki's army tried to
carry out in December 1870. The coincidence may have been
more than accidental. Engels became so enthusiastic about
his plans that he actually wanted to go to France to offer his

services to Gambetta. Marx, however, was sceptical. 'Do not
trust these bourgeois republicans,' he said to him, according
to Charles Longuet, 'whether you are responsible or not, at the
first hitch you will be shot as a spy.'

The General Council discussed the prospects of British
intervention. Short reports of meetings that appeared in a
local London paper, the *Eastern Post*, only give the barest
outline of Marx's views. At the end of September he seems
to have regarded the prospects of British intervention as very
slight. Privateering, England's most powerful weapon against
the Prussians, had been forbidden by the Declaration of Paris
in 1856. But the situation changed on 20 October, when Russia
denounced the Treaty of Paris as far as the Black Sea was
concerned. The transactions of the General Council on 1 January 1871 show how Marx regarded the distribution of forces
then. Engels said that if England had declared war on Russia
after 20 October, Russia would have joined forces with Prussia.
Austria, Italy and Turkey would have adhered to the side
of England and France. Turkey would have been strong
enough to defend herself against Russia, and Europe would
have expelled Prussia from France. Such a European war
would have meant the saving of France and Europe and the
downfall of absolutism. At a meeting on 14 March Marx was
still in favour of British intervention and a ruthless privateer
ing war. But by the middle of March the war was over. Four
days later the Commune was proclaimed in Paris.

On 28 January the Provisional Government had signed an
armistice with Prussia, in spite of Bismarck's monstrous de
mands. The population of besieged Paris was on the point of
starvation, all the French armies had been defeated, and all
prospect of the fortune of war changing seemed to have van
ished. Was there really no way of saving France from dis
honour? Had every possible thing been done? The Provisional
Government had been accused of indecision, cowardice and
even treachery before – treachery was the favourite accusation
the Bakuninists and Jacobins directed at 'cette vermine bour
geoise' – and hundreds of thousands of Paris workers an

members of the petty bourgeoisie now started wondering whether these accusations, which they had scarcely listened to before, were not, perhaps, justified after all. They started listening to them with an attentive ear. Once more they turned over in their minds all their dreadful experiences in those four and a half months of siege, and found much that was strange and difficult to understand, and much that had never seemed very plausible to them, though they had accepted it at the time as military necessity, not intelligible to them with their limited view over but a sector of the front. But now they suddenly looked at everything with different eyes. It is known today that after the Battle of Sedan it was absolutely impossible for the French to have won the war without external aid. The question whether a revolutionary war might or might not have forced the Prussians to reduce their demands – Marx still believed this possible as late as February – is scarcely one that can be settled now. But one thing is known now. The Parisians were justified in their suspicions. Paris was not defended as it might have been. The military command was crippled not only by disbelief in the possibility of success. There were large sections among the officers who were bitterly opposed to putting arms into the hands of the 'rabble', particularly the workers, for fear that though they might fight against the external enemy today, tomorrow they might turn their arms against the enemy within. And the more violently the extremists agitated – the possessing classes regarded as an extremist anyone who did not devotedly accept everything that came from above – the more acute their fear of the future became. The Prussians were their enemies today, but they might be friends and allies in the revolution tomorrow. Towards the end of the siege the most shameless of these people made no more secret of the fact that they would prefer the Germans to march in to having a revolution in Paris. Fear of the imminence of insurrection was not the least of the factors that led the Provisional Government to conclude an armistice. The Germans were perfectly well aware of this. Side by side with the peace negotiations there took place negotiations concerning the assistance that Bismarck might provide. He was prepared to release immediately as many French prisoners as might be needed to refill the ranks of the 'army of order', and the Provisional Government pledged itself to disarm the workers of Paris as soon as possible. Rumours of this spread quickly and intensified suspicion. From this to conviction of the Provisional Government's treachery to France was but a step. The Bakuninists and their allies, the Jacobins, saw to it that the step was taken.

This is not the place to write the history of the Paris Commune. Spontaneous mass movements and the deliberate actions of organized groups were so inextricably intermingled that in spite of all that has been written about it and all the research that has been done, the tangle has never been completely unravelled.[42] But one thing is sure. The theory that the March revolution in Paris was an entirely spontaneous rising, entirely unorganized and unprepared, does not correspond to the facts.

True, Bakunin, the arch-conspirator, took no part in it. His strength was broken by the reverse he suffered at Lyons. While still there he wrote to a friend in deep despair: 'Farewell liberty, farewell socialism, farewell justice for the people, and farewell the triumph of humanity!'[43] All his hopes of France had been in vain. 'I have no more faith in the revolution in France', he wrote at the end of October 1870. 'The country is no longer revolutionary at all. The people has become as doctrinaire and as bourgeois as the bourgeois. The social revolution might have saved it, and the social revolution alone was capable of saving it.' The people had shown itself incapable of embracing its own salvation. 'Farewell all our dreams of imminent emancipation. There will be a crushing and overwhelming reaction.'[44]

Great as Bakunin's influence on his friends was, on this occasion they did not follow him – his friends in Paris in particular. What bound them to him was not a thought-out programme – to say nothing of a comprehensive interpretation of society – but a will to action that flinched at no obstacles recognized no obstacles; they were united less by community of conviction than by community of mood; and moods in besieged Paris were necessarily different from what they were at Lyons. Certainly Lyons had been a fiasco, and hard as it might be, they must be better prepared next time. That was what they thought in Paris. They did not rise but made their preparations first. They regarded the incident at Lyons, which had been a terrible blow to Bakunin, as but a preliminary skirmish. Their battle was still to come. They drew up their ranks. Their leader was Varlin.

He was not a particularly gifted speaker, but he set no great store by oratory. An able organizer, energetic and clearsighted, he took up the cause of his class with complete devotion and utterly without personal ambition. General Cluseret called him 'the Christ of the working class', a phrase that sounded false only to those who did not know the details of his life. The workers loved him as their best friend. His work on the *Marseillaise* had brought him into contact with the revolutionary intelligentsia, particularly with the leading men among the Jacobins. With some of them he was on terms of personal friendship and he was exceptionally fitted to reestablish political liaison between them and the Bakuninists, to whose ranks he himself belonged.

On 4 September 1870 Varlin was still in Brussels, to which he had been compelled to flee to escape the attentions of the Bonapartist police. On 5 September he made a speech to the workers of Paris. He very soon resumed the prominent position he had previously occupied in the regional council of the International, and there was more than enough for him to do. The minutes of the regional council's meetings in January 1871, i.e. after a period of three months' intensive work, show that a delegate complained that the sections had been broken up and their members scattered – which gives an indication of the state the Paris sections must have been in during the first few weeks of the republic. Another delegate was of the opinion that the International had been wrecked by the events that followed the proclamation of the republic. In spite of exaggerations, due to reaction after perhaps excessive hopes, in the main these statements were correct. The International in Paris did not develop along the lines that Marx had indicated for it. Difficult the task that confronted the leaders of the Paris sections was – it was no light task, in the midst of the feverish excitement of a besieged city, to attempt to persuade members of the profoundly agitated and half-starving working-class masses to join an organization which was not concerned with their immediate and most pressing interests. But exceptional as the obstacles were, some if not all of them might have been overcome if Varlin and his comrades had not set themselves aims which, though important, were less important than the resuscitation of the sections. He who aimed at overthrowing the Government of National Defence in the midst of war had no time to lose with secondary things but had necessarily to go straight forward towards his goal; and conferring with the Jacobins on preparations for an insurrection was obviously more important than the troublesome effort of trying to build up the still weak sections of the International.

The most important revolutionary organization in Paris was the central committee of the twenty *arrondissements*, which was intended from the first not merely to be a popular check on the Government but to be a definite substitute for it when the proper moment came. The committee was in the hands of the Bakuninists and their allies, the Jacobins, and its paper was *Le Combat*, which was edited by Félix Pyat. There were plenty of differences between the Bakuninists and the Jacobins, but they faded into the background behind their common goal, the overthrow of the Government and the setting up of the revolutionary Commune. Bakunin at Lyons had associated himself with General Cluseret, though he had very soon regretted the decision. But the Bakuninists in Paris remained faithful to their alliance with the Jacobins almost to the last day of the Commune. Little detailed information is extant concerning the activities of the central committee. It had contacts with Lyons, and General Cluseret went there on its behalf, though it did not identify itself with Bakunin's attempted rising. But it did learn from it that the time to strike had not yet come. A circular signed by Varlin and Benoît Malon stated:

By every possible means we are cooperating in national defence, the supreme task of the moment ... The public meetings that we are organizing in every quarter, the organization of republican committees that we are hastening, the active part we are taking in the work of republican municipalities ... have no other aim than that.

Nevertheless we are not neglecting necessary precautions against the scattered and threatening reaction. We are therefore organizing our vigilance committees in every quarter, and we are pressing forward to the foundation of the districts that were so useful in 1793.

Believe us, you must act as follows: (1) stimulate by every possible means the patriotism that must save revolutionary France; (2) take energetic measures against the bourgeois and Bonapartist reaction; press for the acceptance of great defensive measures by the organization of the republican committees, the first elements of the future revolutionary communes.[45]

The armistice got rid of the Prussian millstone for them, or so, at least, they thought, and now the time for action had come. The first task was to win over the National Guard, whose numbers had grown enormously and whose composition had fundamentally altered during the siege. Whereas previously it had been an instrument of the possessing classes, scarcely yielding in loyalty to the Imperial Guard itself, its ranks were now filled with workers and members of the petty bourgeoisie. After the armistice Paris had a garrison of 12,000 regular troops, but there were 256 battalions of the National Guard. If they came over to the side of the revolution, victory, at any rate in Paris, was assured.

The National Guard had formed its own central committee. Within a short time Varlin and his friends had succeeded in gaining influence upon the battalions and the central committee. A meeting of the delegates of the National Guard was held on 10 March 1871 and presided over by Pindy, the Bakuninist who had attempted a rising on 9 August in the previous year. One battalion after another declared itself for the revolution. Varlin was full of confidence. P. L. Lavrov, the Russian philosopher and revolutionary, who was living in Paris and knew Varlin, describes in a letter a conversation he had with him a few days before 18 March. 'Another week,' Varlin said, 'and seventeen of the twenty *arrondissements* will be ours; the other three will not be for us, but they will not do anything against us. Then we shall turn the prefecture of police out of Paris, overthrow the Government and Frances will follow us.'[46]

Varlin had foreseen well. A Government attempt to take away the rifles of the National Guard precipitated the outbreak of the revolution by a few days. Nevertheless Varlin's calculation was correct. On 18 March fifteen of the twenty *arrondissements* acknowledged the authority of the central committee of the National Guard; 215 of the 256 battalions adhered to it. The Commune was proclaimed in Paris.

'The International did not raise a finger to make the Commune', Engels later wrote to Sorge.[47] Varlin was one of the two secretaries of the Paris regional council; but his work for the Commune was not done as secretary of the International. The minutes of the meetings of the regional council during this period have been preserved, and the meagreness of references to the movement that led to the Commune is astonishing. To Lavrov, who was a comparatively slight acquaintance, Varlin made no secret of what was going forward, while at the same time those delegates of the regional council who were not his associates had no idea of what the morrow might bring forth. On 17 March, the day before the rising, a delegate wrote in answer to Gambon, who wanted to know what the attitude of the regional council was to the assembly at Versailles: 'In view of the obscurity of the political situation, the regional council, like you, is in perplexity. What is to be done? What do the people really feel at heart'?[48] All the same, the organizers of the Commune were leading Paris members of the International, though the General Council in London did not 'raise a finger'. There is no reference in any documents or in any letter of Marx or Engels, even in those of the most confidential nature, that gives the slightest indication that the rising in Paris was demanded, much less organized by London.

But nevertheless, as Engels wrote in the same letter to Sorge, the Commune was 'unquestionably the spiritual child of the International';[49] not because Marx and Engels declared complete solidarity with Varlin and his Bakuninist comrades or with the Blanquists or with Pyat and his Jacobins – they knew practically nothing whatever about the activities of these groups in February and the first half of March; not because the Commune was 'staged' by the International, which it was not; but because the Commune, with all the limitations of its time and place, with all its illusions and all its mistakes, was the European proletariat's first great battle against the bourgeoisie. Whether it was a mistake at that juncture to resort to arms, whether the time was misjudged, the leaders deluded, the means unsuitable, all such questions receded before the fact that the proletariat in Paris was fighting for its emancipation and the emancipation of the working class. The latter was the battle-cry of the International. Marx's attitude to the Commune was determined by that fact.

Unfortunately only a few of Marx's utterances during those months have survived, but all the indications available go to show that from the first he regarded the Commune's prospects of success as very slight. Oberwinder, an Austrian socialist, who later became a police agent, says in his memoirs that 'a few days after the outbreak of the March rising in Paris Marx wrote to Vienna that the course it had taken precluded all prospects of success.' The utmost that Marx hoped for was a compromise, an honourable peace between Paris and Versailles.

Such an agreement, however, was only attainable if the Commune forced it upon its enemy. But this it failed to do. 'If they succumb', Marx wrote to Kugelmann, 'only their kind-heartedness is to blame.'[50] On 6 April he wrote to Liebknecht:

'If the Parisians are beaten it looks as if it will be by their own fault, but a fault really deriving from their excessive decency.' The central committee and later the Commune, he said, gave the mischievous wretch, Thiers, time to centralize the hostile forces (1) by foolishly not wishing to start civil war, as though Thiers himself had not started it by his attempted forcible disarming of Paris, and (2) by wishing to avoid the appearance of usurping power, wasting valuable time electing the Commune – its organization, etc., wasted still more time – instead of marching on Versailles immediately after the forces of reaction had been suppressed in Paris.[51] Marx believed the Government would only consent to a compromise if the struggle against Versailles – military, economic and moral – was conducted with extreme vigour. Marx regarded as one of the Commune's greatest mistakes the fact that it treated the Bank of France as a holy of holies off which it must piously keep its hands. Had it taken possession of the Bank of France it would have been able in case of need to threaten the country's whole economic life in such a fashion as to force the Versailles Government very quickly to give in. Once civil war had broken out it must be continued according to the rules of war. But during the first few weeks the Commune conducted it sluggishly, and worse, in the face of an imminent attack it failed to consolidate the position of its weak but important outposts outside Paris. Even the steps taken in the rest of the country to weaken the enemy at the gates of Paris were only half-heartedly carried out, if not altogether neglected. 'Alas! in the provinces the action taken is only local and pacific', Marx wrote on 13 May to Fränkel in Paris.[52] The action in the provinces which Marx considered so necessary had, of course, nothing in common with some adventurous plans which were being hatched in Switzerland. There the old insurrectionary leaders, J. P. Becker and Rüstow, were planning an invasion of the South of France by Swiss members of the International. They believed they would carry the people with them and rescue Paris. In other words they planned a repetition of Herwegh's expedition of 1848. The 'Legion of Internationalists' would have benefited no one but the Commune's enemies. Becker complained later that 'London' would have nothing to do with the enterprise, and 'London' meant Marx. When the Commune was on the point of collapse Marx advised the leaders with whom he was in contact to transfer 'papers that would be compromising to the *canaille* at Versailles' to a safe place. He believed that the threat of publishing them might force them to moderation. All that Marx did, all the advice that he gave, was directed to one end. 'With a small amount of common sense', he wrote ten years later to the Dutchman, Domela Nieuwenhuis, 'the Commune could have attained all that was attainable at that time, namely a compromise that would have been useful to the whole mass of the people.'[53]

Bakunin, however, hoped not for a compromise but for a heroic defeat. He had as little faith as Marx in victory for the people of Paris. 'But their deaths will not be in vain if they do their duty', he wrote to his friend Ozerov at the beginning of April. 'In perishing let them burn down at least the half of Paris.'[54] He could not contain himself with joy at the thought of the day 'ou le diable s'éveillera' and a bonfire would be made of at least a part of the old world. At Locle, where he was living at the time, he waited impatiently for 'heroic' deeds. One of his followers describes how

he foresaw the Commune's downfall, but what he wanted above all else was that it should have a worthy end. He talked about it in advance and said: 'My friends, is it not necessary that the Tuileries be burned down?' And when the Tuileries were burned down, he entered the group room with rapid strides – though he generally walked very slowly – struck the table with his stick and cried: 'Well, my friends, the Tuileries are in flames. I'll stand a punch all round!'[55]

Bakunin had no contacts with Paris. What happened there happened without him, without his advice or help.

Marx's opportunities of influencing the course of events in Paris were not much better. The Paris regional council's messages to the General Council were more than meagre. Towards the end of April, Marx complained that the General Council had not received a single letter from the Paris section. True, he had had a special emissary, the shoemaker Auguste Serraillier, in Paris since the end of March, but Serraillier could do nothing in the face of the ranting of the Jacobins. Pyat and Vésinier were particularly prominent in this direction, and the help which Serraillier besought of the General Council did not avail him very much. The otherwise excellent and enthusiastic Serraillier was not even adequate as a reporter, and Marx learned practically nothing from him. The difficulties of keeping up a regular correspondence between London and blockaded Paris were, of course, very great. Marx managed occasionally to smuggle information through to Paris by making use of a German businessman, and two or three letters even reached Varlin and Fränkel, the leading Communards. But these only serve to demonstrate what is also demonstrated by all the rest of the evidence; namely the smallness of the extent to which Marx was able to influence the Commune. But he could at least work for it.[56]

From the very first day, to quote his words in a letter to Kugelmann, 'the wolves and curs of the old society'[57] descended in a pack upon the Paris workers; they lied, cheated, slandered, no means were too filthy, no sadistic fantasy too absurd to be employed. The liberal Press yielded in nothing to the openly reactionary Press, and Bismarck's newspapers used the same phrases as did Thiers's papers and the great English Press. And they were believed. Even those who otherwise looked with favour upon the International wavered and wished to repudiate the Paris 'monsters'. Even some of the English members of the General Council objected to the General Council's defence of the Commune, in spite of the fact that in England there was still some possibility of distinguishing the true from the false. Other countries were entirely without information. The General Council was overwhelmed with inquiries from everywhere. Marx informed Fränkel that he wrote several hundred letters 'to all the corners of the earth where we have contacts',[58] and from time to time he managed to get an article into the Press. But that was not sufficient by far. The General Council had to proclaim the International's attitude to the Commune to the whole world.

Ten days after the rising Marx was instructed by the General Council to write an address 'to the people of Paris'. But at a meeting on 4 April it was decided temporarily to postpone it, as on account of the blockade it would not have reached those to whom it was addressed.[59] It was also intended to issue a manifesto to the workers of other countries, but this too was postponed, and for two reasons. On 25 April Marx wrote to Fränkel that the General Council was still waiting for news from day to day, but the Paris sections remained silent; [60] and the General Council could wait no longer, for the English workers were waiting impatiently for enlightenment. Marx was forced to toil through the English newspapers – French newspapers only reached England very irregularly – to find what he wanted. His notebooks during this period are full of newspaper cuttings.[61] Even the apparently least important details were valuable to him; he kept them all and tried patiently to form a picture of the great event that was happening from the chaotic jumble of truth and half-truth and fiction that confronted him. On top of these difficulties another one came to hamper him. At a time when every ounce of his energy was demanded he became ill. During the first half of May he was unable to attend the meetings of the General Council; he could only report, through Engels, that he was working on the manifesto. On 30 May, when at last he was able to read his address, 'The Civil War in France',[62] to the members of the General Council, the Commune had already been honourably defeated.

In that bloody week of May 20,000 Communards had been killed on the barricades, cut down in the streets by the blood-thirsty Versailles troops, or massacred in the prison yards. Tens of thousands of prisoners awaited death or banishment. This was not the moment for writing an historical treatise, a cool and dispassionate analysis and critique of the Commune. The manifesto was no lament for the dead, no funeral elegy, but a rapturous hymn to the martyrs of the war of proletarian emancipation, an aggressive defence of those who were slandered even in death. Never had Marx, the passionate fighter, fought so passionately. One recalls his scepticism at the beginning of the war. He had written that after twenty years of the Bonapartist farce one was scarcely justified in counting on revolutionary heroism. The Commune had taught him he was wrong. He looked on, astonished and overwhelmed at 'the elasticity, the historical initiative, the self-sacrificing spirit of these Parisians'. In a letter to Kugelmann he wrote:

> After six months of starvation and destruction, at the hands of internal treachery even more than through the foreign enemy, they rose under the Prussian bayonets as though the war between France and Germany had never existed and the enemy were not outside the gates of Paris. History has no comparable example of such greatness.[63]

The address hailed Paris, 'working, thinking, fighting, bleeding Paris, almost forgetful, in its incubation of a new society, of the cannibals at its gates – radiant in the enthusiasm of its historic initiative.'

What had the Commune been accused of? Of acts of terrorism? The shooting of General Thomas and Lecomte? The execution of the hostages? The death of the two officers

> was a summary act of lynch justice performed despite the instance of some delegate of the central committee ... The inveterate habits acquired by the soldiery under the training of the enemies of the working class are, of course, not likely to change the very moment these soldiers change sides.

But the hostages were shot. Yes, that was true.

> When Thiers, as we have seen, from the very beginning of the conflict, enforced the humane practice of shooting down the Communal prisoners, the Commune, to protect their lives, was obliged to resort to the Prussian practice of securing hostages. The lives of the hostages had been forfeited over and over again by the continued shooting of prisoners on the part of the Versaillais ... The real murderer of Archbishop Darboy is Thiers.

A week after the massacre of thousands of Communards criticism of a terror which had provoked another terror was impossible. The observations in Marx's notebooks show what he thought of the senseless actions of the Jacobins. The address, without naming them, talked of people who hampered the real action of the working classes, 'exactly as men of that sort have hampered the full development of every previous revolution. They are an unavoidable evil; with time they are shaken off; but time was not allowed to the Commune.'

But although the Commune had no time to develop, although it only remained 'a rough sketch of national organization', to those who refused to allow their view to be obscured by secondary things, it revealed its 'true secret'. And that was that

it was essentially a working-class government, the produce of the struggle of the producing against the appropriating class, the political form at last discovered under which to work out the economical emancipation of Labour. The Commune was the reabsorption of the state power by society as its own living forces instead of as forces controlling and subduing it, by the popular masses themselves, forming their own force instead of the organized force of their suppression, the political form of their social emancipation instead of the artificial force (appropriated by their oppressors) of society wielded for their oppression by their enemies. The form was simple like all great things.

The workers had no ideals to realize, no ready-made utopias to introduce by decree of the people, but they had to set free the elements of a new society with which the old collapsing bourgeois society was pregnant. 'They know that in order to work out their own emancipation and along with it that higher form to which present society is irresistibly tending by its own economical agencies, they will have to pass through long struggles, through a series of historic processes, transforming circumstances and men.' These sentences recall, even at times in their very phrasing, those that Marx addressed to Willich and his followers – the Jacobins of their time – after the final collapse of the revolution of 1848 and 1849. He warned his followers against illusions, but his warnings were not shackles put upon them, hampering them, but gave power and strength and the unshakable conviction of final victory. The address ended with these stirring words:

Working men's Paris, with its Commune, will be for ever celebrated at the glorious harbinger of a new society. Its martyrs are enshrined in the great heart of the working class. Its exterminators history has already nailed to that external pillory from which all the prayers of their priests will not avail to redeem them.

The final words were like the sounding of the Last Trump. The Commune was defeated, a battle was lost, but the working-class struggle continued.[64]

[20]

The Decline of the International[1]

SOCIALISTS in France in the 1860s were either Proudhonists or Blanquists, with here and there an isolated Saint-Simonist. But there were no French Marxists. Not one in a hundred members of the International in France knew that the leader of the General Council in London was a German named Karl Marx. In the other Latin countries the situation was the same. The name of Lassalle meant a great deal to the German workers, even to those who were not his followers. They sang songs about him and his picture hung upon the walls of their rooms. The older generation in the Rhineland remembered Marx from 1848, but that was nearly a quarter of a century ago, and in the meantime most people had forgotten him. To only a minute proportion of the younger generation did his name mean anything at all. Not till the middle of the 1860s did this situation slowly and gradually begin to alter, but even in 1870 his name was entirely unknown to the general public. In England Marx was less known than anywhere else. Perhaps here and there some Urquhartite or former Chartist could recollect his name, but that was all. Marx, who had no wish for popularity, set no store on his name being associated with the International, and his signature, when it appeared under any of the pronouncements of the General Council, was always tucked in among those of many others. He spoke at practically no public meetings, he wrote no signed articles, and sufficed himself with the immediate task before him, that of 'influencing the workers' movement behind the scenes', as he occasionally wrote to a friend.[2]

The Commune made him 'the best calumniated and the most menaced man of London', as he described himself (the English phrase is his own) in a letter he wrote Kugelmann in the middle of June 1871.[3] 'It really does one good after being stuck in the mud for twenty years', he added. He was constantly pestered by 'newspaper fellows and others' who wanted to see the 'monster' with their own eyes. For the man behind the International, that gigantic conspiracy against the whole world, who publicly declared his solidarity with its atrocious misdeeds in Paris, must necessarily be a monster.[4] The French Government was very well informed about the International, and had had more to do with it than any other government in Europe. It had staged great trials of its members, set an army of spies after it and knew something of Marx's overwhelming influence on the General Council. On the day after the proclamation of the Commune it had an alleged letter of Marx's to the French sections of the International printed in *Le Journal*, containing the most violent criticism of their political acts. The letter reproved them for intervening in politics instead of confining themselves to the social tasks which should have been their only concern. This attempt to represent Marx as the good spirit of the 'good' Internatonal while the Communards were base renegades sadly missed its mark, for no one in Paris took it seriously. So the Versailles Government tried something else. On 2 April *Le Soir* announced that it had been authoritatively ascertained that Karl Marx, one of the most influential leaders of the International, had been private secretary to Count Bismarck in 1857 and had never severed his connection with his former patron. The Bonapartist papers spread this revelation throughout France. So Marx was a hireling of Prussia, and the real leader of the International was Bismarck, at whose instigation the Commune had been set up. This story hardly tallied with another, according to which the International was waging a war on the whole of civilized humanity, which was the reason why the Versailles Government requested and received Bismarck's help against the Commune. As Marx wrote to P. Coenen at the end of March, word was spread to the whole well-disposed Press of Europe 'to use falsehood as its greatest weapon against the International. In the eyes of these honourable champions of religion, order, the family and property there is nothing in the least wrong in the sin of lying.'[5]

It was necessary for the Versailles Government to disguise the warfare it was waging upon the people of Paris. The International was represented as the enemy of France and of the French. Its chief, Karl Marx, was the enemy of the human race. A flick of the hand, and hey presto! Bismarck's agent was converted into a kind of anti-Christ. But this elevation of their political opponent, who after all really did exist in human form, into the demoniacal sphere did not suit the German philistines, who reduced him to more manageable proportions. Thus the Berlin papers invented a fairy-tale of how Karl Marx, leader of the International, enriched himself at the expense of the workers he misled. This story was subsequently often repeated. Soon afterwards the announcement of Marx's death in the Bonapartist *L'Avenir libéral* served for a few days to relieve the terrified population of their nightmare. But their relief lasted a few days only. The hated chief of the hated International lived on. His name re-echoed across Europe, through which the spectre of communism once more stalked abroad.[6]

The Commune made a myth of the International. Aims were imputed to it that it never pursued, resources were ascribed to it that it never possessed, power was attributed to it of which it had never dared to dream. In 1869 the report of the General Council to the Basle congress had poured ridicule upon the alleged wealth with which the busy tongues of the police and the wild imaginations of the possessing classes had endowed it. 'Although these people are good Christians,' it stated, 'if they had lived at the time of the origins of Christianity they would have hurried to a Roman bank to forge an account for St Paul.' The panic of Europe's rulers elevated the International to the status of a world power. 'The whole of Europe is encompassed by the widespread freemasonry of this organization', said Jules Favre in a memorandum he sent on 6 June 1871 to the representatives of France abroad, directing them to urge the governments to which they were accredited to common action against the common foe. England declined the invitation, but Lord Bloomfield, the British Ambassador at Vienna, illustrating British concern, made diplomatic inquiries with regard to the extent of the activities of the International in the Austrian Empire. In the course of Bismarck's conversations at Gastein with Count Beust, the Austrian Chancellor, the subject of the struggle against the International was discussed at length. Beust mentioned with satisfaction in his memorandum that both governments had spontaneously expressed a desire for defensive measures and common action against it, after the

sensational events that characterized the fall of the Paris Commune, in view of its expansion and the dangerous influence it is beginning to exert on the working class and against the present foundations of the state and society. The thought inevitably arises whether it might not be well to counter this universal association of workers with a universal association of employers, oppose the solidarity of possession to the solidarity of non-possession, and set up a counter-International against the International. The power of capital is still an assured and well-buttressed factor in public life.

The situation, however, was not nearly so threatening as some feared and others hoped. If Bismarck behaved to some extent as though he were preparing to bow before the storm of a Commune in Berlin, he was actuated less by fear of an immediate outbreak than by his wish to frighten the liberal bourgeoisie from forming even the loosest of alliances with the socialist workers against the ruling *Junkers*. But in spite of all exaggerations and overestimates, whether entirely fabricated or genuinely believed, one fact remained. Revolutionary workers had remained in power in Paris for more than two months. Whether the Commune had in every respect acted rightly might justifiably be doubted, but the time for criticism was not yet. One fact dominated everything else, and, in Marx's words, made the Commune 'a new point of departure of world-historical significance'.[7] Workers had seized the power for the first time.

Hitherto the International had concerned itself primarily, though not of course exclusively, with economic matters such as the shortening of the working day, the securing of higher wages, supporting strikes, defence against strike-breaking, etc., and to the overwhelming majority of its members it had appeared as an organization aiming primarily at the improvement of the economic position of the worker. But the situation had undergone a fundamental alteration now. History itself had placed the proletariat's struggle for the seizure of power upon the order of the day. After the Commune it was impossible for the International to continue to restrict itself to activities which were political only by implication. It was necessary to convert its sections from propagandist organizations and trade-union-like groups into political parties. After the Communards had fought on the field of battle it was impossible for the workers of the International to revert to the narrow struggle for their immediate economic interests in the factories and merely draw public attention to themselves from time to time by issuing a political proclamation from the sidelines, which might be read or not. They must enter the political field themselves, welded into a firm organization, with a party that openly proclaimed its programme – the seizure of the state power by the working class as the preliminary to its economic liberation. The conclusion the governments of Europe drew from the Commune was that the International was a political world power, menacing to them all. The conclusion the International drew from it was that it was the latter that they must become.

With the 'politicalizing' of the International the function of the General Council necessarily altered. In the past the General Council had practically not interfered at all in the life of individual sections, but now a thorough-going coordination of their activities, though within definite limits, had become imperative. That did not involve the assumption by the General Council of a kind of supreme command over the various sections, dictating to them from London the exact details of what they were to do. It did, however, involve a multiplication of the tasks devolving upon it, and the adoption by it of an entirely different position from that which it had adopted, and been compelled to adopt, in the past. And therewith internal questions arose of which not even the preliminaries had existed before.

Marx and Engels devoted the months that followed the collapse of the Commune to the task of energetically reconstructing the International. 'The long-prepared blow', to use Marx's phrase, was struck at a conference held in London in the second half of September 1874. In a number of countries the sections of the International had not recovered from the blows that had descended upon them as a result of the war and its aftermath, and these countries were not represented at the conference. That was the reason for the summoning of a conference instead of a congress. On this occasion Marx presided over the discussions of the International for the first time since 1865. He drafted a resolution concerning the question of the political struggle, which had become the central issue. The resolution observed that a faulty translation of the statutes into French had resulted in a mistaken conception of the International's position. (The statutes provisionally set up by the General Council in 1864 stated: 'The economic emancipation of the workers is the great aim to which all political action must be subordinated as a means.' The statutes were confirmed by the first congress, held in 1866. In the French version of the congress report issued by the Geneva section the words 'as a means' are missing. All the other versions have them. Neither in the surviving minutes of the congress nor in the contemporary Press is there any mention of any alteration of the statutes. The fact that the last two words are missing from the French version is undoubtedly an accident and possibly merely a printer's error.) The conference reminded the members of the International 'that in the militant state of the working class its economic progress and political action are indissolubly united'.

Previous congresses had only dealt incidentally with internal International affairs. At this conference, indicating the altered situation, they played the leading role. The conference adopted resolutions concerning the organization of sections in those countries in which the International had been banned, as well as resolutions concerning the split in Switzerland, the Bakuninist Alliance, and other matters. The policy of the International Press was directed to be conducted along certain definite lines – a thing quite unprecedented in the past. All the conference's transactions were aimed at strengthening the structure of the International for the approaching political fray.

Marx, and Engels like him, believed that as soon as the period of reaction, which could not but be brief, was over the International was destined for a rapid and immense advance. For this the London conference was intended to prepare the way. But a year later the International was dead.

Of the two countries which had been its main support, France's withdrawal from the movement lasted not just for a few months or for a year but for a full decade. The advance guard of the French proletariat had fallen at the Paris barricades or was languishing in prison or perishing in banishment in New Caledonia. The small groups that survived were insignificant. Those that were not broken up by the police dissolved gradually of their own accord.

In the other of the two countries which had been the International's main support developments were unfavourable too.[8] In England the workers' movement had no need to be urged to take the political road. Even before the reorganization of the International it had taken that road itself, and was now pursuing definite if narrowly-circumscribed political aims; but at the very moment when it should have been marshalling its ranks for a general attack on the power of the possessing classes, it withdrew from the struggle. So many of its demands had been granted that it started feeling satisfied. Stormy meetings and uproarious demonstrations had demanded universal suffrage, and universal suffrage had been attained. England's economic strides relieved the situation to such an extent that the Government no longer had cause to fear the consequences of reform. It was able to repeal a whole series of legal enactments that imposed oppressive restrictions on the trade unions, and this deprived the trade union leaders of yet another impulse towards political action. After the collapse of the Chartist movement only relatively small groups had worked to revive an independent political movement among the workers, and such a thing looked entirely superfluous now. Many prominent trade unionists once more drew nearer to the liberals, who took advantage of the opportunity to make the trade union cause their own; or at least acted as if they did, though a debt of gratitude was certainly due to the energy of the radical liberals, men like Professor Beesly and Frederic Harrison. In many constituencies liberals supported the candidature of trade union leaders. In these profoundly altered circumstances not much attention was paid to the General Council's admonition to create an independent political movement. Opposition to the General Council, weak at first but definite nevertheless, reared its head among the trade union leaders. Several other factors contributed to this. Objection was taken to Marx's definitely pro-Irish attitude, and the General Council's uncompromising partisanship of the Commune was felt as inopportune and disturbing by labour leaders who had started associating themselves with the ruling system and, though the influence of this may at first only have been slight, in some cases had become members of royal commissions.

Opposition to the General Council first expressed itself in a demand for the formation of a special regional council for England. This demand was thoroughly justified according to the statutes. All the other countries had their own councils, but up to 1871 the General Council served also as regional council for England. This had come about quite spontaneously. London was the headquarters of the International and no one – least of all Marx – felt there was any necessity for a special council for England apart from the General Council. He formulated his reasons in a 'confidential communication' at the beginning of 1870. Although the revolutionary initiative was probably destined to start from France, he stated, England alone could provide the level for a serious economic revolution. He added that the General Council being placed in the happy position of having its hand on that great lever of the proletarian revolution, what madness, they might almost say what a crime it would be to let it fall into purely English hands! The English had all the material necessary for the social revolution. What they lacked was generalizing spirit and revolutionary passion. The General Council alone could supply the want and accelerate the genuine revolutionary movement in that country and consequently everywhere ... If one made the General Council and the English regional council distinct, what would be the immediate effects? Placed between the General Council of the International and the General Council of the Trades Unions, the regional council would have no authority and the General Council would lose the handling of the great lever.[9]

This argument was as valid in the autumn of 1871 as it had been in the spring of 1870, but in the meantime the centrifugal forces in England had grown so strong that it was necessary to make concessions if the International as a whole were not to be jeopardized. The London conference decided that a British regional council should be formed. The immediate consequences appeared entirely favourable. The number of British sections increased rapidly, and relations between the regional council and the trades unions became closer and better. On the other hand the General Council lost its influence in England, and within a short time it became evident that there was a danger of the General Council severing its connection with the International altogether.

Though there were some countries in which the strength of the International had increased in 1870 and 1871, the result of the withdrawal of France and the altered situation in England was that it was extraordinarily weakened as a whole. For the advance of the German workers' movement and the shifting of the centre of gravity across the Rhine was an inadequate compensation.

These years saw the emergence in Germany of a workers'

party which was the archetype and pattern of continental workers' parties up to the First World War. It approximated closely to what Marx insisted should be the form of the political movement of the proletariat, though it failed to fulfil his demands in every way. Sharp, sometimes over-sharp criticism appeared in the letters Marx addressed to the leaders of the German party. Nevertheless, Marx on the whole approved of the path that the German socialists had struck out upon. He approved of their work of organization and propaganda, and of their attitude in Parliament and to the other parties. The party visibly grew from year to year and it was to be expected that within a short time it would play a leading role in the International. It never did so, for two reasons. The first was the severity of German legal restrictions on the right to form associations; the Government were constantly on the watch for an opportunity of suppressing the German workers' party, and its leaders therefore assiduously avoided doing anything that might have given them the opportunity of doing so under cover of legal forms. In the second place the German party was completely absorbed with its work in Germany. The German socialists proclaimed their complete solidarity with the International, but that was practically all. The German party remained practically without significance as far as the inner life of the International was concerned.

Marx blamed Wilhelm Liebknecht for the 'lukewarmness' with which he conducted the 'business of the International' in Germany. But it is doubtful whether anyone could have done better than Liebknecht, who was absolutely tireless and was completely devoted to Marx. After the London conference Marx informed Liebknecht that the General Council wished him to establish direct contact with the principal places in Germany.[10] This task Liebknecht had already begun. He actually succeeded in forming sections in Berlin and other towns. These, however, led a very precarious existence and were not of much use to the General Council. In spite of all the sympathy with which the German socialists regarded the International, they were prevented from helping the General Council by the fact that they embodied in a pronounced fashion the very thing which, in the eyes of its opponents, made the General Council unworthy of continuing to lead the International – namely 'authoritarian socialism'. For such acts of 'subservience to the state' as participating in elections not only failed to impress but actually went far to repel many members of the International in those countries in which Bakunin's 'anti-authoritarian socialism' was now triumphant.

The Commune had by no means corresponded to Bakunin's ideals. He had had no great hopes of it himself, and his friends in Paris had had to acquiesce in actions that conflicted sharply with what Bakunin demanded of a revolution. This, however, did not prevent Bakunin from annexing the Commune for his own 'anti-authoritarian communism' and declaring that Marx's ideas had been thoroughly confuted by it. The pitiful end of the rising at Lyons had made him despair of the workers' capacity for revolt, but the glow of the burning Tuileries once more illumined the future in his eyes. So all strength and passion had not yet departed from the world. The revolution was not postponed into the indefinite future but was as imminent as it had been before Sedan. It was bound to come soon, quite soon, perhaps tomorrow. To confine oneself to petty, philistine 'politicalizing' as the German social democrats did was equivalent in Bakunin's eyes to a renunciation of the revolution. He resumed the work that he had interrupted for some months, and started spinning his web of secret societies anew. The Commune had made good the wrong done the world by the triumph of Prussia, and the workers' hatred of the butchers of Versailles was a guarantee of ultimate victory. That hatred must not be allowed to cool. Bakunin flung himself zealously into his task.

The Latin countries, especially Spain and Italy, seemed to him to hold out the most favourable prospects for the social revolution. Spain had been the scene of a lively struggle between republicans and constitutionalists since the expulsion of the Bourbons in 1868. The constitutionalists intended the vacant throne for some foreign prince. The struggle broke out sporadically into civil war, and war to the death was declared on the Catholic Church as the mainstay of reaction; and everywhere the workers were stirring. Their new-won national unity brought the people of Italy no peace. The struggle with the dispossessed Pope kept the whole country on tenterhooks. Workers and peasants were as near as ever to starvation in the new kingdom that had been united after such suffering and sacrifice, and the intellectuals were deeply disappointed by what they had so ardently longed for. Bakunin rested his brightest hopes upon Italy and Spain. Sparks from the burning South would leap across into France, Belgium and Latin Switzerland.

Of Germany Bakunin had no hopes whatever. His hopes of that country had been weak before. Now, after the German victory, he felt compelled to abandon them altogether. For were the German socialists not manifestly paying the state the same idolatry as the German bourgeoisie? Where were they when they should have been attacking the brutal victor, Bismarck? What had they done to save the Commune? That Bebel and Liebknecht had voted against war credits, that their protest against the mad orgies of unleashed militarism[11] had caused them to be put on trial for high treason was forgotten or did not count. In his struggle for domination of the International Bakunin exploited with great skill the chauvinistic anti-German undercurrents that had been stimulated by, and had survived, the war. Germany meant Bismarck, but it meant Liebknecht and Bebel too. A German, citizen of a country inclined to despotism by its very nature, was leader of the General Council, and he was the inventor and advocate of 'state socialism', a conception that corresponded exactly with the German temperament. The International was in the hands of a pan-German, and the 'League of Latin and Slavonic Races' must rescue it. In his private letters Bakunin placed no bridle upon his hatred of the Germans, and fanned chauvinistic inclinations to the utmost of his power, though in his public utterances he was noticeably more cautious.

The situation in Europe was as favourable for Bakunin's

renewed struggle for the control of the International as it was unfavourable for his conception of the social revolution. Everything conspired to help him; the abstention of the Germans, the chauvinism of the Latin countries, the backwardness of Italy and Spain, where revolutionary romanticism flourished exuberantly because of the weakness of the young proletariat and the strength of the old carbonari traditions.

Bakunin quickly realized the most effective way of conducting his attack on the General Council. The most heterogeneous elements could be united in an attack on Marx if they could be given a single aim, namely the revocation of the decisions of the London conference. The watchword of Bakunin's campaign was: 'Down with the General Council, who aim at forcing the sections of the International into the political struggle and usurping power over them. Down with the "dictatorship" of the General Council!'

The attack opened in Latin Switzerland, Bakunin's surest stronghold now as in the past. In 1870 there had been a split between the 'anti-authoritarians' and the groups that adhered to the General Council. The 'anti-authoritarians' had created their own regional council and become a kind of international centre of the Bakunist movement. As soon as the decisions of the London conference were known this regional council summoned a regional congress to protest against them, and more particularly against 'the General Council's dictatorial attitude towards the sections'. The congress met at Sonvilliers on 12 November 1871 and openly declared war on the General Council. It addressed a circular to all the sections of the International, skated cleverly over the fact that the Geneva Council had assigned the working class the duty of the conquest of political power and expanded itself at length on the latter's alleged attempt to dominate the sections. The circular stated that it was a fact, proved by experience a thousand times, that authority invariably corrupted those who exercised it. 'The General Council could not escape from that inevitable law.' The General Council wanted the principle of authority introduced into the International. The resolutions carried by the

London conference, which had been irregularly and unconstitutionally summoned,

are a grave infringement of the general statutes and tend to make of the International, a free federation of autonomous sections, a hierarchical and authoritarian organization of disciplined sections, placed entirely under the control of a General Council which may at its pleasure refuse them membership or even suspend their activities.

Finally the circular demanded the immediate summoning of a general congress.[12]

Bakunin's posing as the advocate of complete sectional autonomy was a clever move. The difficulties and inevitable friction involved in the reorganization of the International and the transfer of the chief emphasis to the political struggle created sympathy for Bakunin's demands among groups that otherwise had not the least use for his social-revolutionary programme. Bakunin's calculations now and subsequently proved themselves to be entirely correct.

A private circumstance compelled Bakunin to open his attack on the General Council soon after the London conference, when his preparations were not so advanced as they ought to have been. He knew that the Nechaiev affair had been raised at the conference. The conference had authorized the General Council to 'publish immediately a formal declaration indicating that the International Working Men's Association had nothing whatever to do with the so-called conspiracy of Nechaiev, who had treacherously usurped and exploited its name.'[13] In addition, Utin, a Russian *émigré* living in Switzerland, was authorized to prepare a summarized report of the Nechaiev trial from the Russian Press and publish it in the Geneva paper *L'Égalité*.

The Nechaiev affair plays such an important role in the history of the International, or rather in the history of its decline, that it deserves to be recounted at some length.[14]

Nechaiev was the son of a servant in a small Russian provincial town. He put to such good use the few free hours tha his work as a messenger in the office of a factory left him that he succeeded in passing his examinations as an elementary school teacher. He starved and scraped until he had saved enough money to go to St Petersburg, where he had himself entered as an external student at the university. In his first winter term, in 1868, he entered the student movement, in which his energy and the radical nature of his views soon earned him prominence. But that was not enough for him. He wanted to be foremost, and in order to enhance his reputation as a revolutionary he started inventing stories of his adventurous past. First he said he had been a prisoner in the fortress of Petropavlovsk. Then he added an account of his daring escape. The majority of his listeners accepted all this unquestioningly; they were filled with indignation at the stories he told of his treatment by the prison warders, and a students' meeting was actually called and a delegation actually approached the university authorities. Nevertheless there were some who doubted. Some of the details of Nechaiev's prison experiences sounded improbable to the more experienced among his colleagues, and the officials declared that Nechaiev had never been under arrest.

Before this fact had been established, however, Nechaiev illegally went abroad to make contact with the Russian *émigré* leaders. He reached Geneva in March 1869 and made the acquaintance of Herzen and Ogarev, the patriarchs of the 'emigration', as well as of the representatives of the younger generation of refugees. He made an extraordinary impression upon them all. Herzen, who had grown old, tired and sceptical, said that Nechaiev went to one's head like absinthe. But the young student was not satisfied with praise and honour. He added details of his own. He said that Russia was on the eve of a tremendous revolutionary outbreak, which was being prepared by a widespread secret society. Of this society he was a delegate. And he repeated the story of his imprisonment and flight. In Geneva also there were a few people who refused to be taken in so easily. A number of *émigrés* had been prisoners in the fortress of Petropavlovsk themselves and knew how impossible it was to escape, and letters came from St Petersburg from people who ought to have known, saying that the secret society did not exist, or at any rate gave not the slightest sign of its existence. But those who regarded Nechaiev with suspicion belonged to groups who were hostile to Bakunin. It was these who not long afterwards formed a 'Russian section' of the International and made Marx their representative on the General Council. This, however, cannot have been the deciding factor in causing Bakunin to ignore their warnings. He knew the fortress of Petropavlovsk himself and knew – could not possibly have helped knowing – that Nechaiev was a liar. But what did it matter? Lies could be useful in revolutionizing the slothful, and after all this Nechaiev was a marvellous fellow. Bakunin wrote a regular panegyric about him in a letter to Guillaume, describing him as

one of those young fanatics who hesitate at nothing and fear nothing and recognize as a principle that many are bound to perish at the hands of the Government but that one must not rest an instant until the people has risen. They are admirable, these young fanatics – believers without God and heroes without phrases!

Bakunin and Nechaiev became fast friends.

Bakunin did not apparently formally admit Nechaiev to his secret society. The idea of his association with Nechaiev being surveyed by its otherwise fully initiated members was an uncomfortable one to him. The Bukanin–Nechaiev society was a quite intimate super-secret society, such as the old conspirator loved. Its object was the revolutionizing of Russia.

In the spring and summer of 1869 Bakunin wrote as many as ten pamphlets and proclamations, and Nechaiev had them printed. Among them was the subsequently famous *Revolutionary Catechism*,[15] which was intended to be a reply to the question of what were the best ways and menas of hastening the outbreak of the revolution in Russia. The answer was to be found by the consistent application of two principles. The first was 'the end justifies the means' and the second was 'the worse, the better'. Everything – and by that Bakunin meant everything without any exception whatever – that promoted the revolution was permissible and everything that hindered it was a crime. The revolutionary must concentrate on one aim, i.e. destruction. 'There is only one science for the revolutionary, the science of destruction. Day and night he must have but one thing before his eyes – destruction.' That was Bakunin's own summary of the duties of a revolutionary. Within the revolutionary organization the strictest centralization and the most rigorous discipline must prevail, and the members must be completely subordinate to their leaders. The object of this organization was 'to use all the means in its power to intensify and spread suffering and evil, which must end by driving the people to revolt'. The *Catechism* even defended terrorism, which, however, it did not recommend against the worst tyrants, because the longer such tyrants were allowed to rage the better it would be for the revolutionizing of the people.

Towards the end of the summer of 1869 Nechaiev travelled illegally to Russia, taking with him a mandate from the 'central committee of the European Revolutionary Alliance', written and signed by Bakunin, recommending him as a reliable delegate of that organization. Bakunin had actually had a special stamp prepared, with the words: 'Office of the foreign agents of the Russian revolutionary society Narodnaia Rasprava.'

Nechaiev remained in Russia for more than three months. He succeeded in forming an organization based on, or alleged to be based on, the *Revolutionary Catechism*. Revolutionary-minded young men were not so very difficult to find, and his letter of recommendation, signed by Bakunin, whose name was universally honoured, earned him the greatest respect. He chose Moscow as his centre and it was not long before he had gathered a group about him. Had he assigned it practical aims and objects, its fate would have been the usual fate of such organizations in Russia. It would eventually have been discovered and dissolved by the police, but two or three new groups would have arisen to take its place. To Nechaiev, however, that would have appeared an idle pastime. He wished his followers to believe that there was a secret revolutionary committee which they must unconditionally obey, and, true to the injunctions of the *Catechism*, he used every means that tended to serve his aim. Once, for instance, he persuaded an officer he knew to pose as a supervisory party official sent from the secret headquarters on special duty. That ruse might pass at a pinch. But Nechaiev did not shrink from even cruder mystifications, so crude that he ended by perplexing some of his own followers. Finally a student named Ivanov announced to other members of the group that he no longer believed in the existence of any committee, that Nechaiev was lying to them and that he wished to have nothing more to do with him. Nechaiev decided that the 'criminal' must die. He succeeded in persuading the rest of his followers that Ivanov was a traitor and that only his death could save them. On 29 November 1869 they lured Ivanov to a dark corner of a park and murdered him. Ivanov defended himself desperately and bit Nechaiev's hand to the bone as he was strangling him with a shawl. Nechaiev bore the scar for the rest of his life. The murderers were soon discovered and arrested, and only Nechaiev succeeded in escaping abroad.[16]

Detailed reports of Ivanov's murder appeared in the papers, and the crime was remembered for many years. It armed the Russian revolutionaries against Nechaiev-like methods.

Bakunin knew the whole story in detail, but it only enhanced Nechaiev's reputation in his eyes. On learning that Nechaiev had arrived in Geneva – he was living at Locarno at the time – he leapt so high with joy that he nearly broke his old skull against the ceiling, as he wrote to Ogarev. He invited Nechaiev to Locarno, looked after him and was his friend as before. 'This is the kind of organization of which I have dreamed and of which I go on dreaming', he wrote to his friend Richard.[17] 'It is the kind of organization I wanted to see among you.' At this time Bakunin had already started his struggle against the General Council of the International on the ground of its 'dictatorial arrogance'.

To the same period there belongs the incident which, apart

from the other reasons, led directly to Bakunin's expulsion from the International. His financial position had always been precarious, but in the autumn of 1869 he was in particularly desperate straits. Through some Russian students who were followers of his he was put into touch with a publisher who offered him 1,200 roubles – far more than the author himself ever got for it – for translating Marx's *Das Kapital*. Bakunin accepted the offer gladly and received an advance of 300 roubles. He did not show himself to be in any hurry to complete the task, however, and three months later he had only done sufficient to fill thirty-two printed pages. He readily let himself be convinced by Nechaiev that he had more important matters to fill his time and that he belonged to the revolution and must live for the revolution only. So he laid the work aside and gave Nechaiev full authority to come to an arrangement with the publisher. Nechaiev set about this task in an inimitable manner. It was impossible for Bakunin to communicate directly with the publisher himself on account of the police, and a student named Liubavin had undertaken to do so on his behalf. The contract had been formally made out in Liubavin's name and in the publisher's books Liubavin was nominally liable for the 300 roubles' advance. One day Liubavin received a letter bearing the stamp of Nechaiev's organization. Its most remarkable passages are quoted below:

DEAR SIR, On behalf of the bureau I have the honour to write to you as follows. We have received from the committee in Russia a letter which refers among other things to you. It states: 'It has come to the knowledge of the committee that a few young gentlemen, dilettanti liberals, living abroad, are beginning to exploit the knowledge and energy of certain people known to us, taking advantage of their hard-pressed financial straits. Valuable personalities, forced by these dilettanti exploiters to work for a day labourer's hire, are thereby deprived of the possibility of working for the liberation of mankind. Thus a certain Liubavin has given the celebrated Bakunin the task of translating a book by Marx, and, exploiting his financial distress just like a real exploiting bourgeois, has given him an advance and now insists on the work being completed. Bakunin, delivered in this manner to the mercy of young Liubavin, who is so concerned about the enlightenment of Russia, but only by the work of others, is prevented from being able to work for the supremely important cause of the Russian people, for which he is indispensable. How the behaviour of Liubavin and others like him conflicts with the cause of the freedom of the people and how contemptible, bourgeois and immoral their behaviour is compared with that of those they employ and how little it differs from the practices of the police must be clear to every decent person.

The committee entrusts the foreign bureau to inform Liubavin:

'(1) That if he and parasites like him are of the opinion that the translation of *Das Kapital* is so important to the Russian people at the present time they should pay for it out of their own pocket instead of studying chemistry and preparing themselves for fat professorships in the pay of the state . . .

'(2) It must immediately inform Bakunin that in accordance with the decision of the Russian revolutionary committee he is exempt from any moral duty to continue with the work of translation . . .'

Convinced that you understand, we request you, dear sir, not to place us in the unpleasant position of being compelled to resort to less civilized measures . . .

Amskiy,
Secretary to the Bureau.

Bakunin subsequently stoutly denied that he knew anything of the contents of this letter, and there is every reason to believe him. But when Liubavin sent him a letter indignantly protesting against these threats, Bakunin, instead of talking to Nechaiev about it, for he must have guessed who was behind it all, took occasion to be offended at Liubavin's intelligibly not very courteous tone. He wrote to Liubavin that he proposed to sever relations with him, that he would not continue the translation and would repay the advance. He never did repay the advance and must have known that he would never be able to do so.

In Nechaiev's opinion this species of blackmail was not only permissible to a revolutionary but was actually demanded of him. At every opportunity he threatened denunciation or the use of force, and stole his opponents' letters in order to be able to compromise them with the police. He shrank at nothing. He caused revolutionary appeals to be sent to one of his greatest enemies, a student named Negrescul, who was being kept under police observation, and, as Nechaiev expected, the material fell into police hands and Negrescul was arrested. He succumbed to tuberculosis in prison and died a few months after his release.

Bakunin knew what Nechaiev was capable of, as many others did by this time, but he remained loyal to him as before. Not till Nechaiev actually started threatening people whom Bakunin held dear – Herzen's daughter for instance – did Bakunin raise his voice against him. The final impulse that caused Bakunin to break with him seems to have been provided by Nechaiev's plan to form a gang for the specific purpose of robbing wealthy tourists in Switzerland. He even tried to force Ogarev's stepson to join him, whereupon Bakunin protested. At that Nechaiev appropriated a strongbox of Bakunin's containing correspondence, secret papers, and the statutes of his revolutionary organizations – including the original manuscript of the *Catechism* – and threatened Bakunin with publication should he take any steps against him.

That was the end of Bakunin's friendship with Nechaiev. Bakunin was horrified at the practical conclusions that Nechaiev drew from principles that he himself had helped him to formulate. The story that Nechaiev told some of his acquaintances, namely, that when he first came abroad he was an 'unspoiled, good and honourable youth' and that it was Bakunin who corrupted him, was, of course, not true. Nechaiev had started his mystifications in Russia before his first journey abroad. But Bakunin not only made no attempt to counteract Nechaiev's inclinations, he actually encouraged them by giving them a kind of theoretical foundation. Their quarrel is not sufficient to obliterate the fact that Nechaiev was very strongly influenced by Bakunin and that it was Bakunin himself who evolved the theory by which all things were permitted.

Not much more needs be said about Nechaiev's further career. He lived two more years abroad, first in London, then in Paris and finally in Switzerland. He published more revolutionary literature and threatened and blackmailed as before. Bakunin refused to have anything more to do with him and was so embittered against him that he would have liked to denounce him as a 'homicidal maniac, a dangerous and criminal lunatic, whom it was necessary to avoid'. Nechaiev was finally betrayed by a Polish *émigré* in the service of the police. He was arrested in Zürich in the middle of August 1872 and repatriated to Russia as a common criminal. On 8 January 1873 he was condemned to twenty years' hard labour in the mines of Siberia. He was not sent to Siberia, however, but confined in the fortress of Petropavlovsk. Such was his power over people that he actually succeeded in winning over the soldiers who kept guard over him, and they helped to put him in touch with revolutionaries outside. He devised a plan for seizing the fortress during a visit of the Tsar's, but he was betrayed by one of his fellow prisoners and transferred to severe solitary confinement. He died of scurvy on 21 November 1882.

Marx had been a close student of Russian affairs since the 1850s. At first he paid attention chiefly to Russian foreign policy, but later he devoted himself with ever-increasing interest to the social movement in Russia itself.[18] At the end of the 1860s he learned Russian in order to be able to study the sources in the original. The activities of Bakunin and Nechaiev attracted his attention early. More detailed information was first supplied him by Hermann Lopatin, a respected Russian revolutionary, who settled in London in the summer of 1870 and established close terms of friendship with Marx. Lopatin had previously lived in St Petersburg, where he had had the opportunity of observing Nechaiev's first steps at close quarters. After his first conversations with Lopatin Marx wrote to Engels: 'He told me that the whole Nechaiev yarn is a mass of lies. Nechaiev has never been in a Russian prison and the Russian Government has never tried to have him murdered; and so on and so forth.'[19] Lopatin was the first to tell Marx of the murder of Ivanov. From the autumn of 1871 onwards another Russian *émigré*, Utin, kept him informed of everything, as we know today in all essentials correctly.[20]

If the International were to survive it was necessary to purge it of Bakunin and Bakuninism. It was no longer an abstract question of 'anarchy or authority'. The International must not be a screen for activities *à la* Nechaiev. Even if Bakunin himself were incapable of drawing the practical consequences of his own teaching, as Nechaiev had done, the Nechaiev affair had demonstrated that people might always be found who would take his theories seriously. One crime like Nechaiev's carried out in Europe in the name of the International would suffice to deal the workers' cause a reeling blow. The struggle against Bakunin had become a matter of life and death for the International.

The struggle had to be fought under very unfavourable circumstances. The French sections had been swept away by the white terror after the Commune. Those who had been able to flee were refugees in Switzerland, England or France. An immense amount of work devolved on the refugee committee of the General Council, and Marx, on whom the main burden fell, was occupied for months raising money for them, securing them work, giving them advice. He made the personal acquaintance of practically every refugee, and a number of them became his friends. The most important of the refugee Communards were admitted to the General Council, including Vaillant, Ranvier and other Blanquists. These were socialists who, in whatever else they differed from Marx, agreed with him on the most important point of all, i.e. the necessity of the International taking its place in the political struggle. Among the multitude of refugees there were, as Engels wrote to Liebknecht, 'of course the usual proportion of scum, with Vermersch, editor of *Père Duchêne* [a paper published during the Commune], as the worst of the lot'.[21] The Jacobins formed a 'section française de 1871' and relapsed into their favourite role of theatrical and bloodthirsty revolutionism. The General Council were far too spineless for them, and they soon started attacking it vigorously in *Qui vive?*, a paper edited by Vermersch.

In their eyes the General Council was Marx. Marx, they maintained, was living in luxury at the expense of the workers. He embezzled the workers' money, and had made the International a 'German aristocratic' domain. He was a pan-German and a crafty servant of his master, Bismarck. All this had been said before, but by the reactionary Press. But now it was repeated and decked out with fondly invented details by the ultra-revolutionaries, the enemies of 'authority'. Their particular complaint was that the International was in German control and they played as usual on all the chauvinistic instincts, old and new. There was not a semblance of justification for their complaint. There were three times as many English as Germans on the General Council, and the Germans were outnumbered even by the French. The number of members represented by the French was certainly not very large, and the Blanquists could certainly not be reproached with harbouring affection for the new German Empire.

The French *exaltés* cost the General Council a great deal of time and a great deal of trouble, and at the same time it was compelled to occupy itself with a number of disagreeable internal disputes. Marx had secured the election of his old friend Eccarius as general secretary. The International was poor, and all it could pay its general secretary was fifteen shillings a week, and even this he did not receive regularly. So he added to his income by journalistic work, reporting International affairs for *The Times* and other newspapers. Occasionally he mentioned things that were not intended for publication, and this repeatedly led to heated arguments at General Council meetings, and sometimes Marx had difficulty in protecting Eccarius from the general indignation. Then came the London conference. It was decided that its sessions should be private and that no communications should be made to the Press, including the party Press, and everyone but Eccarius abided by this decision. A storm of indignation arose, and Eccarius was violently attacked. This time even Marx could not help him, and ever afterwards Eccarius felt that Marx had let him down.

He had long been closely associated with the English trade union leaders, and as soon as they started opposing Marx he sided with them and did a great deal to intensify personal animosities on the General Council. Occasionally its meetings were very lively indeed.

The meetings in High Holborn, where the General Council met at that time [Lessner writes in his memoirs],[22] were the most tempestuous and exhausting that can be imagined. It was no light task to stand up to the babel of tongues and the profound differences of temperament and of ideas. Those who criticized Marx for his intolerance ought to have seen the skill with which he got to the heart of people's ideas and demonstrated the fallacies of their deductions and conclusions.

The refugee Communards brought more than enough temperament with them. Of the English members of the General Council, Odger and Lucraft had resigned, having taken advantage of the International's pro-Communard manifesto to dissociate themselves from an organization in which they, as cautious and far-sighted individuals and members of royal commissions and friends of some of the very best people, had long since begun to experience a sensation of discomfort. (Odger had a magnificent career, and ended by being knighted and awarded the Nobel Peace Prize.) Those Englishmen who remained on the General Council coquetted with the liberals, split on purely personal grounds into two and sometimes into three factions and did nothing to lessen the general friction. Engels definitely settled in London in the middle of September and Marx proposed his election to the General Council, but even his admission to that body, valuable as it was, only had negative consequences. To the Londoners Marx was an old friend. They knew him, his wife and his children, and they knew how unspeakably hard his life had been during all these years, and even those who did not like him respected him for his selfless work for the common cause. But Engels was a rich manufacturer from Manchester, a distinguished-looking gentleman, with excellent manners, and somewhat cool and distant. Certainly he was very clever and educated and a good socialist, and many years ago he had written a book; that they either knew or heard for the first time now; but in their eyes he was first of all a stranger. And he was not always a very nice stranger either. In later years Engels himself told Bernstein that Marx generally played the role of peace-maker and conciliator, but when he, Engels, was in the chair the General Council meetings generally ended with a colossal row. In the editorial chair of the *Neue Rheinische Zeitung* it had been the same. The downfall of the International is not attributable to the friction on the General Council, but efficiency was certainly not promoted by it.

Just at this moment of internal tension it was called upon to withstand a serious test. The vigorous attack on the General Council contained in the circular issued by the Bakuninist congress at Sonvilliers attracted a great deal of attention. It was printed and reprinted and long extracts appeared in the bourgeois Press. ('The International monster is devouring itself.') In France, where everything in any way connected with the International was wildly persecuted, it was posted up on the houses. The General Council replied with another circular, 'The Alleged Split in the International', revealing the secret history of the Bakunin Alliance for the first time.[23] This made the Bakuninists very angry indeed. They said a general congress must be summoned at once. Certainly, the General Council replied, things could not continue like this. Invitations were sent out on 10 July 1872 for a congress to take place on 2 September at the Hague. Marx wrote to Sorge that the life or death of the International was at stake.[24]

The Bakuninist sections in the Latin countries promptly protested at the choice of the Hague. The Fédération jurassienne wrote that the congress ought not to meet in a 'milieu germanique' and suggested Switzerland instead. From their own point of view they were quite right. The sections' limited funds meant that to a certain extent the composition of the congress depended on where it took place, for the cost of travelling necessarily limited the number of delegates who could travel from a great distance. It was therefore intelligible that the Swiss were in favour of Switzerland. They expected their argument that Bakunin would not be able to travel to Holland either through France or through Germany, because in both countries he would be liable to arrest, to carry particular weight. But Marx was in a similar position. The same reasons would make it impossible for him, as well as other members of the General Council, to travel to Switzerland. But antagonism had by this time become far too profound for material considerations to carry any weight. The Bakuninists considered the advisability of being represented at the congress at all. On 4 August the Italians at Rimini decided not to be represented at the Hague, and proposed the summoning of an opposition congress at Neuchâtel, also on 2 September.[25] The Swiss Bakuninists did not go so far as that. They decided, with Bakunin's consent, to be represented at the Hague. Even the moderate spirits among them could no longer conceal from themselves the fact that a split was inevitable. In the last resort the differences between Marx and Bakunin boiled down to the differences between the historical tasks necessarily confronting the proletariat in countries in which capitalism was fully developed and the illusions to which the semi- and demi-semi-proletarians living in countries in which capitalist development was only just beginning were equally necessarily subject. Even the most intelligent of the Bakuninists formed a most distorted picture of the situation. Malon, for instance, had for a long time resisted the tendencies making for a split. Now he reconciled himself to it. 'Now that I am calm and alone, I see that the split was inevitable', he wrote to a friend at the end of August.[26] In his opinion it was inevitable because of the temperamental differences between the Latin and the German races. One day this, like everything else that divided the nations, would disappear 'into the infinite of the human race'. But now these differences still existed, and the recent war had only intensified them. It would be in vain to go on trying to unite the incompatible. Everyone who attended it knew that the Hague congress would be the last of the united International.

When it met at the Hague on 2 September, the town was

K.M.—13*

swarming with journalists and secret agents. No assembly of
the International had roused the world's attention like this
one. It was the first after the Commune – a 'declaration of war
of chaos on order'. An attempt had been made to persuade
the Dutch Government to forbid the congress. Jules Simon
had travelled from Paris to the Hague to present his Government's request to this effect, but he had as little success as
others who wanted the same. Next it had been announced
that the congress would resolve on acts of terrorism, and that
it was a rendezvous of regicides. But the Dutch Government
refused to be intimidated. Next an attempt had been made to
incite the population against the congress. The *Haager Dag-
blaad*, for instance. warned the citizens of the Hague not to
allow their wives and daughters to go out alone during the
sessions of the congress, and called on all the jewellers to draw
their shutters. The police, however, took no action and seemed
actually to regard the congress with benevolence. A Berlin
secret police agent reluctantly reported that up to 5 September
all the meetings were strictly private, and

not only does the Dutch police keep no watch whatever on them
but protects the meeting-place in the Lombardstrasse so scrupulously that the public is not even allowed a look into the ground
floor where the meetings are held, or even so much as make an
attempt to overhear through the open window a single word of
what is taking place within.

As long as the sessions remained secret there was nothing
for the journalists to do but wander round the meeting-hall
and describe their 'impressions'. A few of them faked interviews with Marx. Others described the delegates, and Marx
in particular. The correspondent of the *Indépendence belge*
wrote that the impression that Marx made on him was
that of a 'gentleman farmer', which was friendly at any
rate.

The congress was not very numerously attended. No more
than sixty-five delegates were present. Congresses of the International had been better attended in the past, and among the

delegates were many who were not known from before. But it was the first International congress attended by Marx and Engels. The first and private sessions were devoted to examination of the delegates' mandates, and there was bitter strife about each one, for each one was important. At previous congresses this part of the proceedings had been regarded as but a superfluous formality. It soon became clear that there was a majority for Marx, with forty votes to twenty-five. There were two opposing factions, each united as far as internal questions affecting the International were concerned, but far from united politically. The opposition was held together by antagonism to Marx. It consisted of all the Belgian, all the Dutch, all the Jurassian and nearly all the English and Spanish delegates. The majority was more united, consisting of the Germans, the German-Swiss, the Hungarians, the Bohemians, the German *émigrés* from America, but it included many French *émigrés* and delegates of illegal sections in France too. The Blanquists were particularly well represented among the French *émigrés*.[27]

This grouping by no means bore out the theory of the contrast between the state-worshipping Germanic races who were loyal to Marx and the freedom-loving, anti-authoritarian Latins. Guillaume, leader of the Jurassian section, was extremely astonished when Eccarius told him 'que le torchon brûlait au Conseil général'. He had believed that the English delegates, who were trade unionists, were devoted followers of Marx. He now found out that they were 'en guerre ouverte avec ceux qui formaient la majorité'.[28] He was just as surprised when he found there was Dutch opposition to the General Council. Attempts to unite the opposition were made before the opening of the congress, but it was only towards its close that the fundamental political differences between the various groups made it possible to come to a common understanding.

Violent disputes took place during the examination of the mandates. The English delegates were unwilling to admit their fellow countryman, Maltman Barry, who was provided with a mandate from an American section, on the ground that he was not a known trade union leader. At that Marx sprang indignantly to his feet. It was an honour to Citizen Barry that that was so, he exclaimed, because almost all the English trade union leaders were sold to Gladstone or some other bourgeois politician. That remark was held against Marx for a long time. The mandates of the delegates of the German sections were also disputed. During their trial for high treason at Leipzig in 1872 Bebel and Liebknecht had declared the solidarity of their party with the International, though the party did not belong to the International and its local groups were not sections of the International.[29] This was formally correct. To prevent their party from being banned Bebel and Liebknecht could not have done otherwise. The Bakuninists, relying on this statement, demanded that the German delegates' mandate should not be recognized. Now the sections the German delegates represented were not very big and had only been formed specially for the congress, but behind many a Bakuninist mandate there was not exactly a mass organization either. The German mandate was accepted.

Fully three days were occupied with these and similar matters. The real congress did not begin until 5 September. It met in a working-class quarter of the town. A French newspaper remarked sarcastically that next to the congress hall was a prison, 'then laundries, small workshops, many pothouses, tap-rooms, here called *taperij*, and clandestine establishments such as are used, as one would say in congress style, by the Dutch proletariat'. The sessions took place in the evening, in order to enable workers to attend. 'The workers certainly did not fail to put in an appearance. Never have I seen a crowd so packed, so serious, so anxious to see and hear.' The events of the evening of 5 September were described by *Le Français* as follows:

At last we have had a real session of the International congress, with a crowd ten times greater than the hall could accommodate, with applause and interruptions and pushing and jostling and tumultuous cries, and personal attacks and extremely radical but nevertheless extremely conflicting declarations of opinion, with recriminations, denunciations, protests, calls to order, and finally a closure of the session, if not of the discussion, which at past ten o'clock, in a tropical heat and amid inexpressible confusion, imposed itself by the force of things.

The first question discussed was that of the extension of the General Council's powers in accordance with the resolution passed at the London conference. The opposition not only wanted no extension of the General Council's powers, but objected to the powers the General Council already possessed. They wanted to reduce it to a statistical office, or even better, to a mere letterbox, a correspondence office. These advocates of autonomy were opposed by Sorge, who had come from New York. He said that the International not only needed a head, but one with plenty of brains. Guillaume, who describes the scene, says that at this people looked at Marx and laughed. The congress gave the General Council its extended powers. The resolution stated that it was the duty of the General Council to carry out the decisions of the International congress and to see that the principles and general intentions of the statutes were observed in every country, and that it had the power to suspend branches, sections, committees and federations until the next congress. Thirty-six delegates voted for this resolution, with fifteen against and six abstentions.

When the ballot was over Engels rose and proposed in his own and Marx's name that the headquarters of the General Council be transferred from London to New York. This caused an indescribable sensation. A few weeks previously, when somebody had suggested removing the headquarters of the International from London, Marx had opposed it strenuously, and now here he was proposing it himself. Vaillant, speaking for the Blanquists, made a passionate protest. So far as he was concerned, transferring the General Council to New York was equivalent to transferring it to the moon. The Blanquists could not possibly have any influence on the General Council unless it remained where it was, i.e. in his place of exile, London. But Marx had calculated rightly. If the Blanquists, who otherwise supported him, opposed him in this, there were plenty of opposition delegates to support him. A General Council in America would obviously mean a General Council without Marx. And so they voted for the resolution. It was carried by twenty-six votes to twenty-three.

Then the political debate began. The General Council proposed that the following resolution of the London conference be incorporated in the statutes.

In its struggle against the collective power of the possessing classes, the proletariat can only act as a class if it constitutes its own distinct political party, opposed to all the old parties formed by the possessing classes. The forming of a political party by the proletariat is indispensable in order to assure the triumph of the social revolution and its ultimate object, the abolition of all classes. The coalition of working-class forces, already obtained in economic struggles, must also serve as a lever in the hands of that class in its struggle against the political power of its exploiters. The lords of the earth and the lords of capital always use their political privileges to defend and perpetuate their economic monopolies and to enslave Labour, and therefore the conquest of political power is the great duty of the proletariat.[30]

Every point of view was represented in the discussion, from that of the extremists opposed to political intervention of any kind on the one hand to that of the Blanquists, who had no patience with the economic struggle, on the other. The Blanquists accepted the principle of the strike as a means of political action, but their real interest remained the barricade. They wanted to put 'the militant organization of the revolutionary forces of the proletariat and the proletarian struggle' on the programme of the next congress. Guillaume, as spokesman of the 'anti-authoritarians', stated that the majority wanted the seizure of political power and the minority wanted its annihilation. The General Council resolution was carried by twenty-nine votes to five, with eight abstentions. By this time many delegates had left, being unable to remain at the Hague any longer, and others no longer took part in the voting, having lost interest. The Blanquists attacked the General Council for having caused the revolution to take flight across the ocean and left the congress. The Bakuninists, however, decided after reflection that the situation was far better than it had seemed at first. 'The authority of the General Council, voted for in principle by the majority, is in fact abolished by the choice of New York', Guillaume wrote in triumph.

On the last day the congress discussed the desirability of expelling members of the Bakuninist Alliance from the International. A special committee was appointed to examine the evidence submitted to it by the General Council. Guillaume was invited to appear before it but refused, giving the same explanation as he had given at the congress in Latin Switzerland in April 1870. 'Every member of the International has the full and complete right to join any secret society, even the Freemasons. Any inquiry into a secret society would simply be equivalent to a denunciation to the police,' he maintained. The utmost to which he would consent was to a 'private conversation' with members of the committee. Clever as he was, he could not answer the weighty evidence against him. Nechaiev's letter to Liubavin made a great impression. Bakunin and Guillaume were expelled from the International.

The congress ended on 7 September. On 8 September a meeting, organized by the local section, took place at Amsterdam. Among the speakers were Marx, Engels, Lafargue, Sorge, Becker and others. Marx's speech was reported in *La Liberté*, the Brussels organ of the International, and in the *Allgemeen Handelsblad* of Amsterdam, and was by far the most important made by him at the time of the congress. In it he summed up its results.

He proclaimed the necessity of the working classes fighting the old, decaying society in the political field and in the social field alike. The worker must one day seize political supremacy in order to establish the new organization of labour. He must overthrow the old politics sustaining the old institutions.

The International had proclaimed the necessity of the political struggle and repudiated pseudo-revolutionary abstention from politics. But he indicated the future path in general outline only. No prescription for the seizure of political power was valid for all countries and all times, as the Blanquists, and others too, pretended.

But we have never said that the means to arrive at these ends were identical. We know the allowance that must be made for the institutions, manners and traditions of different countries. We do not deny that there exist countries like America, England, and, if I knew your institutions better, I would add Holland, where the workers may be able to attain their ends by peaceful means. If that is true we must also recognize that in most of the countries of the Continent force must be the lever to which it will be necessary to resort for a time in order to attain the dominion of labour.[31]

Marx ended his speech with a defence of the decision to transfer the General Council to America. America was the land of the workers, to which hundreds of thousands emigrated every year, whether banished or driven by want, and in America a new and fruitful field was opening for the International. As far as he himself was concerned, he was retiring from the General Council, but he denied the rumours that he was retiring from the International. On the contrary, freed from the burden of administrative work, he would devote himself with redoubled energy to the task to which he had devoted twenty-five years of his life and would continue with until his last breath, namely his work for the liberation of the proletariat.

Marx's motives for transferring the General Council to New York have been much discussed. At the congress he had done all in his power to gain the victory, and he had gained it, though in some things his victory was more apparent than real. He had conducted a ruthless struggle against the Bakuninists and seemed determined to conduct it to the very end, i.e. the complete extermination of anarchism. And then all of a sudden he caused the General Council to be banished from Europe. He must obviously have realized that his influence on the life of the International would be very seriously impaired. It has been suggested that Marx had grown weary of the strain and the petty cares that his work on the General

Council involved, of the ever-increasing burden of correspondence that he had to conduct, the exhausting and fruitless debates with the English members, the meetings and conferences and visits, and the whole troublesome, time-robbing labour that devolved mainly upon his shoulders. It has been suggested that he wished to be free of all this and to return to his most important task, the completion of *Das Kapital*. Certainly Marx often complained of how little time his work on the General Council left him for his scientific work. But he always laid everything else aside when the International demanded it. 'He was above all a revolutionary.' One recalls those words of Engels.[32] Besides, after the Hague congress, Marx could have done much more scientific work without sacrificing any of his political work whatever, for Engels now lived in London and could have represented him on the General Council and carried out his wishes. But in spite of this he insisted on the General Council moving away from London.

Marx had other reasons. For the General Council to have remained in London would have spelled the ruin of the International. Bakunin had been expelled, but the spirit of Bakunin lived on. Nearly all the sections in Southern Europe, in Italy and Spain, were 'anti-authoritarian'. The Commune inspired and inflamed them, and their watchword was action, action all the time. They wanted all or nothing, and their only battle-cry was the social revolution. Marx and Engels saw the danger. 'Spain is so backward industrially that there can be no talk of an immediate, complete emancipation of the working class. Spain must pass through various stages of development before it comes to that, and a whole series of obstacles must be cleared out of the way.' The Bakuninists violently attacked the young Spanish republic, which was threatened on all sides as it was. Marx and Engels regarded the blind, impetuous radicalism of the Bakuninists as fatal. 'The republic offered the opportunity of compressing those preliminary stages into the shortest possible time, and of rapidly removing those obstacles.'[33] But the Bakuninists did not listen and did not look. Anything but attack and again attack and barricades was 'politics', 'idolizing the state', cowardly and counter-revolutionary. It was necessary for the International to part from them. 'If we had been conciliatory at the Hague', Engels wrote to Bebel at the end of June 1873, 'if we had hushed up the split, what would the consequences have been? The sectarians, namely the Bakuninists, would have had a whole year's time to commit far greater stupidities and infamies in the International's name.' [34]

The Hague congress had also shown that all the Proud-honist groups, the Dutch, the Belgians and others as well, would have been ready to follow the Bakuninists as soon as they left or were expelled from the International, and all that would have remained would have been the group that supported Marx during the congress. It would very soon have melted away. The German party was bound to avoid anything that might imperil its legal status, particularly after the outcome of the Leipzig high treason trial. Marx approved of their policy in this. It would be impossible for them to share in the life of the International, at least for a long time to come. Of Marx's majority at the congress that only left the Blanquists.

Marx esteemed Blanqui very highly and had a high opinion of the Blanquists' courage, and he had not a few personal friends among them. But a whole world divided him from them politically. He had had several serious disputes with them even before the congress. At the congress they had followed him as long as it was a question of fighting against the 'anti-politicians', the 'destroyers of the state'. The Blanquists stoutly asserted the omnipotence of the state. It must not be destroyed but seized, but there was only one way of seizing it, and that was the barricade – whether in Spain or France, England or Germany made no difference. In their eyes the single duty of the International was to organize armed risings.

We shall return to Marx's Amsterdam speech in another connection. It alone gives the explanation of the decision to transfer the General Council to New York. Had it remained in London, Marx would only have been able to maintain his ground with the aid of the Blanquists. The International would have become Blanquist, and its programme would have shrunk to the single word: barricade.

The congress had decided to transfer the General Council to New York for the year 1872–3. Marx was convinced that developments in Europe would be so rapid and so favourable that after a year the General Council would be able to return from exile. This was a mistake. Marx correctly estimated the direction the workers' movement was taking; as happened more than once, he was mistaken about its tempo. He soon recognized his error. A year after the Hague congress he gave up the International for lost. Its history in America is that of its gradual death. Its slow decline was occasionally interrupted by petty crises, by splits and splits again, and it is impossible to establish for certain even the date when it finally expired. When Engels rose at the Hague congress and proposed that the General Council be transferred to America, the International ceased to exist.

[21]

The Last Ten Years

MARX was so identified with the International in the public eye that people refused to believe that the chief of the general staff would remain in London after the general staff had been transferred to New York. English newspapers announced that Marx was preparing to emigrate to America. In 1876 Professor Funck-Brentano actually told the Le Play Society in Paris that Marx had been living in the United States ever since the Hague congress.

Marx, however, remained in London, still occupied with work for the International, though to a smaller extent than before. His first task was to supervise the publication of the decisions of the Hague congress. His friend Sorge kept plying him from New York with requests for instructions. The furious attacks of the Bakuninists, who now shrank at nothing, had at least occasionally to be answered with a few sharp blows. A split occurred in the British regional council and Marx had passages of arms with Hales, Mottershead, Jung and Eccarius.

From the spring of 1873 onwards it became clearer every month that what had at first appeared to be only the liquidation of a phase in the life of the International culminating in the Hague congress was in fact the liquidation of the International itself. In September Marx advised Sorge to 'let the formal organization of the International recede into the background for the time being, but not to let the headquarters at New York out of his hands, in order to prevent idiots or adventurers from gaining control and compromising the cause.'[1] Events and the inevitable evolution of things would lead to the resurrection of the International in an improved form; for the time being it was sufficient not to let the connections with the best men in the various countries lapse. Marx

summed up the situation in a letter to Sorge in April 1874.[2]
He said there could be no question at the moment of the working classes playing a decisive role in Europe. In England the
International was for the time being (once more 'for the time
being') as good as dead, the new French trade unions were but
points of departure from which development would take place
when freer movement became possible again, and in Spain,
Italy and Belgium the proletariat was to all intents and purposes impotent. Germany, practically the only country in
which the workers' movement was in the ascendant, did not
count in the International. Contrary to his hopes, for practically a year after the Hague congress Marx had no time to resume his theoretical work but had to devote himself almost
entirely to International affairs; and what time was left to him
he had to devote to the settling of matters he believed to have
been settled already.

Das Kapital was to have been translated into French at the
end of 1867 Élie Reclus, brother of Élisée Reclus, an anarchist
who subsequently became a well-known geographer, undertook the task, but soon abandoned it. Two years later another
Frenchman undertook it but did not get very far. Not till the
winter of 1871 was a French publisher found who was willing
to take the risk (for a risk it was at that time). There were
difficulties of all kinds from the first. The publisher, a book-
seller named Lachâtre, lived abroad, having been condemned
to twenty years' imprisonment for his part in the Commune,
and his business was managed by a legal administrator. Next
there was a shortage of funds. Marx invited his cousin, August
Philips, who lived in Amsterdam, to share in the cost of publication, but Philips said he would not think of furthering
Marx's revolutionary aims. In the end *Das Kapital* was published in French, though it only came out in instalments
published at intervals. Marx wrote to Lachâtre that this
method of publication gave him particular satisfaction. 'Sous
cette forme l'ouvrage sera plus accessible à la classe ouvrière
et pour moi cette considération l'emporte sur toute autre.' * [3]

* 'The work will be more accessible to the working classes in that
form, and for me that consideration takes precedence over all others.'

Roy, the translator, did his work well, but Marx had 'the deuce of an amount' to do all the same; not only had he to revise the translation, which was no light task in view of the condensed style of the original and the play made with Hegelian phraseology in the chapter on the theory of value, but he simplified passages here and expanded passages there, amplifying the statistical data and indulging in controversies with French economists. The final instalment did not appear till May 1875, for there were periods when he had to stop work on it altogether and others when he could only continue by exerting himself to the utmost, for he was a sick man.

In autumn 1873 he broke down altogether. He had been suffering from headaches and insomnia during the summer and was ordered by his doctor not to work more than four hours a day. Then his health improved somewhat, but in November it grew worse again. The 'chronic mental depression' grew worse and worse. The doctor ordered complete cessation of work, and his friends feared the worst. Once more he recovered, but in the summer of 1874 he again had to take a 'complete rest'. After years of superhuman toil on *Das Kapital*, carried out under the most adverse circumstances in the hunger and poverty of exile, harassed by cares about tomorrow's bread to feed his wife and children, followed by the work of building up the International and the exhausting struggle to hold it together into which he cast the last ounce of his resources, his old liver trouble broke out again. He never again shook it off completely, though three visits to Carlsbad and a cure at the German resort of Neuenahr caused such an improvement that it never became threatening again. His first visit to Carlsbad in the summer of 1874 was somewhat risky, as it was by no means certain that the German and Austrian police would allow the 'chief of the Red International' to go unmolested. In August 1874 Marx applied to the Home Office for British citizenship, but the application for naturalization was refused on the grounds (which of course Marx never knew) that 'this man was not loyal to his king'. In Carlsbad, as the police boasted, he was 'continually and uninterruptedly

watched', but gave 'cause for no suspicion', so they did not
trouble him any more. After the enactment of the Socialist
Law of 1878 the route through Germany was closed to him,
but he no longer needed the German and Bohemian watering
places. The headaches and insomnia, the 'nervous exhaustion'
as Engels called it, remained.

After 1873 Marx never regained his old capacity for work.
He remained the insatiable reader that he had always been;
he continued indefatigably making extracts from what he read,
he went on collecting material, but he no longer had the
capacity to organize it. Again and again he sat down and
started and in the autumn of 1878 believed that the second
volume of *Das Kapital* would be finished within a year, but
he never completed more than a few pages of the fair copy.
Marx had learned Russian. England had served as the main
illustration of theoretical development in the first volume of
Das Kapital, and he intended to use Russia as the basis of his
treatment of ground rent in the second volume. Marx could
not get enough Russian literature. After his death Engels
found two whole cubic metres of Russian statistical material.
It was not conscientiousness alone that drove Marx on in his
everlasting search for new material. He used it also to hide
from himself the crippling of his creative powers. Engels
hated those piles of Russian books and once said to Lafargue
that he would have liked to burn them. For he suspected Marx
of sheltering behind them in order to find peace from the
pricks of his own conscience and the urging of his friends. But
Engels did not discover how little had been completed of what
he had believed to have been completed, in spite of all his
suspicions, until after Marx's death, when he examined his
manuscripts. 'If I had known,' he wrote to Bebel in the late
summer of 1883,

I would have given him no peace by day or night until the whole
thing had been finished and printed. Marx himself knew this better than anyone, and he also knew that if it came to the worst, as it
has, the manuscript could be edited by me in his spirit. He
actually said so to Tussy.[4]

The second volume of *Das Kapital* was completed by Engels and published in 1885. The third volume appeared in 1894. After 1877, when he wrote a contribution to Engels's attack on Eugen Dühring, as well as a few articles opposing Gladstone's Russian policy, Marx published practically nothing.

The latter appeared in conservative newspapers. There was no socialist Press in England, but when it came to attacking Russia, Marx was willing to enter into alliance with the devil himself. The Franco-Prussian War had enormously strengthened Russia's position in Europe, and Russia remained the 'so far unassailed bulwark and reserve army of the counter-revolution'.[5] Russia was still an oppressive nightmare over Europe. Anyone who fought Russia was objectively fighting in the service of the revolution.

The International was broken. In the middle of the 1870s there was no proletarian army anywhere but in Germany. Under Marx's leadership it did all in its power to denounce Bismarck's servility towards the Tsar, in the Reichstag, in its newspapers, in pamphlets like Liebknecht's 'The Oriental Question, or shall Europe become Cossack?'[6] which Marx approved of, although he usually did not see eye to eye with Liebknecht. But the German party was far too weak to affect German foreign policy in the slightest degree. The European proletariat, split, scattered or not organized at all, was powerless. Marx was convinced that the future belonged to it, and whatever happened in Europe nothing could shake his conviction of its ultimate victory. 'So far I have always found', he once wrote to Johann Philipp Becker, 'that all really sound men who have once taken the revolutionary road invariably draw new strength from defeat and become ever more resolute the longer they swim in the stream of events.' The bourgeois world was destined to destruction, though how and when was uncertain, for it depended on factors over which the proletariat so far had no control. 'General conditions in Europe are of such a kind that they are heading more and more towards a European war. We must go through it before there can be any thought of the European working classes having decisive influence.'[7] That was what Marx thought in the spring of 1874. War might advance the rise of the proletariat to power or might impede it. Marx closely followed the foreign politics of the great European countries. In February 1878, when his wife was ill and he was suffering from headaches by day, insomnia by night, and bad fits of coughing, he wrote two long letters to Liebknecht which show how carefully he followed political and military events during the Russo-Turkish war, which ended with the preliminary peace of Adrianople at the end of January.[8]

In 1874 Marx still expected a resurrection of the European workers' movement as a result of a general European war. For as long as the stronghold of the counter-revolution had not fallen, as long as its shadow still lay over Europe, all hope of a victory for the revolution was in vain. The movement might gain success in one or other or all the countries of Central and Western Europe, but the last word would still be spoken by the Tsar. And the Tsar could only be overthrown in a war with another great power. The foundations on which Russian absolutism rested were still too strong to be shaken by anything less than a European war. Up to the middle of the 1870s Marx was extremely sceptical of all news of revolutionary movements in Russia, and the Nechaiev affair was not calculated to make him change his mind.

But the more thoroughly he studied Russia, the more Russian literature he read, the more Russian statistics he examined, the more probable it began to appear to him that this colossus with feet of clay only needed a slight blow from without to cause it to collapse. When Russia declared war on Turkey in 1877 he felt practically certain of a Turkish victory, which would be followed by a Russian revolution. And when the Turks really did gain a victory he believed revolution in St Petersburg to be at hand. 'All classes of Russian society are economically, morally, intellectually in complete decay', he wrote to Sorge at the end of September 1877. 'This time the revolution will begin in the East.'[9] On 4 February 1878 he explained to Liebknecht that we are definitely on the side of the Turks for two reasons: (1) because we have studied the Turkish peasant, i.e. the Turkish masses, and we have learnt that the Turkish peasant is without doubt one of the most capable and moral representatives of European peasantry [this argument could of course also have been used of Serbian and Bulgarian peasants whom the Turks oppressed]; (2) because the defeat of the Russians will considerably hasten the social revolutions in Russia, the elements of which already to a great extent exist, and thereby also hasten the revolution in all Europe.[10]

When Marx wrote this Turkey had already been defeated. But Marx did not abandon his idea of the necessity of a European war.

There was now a revolutionary movement in Russia that was incomparably stronger than could have been hoped for two years previously. The Narodnaya Volya (People's Will) party attacked absolutism with the only weapon the revolutionaries had. That weapon was terrorism. In 1879 and 1880 members of this party made several abortive attempts on the life of the Tsar. Many paid for them with their lives. Those who managed to escape abroad (Leo Hartman, N. Morosov, and others) were received by Marx as friends. Alexander II was assassinated by a member of the Narodnaya Volya party in March 1881. On 11 April Marx wrote to his daughter Jenny that the terror was 'a historically inevitable means of action, the morality or immorality of which it was as useless to discuss as that of the earthquake at Chios'.[11] The Russian terrorists were 'excellent people through and through, *sans phrase mélodramatique*, simple, straightforward, heroic.' It was no longer necessary for the fortress to be stormed from without, for it was crumbling by itself. War had become superfluous. Nay more, it would actually be harmful now.

Engels wrote to Bebel in the middle of December 1879 :

In a few months things in Russia are bound to come to a head. Either absolutism will be overthrown, after which, the stronghold of reaction having collapsed, a wind of a different kind will blow through Europe, or there will be a European war which will bury the present German party in the struggle which every country will have to fight for its national existence.[12]

On 12 September 1880 Marx wrote to Danielson that he hoped that there would be no general European war. 'Although in the long run it could not hold up social development, and in that I include economic development, but would rather intensify it, it would undoubtedly involve a futile exhaustion of forces for a longer or shorter period.'[13] Three months before Marx's death Engels wrote to Bebel, repeating Marx's views as follows:

I would consider a European war a misfortune; this time a terrible misfortune. It would inflame chauvinism everywhere for years, as every country would have to fight for its existence. The whole work of the revolutionaries in Russia, who stand on the eve of victory, would be annihilated and made in vain, our party in Germany would be temporarily swamped and broken up in the chauvinist flood, and the same thing would happen in France.

Russia was 'sinking into a morass'. Tsarism was succumbing in peaceful putrefaction and its last supports were being smashed by the revolutionaries' bombs. Marx overestimated the disintegration of Russian society and the strength of the revolutionary movement. The power of absolutism, though weakened, was not shaken nearly to the extent that Marx believed. It had become improbable that Russia would actively intervene as in 1849 and give military aid in suppressing a Central European revolution. The weight with which Russia had overlain Europe for decades had become lighter. Europe could go its own way without the fear of finding it barred at all decisive points by Russian troops – but only if peace were kept, and a struggle of warring peoples did not come to bar the way and hold up the struggle of the rising proletarian class, throwing it back for ten, twenty years or even more.

In the 1870s and at the beginning of the eighties the European workers' movement took great steps forward and advanced faster than Marx expected after the death of the International; and it did so without passing through a general European war. True, it did not always take the path that Marx considered the right one. He found much to criticize in the German party, and later in the French. But in spite of its faltering and its uncertainties and all its temporary deviations it was on the right track.

The 1874 elections showed that the 'Eisenacher', the followers of Liebknecht and Bebel, and the followers of Lassalle were practically equal in strength. During the decade that followed Lassalle's death the movement he had founded lost a great deal of its sectarian character. The specific Lassallean demands still remained on its programme, but they were not believed in with much conviction and in the end survived practically only out of sheer tradition. The two German workers' parties grew nearer and nearer to each other. They both fought the same enemy, they were both persecuted alike, and gradually the wish to surmount the breach and unite became so strong that towards the end of 1874 amalgamation into one great German workers' party was decided on. Marx and Engels were indignant at the news. When Marx was sent a draft of the programme of the new party, he wrote his observations on it and sent them to the 'Eisenacher'. He took the programme point by point, subjecting each to devastating criticism, proving the whole to be a hash of ill-understood scientific socialism, vulgar democratic phraseology and long-obsolete Lassallean demands, and he ended by threatening to attack it publicly if it were adopted. It was adopted, and became the programme of the German Social Democratic Workers' party, founded at Gotha at the end of May 1875. Marx, in spite of his threat, made no public attack on it, because the programme was regarded as communist by workers and bourgeoisie alike.[14] Nor did the split, which Marx regarded as inevitable, occur. The party remained united, and in 1891, at Erfurt, adopted a pure Marxist programme.

Marx had made a mistake and recognized it. He never regarded himself as infallible. Engels, in a letter to Bebel of 4 November 1875, described the place that Marx and he assigned themselves in the international workers' movement. Their task, he said, was 'uninfluenced by details and distracting local conditions of the struggle, from time to time to measure what had been said and done by the theoretical prin-

ciples that are valid for all modern proletarian movements.'
They demanded one thing only from the party; that it remain
true to itself.[15] Bakuninists and bourgeois politicians accused
Marx of enthroning himself as red Tsar in London, sending
out ukases for which implicit obedience was required; and
they said that these often led to prison, death and destruction.
Nothing could have been farther from the truth. 'It is easy
for us to criticize', Engels acknowledged in a letter to Frau
Liebknecht, when Wilhelm Liebknecht was once again in
prison, 'while in Germany every imprudent or thoughtless
word may lead to imprisonment and a temporary interruption
of family life.'[16] Another time he wrote to Bebel: 'We are not
unaware of the fact that it is all very well for us to talk, but
that your position is much more difficult.'[17]

After the enactment of Bismarck's Socialist Law in 1878,
when the party spent some time in doubt and uncertainty and
many thought that the right policy was to be absolutely loyal
and not provoke the enemy, in the hope of causing him to
moderate his severity, Marx attacked them furiously. Though
once more he threatened to attack them publicly, he did not
do so.[18] On 5 November 1881 he wrote to Sorge that the
'wretched' attitude of the *Sozialdemokrat*, the paper the party
published at Zürich and smuggled into Germany, led to constant disputes with Liebknecht and Bebel in Leipzig, and that
these disputes often became very violent indeed. 'But we have
avoided intervening publicly in any way', the letter continued.
'It would not be decent for people living abroad in comparative
peace to provide an edifying spectacle for the bourgeoisie and
the Government by aggravating the position of men working
in the most difficult conditions and at great personal sacrifice.'[19]
The same trust in the logic of development that had guided
Marx as leader of the General Council of the International
determined his attitude to the growing German party
now.[20]

In France the socialist ranks that had been scattered by the
Commune gradually re-formed towards the end of the 1870s.
A fair number of them were former Bakuninists who drew

nearer and nearer to Marxism. Prominent among them were Jules Guesde and Benoît Malon. In November 1877 Guesde founded *L'Égalité*, a weekly to which Bebel and Liebknecht contributed from Germany. Although not at all clear in its views, the circle grouped round *L'Égalité* nevertheless contributed substantially towards the propagation of the basic ideas of modern socialism. So rapidly did the movement grow that in October 1879 the Fédération du Parti des Travailleurs Socialistes was founded at a congress at Marseilles. Its programme, adopted at a congress at Le Havre in November 1880, was fundamentally based on Marx. Guesde visited London and the new party's minimum programme was the joint labour of Marx, Engels, Guesde and Lafargue. It did not correspond with the wishes of Marx and Engels in every way. Among other things Guesde insisted on inserting a demand for a minimum legal wage. Marx opposed this, saying that if the French proletariat were still childish enough to need such a bait it was not worthwhile drawing up a programme for them at all. But Guesde insisted and the demand remained in the programme. But this did not cause Marx to withdraw his advice and help from the new party, any more than he had done in the case of the German party when it drew up its Gotha programme. He knew that it would overcome these infantile ailments. He did not believe the young party to be united enough to survive for long. This time he was right. No sooner had it been founded when it split into two. Marx's connection with the Parti ouvrier, led by Guesde, was a very slender one. Engels wrote to Bernstein in October 1881 that Marx had given Guesde advice from time to time through Lafargue, but it was scarcely ever followed.[21] In the violent dispute that broke out between the two groups after the split at the congress at Saint-Étienne in September 1882, Guesde and his friends were continually attacked for 'submitting to the will of a man who lived in London outside any party control'.[2] They did not submit to his control and had no justification whatever for their claim that theirs was the scientific socialism that Marx had founded. A remark that Marx once made to

Lafargue has often been quoted: 'Ce qu'il y a de certain, c'est que moi, je ne suis pas marxiste.'[23]

Nevertheless the movement in France made progress while the working classes in England, the most industrialized country in the world and the country in which Marx lived, remained silent and inactive. Occasionally the British working classes seemed to stir, but no attempt to form a proletarian party ever got beyond the preliminary stages. In the spring of 1881 Marx tried to bring the trade union leaders into contact with the radical politicians. Engels, optimistic as ever, already visualized a 'proletarian-radical party' led by Joseph Cowen, M.P. for Newcastle, 'an old Chartist, half, if not a whole communist and a very fine fellow'. A year later he wrote to Kautsky: 'There is no workers' party here, there are only conservatives and liberal-radicals.'[24] Yet Marx's ideas gradually penetrated even in England. The first and by far the most important English Marxist was H. M. Hyndman. He had read *Das Kapital* in French and was converted at once. He attached himself to Marx, they frequently exchanged visits, and at Marx's quiet retreat in Maitland Park Road, they would often talk till late into the night. But in the summer of 1881 the friendship abruptly terminated. Hyndman wrote a book, *England for All*, in which he popularized *Das Kapital* and did so very well. But he did not mention Marx's name, though he incidentally remarked that he owed a great deal to an important thinker. Marx took this seriously amiss and refused to accept the excuse that Englishmen did not like being taught by foreigners. Hyndman was a vain man, with a strong inclination to political adventurism, and his silence about Marx was not due to objective reasons alone. Hyndman's alleged sole motive for silence about Marx was paralleled by Guesde, who gave the same reason for asking Malon to give out his programme, which Marx had cooperated in drafting, as his own. Hyndman said that Engels's jealousy was to blame for the breach. Objective and personal reasons may have been combined. To the end of his life Marx remained practically unknown in England.

The old International was incapable of resurrection. In February 1881 Marx wrote to Domela Nieuwenhuis, the Dutch socialist, that the right moment for the formation of a new workers' association had not yet come.[25] But the right moment was drawing nearer every year. The old General Council was dead, and the new was only in the making. There were no congresses, no resolutions to which the movements in the various countries could adhere. But Marx was alive. His significance for the proletarian movement after the dissolution of the International cannot be better illustrated than by a few sentences from a letter Engels wrote to Bernstein in October 1881.

By his theoretical and practical work Marx has acquired such a position that the best people in the workers' movements in the various countries have full confidence in him. They turn to him for advice at decisive moments, and generally find that his advice is the best. He holds that position in Germany, France and Russia, not to mention the smaller countries. Marx, and in the second place myself, stand in the same relation to the other national movements as we do to the French. We are in constant touch with them, insofar as it is worthwhile and opportunity is provided, but any attempt to influence people against their will would only do harm and destroy the old trust that survives from the time of the International. In any case, we have too much experience in revolutionary matters to attempt anything of the sort. It is not Marx who imposes his opinions, much less his will, upon the people, but it is they who come to him. That is what Marx's real influence, which is of such extreme importance for the movement, depends on.[26]

Marx issued no orders and set no patterns which the class war should follow. Just as he believed the idea of commanding the European workers' movement from London to be absurd, so did he obstain from devising a plan of action that should be valid for all countries and all times. The speech he made at Amsterdam after the Hague congress has already been mentioned. It had an unusual fate. When it appeared in the *Volksstaat* in October 1872, those passages in which Marx spoke of force as the lever of the revolution in most continental countries were missing. It had been necessary to omit them for fear of police persecution. In recent years it has again been quoted, but once more in abbreviated form, though needlessly now; and this time the omitted passage is that in which Marx spoke of the possibility of a peaceful seizure of the state power by the proletariat in England and America. Only the whole speech is the whole Marx. In 1881, the year in which Marx welcomed the Russian terrorists' attempted assassination of the Tsar, he said to Hyndman:

If you say that you do not share the views of my party for England I can only reply that that party considers an English revolution not necessary but – according to historic precedence – possible. If the unavoidable evolution turns into a revolution, it would not only be the fault of the ruling classes, but also of the working class. Every pacific concession of the former has been wrung from them by 'pressure from without'. Their action kept pace with that pressure and if the latter has more and more weakened, it is only because the English working class know not how to wield their power and use their liberties, both of which they possess legally. In Germany the working class were fully aware from the beginning of their movement that you cannot get rid of a military despotism but by a revolution. England is the one country in which a peaceful revolution is possible, but [he added after a pause] history does not tell us so.

Hyndman quoted this conversation correctly.[27] Three years after Marx's death Engels wrote in the foreword to the English translation of *Das Kapital*:

Surely, at such a moment the voice ought to be heard of a man whose theory is the result of a life-long study of the economic conditions of England, and whom that study led to the conclusion that at least in Europe, England is the only country where the inevitable social revolution might be effected entirely by peaceful and legal means. He certainly never forgot to add that he hardly expected the English ruling classes to submit without a 'pro-slavery rebellion' to this peaceful and legal revolution.

The proletariat would win, peacefully perhaps in the

countries where there was an old and deeply-rooted democracy, but by force in those countries that were in the hands of despotism. When his daughter Jenny gave birth to a son in April 1881, Marx wrote to her:

My 'women folk'[28] hope that the 'newcomer' will increase the 'better half' of humanity; so far as I am concerned at this turning point in history, I favour children of the masculine sex. They have before them the most revolutionary period mankind has ever known. It is bad to be an old man at this time, for an old man can only foresee instead of seeing.

With this unflinching confidence Karl Marx died.

His was a painful dying but an easy death. Both his elder daughters lived in France. Jenny was married to Charles Longuet, Laura to Paul Lafargue. Eleanor, known to everyone as Tussy, looked after her parents. Marx was ill and his wife was wasting away with an incurable cancer. In summer 1881 they visited Jenny Longuet at Argenteuil. Frau Marx came back to London in a state of collapse, was confined to bed and died on 2 December 1881. For a long time Marx had known she was incurable, but her death was a heavy blow. 'The Moor has died too,' Engels said when he received the news of Frau Marx's death.

Marx was forbidden to attend the funeral, being bedridden after an attack of pleurisy. As soon as he was well enough to travel the doctors sent him to the south. At the end of February 1882 he went to Algiers but succumbed to pleurisy again. An exceptionally cold winter and a wet spring aggravated his condition. He went to Monte Carlo in the hope of an improvement, but succumbed to pleurisy for the third time. Not until he reached Argenteuil and later Lake Geneva did he recover sufficiently to be able to return to England. London fog drove him to the Isle of Wight. He caught cold again, had to keep to his room for a long time, tortured by a cough and barely sleeping four hours a night.

Jenny Longuet died unexpectedly in Paris on 11 January 1883. Marx hurried back to London. He scarcely spoke for days. He put up no more resistance to the advance of illness. Laryngitis made it almost impossilbe for him to swallow. He died on 14 March 1883 of a pulmonary abscess. Engels wrote to the faithful Sorge:

For the past six weeks I was in mortal terror as I turned the corner each morning lest I should find the blinds pulled down. Yesterday afternoon at half past two, the best time of day for visiting him, I went there. The whole house was in tears, it seemed to be the end. I made inquiries, tried to find out what was happening, to console. There had been a slight haemorrhage, but then there had been a sudden collapse. Our excellent old Lenchen, who had nursed him better than a mother, came down. He was half asleep, and she said I could go up with her. When we entered the room he lay there asleep, never to reawaken. His pulse and breathing had stopped. In those two minutes he had peacefully and painlessly passed away.[29]

He was buried in the cemetery at Highgate on 17 March. Liebknecht spoke for the German workers, Lafargue for the French workers, Engels for the workers of the world.[30]

His name and his work will re-echo down the centuries.

Appendix I

MARX'S ANTECEDENTS AND
HIS ATTITUDE TO JUDAISM

Various authors have taken an interest in Marx's antecedents.[1] The question arises whether Marx suffered from anti-Semitism, and in particular whether he experienced any hostility from the Westphalen family in this respect. Whatever the reality may have been, the appearances are that he did not. The reader will have noted on p. 70 that he denied his son-in-law Charles Longuet's allegation of 'race prejudice'. Let us quote the letter he wrote to his daughter Jenny Longuet on 7 December 1881 after Jenny Marx's death:

Je reçois à l'instant *La Justice* du 7 décembre, où je trouve, dans la rubrique 'Gazette du jour', une notice nécrologique disant entre autres: 'On devine que son (*il s'agit de votre mère*) *mariage* avec Karl Marx, fils d'un avocat de Trèves, *ne se fit pas sans peine.* Il y avait à vaincre *bien des préjugés, le plus fort de tous étant le préjugé de race.* On sait que l'illustre socialiste est d'origine israélite.' Toute cette histoire is a *simple invention*; there was *no préjugés à vaincre.* I suppose I am not mistaken in crediting Mr Ch. Longuet's inventive genius with literary 'enjolivement'.[2]

Let us recall that some of his opponents, such as Ruge, Proudhon, Bakunin, and Dühring, attacked him as a Jew.

In May–June 1843, finding the view of Bruno Bauer 'too

1. Notably B. Wachstein, 'Die Abstammung von Karl Marx', *Festskrift i anlening af Professor David Simonsen 70-aarige fodseldag*, Copenhagen, 1923, p. 277 ff.; E. Lewin-Dorsch, 'Familie und Stammbaum von Karl Marx', *Die Glocke*, Berlin, 1923, ninth year, I, p. 309 ff., 340 ff.; H. Horowitz, 'Die Familie Lwow', *Monatschrift für Geschichte und Wissenchaft des Judentums*, Frankfurt, 1928, p. 487 ff.; A. Cornu, 1955, vol. I, p. 54; W. Blumenberg, 1962, ch. I.
2. MEW, XXXV, p. 241 f.

abstract' and notwithstanding his aversion to the 'Jewish faith', he supported a petition to the Rhenish Diet for equality of civil and political rights for the Jews.[3]

Marx has been held to have been anti-Semitic, not only because of certain passages in *The Jewish Question* (1844), but also because of personal antipathies to which his correspondence testifies. Calling Lassalle a 'Jewish Negro'[4] did not show any great delicacy in this respect. Such intemperate language was not unusual in the working-class movement, in which Jews often identified themselves with capitalists. In this matter progressives tended to be at one with the chauvinist bourgeoisie.

On the core of the problem, let us quote Engels's view of the matter, which we can assume to have been also that of Marx:

Anti-Semitism is nothing but a reaction of medieval and declining social strata against modern society, which essentially consists of capitalists and wage-earners; it merely serves reactionary aims under a socialist cloak; it is merely a debased form of feudal socialism with which we must have nothing whatever to do. If its existence is possible in a country, it shows it does not have enough capital . . . [It] falsifies all the realities of the problem. It does not even know the Jews it bawls at . . . There are thousands and thousands of Jewish proletarians . . . Besides, we owe only too much to the Jews. As for myself, whom the *Gartenlaube* [a weekly] has turned into a Jew, I should, if I had to choose, rather be a Jew than a 'Herr von'.[5]

Nevertheless Marx's phraseology has been the cause of concern to some readers, such as S. Bloom;[6] an Israeli author, E. Silberner, claims there is an 'anti-Semitic tradition in modern socialism, in which Marx occupies a central position'.[7]

3. cf. Helmut Hirsch, *Archiv für Sozialgeschichte*, vol. VIII, 1968.

4. Letter to Engels, 30 July 1862, MEW, XXX, p. 257.

5. Letter dated 19 April 1890, published by the Vienna *Arbeiter Zeitung*, 9 May 1890. MEW XXII, p. 45.

6. Solomon F. Bloom, 'Karl Marx and the Jews', *Jewish Social Studies*, IV, January 1942.

7. Edmund Silberner, 'Was Marx an Anti-Semite?', *Judaica*, XI, April 1949.

W. Blumenberg replies to these suspicions by denying that Marx was an anti-Semite, but claims, as certain psychologists have done, that he was characterized by a typical 'self-hatred'.[8] M. Rubel was not far from believing this.[9] Arnold Künzli devotes a whole chapter to this alleged *Selbsthass*, this 'Jewish self-hatred' which we mention here merely for the sake of completeness.[10]

Since we here enter the field of psychological inference, we must mention the position adopted many years ago by Gustav Mayer in 'The Jew in Karl Marx'. Though Marx, who was baptized at the age of six, knew nothing of the 'psychical and spiritual treasures of Judaism' and hid his personal problems behind a screen of discretion (what does an individual amount to, after all, to a believer in historical materialism?), the question nevertheless arises – though we must not exaggerate its implications – of what was the motivation of 'his interpretation of his own origins'. In *The Jewish Question* he denounces 'Jewish trafficking'. Why confuse this with Jewish religiosity? Why this caricature, this bias, this lack of historical and psychological understanding? To G. Mayer, Marx, without being conscious of it, embodies the 'primal force' (*Urkraft*) that 'assures Judaism its high rank in the history of humanity'; his models, though he was unaware of it, were the prophets of Israel; like them, he had faith in the ascent of humanity, and accordingly he must not be treated as a destroyer and denier of values, a *Wertnihilist*, for his thought was merely clothed in scientific form, and the emancipation of the proletariat was a genuine prophetical idea. To Franz Mehring, however, *The Jewish Question* reveals a man 'liberated from all bias (*Gefangenheit*), from all Jewish preoccupation'. Thus G. Mayer differs from Marx's biographer.[11]

8. Blumenberg, *Marx*, 1962, pp. 86–7.
9. *Biographie intellectuelle*, 1957, p. 88.
10. A. Künzli, *Karl Marx, eine Psychographie*, Europa Verlag, 1966, p. 195 ff.
11. G. Mayer, 'Der Jude in Karl Marx', *Neue jüdische Monatshefte*, vol. II, Berlin, 1917–18. The article is reprinted by Albert Massiczek as an appendix to his *Der menschliche Mensch. Karl Marx' jüdischer*

The most recent commentators consider that Marx was aiming through the Jewish religion at a certain way of living. The bourgeoisie, whether Christian or Jewish, made money a universal power, and their God was 'practical need, egoism'. The 'Jews' of *The Jewish Question*[12] are, for instance, the Christians of America who prostrate themselves in the face of money, as Marx read about them in Hamilton, Beaumont and Tocqueville; in fact they were the bourgeoisie in general, in relation to whom Heine said: 'Money is the god of our time and Rothschild is his prophet.' Thus the appropriate term here is anti-Judaism – and anti-Christianism.[13]

Humanismus, Europa Verlag, Vienna, 1968. This author sets out to establish a 'basic Jewish personality' (using the methods of the Linton and Kardiner school of anthropology) and goes on to present us with a 'radically different' Marx, who 'can be understood only as a Jew'. The view that Marx was a prophet and not a scientist has of course been maintained by many authors, e.g., Albert Camus.

12. Zur Judenfrage. 1. Bruno Bauer, *Die Judenfrage*. 2. Bruno Bauer, 'Die Fähigkeit der heutigen Juden und Christen, frei zu werden', *Deutsch-Französische Jahrbücher*, I-II, Paris, February 1844. MEW, I, p. 372.

13. Helmut Hirsch, 'Marxiana judaïca I, Les sources américaines de *La Question juive*. II, Les sources judaïques. III, L'antijudaïsme comme source de *La question juive*', *Études de Marxologie*, Économies et Sociétés, August 1963. cf. ibid., Roman Rosdolsky's 'La *Neue Rheinische Zeitung* et les Juifs'. cf. also D. McLellan, 1969 (see Appendix II).

Appendix II

'TRUE SOCIALISM'

A number of references to 'true' socialism are made in the course of this work (pp. 20, 110, 218, etc). What is meant by this is the speculative socialism 'translated' from the French, which was concerned to put an end to the 'alienation' of man, tended to rise above the level of concrete situations, and spread among the German petty bourgeoisie. After the attacks made on it in *The German Ideology*, the description of it in the Communist Manifesto, III, *c*. will have been recognized.

Engels and Marx attacked this chimera from the beginning of 1847, at the end of which the Manifesto was composed. Engels wrote an MS. called *The True Socialists*.[1] In September Marx commented sharply on a book by Karl Grün in an article called 'The Historiography of True Socialism'.[2] Then Engels attacked Karl Beck and Karl Grün in a series of articles called 'German Socialism in Verse and Prose'.[3]

On the struggle against 'true socialism', cf. Herwig Förder, *Marx und Engels am Vorabend der Revolution*, Akademia Verlag, Berlin, 1960.

This school of thought has been studied by a number of modern authors:

D. Koigen, *Zur Vorgeschichte des modernen philosophischen Sozialismus in Deutschland*, Berne, 1901.

1. *Die wahren Sozialisten*, unpublished until 1932. MEW, IV, pp. 248–90.
2. 'Karl Grün, *Die soziale Bewegung in Frankreich und Belgien* (Darmstadt, 1845), oder: Die Geschichtsschreibung des wahren Sozialismus'; *Westfälisches Dampfboot*, August–September 1847. Marx thought of using this article as a supplement to *The German Ideology*. MEW, III, pp. 473–520.
3. 'Deutscher Sozialismus in Versen und Prosa', *Deutsche Brüsseler Zeitung*, 12 September 1847 and 9 December 1847. MEW, IV, pp. 207–47.

A. Cornu, 'German Utopianism: "True" Socialism', *Science and Society*, 12, 1948; *K. Marx et F. Engels*, 1958, vol. II.

John Weiss, *Moses Hess, Utopian Socialism*, Detroit, Wayne State University Press, 1960.

Lloyd D. Easton, 'Alienation and History in the early Marx', *Philosophy and Phenomenological Research*, 22, 1961.

Émile Bottigelli, *Genèse du socialisme scientifique*, Éditions Sociales, Paris, 1967.

David McLellan, *The Young Hegelians and Karl Marx*, Macmillan, 1969.

Appendix III

COULD MARX DISSOLVE
THE COMMUNIST LEAGUE?

THE authors state on p. 174 that Marx 'made use of his discretionary powers and dissolved the League' in May–June 1848. This statement relies on a document not produced in the English first edition, the deposition made by Peter Gerhardt Röser, president of the Cologne Association of Workers, who was convicted at the trial of Cologne communists in 1852–3. Röser agreed to making some disclosures, no doubt having been cornered into seeking an agreement with the police. (Incidentally, it is worth noting that the case was followed very carefully by the Prussian Minister of the Interior, who was no other than Ferdinand von Westphalen, Jenny Marx's brother.) Röser declared, and Nicolaievsky fully accepted his statement, that Marx did not want the adventure in which men like Willich and Schapper were involving themselves.[1] This refusal was associated with a general appreciation of the period and the chances of the revolutionary movement. According to Nicolaievsky, another document tends 'fully to confirm Röser's story'. This is a statement by Marx himself: 'We devote ourselves to a party which – so much the better for it – cannot yet take power. If it did so, it would take measures which would be not directly proletarian, but petty bourgeois. Our party will be able to attain power only when conditions enable it to carry out *its* ideas.'[2]

1. cf. above, pp. 229–30. B. Nicolaievsky used the document as an annex to the German (abbreviated) edition of the present work, *Karl und Jenny Marx*, Berlin, 1933, pp. 149–62.

2. Report of the last meeting of the central committee (*Central-Behörde*) of the League, London, 15 September 1850. Marx was referring to the changing of the rules of the League in 1848. (Document preserved at the International Institute of Social History, Amsterdam.)

These facts and statements carried weight in Nicolaievsky's mind, and later he did not hesitate to write: 'For the history of the League and the years 1848–9 in Marx's life is the first question to be studied'; he said that the present biography had 'far from exhausted the question' (article of 1961 cited below), and he criticized various Soviet historians for failing to draw attention to it 'because of party-political considerations'.[3]

One of these historians, E. P. Kandel, whose works on Marx's early years and the League are authoritative in Russia,[4] declared that the deposition by the traitor Röser was valueless; that Röser, in betraying his friends, tried to minimize the role played by some of them; and that accepting the view that the League was dissolved meant accepting 'the Menshevik interpretation of Marx's and Engels's policy in 1848–9'. Kandel claims that if the League disintegrated in 1848, this was only temporary, and 'it continued to exist in the form of ideological and political leadership' in the *Neue Rheinische Zeitung*, the editors of which were Marx and Engels; and it then 'continued to live in the party cadres, the members of the League, who locally organized and directed the associations of workers.'[5]

Nicolaievsky regarded this as laying down the official Soviet position. Marx, as the predecessor of Lenin, having in mind a 'new kind of party' based on 'professional revolutionaries', would never have dreamt of dissolving his organization. On the other hand, the historian could not ignore this document. 'Without Röser, the history of the League in the years of the

3. B. Nicolaievsky, 'Toward a History of the Communist League, 1847–1852', *International Review of Social History* (published by the International Institute of Social History, Amsterdam), Part II, 1956, pp. 234–52. The discussion of this point is on p. 237.

4. E. P. Kandel, *Marx and Engels. The Organizers of the Communist League*, Moscow, 1953. B. Nicolaievsky (1961) also attributed to him the article on the 'Communist League' in the *Great Soviet Encyclopaedia*, 2nd ed., 1958.

5. E. P. Kandel, 'The distortion of the history of Marx's and Engels's struggle for the proletarian party in the works of certain right-wing socialists', *Voprosy Istorii*, 5, 1958.

revolution would remain a series of incomprehensible movements, tossed by every wind.' Now, all that the Soviet historians seem to know of the document is that part of it which was
published by Nicolaievsky in the 1933 German edition of his
work; in it he printed an unpublished passage where Röser
repeated the contents of a letter from Marx. The passage is as
follows:

> In conclusion, I should like to add this. It is alleged that both
> Marx and Schapper want communism. This does not alter the
> fact that they are opponents or even enemies as soon as it comes
> to the methods by which communism is to be attained. The sup-
> porters of Schapper and Willich want communism introduced at
> the present stage of development, if necessary by force of arms,
> in the course of the imminent revolution. To Marx, communism
> is possible only as a result of an advance in education and general
> development; in one of the letters he addressed to us he distin-
> guished the four phases through which it will be necessary to pass
> before it is achieved. He says that from now to the next revolu-
> tion the petty bourgeoisie and the proletariat march together
> against the monarchy. They will not carry out that revolution
> themselves, but it will result from class relations and will arise
> from poverty. The periodical commercial crises will make it inevit-
> able.   After the next revolution, the petty bourgeoisie having
> acceded to power, the communists will begin their own action
> and will go over to the opposition. Then the social republic will
> come, followed by the socialist–communist republic, and finally
> the ground will be cleared for a purely communist republic
> [Deposition of 3 January 1854].

However that may be, so far as Nicolaievsky was concerned,
the central committee disintegrated in May–June 1848 because of the dissension between two main groups, the 'communist democrats' who followed Marx, and the leaders of the
former League of the Just. Thus the Communist League had
reached an *impasse*, and Marx merely 'cut the Gordian knot'.
No contradiction with the activity in London should be seen
in this; it was the result of the activity of the former leaders of
the League of the Just, who did not give up hope of reaching

agreement again with Marx's group, as was to be seen in 1850.[6]

Claiming that the organization was formally dissolved, or stating more simply that the proposal to dissolve it was followed by its dissolution *de facto*, presents us with one concept of the organization and its tasks; claiming that its existence was continuous presents us with another. That seems to be the essence of this controversy, into which we shall not enter further here.

All that needs be added is that E. P. Kandel replied, maintaining his previous stand;[7] that W. Blumenberg published the complete text of Röser's deposition, inclining, in spite of some reservations about the insufficiency of the documents, to grant him 'credibility';[8] and finally that other evidence is quoted in an article by S. Na'aman which temporarily closes the discussion.[9]

In conclusion, it may be hoped that the following lines written by Marx himself in 1860 will not be overlooked: 'When the February revolution broke out, the central committee in London entrusted me with control (*Oberleitung*) of the League. During the period of the revolution in Germany, its activity died of itself, since more effective ways of attaining its ends presented themselves'. Later Marx speaks of the 'reconstitution' of the League in London.[10]

6. B. Nicolaievsky, 'Who is distorting history? *Voprosy Istorii* and K. Marx in 1848–1849', *Proceedings of the American Philosophical Society*, vol. 105, no. 2, Philadelphia, April 1961.

7. E. P. Kandel, 'Eine schlechte Verteidigung einer schlechten Sache', *Beiträge zur Geschichte der Arbeiterbewegung*, V/2, Berlin, 1963.

8. Werner Blumenberg, 'Zur Geschichte des Bundes der Kommunisten; die Aussagen des Peter Gerhardt Röser', *International Review of Social History*, vol. IX, 1964, p. 81 ff.

9. Shlomo Na'aman, 'Zur Geschichte des Bundes der Kommunisten in der zweiten Phase seines Bestehens', *Archiv für Sozialgeschichte*, V, Hanover, 1965.

10. *Herr Vogt*, MEW, XIV, p. 439 f.

Appendix IV

WORKS OF BAKUNIN AND SELECTED BIBLIOGRAPHY OF WORKS ABOUT HIM

Marx's and Engels's writings about Bakunin can be consulted in part in *Contre l'anarchie*, Paris, 1935, in particular Marx's notes, 'Statism and Anarchy', on Bakunin's ideas about the state, the dictatorship of the proletariat and the agrarian question. See below, 1959.

Bakounine, *Œuvres*, Stock, Paris, 1895–1913, 6 vols.

Albert Richard, 'Bakounine et l'Internationale', *Revue de Paris*, September 1896.

Pisma M. A. Bakunina, Geneva, 1896 (Correspondence).

Correspondance, ed. Michel Dragomonov, translation (not very reliable) by Marie Stromberg, Perrin, Paris, 1896.

Max Nettlau, *The Life of Michel Bakounine* (German, *Michael Bakunin. Eine Biographie*). Privately printed by the author, London, 1896–1900, 3 vols.

J. Guillaume, *L'Internationale*, 1905–10, quoted *passim*.

Eduard Bernstein, *Karl Marx und Michael Bakunin*, Tübingen, 1910.

Fritz Brupbacher, *Marx und Bakunin*, 1913.

N. Riazanov, 'Sozialdemokratische Flagge und anarchistische Ware. Ein Beitrag zur Parteigeschichte', *Die Neue Zeit*, XXXII, vol. I, no. 9, 28 November 1913, p. 332 ff.; no. 10, 5 December 1913, p. 360 ff.

G. M. Steklov, *M. A. Bakunin, his life and work* (in Russian), 1926–7, 4 vols.

Arthur Lehning, 'Marxismus and Anarchismus in der Russichen Revolution', *Die Internationale*, Berlin, 1929.

M. Bakounine, *Confession (1857)*. Traduite du russe par Paulette Brupbacher, avec une Introduction de Fritz

Brupbacher et des annotations de Max Nettlau. Rider, Paris, 1932.

Benoît-P. Hepner, *Bakounine et le panslavisme révolutionnaire. Cinq essais sur l'histoire des idées en Russie et en Europe*, Rivière, Paris, 1937.

E. H. Carr, *Michael Bakunin*, London, 1937.

H. E. Kaminski, *Bakounine, la vie d'un révolutionnaire*, Aubier, Paris, 1938.

Fritz Brupbacher, 'Marx et Bakounine' (translation of the 1913 version), *Socialisme et Liberté*, Éditions de la Baconnière, Neuchâtel, 1955.

Eugène Pyziur, *The Doctrine of Anarchism of Michael Bakunin*, Marquette University Press, 1955.

Henry Mayer, 'Marx on Bakunin', *Études de marxologie*, no. 2, 1959. English version of the notes on 'Statism and Anarchy'.

Michele Bakunin, *Scritti napoletani* (1864–7), ed. P. C. Masini, Bergamo, 1963.

Archives Bakounine, édition établie pour l'Institut international d'Histoire sociale d'Amsterdam par Arthur Lehning. In course of publication, E. J. Brill, Leyden, since 1961. Four vols. published.

La Liberté, selected writings, 1965.

Daniel Guérin, *L'Anarchisme*, Gallimard, Paris, 1965.

Various items on and by Bakunin in D. Guérin, *Ni Dieu ni maître, anthologie historique du mouvement anarchiste*, Éditions de Delphes, Paris, 1966; republished, La Cité, Lausanne, 1969 (pp. 164–275).

A. Lehning, 'La lutte des tendances au sein de la Première Internationale: Marx et Bakounine', *La Première Internationale: l'institution, l'implantation, le rayonnement*. Colloques internationaux du C.N.R.S., Paris, 1964, published in 1968.

Pierre Ansart, *Marx et l'anarchisme*, Presses Universitaires de France, 1969.

Daniel Guérin, *Pour un marxisme libertaire*, Laffont, Paris, 1969.

Appendix V

MARX AND RUSSIA

We have seen that Marx always took a lively interest in Russian politics – his anti-Tsarism made it a largely hostile interest, mounting, in the eyes of Bakunin, for instance, to 'explicit Russophobia and implicit Slavophobia'.[1]

Such a picture would be misleading unless supplemented by a brief reminder of Marx's influence in Russia. The reader will recall his relations with Annenkov, for instance, and Bakunin himself, it is generally agreed, was the first Russian translator of the Communist Manifesto (1859); Bakunin also tried to translate *Das Kapital*. Marx was not lacking in Russian readers, both of *The Poverty of Philosophy* and *The Critique of Political Economy*.[2] By an 'irony of fate', as he wrote to Engels, the first proposal to publish a translation of *Das Kapital* came from Russia, through a 'populist' socialist, the

1. In connection with the last paragraph of the *Inaugural Address* of 1864; speeches made in 1871 and quoted by A. Lehning in his article of 1968 (cf. Appendix IV). To the titles already cited there may be added Paul W. Blackstock and Bert F. Hoselitz, *The Russian Menace to Europe: A Collection of Articles, Speeches, Letters and News Dispatches*, Free Press, Illinois, 1952, covering the whole period 1848–90. The articles of 1835–50 have been studied by M. Rubel, *Marx et Engels devant la révolution russe*, Payot, Paris, not yet published. cf. also L. Netter, introduction to the *Nouvelle Gazette Rhénane* [*Neue Rheinische Zeitung*], Éditions Sociales, 1963, pp. 22–3. Note also the articles published in 1865 in the *Free Press*, 'Revelations on the History of Diplomacy in the Eighteenth Century', cf. the Bibliography, 'Hepner' and 'Hutchinson', and pp. 246–7 above. Complete bibliography of these writings in H. Krause, *Marx und Engels und das zeitgenössische Russland, Giessen*, 1958.

2. Let us mention the artisan-philosopher Joseph Dietzgen, who made a close study of *The Critique* and of *Das Kapital*, as he wrote to Marx from St Petersburg on 5 November 1867.

economist Danielson, who, after H. Lopatin gave up the task, translated and published it in 1882.[3] Though he disliked Herzen as a follower of Proudhon (who also exercised great influence in Russia), he was not drawn towards the Russian socialists who called themselves 'Marxists'. He admired Chernichevsky, who was arrested and exiled in 1862, and in 1869 he began learning Russian in order to be able to read his writings, as well as those of Flerovsky.[4] Most of his correspondents were *narodniki,* or populists, but they also included Lavrov, who was a Proudhonian,[5] as well as Tkatchev and Mikhailovsky.[6]

Marx criticized the attitude of the Russian liberals from as early as 1858: 'To declare themselves opposed to serfdom, but to accept emancipation only on conditions that make it an imposture . . .' (*New York Tribune,* 19 October 1858, 29 December 1858, 17 January 1859).

In 1874 Tkatchev wrote to Engels that he seemed to make little of the revolutionary merits of the *obshchtina,* the Russian peasants' commune. The Russian people, he said, was 'communist by instinct, by tradition'; Russia had no bourgeoisie, and the state was powerless. 'An easier and more agreeable revolution could not be imagined', Engels replied.[7]

Here we recognize the great subject of debate among the populists. Could Russia build a communal society on the ancient foundations of collective land ownership (the *mir*)? Or was capitalism a stage that was universally necessary?

3. Marx conducted a protracted correspondence with his translator. cf. *Die Briefe von K. Marx und F. Engels an Danielson (Nicolaï-on),* letters published by G. Mayer and Kurt Mandelbaum, Leipzig, 1929. cf. M. Rubel, 'La Russie dans l'œuvre de Marx et d'Engels. Leur correspondance avec Danielson', op. cit.

4. N. Flerovsky, *The Situation of the Working Class in Russia,* 1869.

5. About twenty letters, from 1871 to 1882, MEW, XXX.

6. On Russian populism cf. Venturi's basic work, *Il popolismo russo,* 1952. See also *Populism,* ed. G. Ionescu and E. Gellner. The Nature of Human Society, Weidenfeld & Nicolson, 1969.

7. Engels replied for Marx and for himself. 'Soziales aus Russland', *Der Volksstaat,* 1875. French translation by M. Rubel in *Économies et Sociétés,* op. cit.

Mikhailovsky submitted the problem to Marx, who replied in French.[8]

The problem of primitive institutions had been long familiar to Marx and he did a great deal of reading on the subject, including M. Kovalevsky's book on *Communal Property* in Russia, which was sent him by the author in 1879.

Among the Russian populists a number of theorists were beginning to stand out, including Axelrod, Deutsch and the Plekhanov of *Socialism and the Political Struggle*.[9] The militant revolutionary Vera Zassoulitch, who had taken refuge in Geneva after making an assassination attempt and was an associate of these men, wrote to Marx in their name on this 'question of life or death'. Was the *mir*, the rural commune, viable or not? Should the revolutionaries struggle for its liberation or disinterest themselves in it to devote themselves to the town workers? Her letter provided the occasion for this most remarkable reply by Marx: 'To save the Russian commune a Russian revolution will be necessary.'[10] The Russian commune did not of course survive 1917.

8. 'L'avenir social de la Russie', posthumously published by V. Zassoulitch in 1884. La Pléiade, II, pp. 1552–5. cf. M. Rubel, op. cit.

9. cf. Dietrich Geyer, *Lenin in der russischen Sozialdemokratie*, Cologne, 1962, pp. 16–35; *Revolutionary Russia*, ed. R. Pipes, Harvard, 1968.

10. Letter of Vera Zassoulitch to Marx of 16 February 1881; reply and rough notes for it, 8 March 1881. La Pléiade, II, pp. 1556–73. Engels later sent to Zassoulitch the reply to Mikhailovsky quoted above. M. Rubel, op. cit. On this point, cf. Part VIII of *Das Kapital* on 'primitive accumulation', end of ch. XVI; and Marx's and Engels's foreword to the new Russian edition of the Communist Manifesto, 1882, La Pléiade, I, p. 1483. Other documents in *Économies et Sociétés*, July 1969. cf. also K. Papaioannou, 'La Russie et l'Occident', *Le Contrat social*, XII, nos 1 and 2–3, 1968.

Bibliography

I. BIOGRAPHICAL

(a) *Chronology.*

Karl Marx. Chronik seines Lebens in Einzeldaten, Marx-Engels-Lenin Institute, Moscow, 1934 (based on documents previously assembled by D. Riazanov).

'Chronologie' established by M. Rubel, in K. Marx, *Œuvres*, La Pléiade, vol. 1, 1963.

B. Andreas and W. Mönke, 'Neue Daten', *Archiv für Sozial-geschichte*, VIII, 1968.

Marx-Chronik. Daten zu Leben und Werk. Assembled by M. Rubel, Carl Hanser Verlag, Munich, 1968.

(b) *Some Lives of Marx and Engels.*

SPARGO, J.
Karl Marx, his Life and Works, New York, 1912.

MEHRING, FRANZ
Karl Marx. Geschichte seines Lebens, Dietz, Stuttgart, 1918; 5th ed., Leipzig, 1933; re-editions: Zürich, 1946; F. Mehring, *Gesammelte Schriften*, vol. III, Dietz, Berlin, 1960. French version in preparation, Maspéro, Paris.

RIAZANOV, DAVID
Karl Marx, homme, penseur et révolutionnaire, Éditions Sociales Internationales, Paris, 1927. Photographic reimpression, Anthropos, Paris, 1968.

RÜHLE, OTTO
Karl Marx, Leben und Werk, Avalun Verlag, Dresden, 1928.

VORLÄNDER, KARL
Karl Marx, sein Leben und sein Werk, Leipzig, 1929.

NICOLAIEVSKY, BORIS, and MAENCHEN-HELFEN, OTTO
Karl und Jenny Marx. Ein Lebensweg, Berlin, 1933.
Karl Marx, Man and Fighter, English translation by G. David and E. Mosbacher, Methuen, 1936; Lippincott, Philadelphia, 1937. (This volume is a republication of this edition.)
Karl Marx, Gallimard, Paris, 1937.
Karl Marx, L'homme et le lutteur, revised ed., Gallimard, Paris, 1970.

Karl Marx, Eine Biographie, Dietz, Hanover, 1963. Italian, Dutch, Swedish and Czech editions.

MAYER, GUSTAV
Friedrich Engels, eine Biographie, 2 vols., M. Nijhoff, The Hague, 1934.

CARR, E. H.
Karl Marx. A study in fanaticism, Dent, 1934.

CORNU, AUGUSTE
Karl Marx, l'homme et l'œuvre. De l'hégélianisme au matérialisme historique (1818–1845), Alcan, Paris, 1934; *La Jeunesse de Karl Marx*, Presses Universitaires de France, Paris, 1934. Revised version in *Karl Marx et Friedrich Engels, leur vie et leur œuvre*, Presses Universitaires de France, Paris; Vol. I: *Les Années d'enfance et de jeunesse. La Gauche hégélienne (1818/1820–1844)*, 1955; Vol. II: *Du libéralisme démocratique au communisme. La 'Gazette rhénane'. Les 'Annales franco-allemandes' (1842–1844)*, 1958.

RUBEL, MAXIMILIEN
K. Marx, Essai de biographie intellectuelle, Paris, 1957.

BERLIN, ISAIAH
Karl Marx. His Life and Environment, Oxford University Press, 1939. French version, *Karl Marx*, translated by Anne Guérin and P. Tilche, Gallimard, Paris, 1962.

BLUMENBERG, WERNER
K. Marx in Selbstzeugnissen und Bilddokumenten, Rowohlt Monographien, Reinbek bei Hamburg, 1962. French version, *Marx*, translated by R. Laureillard, Le Mercure de France, Paris, 1967.

LEFEBVRE, HENRI
Karl Marx, sa vie, son œuvre, avec un exposé de sa philosophie, Presses Universitaires de France, Paris, 1964.

II. THE WORKS OF MARX AND ENGELS
BIBLIOGRAPHY

In general, reference has been made to two works by:

RUBEL, MAXIMILIEN
Bibliographie des œuvres de Karl Marx, avec en appendice un Répertoire des œuvres de Frédéric Engels, Marcel Rivière, Paris, 1956.

Supplément à la *Bibliographie des œuvres de K. Marx*, Marcel Rivière, Paris, 1956.
References to other works in the footnotes *passim*.

WORKS QUOTED

(a) *Original text. Complete editions.*
The two major sources are:
MEGA (Marx–Engels Gesammtausgabe). Published under the editorship of D. Riazanov from 1927 onwards. Interrupted in 1932. Thirteen volumes published (Marx–Engels Institute, Moscow).
MEW (Marx–Engels, *Werke*). Publication begun in 1957; forty-three volumes have appeared. Institute for Marxism-Leninism, Dietz, Berlin. It is to this edition that the reader is generally referred in the footnotes.

(b) *Original version. Partial editions.*
A number of works consisting largely of collections of letters and articles are listed below. Reference has been made in principle to the most recent publications, and most of them are classified under the name of the editor.

(c) *French version. Complete editions.*
OE.C. *Œuvres complètes de Karl Marx*, translated by Jules Molitor, A. Costes, Paris. This series, published from 1923 onwards, includes a number of philosophical works and letters, as well as the *Œuvres complètes de Frédéric Engels*, translated by Bracke (Desrousseaux) and J. Molitor.
E.S.I. Les Éditions Sociales Internationales, founded in 1931 and interrupted in 1940, published a series of works by Marx and Engels. The editors, etc., are generally anonymous.
E.S. Les Éditions Sociales resumed publication of the above from 1945 onwards.
La Pléiade. Karl Marx, *Œuvres*, edited by Maximilien Rubel, Bibliothèque de la Pléiade, Gallimard, Paris. Two volumes have been published: 'Économie', I (1963) and II (1968).

(d) *French versions. Partial editions.*
See under (b).

III. HISTORICAL WORKS AND OTHER SOURCES

The following is of course not a complete bibliography, but is intended solely to aid the reader in referring to works quoted in the notes.

(a) *Selected works and periodicals.*

Die Neue Zeit, weekly founded by Karl Kautsky in 1883; publication continued until 1923.

Aus dem Literarischen Nachlass von Karl Marx und Friedrich Engels, 1841 bis 1850, ed. Franz Mehring, Dietz, Stuttgart, 1902, 4th ed., 1923, 3 vols.

Grünberg-Archiv. Abbreviation for *Archiv für die Geschichte des Sozialismus und der Arbeiterbewegung,* ed. Carl Grünberg, Leipzig, 1910–30. cf. in particular 'Neue Beiträge zur Biographie von Marx', X, 1922.

Archiv für Sozialwissenschaft und Sozialpolitik, ed., Werner Sombart, Max Weber and Edgar Jaffe, Mohr, Tübingen and Leipzig.

Marx–Engels Archiv; Journal of the Institute of Marxism–Leninism, Moscow, ed., D. Riazanov, Frankfurt; vol. I, undated, and vol. II, 1927.

IRSH. *International Review for Social History,* published by the Institute of Social History, Amsterdam, 1936–9 and 1956 onwards.

Beiträge zur Geschichte der Arbeiterbewegung, Institute of Marxism–Leninism, Berlin, 1958 onwards.

Annali dell'Istituto Giangiacomo Feltrinelli, Milan, 1958 onwards.

Études de marxologie. Published by the Institut de Science économique appliquée, edited by M. Rubel, from January 1959 onwards; this publication is now known as *Économies et Sociétés* (ISEA).

Archiv für Sozialgeschichte, published since 1960 by the Friedrich-Ebert Institute, Hanover, Verlag für Literatur und Zeitgeschichte.

Karl Marx, 1918–1968. Neue Studien zu Person und Lehre, published by the Institut für staatsbürgerliche Bildung im Rheinland, Mainz, 1968.

(b) *Works quoted.*

ABRAMSKY, C.
See COLLINS, H.

ADORATSKI, V.
Karl Marx, Eine Sammlung von Erinnerungen und Aufsätzen, Marx–Engels Institute, Moscow; Ring Verlag, 1934.

ALTHUSSER, LOUIS
See FEUERBACH.

ANDLER, CHARLES
Le Manifeste communiste de K. Marx et F. Engels, Introduction historique et commentaire, Rieder, Paris, 1901.

ANDREAS, BERT
Responsible for republication of *Kommunistische Zeitschrift*, London, *1847*. B.S.D. Limmat Verlag, Zürich, undated.
'Briefe und Dokumente der Familie Marx aus den Jahren 1862–1873', *Archiv für Sozialgeschichte*, vol. II, Hanover, 1962.
Le Manifeste communiste de Marx et Engels. Histoire et bibliographie, 1848–1918, Giangiacomo Feltrinelli Institute, Milan, 1963.
'Zur Agitation und Propaganda des Allgemeinen Deutschen Arbeitervereins 1863–1864', *Archiv für Sozialgeschichte*, III, 1963 (with a bibliography of Lassalle).
'Marx et Engels et la gauche hégélienne', *Annali dell'Istituto Giangiacomo Feltrinelli*, VII, 1964–5, pp. 353–526.
See above, section Ia.

ANNENKOV, PAUL
See ch. 9, note 11.

ANSART, PIERRE
See Appendix IV, BAKUNIN.

ARTICLES BY MARX AND ENGELS, selections and republications.
See AVELING, AVINERI, BOTTIGELLI, CHALONER, CHRISTMAN, DRAPER, DUTT, HEPNER, HUTCHINSON, NETTER, RIAZANOV, RUBEL, TORR. See *Œuvres complètes, Œuvres politiques*; see Éditions Sociales, section II(c), above; see also Appendices IV, Bakunin, and V, Russia.

AVELING, EDUARD and ELEANOR (E. MARX)
ed. *The Eastern Question*. A reprint of letters written in 1853–6 dealing with the events of the Crimean War, by K. Marx, S. Sonnenschein, London, 1897.

AVELING, ELEANOR
'A Few Stray Notes', reminiscences written in English and published in German in the *Oesterreichischer Arbeiterkalender für das Jahr 1895*, Brünn. See ADORATSKI. English version in *Reminiscences of Marx and Engels*, Moscow, undated.

K. Marx, *Secret Diplomatic History of the Eighteenth Century*, ed. Eleanor Aveling, London, 1899 (see HEPNER, HUTCHINSON).

K. Marx, *The Story of the Life of Lord Palmerston*, ed. Eleanor Marx, London, 1899 (see HUTCHINSON).

AVINERI, SHLOMO

Karl Marx on Colonialism and Modernization. His dispatches and other writings on China, India, Mexico, the Middle East and North Africa. Edited with an introduction by S. Avineri, Doubleday, New York, 1968.

BADIA, G., and FRÉDÉRIC, J.

See ch. 8, note 12.

BAKUNIN, MICHAEL

See Appendix IV.

BEBEL, AUGUST

Aus meinem Leben, 3 vols., Dietz, Stuttgart, 1910–14. See W. BLUMENBERG, 1965.

BERNSTEIN, SAMUEL

'Marx in Paris, 1848: A neglected chapter', *Science and Society*, New York, III, 3, 1939; IV, 2, 1940.

The First International in America, Kelley, New York, 1962.

BESTOR, A. E.

'Albert Brisbane, propagandist for Socialism in the 1840s', *New York History*, XVIII, April 1947, pp. 128–58.

BIGLER, ROLF R.

Der libertäre Sozialismus in der Westschweiz. Ein Beitrag zur Entwicklungsgeschichte und Deutung des Anarchismus, Kiepenheuer und Witsch, Cologne, 1963.

BLACKSTOCK, PAUL W., and HOSELITZ, BERT F.

See Appendix V, Russia.

BLITZER, C.

See CHRISTMAN.

BLOOM, SOLOMON F.

See Appendix I, Judaism.

BLUMENBERG, WERNER

'Ein unbekanntes Kapitel aus Marx' Leben. Brief an die holländischen Verwandten', *International Review of Social History*, vol. I, 1956, part 1, pp. 54–111.

August Bebel, *Briefwechsel mit Friedrich Engels*, ed. Werner Blumenberg, Mouton & Co., The Hague, Paris, 1965.

See above, section Ib.

See Appendix III, The League.

BLUNTSCHLI, J. C. VON
Die Kommunisten in der Schweiz, 1843.

BOBINSKA, CELINA
Marx und Engels über polnische Probleme, Dietz, Berlin, 1958 (translated from the Polish).

BÖRNE, LUDWIG
Gesammelte Schriften, Tendler, Vienna, 1868.

BÖRNSTEIN, HENRI
Fünfundsiebzig Jahre in der alten und neuen Welt. Memoiren eines Unbedeutenden, 2 vols., Leipzig, 1881.

BORN, STEFAN.
Erinnerungen eines Achtundvierziger, Leipzig, 1898.

BOTTIGELLI, ÉMILE
Published in French, with Laure Lentin: F. Engels, *La Révolution démocratique bourgeoise en Allemagne*, Éditions Sociales, Paris, 1951.

Lettres et documents de Karl Marx, 1856–1883. *Annali dell'Istituto Giangiacomo Feltrinelli*, Milan, 1958, pp. 149–219.

See also *La Pensée*, 1957, nos 74 and 75.

BRACHT, W.
Trier und K. Marx, Treviriensa Verlag, 1947.

BRACKE, WILHELM
K. Marx, F. Engels, *Briefwechsel mit Wilhelm Bracke (1869–1880)*, Dietz. Berlin, 1963.

BRUEGEL, L.
Geschichte der österreichischen Sozialdemokratie, Vienna, 1922–5, 5 vols.

BRÜGEL, FRITZ, and KAUTSKY, BENEDICT
Der deutsche Sozialismus von L. Gall bis K. Marx. Ein Lesebuch, Hess & Co., Vienna and Leipzig, 1931.

BRUPBACHER, FRITZ
See Appendix IV, Bakunin.

BÜRGERS, HEINRICH
'Erinnerungen an F. Freiligrath', *Vossische Zeitung*, Berlin, 10 and 17 September 1876, 26 November 1876 and 3 December 1876.

CAILLÉ, F.
Wilhelm Weitling, théoricien du communisme (1808–1870), Paris, 1905.

CANNAC, RENÉ
Aux sources de la révolution russe: Netchaïev, du nihilisme au terrorisme, Payot, Paris, 1961.

CARR, E. H.
See above, section Ib.
See Appendix IV, Bakunin.

CARRIÈRE, MORITZ
'Lebenserinnerungen', *Archiv für Hessische Geschichte*, 1914.

CHALONER and HENDERSON
Engels as a Military Critic, Manchester, 1959.

CHRISTMAN, HENRY M., and BLITZER, CHARLES
The American Journalism of Marx and Engels. A Selection from the New York Daily Tribune, ed. Henry M. Christman. Introduction by Charles Blitzer. The New American Library, New York, 1966.

COGNIOT, ERNA
Translator of K. Marx, *La Sainte Famille*, Éditions Sociales, Paris, 1969.

COLLINS, HENRY, and ABRAMSKY, CHIMEN
Karl Marx and the British Labour Movement. Years of the First International, Macmillan, 1965.

CORNU, AUGUSTE
See above, section Ib.
On 'True socialism', see Appendix II.
Moses Hess et la gauche hégélienne, Presses Universitaires de France, Paris, 1934.
Editor of Moses Hess, *Philosophische und sozialistische Schriften, 1837–1850. Eine Auswahl*, Akademia-Verlag, Berlin, 1961 (in collaboration with W. Mönke).

CONZE, WERNER
Karl Marx, Manuskripte über die polnische Frage (1863–1864). Edited with an introduction by Werner Conze and D. Hertz-Eichenrode, Mouton & Co., The Hague, 1961.

CUNOW, H.
'Zum Streit zwischen K. Marx und K. Vogt', *Die Neue Zeit*, vol. 37, no. 1, 1918, p. 620 ff.

CZOBEL, E.
'Zur Geschichte des Kommunistenbunds', *Grünberg-Archiv*, 11 (1925).

See KUGELMANN.

DESROCHE, HENRI

Ed. Marx et Engels, 'Circulaire contre Kriege', *Études de marxologie*, Institut de Science économique appliquée, January 1962, pp. 35–60.

Socialismes et Sociologie religieuse, Cujas, Paris, 1965. Extracts from the works of Friedrich Engels, translated and presented with the aid of G. Dunstheimer and M.-L. Letendre. (Part is devoted to Engels's religious correspondence, 1838–41; another to atheism in the works of Marx and Engels; the book also contains the circular against *Kriege* of May 1846.)

DOCUMENTS OF THE FIRST INTERNATIONAL, 1870–71, 4 vols., Lawrence & Wishart. (Institute of Marxism–Leninism of the Central Committee, Communist Party of the Soviet Union.)

DOLLÉANS, ÉDOUARD

Le Chartisme, 1830–1848, 2 vols., Fleury, Paris, 1912–13.

Le Chartisme, 1831–1848, new and revised edition, Bibliothèque d'Histoire économique et sociale, Marcel Rivière, Paris, 1949.

DOMMANGET, MAURICE

Les Idées politiques et sociales d'Auguste Blanqui, Rivière, Paris, 1938.

L'Introduction du marxisme en France, Rencontre, Lausanne, 1969.

DORNEMANN, LUISE

Jenny Marx, Der Lebensweg einer Sozialistin, Dietz, Berlin, 1968.

DRAPER, HAL

'Marx and the Dictatorship of the Proletariat', *Études de marxologie*, September 1962.

'Marx, Engels and the *New American Cyclopaedia*', *Cahiers de marxologie*, Économies et Sociétés, December 1968.

DUTT, R. P.

Ed. K. Marx, *Articles on India*, People's Publishing House, Bombay, 1943.

EASTON, LLOYD D.

'August Willich, Marx and Left-Hegelian socialism', *Études de marxologie*, August 1965.

On 'True Socialism', see Appendix II.

ECKERT, GEORG

Ed. Wilhelm Liebknecht, *Briefwechsel mit Karl Marx und Friedrich Engels*, Mouton & Co., The Hague, 1963.

100 Jahre Braunschweiger Sozialdemokratie. I. *Von den Anfängen bis zum Jahre 1890,* Dietz, Hanover, 1965.

FEUERBACH, LUDWIG

Manifestes philosophiques. Textes choisis; translated by Althusser, Paris, 1960.

FLEURY, V.

Le Poète Georges Herwegh, Paris, 1911.

FÖRDER, HERWIG

Marx und Engels am Vorabend der Revolution, Akademia-Verlag, Berlin, 1960.

FREILIGRATH, FERDINAND

See MEHRING, HAECKEL, BÜRGERS.

FREYMOND, JACQUES

La Première Internationale, recueil de documents publiés sous la direction de J. Freymond, 2 vols., Droz, Geneva, 1962.

Études et Documents sur la Premiére Internationale en Suisse, publiés sous la direction de J. Freymond, Droz, Geneva, 1964.

FRIBOURG, E. E.

L'Association Internationale des Travailleurs. Origines. Paris, Londres, Genève, Lausanne, Bruxelles, Berne, Bâle. Notes et pièces à l'appui, Le Chevalier, Paris, 1871.

FRÖBEL, JULIUS

Ein Lebenslauf, 2 vols., Stuttgart, 1890.

GALL, LUDWIG

See BRUEGEL and KAUTSKY

GERTH, HANS

The First International. Minutes of the Hague Congress of 1872, with related documents. Edited and translated by Hans Gerth, University of Wisconsin Press, Madison, 1958.

GRÜNBERG, CARL

See *Grünberg-Archiv,* section IIIa above.

Reprint of the London communist journal: *Die Londoner Kommunistische Zeitschrift und andere Urkunden aus den Jahren 1847–1848.* Eingeleitet und mit Anmerkungen versehen von Carl Grünberg, *Grünberg-Archiv,* Leipzig, 1921.

'Bruno Hildebrand über den Kommunistichen Arbeiterbildungsverein in London. Zugleich ein Beitrag zu Hildebrands Biographie', *Grünberg-Archiv,* X, 1925.

GUÉRIN, DANIEL

See Appendix IV, Bakunin, and ch. 18, note 8.

GUILLAUME, JAMES
L'Internationale, documents et souvenirs, 1870–1871, 2 vols.,
Société nouvelle de Librairie et d'Édition, Paris, 1905–10.

HAECKEL, MANFRED
Ed. *Freiligraths Briefwechsel mit Marx und Engels*, 2 vols.,
Akademia-Verlag, Berlin, 1968.

HANSEN, J.
*Rheinische Briefe und Akten, an der Geschichte der politischen
Bewegung, 1800–1850*. Publikation der Gesellschaft für rhein-
ische Geschichtskunde, 2 vols., Essen and Bonn, 1919.

HAUPT, G.
See ROUGERIE, J.
See ch. 17, note 1.

HEINE, HEINRICH
See ch. 10, note 5.

HEIGEL, K. T.
'Das Hambacher Fest', *Historische Zeitschrift*, 1913.

HENDERSON
See CHALONER

HEPNER, BENOÎT-P.
Ed. Karl Marx, *La Russie et l'Europe*, première édition intégrale
présentée avec une introduction, 'Marx et la puissance russe',
par B.-P. Hepner, Gallimard, Paris, 1954 (see L. HUTCHINSON).

HERTZ-EICHENRODE, D.
See CONZE

HESS, MOSES
See SILBERNER, CORNU
See Appendix II, 'True Socialism'.

HIRSCH, HELMUT
'Marxiana judaïca', see Appendix I, Judaism.
'Marx in den Augen der Pariser Polizei', *Denker und Kämpfer*,
Europäische Verlagsanstalt, 1955.
'Marxens Milieu. Zu dem Werk von Heinz Monz: *Karl Marx
und Trier*', *Études de marxologie*, August 1965.
See Appendix I, Judaism.

HÖLSCHER, H.
Andenken an Dr Andreas Gottschalk, Cologne, 1849.

HOROWITZ, H.
'Die Familie Lwow', see Appendix I, Judaism.

HOSELITZ
See BLACKSTOCK.

HUTCHINSON, LESTER
Ed. Karl Marx, *Secret Diplomatic History of the Eighteenth Century* and *The Story of the Life of Lord Palmerston,* Lawrence and Wishart, 1967 (see HEPNER).

HYNDMAN, H. M.
The Record of an Adventurous Life, London, 1911.

JAECKH, G.
Die Internationale, 1904.

JONES, ERNEST
See SAVILLE

KAHN, S. B.
'On the Causes of the Ban on the *Rheinische Zeitung*', *Contributions to the History of the Working Class and the Revolutionary Movement,* publications of the Academy of Sciences of the U.S.S.R., Moscow, 1958, pp. 648–62 (in Russian).

KAISER, BRUNO
Ed. *Ex libris, Karl Marx und Friedrich Engels, Schicksal und Verzeichnis,* Dietz, Berlin, 1967.

KAMINSKI, H. E.
See Appendix IV, Bakunin.

KANDEL, E. P.
See Appendix III, The League.

KAUTSKY, BENEDICT
See BRUEGEL, L.

KAUTSKY, K.
See section IIIa, above.
See KUGELMANN

KLUTENTRETER, W.
'*Die Rheinische Zeitung* von 1842/1843', *Dortmunder Beiträge zur Zeitungsforschung,* 10/1 and 10/2.

KOIGEN, D.
On 'True socialism', see Appendix II.

KÖNIG, HERMANN
'Die Rheinische Zeitung von 1842–1843 in ihrer Einstellung zur Kulturpolitik des Preussischen Staates', *Münstersche Beiträge zur Geschichtsforschung,* Neue Folge, 39, 1927.

KRAUSE, H.
See Appendix V, Russia.

KUGELMANN, LUDWIG
K. Marx, *Lettres à Kugelmann* (1862–74). First published incomplete by K. Kautsky, *Die Neue Zeit*, 1902. Russian translation, with a preface by Lenin, 1907. Complete French version based on documents of the Marx-Engels Institute, Moscow: *Lettres à Kugelmann*, preface by Lenin, introduction by E. Czobel, translated by Rose Michel, Éditions Sociales Internationales, 1930. Photographic reimpression, Anthropos, Paris, 1968.

KÜNZLI, ARNOLD
See Appendix I, Judaism.

KUYPERS, JULIEN
'Wilhelm Wolff und der deutsche Arbeiterverein (1847–1848) in Brüssel. Ein Fund aus dem belgischen Landesarchiv', *Archiv für Sozialgeschichte*, III, 1963.

LAFARGUE, PAUL and LAURA
P. Lafargue, 'Persönliche Erinnerungen', *Die Neue Zeit*, IX, vol. I, nos. 1-2, 1890–91. French version, *Souvenirs sur Marx et Engels*, see below.
F. Engels, P. et L. Lafargue, *Correspondance, 1868–1895*. Éditions Sociales, 3 vols., 1956 and 1959.

LASSALLE, FERDINAND
See G. MAYER

LEDIGKEIT, KARL-HEINZ
Wilhelm Liebknecht und August Bebel in der deutschen Arbeiterbewegung, 1862–9, 2nd ed., Rütten & Loening, Berlin, 1958. (Schriftenreihe des Instituts für deutsche Geschichte an der Karl Marx Universität, Leipzig, vol. III.) Ed. *Der Leipziger Hochverratsprozess vom Jahre 1872*, Neu herausgegeben von K.-H. Ledigkeit, Rütten & Loening, Berlin, 1960.

LEFEBVRE, HENRI
See section Ib above.

LEHNING, ARTHUR
See Publisher's Note and Appendices IV, Bakunin, and V, Russia.

LENIN
See Kugelmann, L.

LEWALD, FANNY
Meine Lebensgeschichte, in her *Œuvres complètes*, O. Janke, Berlin, 1871.

LEWIN-DORSCH, E.
'Familie und Stammbaum von K. Marx', see Appendix I, Judaism.

LIEBKNECHT, WILHELM
Karl Marx zum Gedächtnis, Nuremberg, 1896. French version, *Souvenirs*, translated by G.-G. Prodhomme and C.-A. Bertrand, Paris, 1901. In the same volume, *Souvenirs de jeunesse*.
See ECKERT

LONGUET, JEAN
La Politique internationale du marxisme, Alcan, Paris, 1918.

LUCAS, ALPHONSE
Les Clubs et les clubistes, Dentu, Paris, 1851.

MANDEL, ERNEST
'La formation de la pensée économique de Karl Marx, de 1843 jusqu'à la rédaction du *Capital*.' Étude génétique, Maspéro, Paris, 1967.

MANDELBAUM, KURT
See Appendix V, Russia.

MARX, ELEANOR
See AVELING

MARX, JENNY
'Brève esquisse d'une vie mouvementée', *Souvenirs sur Marx et Engels*. Moscow, undated.

MARX, LAURA
See LAFARGUE

MASSICZEK, ALBERT
See Appendix I, Judaism.

MAYER, GUSTAV
'Der Untergang der *Deutsch-Französischen Jahrbücher* und des Pariser *Vorwärts*', *Grüberg-Archiv*, vol. III, 1913, p. 415 f.
Ed. The Marx-Lassalle correspondence, 'Der Briefwechsel zwischen Lassalle und Marx', in F. Lassalle, *Nachgelassene Briefe und Schriften*, vol. III, Deutsche Verlagsanstalt, Stuttgart and Berlin, 1922.
Bismarck und Lassalle, Ihr Briefwechsel und ihre Gespräche, Dietz, Berlin, 1928.
See section Ib above, Life of Engels.
See Appendix I, Judaism, and Appendix V, Russia.

MAYER, PAUL
'Die Geschichte des Sozialdemokratischen Parteiarchivs und das Schicksal des Marx-Engels Nachlasses', *Archiv für Sozialgeschichte*, Hanover, vols. VI-VII, 1966-7.

MCLELLAN, DAVID
See Appendices I, Judaism, and II, 'True Socialism'.

MEHRING, FRANZ
See sections Ib and IIIa above.

Ed. Marx's letters to Freiligrath, 'Freiligrath und Marx in ihrem Briefwechsel', Ergänzungshefte zur *Neuen Zeit*, no. 12, 12 April 1912.

Republished and introduced the two addresses of the central committee to the League of March and June 1850, *Sozialistiche Neudrucke*, no. 6, Berlin, 1914.

'Georg Herwegh', *Grünberg-Archiv*, IV, 1914.

Geschichte der deutschen Sozialdemokratie, 6th ed., 1919.

MEYER, H.
'Karl Marx und die deutsche Revolution von 1848', *Historische Zeitschrift*, Munich, no. 3, December 1951.

MÖNKE, WOLFGANG
Neue Quellen zur Hess-Forschung, Akademia-Verlag, Berlin, 1964.

Das Literarische Echo in Deutschland auf F. Engels' Werk 'Die Lage der arbeitenden Klasse in England,' Akademia-Verlag, Berlin, 1965.

See above, section Ia, B. ANDREAS.

See CORNU.

MOLNAR, MIKLOS
Le Déclin de la Première Internationale. La Conférence de Londres de 1871, Publications de l'Institut des Hautes Études internationales, no. 42, Droz, Geneva, 1963.

MONZ, HEINZ
Karl Marx und Trier, Verhältnisse-Beziehungen-Einflüsse, Trier, 1964.

Das Karl-Marx-Geburtshaus in Trier. Published by the Karl Marx Haus Verwaltung, Trier, 1967.

'Unbekannte Kapitel aus dem Leben der Familie Johann Ludwig von Westphalen', *Archiv für Sozialgeschichte*, vol. VIII, 1968, pp. 247-60.

'Die rechtsethischen und rechtspolitischen Anschauungen des Heinrich Marx', *Archiv für Sozialgeschichte*, vol. VIII, 1968, pp. 261-83.

NA'AMAN, SHLOMO
See Appendix III, The League.

'Lassalle et la Révolution française: Analyse de son œuvre post-hume, Histoire du développement social', *Études de marx-ologie*, no. 4, 1961.

'Lassalles Beziehungen zu Bismarck – ihr Sinn und Zweck: zur Beleuchtung von Gustav Mayer, Bismarck und Lassalle', *Archiv für Sozialgeschichte*, vol. II, 1962.

'Zur Geschichte des Bundes der Kommunisten in der zweiten Phase seines Bestehens', *Archiv für Sozialgeschichte*, vol. V, 1965.

Ferdinand Lassalle, Deutscher und Jude, Hanover, 1968.

NERRLICH

See RUGE.

NETTER, LUCIENNE

K. Marx, F. Engels, *La Nouvelle Gazette rhénane* (articles). Trans-lation, introduction and notes by Lucienne Netter, Editions Sociales, Paris, 1963; vol. I, 1 June–5 September 1848.

NETTLAU, MAX

See Appendix IV, Bakunin.

Speech of Weitling, 1845, in 'Londoner deutsche kommunistiche Diskussionen, 1845. Nach dem Protokollbuch des C.A.B.V.', *Grünberg-Archiv*, X, pp. 362–91.

NICOLAIEVSKY, BORIS

See section Ib above.

See Appendix III, The League.

'August Willich, ein Soldat der Revolution van 1848', *Der Abend*, Berlin, 4 May 1931.

OLLIVIER, MARCEL

'Karl Marx poète', *Le Mercure de France*, 15 April 1933.

PAPAIOANNOU, KOSTA

See Appendix V, Russia.

PROUDHON, PIERRE-JOSEPH

Le Système des contradictions économiques ou Philosophie de la misère, introduction and notes by Roger Picard, 2 vols., *Œuvres complètes*, published under the direction of C. Bouglé and H. Moysset, Éditions Marcel Rivière, Paris, 1923.

PYZIUR, EUGÈNE

See Appendix IV, Bakunin.

RAMM, THILO

Ferdinand Lassalle als Rechts- und Sozialphilosoph, Westkultur Verlag Anton Hain, Meisenheim, Vienna, 1953.

Reminiscences of K. Marx and F. Engels, Moscow, undated.

RIAZNOV, DAVID
See above, sections Ib and IIa; see also Appendix IV, Bakunin.
'Marx als Verleumder', *Die Neue Zeit*, 2 December 1910.
'Marx und seine russischen Bekannten in den vierziger Jahren', *Die Neue Zeit*, XXXI, vol. I, 1913.
Published the articles from the *New York Tribune*, translated from English into German by Louise Kautsky, in 2 vols. of the *Gesammelte Schriften von Karl Marx und Friedrich Engels* 1917–18 (chiefly the articles of 1852–5).
Published a description of the manuscript of *Die deutsche Ideologie*, in *Marx–Engels Archiv*, I, pp. 205–11 (undated).
'Zur Geschichte der Ersten Internationale', MEGA, vol. I, 1927, p. 119 ff. (an unfinished paper).
'Novy dannie o rousskikh priateliakh Marksa i Engelsa', *Letopisi marksizma*, VI, 1928.
Introduction to the Communist Manifesto in *Œuvres complètes*, translated by Molitor, Costes, Paris, 1934; 2nd ed., 1953.
'Zur Frage des Verhältnisses von Marx zu Blanqui', *Unter dem Banner des Marxismus*, 1938.

RICHARD, ALBERT
See Appendix IV, Bakunin.

RING, MAX
Erinnerungen, Berlin, 1898, vol. I.

ROSDOLSKY, ROMAN
'Karl Marx und der Polizeispitzel Bangya', *International Review for Social History*, vol. II, pp. 229-44, Leyden, 1937.
See Appendix I, Judaism.

ROUGERIE, JACQUES
See Publisher's Note.
'La Première Internationale à Lyon, 1865–1870: problèmes d'histoire du mouvement ouvrier français', *Annali dell' Istituto Giangiacomo Feltrinelli*, IV, 1961, pp. 123–93.
'Quelques documents nouveaux sur le Comité central des vingt arrondissements de Paris', *Le Mouvement social*, no. 37 (on the Commune), October-December 1961.
'Sur l'histoire de la Première Internationale. Bilan d'un colloque et de quelques récents travaux', *Le Mouvement social*, no. 51, April-June 1965, pp. 23-46.

ROUGERIE, JACQUES, and HAUPT, GEORGES
'Bibliographie de la Commune de Paris', *Le Mouvement social*, no. 38, January-March 1962.

RUBEL, MAXIMILIEN
See Publisher's Note.
See section Ia above.
'La pensée maitresse du *Manifeste communiste*', *La Revue social-iste*, February 1948.
Translator of K. Marx's 'Die Bourgeoisie und die Kontrerevolu-tion' (December 1848), under the title 'Bilan de la révolution prussienne', *La Revue socialiste*, May and June 1948, nos. 21 and 22.
Translated K. Marx, 'Méditation d'un adolescent sur le choix d'une profession', *La Nef*, Paris, June 1948, pp. 52–6.
Translated K. Marx, 'Socrate et le Christ', ibid., pp. 57–64.
Translated F. Engels, 'Von Paris nach Bern', *La Revue socialiste*, April 1949.
Published K. Marx, 'La Spree et le Mincio (25 juin 1859)', *Études de marxologie*, June 1960.
Karl Marx devant le bonapartisme, Mouton & Co., Paris and The Hague, 1960 (École pratique des Hautes Études, Sorbonne).
'K. Marx, un discours sur la Pologne', *Etudes de marxologie*, January 1961.
Published F. Engels, 'La Savoie, Nice et le Rhin (1860)', *Études de marxologie*, January 1961.
Published 'Deux interviews de Karl Marx sur la Commune', *Le Mouvement social*, no. 38, January–March 1962.
'Aux origines de l'Internationale', *Le Mouvement social*, no. 51, April–June 1965.
See ch. 17, note 1.
'La Charte de l'Internationale. Essai sur le "marxisme" dans l'A.I.T.', *Le Mouvement social*, no. 51, April–June 1965.
See Appendix V, Russia.
RUGE, ARNOLD
Zwei Jahre in Paris, Leipzig, 1846.
Arnold Ruges Briefwechsel und Tagebuchblätter aus den Jahren 1825–1880, P. Nerrlich, Berlin, 1886.
SAVILLE, JOHN
Ernest Jones, Chartist. Selection from his Writings and Speeches, ed. John Saville, Lawrence and Wishart, 1952.
SCHAFFENHAUR, WERNER
Feuerbach und der junge Marx. Entstehungsgeschichte der marxistischen Weltanschauung, Deutscher Verlag der

Wissenschaft, Berlin, 1965 (correspondence between K. Marx and L. Feuerbach 1843–4 is published as an appendix).

SCHIEDER, WOLFGANG
Anfänge der deutschen Arbeiterbewegung. Die Auslandsvereine im Jahrzehnt nach der Julirevolution von 1830, Klett Verlag, Stuttgart, 1863.

SCHIEL, HUBERT
Die Umwelt des jungen Marx. Die Trierer Wohnungen der Familie Marx. Ein unbekanntes Auswanderungsgesuch von Karl Marx, Trier, 1954.

SCHMIDT, WALTER
Wilhelm Wolff, sein Weg zum Kommunismus, 1809–1846, Dietz, Berlin, 1963.

SCHRAEPLER, ERNEST
'Der Bund der Gerechten. Seine Tätigkeit in London 1840–1847', *Archiv für Sozialgeschichte*, II, 1962.

SCHURZ, KARL.
'Erinnerungen an Karl Marx', *Russkaya Bogatstwo*, 1906, no. 12.

SEIDL-HOPPNER, WALTRAUT
Wilhelm Weitling, der erste deutsche Theoretiker und Agitator des Kommunismus, Dietz, Berlin, 1961.

SEILER, SEBASTIAN
Das Komplott vom 13 Juni 1849, Hamburg, 1850.

SILBERNER, EDMUND
See Appendix I, Judaism.
Published Moses Hess, *Briefwechsel*, Mouton & Co., The Hague, 1959 (Nicolaievsky's attention was drawn to these letters by his correspondent D. Riazanov).
'Moses Hess als Begründer und Redakteur der *Rheinischen Zeitung*', *Archiv für Sozialgeschichte*, IV, 1964.
'Moses Hess und die Internationale Arbeiter Assoziation', ibid., V, 1965.
Moses Hess, Geschichte seines Lebens, Brill, Leyden, 1966.

SLONIM, MARC
De Pierre le Grand à Lénine, Gallimard, Paris, 1933.

SOMERHAUSEN, LUC
L'Humanisme agissant de Karl Marx, Paris, 1946.
Souvenirs sur K. Marx et F. Engels, Moscow, undated.

STEIN, H.
Der Kölner Arbeiterverein, Cologne, 1921.

STEKLOV, G. M.
See Appendix IV, Bakunin.

STIEBER and WERMUTH.
Die Communisten-Verschwörungen des 19. Jahrhunderts. Im amtlichen Auftrag zur Benutzung der Polizeihörden der sämtlichen deutschen Bundesstaaten auf Grund der betreffenden gerichtlichen und polizeilichen Akten dargestellt, Berlin, 1853–4, 2 vols.

TESTUT, OSCAR
L'Internationale et le jacobinisme au ban de l'Europe, Paris, 1872, 2 vols.

TORR, DONA
Published *Marx on China,* 1853–60. Articles from the *New York Daily Tribune.* With an introduction and notes. Lawrence and Wishart, 1951.

TYRAIEV, C. B.
Georg Weerth (et 1848), Moscow, 1963 (in Russian).

VENTURI
See Appendix V, Russia.

VERDÈS, J.
See ch. 17, note 1.
'BA 1175. Marx vu par la police française', *Études de marxologie,* Institut de Science économique appliquée, S.10, April 1966.

VICKERS, T.
August von Willich, Cincinnati, 1878.

VILLETARD, EDMOND
Histoire de l'Internationale, Garnier, Paris, 1872.

VUILLEUMIER, MARC
See ch. 17, note 1.
'Frankreich und die Tätigkeit Weitlings und seiner Schüler in der Schweiz', *Archiv für Sozialgeschichte,* V, 1965.

WACHSTEIN, B.
See Appendix I, Judaism.

WEERTH, GEORG
See TYRAIEV.

WEISS, JOHN
See Appendix II, 'True Socialism'.

WEITLING, WILHELM
See CAILLÉ, CORNU, SEIDL-HOPPNER, VUILLEUMIER, WITTKE

WERMUTH
See STIEBER
WILLICH, AUGUST VON
See EASTON, NICOLAIEVSKY, VICKERS
WITTKE, C.
The Utopian Communist. A Biography of W. Weitling, Nineteenth Century Reformer, Louisiana State University Press, 1950.
WOLFF, WILHELM
See KUYPERS, SCHMIDT

Notes

Foreword

1. 'Das Begräbnis von Karl Marx', *Der Sozialdemokrat*, 22 March 1883. MEW, XIX, p. 335 ff.
2. On the history of the archives of the German Social Democratic Party, cf. Paul Mayer, 1966–7. They are now in the Marx-Engels Collection, International Institute of Social History, Amsterdam.

Chapter 1. Origins and Childhood.

1. On Marx's early life, works by A. Cornu, 1934 and 1955, are now available.
2. On this annexation of Trier and the Lower Rhineland, cf. A. Cornu, 1955, vol. 1, ch. 1.
3. On Trier and Marx, cf. W. Bracht, 1947; H. Monz, 1964; H. Hirsch, 1965.
4. On the Marx family environment and homes, cf. H. Schiel, 1954.
5. On Marx's antecedents, cf. Appendix I.
6. Letter to Ruge, 13 March 1843, MEW, XXVII, p. 418. cf. Appendix I.
7. *The Jewish Question*, February 1844. cf. Appendix I.
8. Marx to Engels, 30 April 1858, MEW, XXXII, p. 75.
9. cf. H. Monz, 1967. The house is now a museum and meeting place.
10. Letter of 2 March 1837, MEGA, I, 2, pp. 204–5; MEW, supplementary vol. I, 1968, pp. 626–9.
11. On Ludwig Gall, cf. F. Brügel and B. Kautsky, 1931; A. Cornu, vol. I, pp. 52–3.
12. The *Gesellschaft für nützliche Forschung*, which took an interest in the past history of Trier.
13. cf. H. Monz, 1964; and his 'Die rechtsethischen . . . Anschauungen', 1968.
14. cf. H. Monz, 1968, p. 89.
15. Eleanor Marx-Aveling, 1895.
16. The Hambacher Fest, as mentioned above, took place on 27 May 1832 near Neustadt (Rhineland-Palatinate). Twenty-five thousand people responded to the appeal of some 'radicals' to celebrate the anniversary of the Bavarian constitution. The day ended with

arrests, followed by convictions. One of those persecuted was Wyttenbach, who was among the speakers. cf. A. Cornu, vol. I, 1955,
pp. 16, 61–2; K. T. Heigel, 1913.
17. MEGA, I, 1/2, p. 164 f.
18. P. Lafargue, *Persönliche Erinnerungen*, 1890–91.
19. 18–29 November 1835, MEGA, I, 1/2, p. 186.

Chapter 2. A Happy Year at Bonn.

1. 18–29 November 1835. MEGA, I, 1/2, p. 185.
2. M. Carrière, *Lebenserinnerungen*, 1914.
3. At the beginning of 1836. MEGA, I, 1/2, p. 189.
4. Marx to Lassalle, 10 June 1858. MEW, XXIX, pp. 562–3. The 'unpleasant fellow' was the *Intendanturrat* Herr Fabrice.
5. MEGA, I, 1/2, p. 192.

Chapter 3. Jenny von Westphalen.

1. For a better knowledge of Jenny von Westphalen's personality the
letters and documents on the Marx family (1862–73), published
by E. Bottigelli, 1958, and B. Andreas, 1962, may be consulted. cf.
also Luise Dornemann, 1968.
2. MEGA, I, 1/1, pp. 3–144.
3. On L. von Westphalen, cf. H. Monz, 'Unbekannte Kapitel', 1968.
4. cf. Appendix III.
5. F. Engels, foreword to first German edition of *Utopian Socialism
and Scientific Socialism*, 1882. MEW, XIX, p. 188.
6. 28 December 1836. MEGA, I, 1/2, p. 198.
7. Marx wrote to Jenny on 15 December 1863 from Trier, where he
went after his mother's death: 'Every day I keep being asked about
the *quondam* prettiest girl in Trier and the belle of the ball. It is
a damnably agreeable thing for a man when his wife goes on living
as a fairy princess in the imagination of a whole town.' MEW,
XXX, p. 643.
8. 2 March 1837. MEGA, I, 1/2, p. 205.
9. 16 September 1837. MEGA, I, 1/2, p. 212. MEW, supplementary
vol. I, 1968, pp. 630–34.
10. MEGA, I, 1/2, pp. 3–57 (poems); pp. 59–75 (*Oulanem*); pp. 76–92
(*Scorpion and Felix*). cf. A. Cornu, vol. I, pp. 74–8, 93–9; M. Ollivier,
1933; H. Lefebvre, 1964.
11. Marx to his father, 10 November 1837. MEGA, I, 1/2, p. 215.

Chapter 4. Student Years in Berlin.

1. On the subjects studied by Marx, and his teachers, cf. A. Cornu, vol. I, 1955, p. 73 ff.
2. Marx to his father, 10 November 1837. MEGA, I, 1/2, p. 212; MEW, supplementary vol. I, 1968, pp. 3–12 (the text in full). This letter made Heinrich Marx fear that his son was engaging in useless studies and compromising his future, and made him angry. He expressed these anxieties and rebuked young Karl for reckless expenditure in his reply (9 December 1837).
3. Max Ring, 1898.
4. Betty Lucas, a childhood friend of Jenny's, tells what she knew about Marx's relations with Bettina in her *Memoirs* (1862). cf. L. Dornemann, 1968, p. 39 f.
5. These notebooks have been preserved in the Marx-Engels collection at the International Institute of Social History, Amsterdam. Description in MEGA, I, 1/2, pp. 107–13.
6. cf. A. Cornu, vol. I, 1955, p. 132 f.
7. On Köppen, cf. Helmut Hirsch, 1955, pp. 19–82.
8. The German version here quotes the following description of Bauer from Varnhagen von Ense's *Diary*: 'A profoundly resolute man, who beneath a cold exterior burns inside. He refuses to recognize obstacles and is more likely to be a martyr to his convictions.'
9. 'Introduction to the Critique of Hegel's Philosophy of Law', 1844. See ch. 6, note 15.
10. 28 December 1836. MEGA, I, 1/2, p. 199.
11. K. Marx to his father, 10 November 1837. MEW, supplementary vol. II, 1967, pp. 283–316.
12. *Friedrich der Grosse und seine Widersacher*, Leipzig, 1840.
13. Anon. (E. Bauer and F. Engels), *Die frech bedräute, jedoch wunderbar befreite Bibel, oder: Der Triumph des Glaubens . . . Christliches Heldengedicht in vier Gesängen*, Zürich, 1842, MEW, supplementary vol. II, 1967, pp. 283–316.
14. W. Liebknecht, 1896.
15. See ch. 3, note 2.
16. Let us add a detail that is not without interest. In 1838 the Trier recruiting commission decided that Marx was 'accepted for voluntary service' in Berlin, but the departmental medical committee declared him to be unfit for service because of pulmonary weakness and blood-spitting; this was repeated in 1839. cf. H. Schiel, 1954, p. 23.

Chapter 5. Philosophy under Censorship.

1. This passage, quoted without reference in the first edition, is from Köppen's book on Frederick the Great referred to in ch. 4, note 12.
2. 'Bemerkungen über die neueste preussische Zensurinstruction. Von einem Rheinländer', *Anekdota zur neuesten deutschen Philosophie und Publizistik*, Zürich, 13 February 1843. MEW, I, pp. 5–25. Arnold Ruge first published his *Jahrbücher* ('Year Books') at Halle, and then, as a result of calling on the King of Prussia (through the pen of Johann Jakoby) to give his consent to political representation of the people, at Dresden; they then became the *Deutsche Jahrbücher*. Finally, to escape the censorship, he published the *Anekdota* at Zürich, with the collaboration of Bruno Bauer, Köppen, Feuerbach, etc.
3. 'Die Verhandlungen des 6. rheinischen Landtags', *Rheinische Zeitung*, Cologne, 5–9 May 1842. MEW, I, p. 28 ff. Marx wrote another, on the Church conflict at Cologne, but this was banned and has subsequently been lost.
4. Georg Jung to Arnold Ruge, 18 October 1841. MEGA, I, 1/2, p. 261 f.
5. Moses Hess to Berthold Auerbach, 2 September 1841. MEGA, ibid., p. 260.
6. On this role as founder and editor of the *Rheinische Zeitung*, cf. the articles by E. Silberner, 1964, and W. Klutentreter.
7. On Moses Hess, cf. A. Cornu, 1934; W. Mönke, 1964; E. Silberner, 1966. A selection of his philosophical and socialist writings was published by A. Cornu and W. Mönke, 1961.
8. Article on freedom of the Press in *Rheinische Zeitung*, 12 May 1842. cf. note 3.
9. cf. article by H. König, 1927.
10. 9 July 1842. MEW, XXVII, p. 406.
11. F. Engels to Richard Fischer, 15 April 1895. MEW, XXXIX, p. 466.
12. cf. letters of Marx, Ruge and Bruno Bauer, MEGA, I, 1/2, p. 285 ff. On Herwegh, cf. V. Fleury, 1911; F. Mehring, 1917.
13. Marx to Engels, 25 July 1877. MEW.
14. Hansen, vol. I, pp. 472–3.
15. From the Preussisches Staatsarchiv, D. 1, No. 153. cf. article by S. B. Kahn, 1958. The Ambassador's reports are dated 10 January 1843 (Kahn, p. 656 f.) and 7 February 1843 (Kahn, p. 661). The censor Saint-Paul's reports are quoted by J. Hansen, 1919. B. Nicolaievsky returned to this point in his article 'Who is distorting history?' (1961; cf. Appendix III). As he says at the beginning of the next chapter, Berlin wanted this ban just as much as St Petersburg; cf. H. König, 1927.

Chapter 6. The Germans Learn French.

1. Leipzig, 1844. cf. below, p. 110.
2. *Introduction to the Critique of Hegel's Philosophy of Law*, 1844. cf. note 15.
3. When he left Cologne Marx left his papers and books with his friend Dr Roland Daniels. The inventory of his library has been preserved. cf. Bruno Kaiser, 1967.
4. 25 January 1843. MEW, XXVII, p. 415.
5. 13 March 1843. MEW, XXVII, p. 417.
6. Marx to Feuerbach, 3 October 1843. MEW, XXVII, p. 419.
7. 13 March 1843. MEW, XXVII, p. 417.
8. Henriette Marx to her son, 29 May 1840. MEGA, I, 1/2, pp. 242–3.
9. cf. Appendix I.
10. cf. Appendix III.
11. On Marx's application for restoration of Prussian nationality, cf. below, p. 176.
12. A. Ruge, 1846.
13. These are the words with which Marx concludes his 'Introduction to the Critique of Hegel's Philosophy of Law', Paris, 1844.
14. cf. Appendix I.
15. 'Introduction to the Critique of Hegel's Philosophy of Law', *Deutsch-Französische Jahrbücher*, I–II, February 1844. MEW, I, pp. 378–91.
16. *The Critique of Political Economy*, MEW, XIII.
17. 'Rechtfertigung des — Korrespondent von der Mosel', *Rheinische Zeitung*, 15–20 January 1843. MEW, I, p. 177.
18. *The Critique of Political Economy*, op. cit., p. 272.
19. 'Introduction to the Critique of Hegel's Philosophy of Law.'
20. ibid.
21. cf. A. Ruge, 1886.
22. cf. the letters quoted by H. Hirsch, 'Marxiana judaïca' (in French; cf. Appendix I).
23. On this project and its failure, cf. Ruge's letter to Marx of 22 September 1843; Jenny Marx, 'Brève esquisse d'une vie mouvementée' (1865), p. 230; A. Cornu, vol. II, 1955, chapter on the *Deutsch-Französische Jahrbücher*.
24. cf. A. Ruge, 1886 (letter from Ruge to Feuerbach of 15 May 1844).
25. cf. A. Ruge, 1886.
26. E. Marx-Aveling, 1883; J. Spargo, 1912, see section 1b of Bibliography.
27. ibid.
28. 'Critical Notes on the article "The King of Prussia and Social Reform, by a Prussian"', *Vorwärts*, 7 and 10 August 1844. MEW, I,

pp. 392–409. The army had just put down the weavers' rising. Ruge
had announced that both rich and poor in Germany lacked a
'political soul' and that a social revolution was impossible. Marx
replied by comparing the Silesians rising to risings by workers in
England. He said that the weavers had risen, not against the King,
but against the bourgeoisie. Note the appearance here of the theme
of the class struggle and criticism of the bourgeois state. On the
weavers' rising, cf. Georg Eckert, 1965.

29. On Marx's first economic reading, cf. *Œuvres*, La Pléiade, vol. II,
p. LIV ff.
30. On the fate of the *Deutsch-Französische Jahrbücher and Vorwärts*,
cf. G. Mayer, 1913; A. Cornu, vol. II, 1955.

Chapter 7. The Communist Artisans of Paris.

1. Ewerbeck was one of the founders of the League of the Just and
translated Cabet's *Voyage en Icarie* into German.
2. On the antecedents of the Communist League, cf. Charles Andler's
historical introduction to the *Communist Manifesto*, 1901.
3. On Weitling, cf. the Bibliography.
4. *Die Menschheit wie sie ist und wie sie sein sollte*, Paris, 1838–9.
Republished in Munich, 1895.
5. cf. M. Vuilleumier, 1965.
6. *Garantien der Harmonie und Freiheit*, 1842 (December); republished by Franz Mehring, Berlin, 1908. The article by Karl Marx
is that of 10 August 1844, 'Critical Notes . . .' cf. ch. 6, note 28.
7. On Georg Weerth, cf. Tyraiev, 1963.
8. cf. 'Economics and Philosophy', MEGA, I, 3, p. 112.
9. ibid., p. 135.
10. *Die Heilige Familie*, 1845, MEW, II, p. 88 ff.
11. A. Ruge, 1886, p. 65.
12. Letter from Marx to J. B. von Schweitzer, February 1865.
13. Marx to Hermann Becker, 8 February 1851. MEW, XXVII, p. 544.
14. On the *Deutch-Französische Jahrbücher* and *Vorwärts*, cf. G.
Mayer, 1913.
15. Börnstein, 1881.
16. H. Bürgers, 1876.

Chapter 8. The Lifelong Friend.

1. On Engels, cf. Gustav Mayer's biography, 1934; also H. Hirsch's
little book, 1968, which contains a number of corrections. On
Engels's early life which forms the subject of this chapter, cf. A.
Cornu, vol. I, 1955, pp. 112-31; H. Desroche, *Socialisme et Sociologie religieuse*, 1965.
2. For the youthful writings, cf. MEGA, I, 2; A. Cornu, 1955.

3. To F. Gräber, 12–27 July 1839. M E W, supplementary vol. II, 1967, p. 403 f. On this question cf. H. Desroche, 1965, which contains Engels's religious correspondence, 1838–41.

4. cf. above, p. 59.

5. cf. G. Mayer, 1934, p. 112.

6. 'Introduction to the Critique of Hegel's Philosophy of Law', op. cit., ch. 6, note 2.

7. 'Umrisse zu einer Kritik der Nationalökonomie', *Deutsch-Französische Jahrbücher*, instalments I and II, Paris, 1844. MEW, I, pp. 499–524.

8. In 1859, in the foreword to the *Critique of Political Economy*.

9. 'Progress of Social Reform on the Continent', The *New Moral World*, no. 19, 4 November 1843. MEW I, pp. 480–96 (in German translation). Quotation from p. 495.

10. At the time when this book was written, Édouard Dolléans's *Le Chartisme*, 1912–13, was, among other works on the subject, already known. Dolléans notes that Engels became acquainted with the 'pre-Marxist formulations of Bronterre O'Brien' and that 'some Chartists expressed very precisely the theory of the industrial reserve army', etc. (p. 325 of 1949 edition).

11. 'Progress of Social Reform on the Continent', The *New Moral World*, no. 19, 4 November 1843. MEW, I, pp. 480–96 (in German translation). Quotation from p. 495.

12. F. Engels, *Die Lage der arbeitenden Klasse in England*, Leipzig, 1845. MEW, I, p. 464 ff. English translation: *The Condition of the Working Class in England*, Stanford University Press, 1968; French translation and notes: *La Situation de la classe laborieuse en Angleterre*, G. Badia and J. Frédéric, Éditions Sociales, Paris, 1960. This work made a certain impact in Germany, as is shown by Mönke, 1965.

13. F. Engels, relating the history of the Communist League in his introduction to the 1885 edition of Marx's *Revelations about the Trial of the Cologne Communists*. The introduction is entitled *Zur Geschichte des 'Bundes der Kommunisten'*. MEW, XXI, p. 212 ff.

14. ibid.

15. 'The beginning of their cooperation' is a reference to their work on the *German Ideology*. cf. ch. 9, note 8.

16. *Die Heilige Familie, oder Kritik der kritischen Kritik*, 1845. MEW, II, pp. 3–224.

17. *Dies Buch gehört dem König*, 1842.

18. Engels to Marx, 26 February 1845 to 7 March 1845. MEW, XXVII, p. 20.

19. Engels to Marx, 17 March 1845. ibid., p. 28.

Chapter 9. Clarification.

1. H. Bürgers, 1876.
2. Marx to Ruge, 30 November 1842. MEW, XXVII.
3. When this book was written few letters from Marx to Freiligrath were known (some nine letters or fragments were published by F. Mehring in 1912). There is now available the correspondence published by M. Haeckel, 1968. cf. letter from Marx to Freiligrath of 23 February 1860, MEW, XXX, p. 461.
4. It is now known, thanks to H. Schiel, 1954, that in October 1845 Marx applied to the burgomaster of Trier for permission to emigrate to the United States.
5. cf. M. Rubel, introduction to K. Marx, *Œuvres*, La Pléiade, vol. II, p. LIV ff; on this project in particular, cf. pp. LXIII–LXVII.
6. cf. note 8.
7. *Zur Geschichte des 'Bundes der Kommunisten'.* cf. ch. 8, note 13. There are a number of references by Engels to the paternity of the materialist theory of history. Apart from this reference, we may mention his foreword to the new edition of the *Peasant War* (1870), and that to the second edition of the *Communist Manifesto* (1883).
8. *Die deutsche Ideologie*, 1845–6, published posthumously. Fragments were published in 1902–3 by E. Bernstein, in 1921 by G. Mayer, and in 1927 by D. Riazanov. First published in full in MEGA, I, 5, 1932. cf. text in MEW, III, pp. 9–350. Suggestions have been made that other authors (Moses Hess, Weydemeyer) were also involved in the work, but B. Andreas and W. Mönke showed in a 1968 article that the sole authors were Marx and Engels.
9. On the nature of this 'egoism' and its affinities with existentialism, cf. H. Arvon, 1954.
10. On 'true socialism', cf. Appendix II.
11. Letter to Paul Annenkov, 28 December 1846. Annenkov was a member of a group of Russian intellectuals with whom Marx was on friendly terms in Paris in 1843–4; their relations are described in articles by D. Riazanov, 1913 and 1928.
12. 'Theses on Feuerbach', two sheets written in a notebook by Marx in 1845 and published after his death by Engels as an appendix to his *L. Feuerbach and the End of Classical German Philosophy*. MEW, III, pp. 533–5.
13. Introduction to the *Critique of Political Economy*, MEW, XIII.

Chapter 10. Face to Face with Primitive Communism.

1. In his *Zur Geschichte* . . . cf. ch. 8, note 13.
2. On Weitling, cf. Wittke, 1950; W. Schieder, 1963; F. Caillé, 1905; A. Cornu, 1955.
3. J. C. von Bluntschli, *Die Kommunisten in der Schweiz*, 1843.
4. *Kerkerpoesien*, Hamburg, 1844.
5. H. Heine, *Geständnisse* ('Confessions'), 1853.
6. cf. ch. 7, notes 4 and 6.
7. London, 15 April 1846. Letter published in article by C. Grünberg, 1925, pp. 455–9, who provides information on H. Hildebrand.
8. F. Engels, *Zur Geschichte* . . . , op. cit., cf. ch. 8, note 13.
9. 23 June. cf. M. Nettlau, *Grünberg-Archiv*, X.
10. cf. H. Förder, 1960.
11. Marx to Proudhon, 5 May 1846. Proudhon's reply was dated 17 May. He said that he did not believe revolutionary action to be a means of bringing about social reform and mistrusted economic dogmatism and the 'religion of reason'. He informed Marx of the forthcoming publication of his 'Philosophie de la misère'. MEW, XXVII, pp. 442–4.
12. On R. Daniels, cf. ch. 6, note 3.
13. On this meeting, cf. H. Förder, 1960. On Annenkov, cf. ch. 9, note 11. His story, 'Ten Memorable Years', was published in Russian in *Vestnyk Europy*, St Petersburg, 1880, and in German in the *Neue Zeit*, 1883.
14. Weitling to Moses Hess, 31 March 1846, in the latter's correspondence published by E. Silberner, 1959, p. 151.
15. MEW, IV, pp. 3–17. cf. also H. Förder, 1960.

Chapter 11. The Communist League.

1. Apart from Engels's *History of the Communist League*, op. cit., ch. 8, note 13, there is a document by two police officials, Wermuth and Stieber, 'The Communist Conspiracies of the Nineteenth Century', 1853–4. Many facts about this period are still obscure. For a general view, cf. H. Förder, 1960.
2. *Herr Vogt*, 1860. MEW, XIV, p. 439.
3. cf. E. Schraepler, 1962, on the activities in London of the League of the Just.
4. MEW, IV, p. 596.
5. Letter from Marx to Blos, 10 November 1877. MEW, XXXIV, p. 308.
6. Republished by C. Grünberg, 1921.
7. In fact it was not Marx who wrote about 'communist colonies' in

this journal, as the anonymity might lead one to suppose, but Engels, who also contributed an article on Fourier in 1846.

8. Marx to Herwegh, 8 August 1847. MEW, XXVII, p. 467.
9. Paris, 1846. Republished 1923.
10. *Misère de la philosophie. Réponse à la 'Philosophie de la misère' de M. Proudhon*, Paris and Brussels, 1847.
11. cf. Appendix II.
12. 'Lohnarbeit und Kapital', *Neue Rheinische Zeitung*, 5–11 April 1849; republished by Engels in 1891 with modifications. MEW, VI, 1959, pp. 397–423. A notebook on 'wage labour' exists, containing Marx's rough lecture notes. It consists of about sixteen pages and is dated 'Brussels, December 1847'; it was published by D. Riazanov in 1924–5. Text in MEGA, I, 6, pp. 451–72.
13. On W. Wolff and this cultural association, cf. H. Förder, 1960 and article by J. Kuypers, 1963.
14. F. Engels, 'Wilhelm Wolff', *Die Neue Welt*, 1 August 1876 and 25 November 1876. MEW, XIX, p. 59.
15. 'Address of the German Democratic Communists of Brussels to Mr Feargus O'Connor', the *Northern Star*, no. 454, London, 25 July 1846. MEGA, I, 6, pp. 25–6.
16. On J. Lelewel, cf. C. Bobinska, 1958, esp. p. 39 f., p. 68 f.
17. *Discours sur la question du libre-échange. Prononcé à l'Association démocratique de Bruxelles dans la séance publique du 9 janvier 1848 par Charles Marx*, La Pléiade, I, pp. 137–56. This follows the lost draft of a contribution that Marx proposed to make to a conference of economists he attended in 1847 but was prevented from making.
18. Unpublished, date uncertain. Amsterdam collection, F21.
19. Letter of 2 February 1846, published in the *Münchner Post*, 30 April 1926.
20. Heinzen advocated a kind of government or 'royal' socialism. S. Born's publication was anonymous, *Der Heinzen'sche Staat, eine Kritik von Stephan*, Berne, end of September 1847. Marx and Engels praised it in their attacks on Heinzen: 'Die moralisierende Kritik und die kritisierende Moral. Beitrag zur deutschen Kulturgeschichte, gegen Carl Heinzen', *Deutsche Brüsseler Zeitung*, five articles from 28 October to 25 November 1847.
21. S. Born, *Erinnerungen eines Achtundvierziger*, Leipzig, 1898.
22. *Grundsätze des Kommunismus*. These 'Principles of Communism', written in October 1847, were published by E. Bernstein in 1914. MEW, IV, p. 363–80.
23. Engels to Marx, 24 November 1847. MEW, XXVII, p. 107. On the origins of the *Communist Manifesto*, cf. H. Förder, 1960.
24. Speech published in the *Deutsche Brüsseler Zeitung*, 9 December

1847. MEW, IV, p. 416. On this meeting, cf. É. Dolléans, 1949, p. 296 f.
25. *Manifest der kommunistischen Partei*, 1848; the title became *Das Kommunistische Manifest* in 1872. MEGA, I, 6, 1832, pp. 527–7. For the circumstances of its publication, cf. the most recent version, La Pléiade, I, 157–95. For a bibliography of the various editions and translations, cf. Bert Andreas, 1963.
26. Engels had sent Marx the *Grundsätze des Kommunismus* from Paris; the idea of the 'transitional programme' (of nationalization) no doubt comes from that document. Engels said later: 'Marx's basic and leading ideas belong solely and exclusively to Marx' (foreword to German republication of 1883).

Chapter 12. The Revolutionary Tempest.

1. F. Freiligrath, 1848.
2. F. Engels, 'Die Bewegung von 1847', *Deutsche Brüsseler Zeitung*, no. 7, 23 January 1848. MEW, IV, pp. 494–503.
3. *Célébration, à Bruxelles, du deuxième anniversaire de la Révolution polonaise du 22 février 1846. Discours prononcés par MM. A.-J. Senault, Karl Marx, Lelewel, F. Engels et Louis Lublinger, avocat*, Brussels, 1848 (15 March). Marx's and Engels's speeches, I, 6, 1932, pp. 409–11.
4. J. Kuypers, pp. 103–7. On the action taken against foreigners in Brussels, cf. K. Marx, correspondence in *La Réforme*, 12 March 1848.
5. Stephan Born, *Erinnerungen*, op. cit., ch. 11, note 21.
6. Manuscript in French. (Archives nationales, documents du gouvernement provisoire, BB30/319.) Facsimile in L. Somerhausen, 1946, p. 173. MEW, IV, pp. 605–6.
7. MEW, XIV, p. 676.
8. Letter to *La Réforme*, Paris, 8 March 1848. MEW, IV, pp. 536–8 (translated from the French).
9. cf. on this period S. Bernstein's articles, 1939–40.
10. In her autobiography, 1871.
11. Engels, 'Von Paris nach Bern', unfinished MS. of October–November 1848, published in *Neue Zeit*, 1898. MEW, V, pp. 463–80.
12. cf. S. Seiler, *Das Komplott vom 13. Juni 1849*, 1850, p. 21.
13. *Les Clubs et les clubistes*, 1851.
14. There seems to be a mistake here. Alphonse Lucas, op. cit., pp. 113–114, mentions a 'Citizen Marx' who, however, was someone other than the subject of this book.
15. 'Flocon offered Engels and me money to found the *Neue Rheinische Zeitung*. We refused, because as Germans we were unwilling to accept subsidies even from a friendly French government.'

(Marx to his lawyer Weber, 3 March 1860.) MEW, XXX, p. 510.
16. 8 March 1848. MEW, XXVII, p. 116.
17. 'Statement by the central committee of the Alliance of German Workers', sent to Cadet at the end of March 1848 to be published by *Le Populaire*, which did not print it. MEW, V, p. 6. On this opposition to Herwegh's and Bornstedt's 'adventurism', cf. S. Bernstein, 1939–40. In his *History of the Communist League*, 1885, Engels wrote: 'We opposed this game ... Importing an invasion, which would be importing revolution from outside by force, would be tripping up the revolution in Germany.' MEW, XXI, p. 218.

Chapter 13. The 'Mad Year' in Cologne.

1. H. Hölscher, *Andenken an Dr Andreas Gottschalk*, Cologne, 1849. After Gottschalk's death Herwegh mourned him as 'one of the most noble and energetic characters he had ever met' (in a letter to his wife, 15 September 1849). In later years, however, Engels, while admitting memory gaps, was less respectful towards him. In a letter to Liebknecht of 29 October 1889 he referred to him as a 'complete demagogue', as the 'prophet Gottschalk', and as a 'curious creature' introduced into the Communist League by Hess. MEW, XXXVII, p. 298. Some letters from Gottschalk to Hess have been published in M. Hess, *Briefwechsel*, 1959. cf. also E. Silberner, *Moses Hess*, 1966, p. 285 ff.
2. *Im preussischen Heere! Ein Disciplinverfahren gegen Premier Lieutenant von Willich*. Mannheim, 1848.
3. Willich, whom Marx and Engels referred to at the time as the 'Hohenzollern knight', was said to be the son of Prince August, brother of Friedrich Wilhelm III – a detail that is of course unverifiable. He subsequently emigrated to the United States. cf. T. Vickers, 1878; article by L. D. Easton, 1965. On the influence of Hegelian ideas on oppositional officers, cf. E. Czobel, 1925. On Willich's role in 1848, cf. B. Nicolaievsky, 1931. On his dissension and rupture with Marx, cf. below, p. 227 f.
4. 5 September 1847. Moses Hess. *Briefwechsel*, p. 174.
5. ibid., p. 176.
6. Unpublished letter, Marx-Engels collection, International Institute of Social History, Amsterdam.
7. *Sitzungsprotokoll der Kölner Gemeinde des Bundes der Kommunisten vom 11. Mai 1848*, signed H. Bürgers and J. Moll. MEW, V, p. 484.
8. Leaflet entitled *Forderungen der Kommunistischen Partei in Deutschland*, printed in Paris 1 April 1848 and reproduced in various newspapers during the following days, signed K. Marx, K.

Schapper, H. Bauer, F. Engels, J. Moll, W. Wolff. MEGA, VII, pp. 3–4. The signatories proposed nationalization of the means of production, banks, transport and education, and the setting up of a workers' army. The object was a transitional system, to establish the confidence of the petty bourgeoisie; this confidence did not last for long.

9. F. Engels, 'Marx und die *Neue Rheinische Zeitung* 1848–1849', *Der Sozialdemokrat*, 13 March 1884. MEW, XXI, p. 18.

10. Peter Gerhardt Röser, one of the principal accused in the Cologne trial. He was arrested in 1851 and interrogated in 1853 (cf. below, p. 229 f; cf. also the reference to his deposition in Appendix III).

11. cf. Appendix III.

12. cf. the monograph by H. Stein, 1921, who cites the small journals (not extant) published by this little group.

13. Article by F. Engels, op. cit. (1884). MEW, XXI, p. 19.

14. ibid.

15. Engels to Marx, 25 April 1848. MEW, XXVII, p. 125.

16. Article by Engels, op. cit. (1884).

17. There was an exception to this, *Wage-Labour and Capital*, the lectures given in December 1847, to which Marx wrote an introduction at the beginning of 1849 (cf. ch. 11, note 12).

18. Except for the articles on the events of June 1848. cf. note 22.

19. Engels to Marx, 25 April 1848. MEW, XXVII, p. 126.

20. Stefan Born, 1898.

21. Communist Manifesto, Part IV. These lines are echoed, for instance, in the article in the *Deutsche Brüsseler Zeitung* of 14 November 1847 in which Engels says that 'the democratic movement ... assumes the existence of a proletariat, a dominant bourgeoisie, an industry that produces the proletariat and has brought the bourgeoisie into power'. MEW, IV, pp. 391–8. Later Marx was to insist that 'members of the proletarian party' must leave the preparation of a revolution against the *status quo* to the 'classes directly interested ... under penalty of renouncing their own party position and the tasks that arise spontaneously from the general conditions of existence of the proletariat'. *Revelations on the Trial of the Cologne Communists*, written in 1852, MEW, VIII, p. 458. cf. below, p. 239 ff.

22. In 'Nachrichten aus Paris' ('News from Paris'), 27 June 1848, and 'Die Junirevolution', 29 June 1848, *Neue Rheinische Zeitung*, Marx described the rising as the 'revolution of the proletariat against the bourgeoisie'. Engels wrote five articles on this subject in June and July 1848. MEW, V, p. 116 and p. 133 ff.

23. Article of 1848, op. cit. On these articles from the *Neue Rheinische Zeitung*, cf. Franz Mehring's introduction to his selection from

them in his *Aus dem literarischen Nachlass*, vol. III, 1902, pp. 3–86.
MEW, VI; cf. also M. Rubel, article of July 1961, and Appendix V.
24. Letter to K. F. Köppen, 1 September 1848; to escape from the farce,
   Marx wanted to return to the 'sleepless night of exile'. MEW,
   XVII, p. 484.
25. F. Engels, 'Marx und die *Neue Rheinische Zeitung* 1848–1849',
   Der Sozialdemokrat, 13 March 1884. MEW, XXI, p. 22.
26. 'The dictatorship of the intelligence.'
27. Report in *Der Wächter am Rhein*, the journal of the Gottschalk
   club, Cologne, 23 August 1848. Not reproduced in MEGA, I, 7. cf.
   H. Meyer, article of December 1951, p. 524, which quotes passages
   from it.
28. K. Schurz, article of 1906.
29. Albert Brisbane, an apostle of Fourierism in the United States, had
   studied philosophy in Berlin and become acquainted with the
   Young Hegelians. According to Riazanov (introduction to the
   Gesammelte Schriften, 1917, I, p. XVIII ff.), he met Marx in Cologne
   in November 1848. See Bestor, 1947.
30. *Neue Rheinische Zeitung*, 8 September 1848. On Marx's journey,
   cf. J. Fröbel, 1890, I, p. 193.
31. *Neue Rheinische Zeitung*, 15 September 1848.
32. ibid., 19 September 1848.
33. H. Bürgers, 1876.
34. Marx had renounced his Prussian nationality on 1 December 1845.
   In 1848 he applied to have it restored, but this was refused (3
   August). He appealed against the decision (22 August); the text
   of the application appeared in the *Neue Rheinische Zeitung* of 5
   September (MEW, V, pp. 382–5). On 11 August he spoke on the
   matter at a meeting of the Association démocratique (report in
   Der Wächter am Rhein, 28 August); he said the Prussian Government still resented his refusal to work for it in 1843 (cf. above,
   p. 71). cf. Grünberg-Archiv, X, p. 64.
35. Published in the *Zeitung des Arbeitervereins*, Cologne, 22 October
   1848. Grünberg-Archiv, XII, p. 178.

Chapter 14. Defeat with Honour.

1. 'Die Kontrerevolution in Berlin', *Neue Rheinische Zeitung*, 11 and
   14 November 1848. F. Mehring, *Aus dem literarischen Nachlass*,
   op. cit., III, pp. 200–205 (article of 11 November). MEW, VI, p. 12
   f.
2. K. Marx, 'Keine Steuer Mehr!' ('No More Taxes!'), *Neue Rheinische Zeitung*, 17 November 1848; the Prussian National Assembly
   forbade the Brandenburg Ministry to raise taxes; the appeals for

active resistance by Marx, Schapper and Schneider were published on 19 November. MEW, VI, p. 30 ff.

3. *Neue Rheinische Zeitung*, 25 February 1849. MEW, VI, p. 252.

4. ibid.

5. 'Die Bourgeoisie und die Kontrerevolution', *Neue Rheinische Zeitung*, 10, 15, 16 and 31 December 1848. F. Mehring, op. cit., III, pp. 206–29. MEW, VI, p. 124.

6. 'Die revolutionäre Bewegung', *Neue Rheinische Zeitung*, 1 January 1849. F. Mehring, op. cit., III, pp. 230–32.

7. 'Komiteesitzung des Arbeitervereines vom 15. Januar 1849', *Freiheit, Arbeit*, Cologne, 21 January 1849. MEW, VI, p. 579. cf. H. Meyer, 1951.

8. *Freiheit, Brüderlichkeit, Arbeit* ('Liberty, Fraternity, Work').

9. 'Montesquieu, LVI', *Neue Rheinische Zeitung*, 21–22 January 1849. MEW, VI, pp. 182–96.

10. ibid.

11. Gottschalk attacked Marx in his own journal, *Freiheit* ..., on 25 February 1849. cf. also his letter of 22 March 1849 to M. Hess in the latter's *Briefwechsel*, p. 216.

12. Röser's deposition, p. 153 (see below, pp. 229–30).

13. 'Der erste Pressprozess der *Neue Rheinische Zeitung*', *Neue Rheinische Zeitung*, 14 February 1849; 'Der Prozess gegen den Rheinischen Kreisausschuss der Demokraten', *Neue Rheinische Zeitung*, 25 and 27 February 1849. MEW VI, pp. 223–39 and 240–57.

14. cf. note 16.

15. Rough drafts of two letters from Marx 'to Colonel Engels, town commandant of Cologne', March 1849. MEW, XXVII, pp. 496 and 498. Engels's account in a letter to Kautsky, 2 December 1885. MEW, XXXVI, p. 399, and note 523, p. 808.

16. In October 1848 the *Neue Rheinische Zeitung* published an appeal, signed 'Hecker' (the name of a well-known republican). Another Hecker, a public prosecutor, accused Marx of high treason; the latter, needless to say, poured ridicule on this situation, with the result that he was charged with insulting the public prosecutor. When Marx appeared before the examining magistrate a demonstration of popular sympathy took place. Engels, Marx and Korff appeared before the Cologne court in February. Marx told the jury that the revolution had in no way changed the political system and denounced the counter-revolution in no uncertain terms. 'The first duty of the Press', he concluded, 'is to undermine all the foundations of the existing political state.' Next day he appeared before the same court on a charge arising out of the appeal to refuse payment of taxes. The National Assembly had voted to ban the raising of taxes, and the Brandenburg Ministry had used threats; hence

the appeal to resistance (*Neue Rheinische Zeitung*, 19 November 1848). Those charged were Marx, Schapper and Schneider, the signatories. Marx said that society should not be based on the law, but that the law should be based on society. cf. 'Assisenverhandlungen gegen den Rheinischen Kreisausschuss der Demokraten', *Neue Rheinische Zeitung*, 19, 25, 27 and 28 February 1849. All these articles are reprinted in MEW, VI. F. Engels republished them with a preface in 1885, *Karl Marx vor den Kölner Geschworenen*.

17. Reports of their statements in the *Neue Rheinische Zeitung*, 15 April 1849 (2nd ed.) and in *Freiheit, Brüderlichkeit, Arbeit*, 22 and 29 April 1849. MEW, VI, p. 426.
18. Richard Wagner, *Mein Leben*. English translation: *My Life*, Dodd, Mead & Co., 2 vols., 1911.
19. The order stated that he had 'disgracefully abused the law of hospitality'.
20. Republished by F. Mehring, Aus dem literarischen Nachlass, op. cit., vol. III, and in K. Marx and F. Engels, *Die Revolution von 1848*, Dietz, Berlin, 1953. MEW, VI.
21. cf., note 20. MEW, VI, p. 519.
22. cf. F. Mehring, *K. Marx*, 1933 ed., p. 218.
23. The authors here quote in the third person a statement made by Engels himself in the first person, in 'Die deutsche Reichsverfassungskampagne', *Neue Rheinische Zeitung-Revue*, March–April 1850. The passage quoted is on p. 21. See also G. Mayer, *F. Engels*, I, p. 345 ff.

Chapter 15. The End of the Communist League.

1. Marx to Eduard Müller-Tellering, 15 January 1849. MEW, VI, p. 492.
2. Marx to Engels, Paris, 7 June 1849. MEW, VI, p. 137.
3. K. Marx, *Die Klassenkämpfe in Frankreich*, consisting of articles published in the *Neue Rheinische Zeitung* in March and April 1850. Engels procured its republication in 1895. The passage quoted is from the third of these articles, 'Consequences of 13 June 1849' MEW, VII, p. 69.
4. Vevey, 25 July 1849. MEW, XXVII, p. 501.
5. cf. F. Engels, 'Die Reichsverfassungkampagne', op. cit.
6. Letter of 1 August 1849. MEW, XXVII.
7. Marx wrote to Weydemeyer on 19 December 1849 that after the crisis Britain would necessarily be 'the ally of the revolutionary Continent'. MEW, XXVII, p. 517. The crisis is predicted in 'Revue Januar–Februar 1850', *Neue Rheinische Zeitung-Revue*, no. 11, February 1850. MEW, VII, p. 220.

8. J. Marx, 'Brève esquisse d'une vie mouvementée', 1865.

9. 23 August 1849. MEW, XXVII. In an open letter to *La Presse* on 30 July Marx stated that his stay in Paris was for scientific purposes only. MEW, VI, p. 529.

10. cf. É. Dolléans, *Le Chartisme*, pp. 309–16.

11. The reference is to the pamphlet that Marx and Engels were to write in 1852 but which was never published. This was *Die grossen Männer des Exils*, the targets of which were Kinkel, Ruge, Heinzen, Meyer, R. Schramm, etc. cf. below, note 34.

12. Document concerning the various committees of aid for the German *émigrés* in MEW, VII, p. 545 ff.

13. Engels to Jenny Marx, 25 July 1949. MEW, XXVII, p. 502. On 'true socialism', cf. Appendix II.

14. K. Marx and F. Engels, *Ansprache der Zentralbehörde an den Bund*. Copies of this circular, as well as that of June 1850, were found in possession of members of the League arrested in May 1851. The text of the two documents was then published by newspapers in Cologne and Dresden on 24 and 28 June, and is reproduced in the report of the police officials Wermuth and Stieber, 1853–4, p. 251 ff. Engels reprinted them in 1885 in the new edition of *Revelations about the Trial of the Cologne Communists*. cf. also F. Mehring, 1914. MEW, VII, pp. 244–54.

15. ibid., MEW VII, p. 244.

16. They were written in French. cf. facsimile in the *Cahiers du bolchevisme*, 14 March 1933. MEW, VII, p. 553 ff. It has been suggested that they were written by Willich (MEW), but it is no less probable that Marx had a hand in them; note the phrase 'permanent revolution', which appears in a different context in the *Jewish Question*.

17. Same title as the first (cf. note 14).

18. On the relations between Marx and Blanqui, cf. D. Riazanov, *Unter dem Banner* (1938); M. Dommanget, 1938.

19. K. Schurz, article of 1906.

20. *Neue Rheinische Zeitung, Politisch-Ökonomische Revue, redigiert von Karl Marx*, London and Hamburg, 1850.

21. 'Die deutsche Reichsverfassungskampagne', cf. ch. 14, note 23.

22. *Die Klassenkämpfe in Frankreich*, cf. note 3.

23. ibid., p. 179.

24. A. Willich, 'Dr K. Marx und seine Enthüllungen', *Belletristisches Journal*, October 1953. cf. article by L. D. Easton, August 1865, p. 118 ff.

25. K. Marx, *Herr Vogt*, 1860. MEW, XIV, p. 416. Marx attacked Willich in *Der Ritter vom edelmütigen Bewusstsein*, pamphlet, New

York, 1854. MEW, V, pp. 489–518. cf. G. Mayer, *F. Engels*, I, pp. 343 and 393.

26. The books reviewed were: A. Chenu, former captain of Citizen Caussidière's guards, *Les Conspirateurs*, Paris, 1850 (on the secret societies, the prefecture of police under Caussidière, and the volunteer corps); Lucien de La Hodde, *La Naissance de la République*, Paris, 1850 (on the events of February 1848). Republished by F. Mehring, op. cit., pp. 426–34. MEW, VII, p. 266 ff.

27. W. Liebknecht, *K. Marx zum Gedächtnis*, Nuremberg, 1896, p. 37. From February or March 1850 onwards Marx used to invite working-class friends such as Pfänder, Eccarius, etc., to his home for talks about economics. Between June and August 1850 he did the same at the German Workers' Club. In September 1850, however, after the split in the Communist League, Marx, Engels and their friends left the club, must of the members of which were supporters of Willich and Schapper. Thus the 1851 'talks' cannot have taken place at the club, though they may have taken place at Marx's home.

28. On Röser's deposition, cf. ch. 13, note 10, and see Appendix III.

29. This document is reproduced and its history traced in B. Nicolaievsky's article 'Towards a History of the Communist League', 1956. cf. also MEW, VIII, 1960, p. 597 f. Marx refers to the circumstances of the split in *Herr Vogt*.

30. Letter to Adam, Barthélemy and Vidil: 'Sirs, we have the honour to inform you that for a long time we have regarded the association of which you speak as *de facto* dissolved. All that remains to be done is to destroy the articles of association. Will MM. Adam and Vidil be kind enough to appear next Sunday, 13 October, at midday at the residence of M. Engels, 6 Macclesfield Street, Soho, to be present at the burning of the articles of association? We have the honour, etc. [Signed] Engels, Marx, Harney. London, 9 October 1850.' MEW, VII, p. 415.

31. 11 February 1851. MEW, XXVII, p. 184 f.

32. This expression was used by the police to designate Marx and his friends, who also used it among themselves.

33. Marx-Engels collection at Amsterdam; 'E' contains a series of documents relating to the facts alleged.

34. It was to Bangya that Marx gave the MS. of *Die grossen Männer des exils* (cf. note 11). Engels and he wrote this pamphlet in May–June 1852. Bangya undertook to get it published but never delivered the MS. Marx related this in an open letter to the *Belletristisches Journal und New-Yorker Criminal-Zeitung*, New York, 5 May, 1853, about another Prussian police spy named Hirsch. A fragment has survived, *die grossen Männer des Exils*, MEW, VIII, p. 23 ff. On this affair, cf. article by R. Rosdolsky, 1937.

K.M.—16

35. Jenny Marx to Adolf Cluss, 28 October 1852. MEW, XXVIII, p. 640 f.
36. K. Marx to F. Freiligrath, 29 February 1860. MEW, XXX, p. 489.
37. Marx to Frau Daniels, 6 September 1855. MEW, XXVII, p. 618. We met R. Daniels above, ch. 6, note 3.
38. K. Marx, *Enthüllungen über den Kommunistenprozess zu Köln*, Basle, January 1853. Serialized in the *Neue-England Zeitung*, a German newspaper published at Boston, Mass., in March–April 1853, and republished in 1875 with a postcript by Marx. Another edition appeared in 1885 after his death, with a preface by Engels to which we have already referred, tracing the history of the Communist League. MEW, VIII, pp. 405–70. A memorandum by the minister Manteuffel concerning copies of the book, dated 20 February 1853, is preserved at Amsterdam (cf. note 33).
39. 'Der Achtzehnte Brumaire des Louis-Bonaparte', *Die Revolution*, New York, 1 May 1852. Republished with an introduction by Marx, Hamburg, 1869, and with a preface by Engels in 1885. MEW, VIII, pp. 111–94.
40. These words occur in a letter from Marx to Friedrich Köppen, 1 September 1848. MEW, XVII, p. 484. See above, ch. 13, note 24.

Chapter 16. The Sleepless Night of Exile.

1. F. Engels, 'Die auswärtige Politik des Zarentums', *Die Neue Zeit*, May 1890. MEW, XXII, p. 13.
2. The authors are here repeating views expressed by Marx in his articles for the *New York Tribune*, 1852–61.
3. This was the *Neue Oder-Zeitung*; about 100 articles are concerned; they are enumerated in M. Rubel, *Bibliographie*. Some had been translated in the French edition of Marx's complete works, vol. VI. The articles deal with political and economic life in England, the corruption of its officials and political figures (Disraeli, Palmerston), the Crimean War and pan-Slavism, the collusion between the Church and the decadent aristocracy, etc.
4. cf. É. Dolléans, 1949, p. 309 ff.
5. Engels to Marx, 17 March 1851. MEW, XXVII, p. 217. The correspondence of 1851–2 contains a number of derogatory opinions. cf. for instance Marx's letter to Engels of 23 February 1851, which paints a ferocious picture of 'dear' Harney; also the letter of 4 February 1852, etc.
6. cf. John Saville, 1952. Extracts from Jones's correspondence with Marx and Engels are quoted in it, p. 231 ff.
7. Letter to the Chartist Parliament. *People's Paper*, London,

18 March 1854. MEW, X, p. 126. cf. also Marx's article 'The Parliament of Labour', *New York Tribune*, 29 March 1854.

8. 'Kirchliche Agitation', *Neue Oder-Zeitung*, June–July 1855. MEW, XI, p. 323.

9. W. Liebknecht, 1896. Marx described the demonstration in a message to the *Neue Oder-Zeitung* dated 25 June 1855 and published 28 June 1855. MEW, XI, p. 322 f. cf. also his letter to Engels of 26 June 1855.

10. cf. John Saville, 1952.

11. His articles on the Near Eastern crisis, edited with comments by D. Riazanov, are available in *Gesammelte Schriften*, 1917.

12. Marx to Engels, 9 March 1853. MEW, XXVIII, p. 218.

13. He did the same in 1860 in *Herr Vogt*, op. cit. cf. also Marx to Engels, 22 April 1854, and to Lassalle, 2 June 1860, on his 'collusion' with Urquhart 'since 1853'.

14. Marx to Engels, 2 November 1853. MEW, XXVIII, p. 306.

15. Eight articles were published in part in the *New York Tribune* (October 1853–January 1854) and in full in the *People's Paper* (October–December 1853). There were several editions of Tucker's pamphlet. None of these pamphlets earned anything for their author. As Tucker mentioned Marx's name in the preface, Marx feared that Palmerston might prosecute him. The articles were republished by Eleanor Marx, London, 1899, and by L. Hutchinson in 1967. Other articles by Marx on Palmerston appeared in the *Neue Oder-Zeitung* in 1855. On the 'Revelations about the History of Diplomatic Secrecy in the Eighteenth Century', cf. L. Hutchinson, 1969.

16. These were the same articles on Palmerston (Tucker pamphlet). The *Free Press*, London and Sheffield, November 1855–February 1856.

17. A selection of Marx's articles was published by H. Christman and C. Blitzer, 1966.

18. cf. above, p 184.

19. *Germany: Revolution and Counter-Revolution*, by Frederick Engels, New York, Marxist Library, vol. XIII, International Publishers, 1933.

20. 'The British Rule in India', *New York Tribune*, 25 June 1853. K. Marx and F. Engels, *On Colonialism*, Foreign Languages Publishing House, Moscow, undated. cf. S. Avineri, 1968.

21. Articles written between July and December 1854. These, as well as others that appeared in *Putnam's Magazine* and the *New American Cyclopaedia*, were republished in *Revolution in Spain*, by K. Marx and F. Engels, International Publishers, New York, 1939.

22. Three articles, June 1853, January and March 1854.

23. Marx to Engels, 5 January 1854. MEW, XXVIII, p. 317. Dana was

also chief editor of the *New American Cyclopaedia*, to which he invited Marx and Engels to contribute, which they did from 1857 to 1860. Strict 'objectivity' was required, and controversial subjects were not entrusted to them. Engels dealt chiefly with military matters. His military writings were collected by Chaloner and Henderson, 1959. For the 'bread and butter' articles written by Marx and Engels for the *New American Cyclopaedia*, see MEW, XIV. cf. Hal Draper, 1968.

24. 23 January 1857. MEW, XXIX, p. 102.
25. 20 March 1850. MEW, XXVII, pp. 608–9.
26. D. Riazanov calculated Marx's income during this period. cf. W. Blumenberg, 1967, ch. VII; also note 66 below.
27. 23 November 1850. MEW, XXVII, p. 144.
28. *Gesammelte Aufsätze von Karl Marx*, Cologne, 1851. This contained the article published in *Anekdota* (cf. above, p. 50) and some of the articles on the debates in the Rhenish Diet (cf. pp. 47–53).
29. Marx to Weydemeyer, 2 August 1851. MEW, XXVII, p. 565.
30. 8 September 1852. MEW, XXVIII, p. 128.
31. Jenny Marx to Engels, 27 April 1853. MEW, XXVIII, p. 645. It was little Edgar Marx, known as 'Musch', who got rid of the baker by this phrase. He was aged six, and died in 1855.
32. 21 June 1854. MEW, XXVIII, p. 370.
33. Informer's report published by G. Meyer, *Neue Beiträge*, 1922, pp. 56–63. On the police spies who trailed Marx and invented the phrase 'the Marx party', cf. the 'Revelations on the Trial of the Cologne Communists', op. cit.
34. W. Liebknecht, *Souvenirs sur Marx et Engels*, 1896, pp. 120–24.
35. 'A Few Stray Notes', *Reminiscences of Marx and Engels*, p. 240–54; Adoratski, 1934, p. 120.
36. ibid.
37. MEW, XXVIII, p. 442.
38. ibid., p. 443.
39. To F. Lassalle, 28 July 1855. ibid., p. 617.
40. Letter to Marx, 27 September 1856. MEW, XXIX, p. 78.
41. To Engels, 13 November 1857. MEW, XXIX, p. 207.
42. To Marx, 15 November 1857. ibid., p. 211.
43. ibid., p. 225.
44. cf. E. Mandel, 1967, and La Pléiade, II, p. LXXIV f.
45. To Engels, 2 April 1851. MEW, XXVII, p. 228.
46. 27 June 1851. MEW, XXVII, p. 559.
47. cf. La Pléiade, II, LXXXIX. He was then writing *Grundrisse der Kritik der politischen Ökonomie*, an important rough draft for *Das Kapital* which was discovered in 1923 and published in 1939–41.

48. 28 January 1858. MEW, XXIX, p. 267.

49. 22 February 1858. ibid., p. 285.

50. 2 April, 1858. ibid., p. 312.

51. 15 July 1858. ibid., p. 340.

52. The same letter.

53. *Zur Kritik der politischen Ökonomie, von Karl Marx, Erstes Heft*, Berlin, 1859. MEW, XIII. On this publication, cf. La Pléiade, I, 1963, pp. 269–70; II, 1968. p. CIII f.

54. cf. M. Rubel, *Karl Marx devant le bonapartisme*, 1960, p. 68 ff.

55. At the end of March 1859 he described to Marx the state of mind prevailing in Austria: the bourgeoisie's hatred of the dynasty, the bellicose intentions of the Austrian army, etc. In June he published a pamphlet, *The Italian War and the Task of Prussia*, which to Marx and Engels seemed Bonapartist and pro-Russian. cf. the letters of Lassalle published by G. Meyer, 1922; F. Mehring, *K. Marx*, 1933, p. 307 ff.; and various articles in the *New York Tribune*. Marx's and Engels's views on the Italian war are expressed in writings such as Marx's article 'The Spree and the Mincio', *Das Volk*, London, 25 June 1859, and Engels's pamphlets *Po und Rhein*, 1859, and *Savoyen, Nizza und der Rhein*, 1860; cf. M. Rubel, June 1960 and January 1961.

56. *Herr Vogt*, London, 1860. cf. the studies of Cunow, 1918, and F. Mehring, *Aus dem Literarischen Nachlass*, 1902.

57. Let us not forget Marx's striking prediction while he was writing *Das Kapital*: 'Whatever happens, the bourgeoisie will remember my boils as long as it exists.' (Letter to Engels of 22 June 1867.)

58. Marx to Engels, 7 May 1861. MEW, XXX, p. 161. Marx's letters to his uncle have been published with comments by W. Blumenberg, 1956.

59. To Engels, 25 February 1862. MEW, XXX, p. 214.

60. To Engels, 18 June 1862. MEW, XXX, p. 248.

61. 7 January 1863. ibid., p. 309.

62. 8 January 1863. ibid., p. 310.

63. 13 January 1863. ibid., p. 312.

64. 24 January 1863. ibid., p. 314.

65. 26 January 1863. ibid., p. 317.

66. On Marx's financial and marital troubles (the birth of his natural son Frederick Demuth [1851–1929]), cf. W. Blumenberg, 1967, and La Pléiade, I, 3rd ed., p. LXXIX ff.

67. 31 July 1865. MEW, XXI, p. 132.

68. 17 April 1867. MEW, XXXI, p. 541.

69. 16 August 1867. ibid., p. 323.

70. *Das Kapital – Kritik der Politischen Ökonomie – Erster Band – Buch I: Der Produktionsprozess des Kapitals*, Hamburg, 1867. cf.

German edition produced by the Marx-Engels-Lenin Institute, Moscow, Verlag für Literatur und Politik, Vienna and Berlin, 1932. Bibliographical details in French edition, La Pléiade, I, p. 539–41. On the writing of the book, cf. La Pléiade, II, Introduction.

71. 30 April 1867. MEW, XXXI, p. 542.

72. Other subjects were the Russo-Turkish war (1854), the Crimean War (1854–5), the Spanish revolution (1854–60), the conflict between Prussia and Switzerland (1856), the abolition of serfdom in Russia (1858), the anti-slavery movement and the American Civil War (1858, 1862), and the wars of Napoleon III. Among the collections of Marx's (and Engels's) articles, etc. are *Revolution in Spain*, 1939; *Articles on India*, 1943; *Marx on China*, 1951; *The Civil War in the United States*, 1937; *The Russian Menace to Europe*, 1952; *The Eastern Question*, 1897.

73. cf. the selected works of Lassalle published by H. Hirsch, 1963. On his ideas, cf. the various works of S. Na'aman, especially his article of 1961, and T. Ramm, 1953. His correspondence with Marx has been published by G. Mayer, *Nachgelassene Briefe*, vol. III, 1922.

74. ibid., vol. I, pp. 227 and 230.

75. 7 May 1861. MEW, XXX, p. 163.

76. 30 July 1862. MEW, XXX, p. 258.

77. cf. the *Critique of the Programme of the German Workers' Party*, (known as the Gotha programme), in which he criticized this 'miraculous cure' in 1875.

78. To J. B. von Schweitzer, 13 October 1868, MEW, XXXII, p. 569.

79. ibid.

80. Published by G. Mayer, 1928. cf. on this point the article by S. Na'aman, 1962.

81. In particular, plagiarism of *Wage-Labour and Capital* (cf. ch. 11, pp. 136–7 and note 12) in the last of Lassalle's writing, *Kapital und Arbeit*, 1864. cf. on this subject Marx's letters to Engels, 6 June 1864, and to Kugelmann, 13 October 1866.

82. On Lassalle's party, cf. the article by B. Andreas, 1963. Details about his work and that of his disciple Wilhelm Bracke will be found in G. Eckert's study of 'Social Democracy in Brunswick', 1965.

Chapter 17. The International Working Men's Association.

1. It is neither possible nor would it be useful to enumerate here all the publications on this subject. Those readers who are interested will find particulars in two biographical articles, 'Études de marxologie', I.S.E.A., August 1964 and August 1965. cf. also M. Rubel,

'Marx et la Première Internationale. Une chronologie', and an assessment by J. Rougerie, M. Rubel, M. Vuilleumier, G. Haupt and J. Verdès in *le Mouvement social*, no. 51, April-June 1965. See also *La Première Internationale: l'institution, l'implantation, le rayonnement*, C.N.R.S., 1968.

2. MEW, XXXI, p. 428.
3. ibid., p. 13.
4. ibid., p. 17.
5. cf. D. Riazanov, who quotes extracts from the speeches in his article on the history of the International, 1927, and M. Rubel's article of April-June 1965, 'Aux origines de l'Internationale'.
6. cf. the MS on the Polish question published by W. Conze and D. Hertz-Eichenrode, 1961; in October 1863 Marx and his friends published a leaflet on the subject, to which Marx returned in 1867. cf. the correspondence between Marx and Engels at the end of 1863, M. Rubel's article of January 1961, and Appendix V, note 1.
7. cf. M. Rubel's article of April-June 1965, 'La Charte de l'Internationale'.
8. *Address and Provisional Rules of the International Working Men's Association*. Pamphlet reproducing the text published in the London weekly The *Bee-Hive*, 5 November 1864.
9. Source untraced. cf. the *Communist Manifesto*, III, 3, and *Herr Vogt*.
10. 23 February 1865. MEW, XXXI, p. 454.
11. 4 March 1865. ibid., p. 90.
12. Letter to Léon Fontaine in Brussels, 15 April 1865. ibid., p. 473.
13. 4 March 1865. ibid., p. 90.
14. 13 March 1865. ibid., p. 100–101.
15. Same letter.
16. To Engels, 29 July 1868.
17. cf. M. Rubel, 'La Charte de l'Internationale', April-June 1965.
18. 'Communication confidentielle', letter written by Marx in French, addressed to the Brunswick committee of the German Social Democratic Party, 28 March 1870, and sent *via* Kugelmann. It consisted of a warning against Bakunin. MEW, XVI, p. 411.
19. K. Marx (and F. Engels), *Les Prétendues scissions dans l'Internationale. Circulaire privée du Conseil général del A.I.T.*, London (printed at Geneva), June 1872. Published in *Le Mouvement socialiste*, July-August 1913. MEW, XVIII; the passage quoted is on p. 34.
20. 'Agli operai italiani', *La Roma del Popolo*, no. 20. 13 July 1871. Mazzini published a series of articles entitled 'Documenti sull' Internazionale' in the same journal at the end of 1871.
21. E. E. Fribourg, *L'Association Internationale des Travailleurs*, 1871,

p. 87. The reference is to the position adopted by the British delegates to the Geneva conference, who sought to make their support for the International conditional on the latter's support in this matter. They wanted the congress to make a declaration on the limitation of working hours, but this proposal was defeated as a result of opposition by the French delegates.

22. ibid., preface, p. 4.

23. This was the defence put forward by E. Varlin in the course of a Paris trial on 22 May 1868. cf. *Procès de l'A.I.T. Première et deuxième Commission du bureau de Paris. Paris, dans les locaux de l'Association et chez les principaux libraires*, 2nd ed., July 1870, pp. 144–65. 'The International Association on principle does not admit strikes; it believes them to be anti-economic; it announced that at Geneva, it has announced it everywhere' (pp. 151–2). But Varlin announced this principle only after long insistence on the aid given to strikers in France, England and Germany.

24. Marx to Liebknecht, 11 February 1878. MEW, XXXIV, p. 320. In this letter he delivers a harsh judgement on the British proletariat which, he says, 'has been increasingly demoralized since 1848' and has ended by being no more than the 'tail of the great Liberal Party, that is, of its oppressors the capitalists', under 'venal' trade union leadership. Also Marx could not forgive the trade union leaders their support of Gladstone's 'Russophile' policy.

25. 2 October 1866. MEW, XXXI, p. 525.

26. *Rapport du Conseil général sur les différentes questions mises à l'étude par la conférence de septembre 1865*. Report for the Geneva conference of the International (3–8 September 1866) drafted by Marx in English and read in French by the delegate Eugène Dupont. Published by two London weeklies in 1867.

27. Marx to Kugelmann, 9 October 1866. MEW, XXXI, p. 525.

28. 'Resolutions of the Congress of Geneva', 1866, and 'Resolutions of the Congress of Brussels', 1868, London. French official text in the *Courrier International*; Freymond, I, pp. 29-36.

29. Freymond, I, p. 109 ff.

30. 10 September 1868. MEW, XXXII, p. 558.

31. cf. *The Nationalization of the Land* (1872), in which Marx restated his 1869 position. French version, La Pléide, I, pp. 1473–9.

32. Paris, 1865. cf. edition supervised by M. Leroy, 1924.

33. The exact numbers were estimated by J. Rougerie in his article of April–June 1965.

34. cf. S. Bernstein, 1962.

35. Guillaume was the author of *L'Internationale*, four vols., 1905–10. He gives a detailed account of the Coullery affair in vol. I. cf. also Rolf R. Bigler, 1963, and Freymond, 1964.

Chapter *18*. Michael Bakunin.

1. cf. Appendix IV, a selected bibliography of works on Bakunin.
2. Bakunin had written to Ruge in 1843. An exchange of letters between them was published in the *Deutsch-Französische Jahrbücher*, the first and only issue, February 1844. Bakunin joined the Association démocratique in December 1847. He stayed in Brussels from the end of December 1847 to the end of February 1848.
3. Or more precisely: 'The pleasure (*Lust*) of destruction is at the same time that of creation'. These words occur in 'The Reaction in Germany, a fragment, by a Frenchman' (signed Jules Élysard), in the *Deutsche Jahrbücher für Wissenschaft und Kunst*, 17–21 October 1842. cf. B.-P. Hepner, 1954, p. 185 f.
4. The attack on Bakunin was published in the *Neue Rheinische Zeitung*, 5 July 1848. Some years later Marx confirmed in a letter to Lassalle (3 March 1860, MEW, XXX, p. 498) that he had published in the *Neue Rheinische Zeitung* a slanderous communication, signed Koscielski, about Bakunin. He had subsequently inserted an *amende honorable* and buried the hatchet with Bakunin, whom he met soon afterwards in Berlin (25–26 August) during the propaganda journey mentioned on p. 184 above. While Bakunin was exiled in Siberia (1849–64) the *Morning Advertiser* (29 August) published another article accusing him of collusion with the Tsar's Government. Marx was not responsible, but Herzen and Golovin suspected him of having instigated the slander. Marx replied by 'breaking a lance' in favour of 'Michael Bakunin' on 2 September 1853 (MEW, IX, pp. 294–6). cf. his letter to Engels, 3 September 1853 (MEW, XXVIII, pp. 280-85). The 1860 letter to Lassalle quoted above also related these facts, but with errors of detail. cf. D. Riazanov, 'Marx als Verleumder', 1910. cf. Bakunin, *Confession*, French version 1932, p. 201 f., p. 209 f. cf. also Appendix IV.
5. It is known, from the letter of 4 November 1864 (MEW, XXXI, p. 16). Bakunin said, among other things, that a peasant revolution would lead to socialism in Poland, and that he proposed to devote himself solely to socialism in future.
6. See the *Confession* of 1857, and Appendix IV.
7. Source unknown.
8. 'Programme et objet de l'Organisation révolutionnaire des Frères Internationaux', *L'Alliance de la Démocratie socialiste et l'Association Internationale des Travailleurs*. Report and documents published by order of the International congress at The Hague; London, 1873, pp. 131–2; reprinted in D. Guérin, *Ni Dieu ni maître*, 1966; 2nd ed., 1969, pp. 197-215.
9. cf. Freymond, vol. I, p. 239 f.

10. This was the first congress of the League of Peace and Freedom, Geneva, 1867. The quotation is from Wyrobov's *Mémoires* (1913).
11. The speech referred to was made by Bakunin on 10 September 1869. There is a passage on Bakunin in *Souvenirs du baron N. Wrangel. Du servage au bolchévisme*, Plon, Paris, 1926.
12. cf. the documents produced by Marx, Engels and Lafargue in *L'Alliance de la Démocratie socialiste et L'Association Internationale des Travailleurs*, July 1873. cf. above, note 8.
13. 15 December 1868. MEW, XXXII, p. 234.
14. 18 December 1868. ibid., p. 236.
15. *Le Conseil général au Conseil fédéral de la Suisse romande à Genève*, January 1870; *Communication confidentielle contre Bakounine*, March 1870. cf. notes 8 and 12, and *Les Prétendues scissions de l'Internationale*, March 1872.
16. 22 December 1868. Marx enclosed this letter with his own letter to Engels of 13 January 1869. MEW, XXXII, p. 757.
17. Undated letter published by M. Nettlau, *The Life . . .* (1895), p. 253; reproduced in J. Guillaume, I, p. 73.
18. Letter published in *Piśma M. A. Bakunina*, Geneva, 1896, pp. 233–8. The quotation seems to be directly from the original and not from the French version, *Correspondance*, pp. 288–95. The résumé preceding it mentions 'scientific socialism', but the phrase does not occur in the letter; Bakunin mentions only the 'great services that he [Marx] has rendered the socialist cause during the past twenty-five years'.
19. These details and those that follow are given by J. Guillaume, vol. I.
20. The report for the Basle congress (6–11 September 1869) was drafted by Marx (in English; it was read in German and French). Subjects proposed by London were, landed property (cf. La Pléiade, I, p. 1473 f.), the law of inheritance, mutual credit, education, the activity of organizations opposed to the emancipation of the workers, etc. Marx's report drew attention to the 'guerrilla warfare between labour and capital, i.e., the strikes which have troubled Europe during the past year', and on 11 September 'resistance funds' were discussed. Another subject proposed for discussion was 'direct legislation exercised by the people'. Report and minutes in *Documents of the First International*, III, pp. 326–42, MEW, XVI, pp. 370–82; Freymond, II, pp. 5–131. cf. J. Guillaume, I, 190.
21. Freymond, vol. II, p. 5 ff.
22. The phrase is A. Ruge's, 1846. cf. E. Silberner, 1965 and 1966.
23. Moses Hess, *Le Réveil*, 2 October 1869; the anonymous reply (it was by J. Guillaume) appeared in *Le Progrès*, Le Locle, 16 October 1869. J. Guillaume, I, p. 222 ff.
24. Varlin to J. Guillaume, 25 December 1869. *Le Progrès*, 1 January

1870. Reprinted, with an account of the circumstances of the foundation of *La Marseillaise*, by J. Guillaume, I, pp. 257–8. MEW, 25. MEW, XXXII, p. 516.

Chapter 19. The Franco-Prussian War.

1. On the antecedents of the Franco-Prussian War, cf. M. Rubel, *Karl Marx devant le bonapartisme*, 1960.
2. Freymond, vol. I, p. 78.
3. M. Rubel, op. cit., pp. 122–3.
4. cf. D. Riazanov, article of 2 July 1915.
5. 7 February 1882. MEW XXXV, pp. 269–70.
6. 20 June 1866. MEW, XXXI, p. 229.
7. ibid., p. 204.
8. ibid., p. 514.
9. Luxembourg was to have been the price of French neutrality. Napoleon III is said to have hoped for more. See the letters of Marx and Engels of 27 March and 4 April 1867.
10. 12 February 1870. MEW, XXXII, p. 443.
11. 17 February 1870. ibid., p. 651.
12. 22 August 1870. MEW, XXXIII, p. 47. On Bebel's and Liebknecht's activity in Germany, cf. K.-H. Ledigkeit, 1958.
13. MEW, XXXIII, p. 38.
14. 20 July 1870. ibid., p. 5.
15. *The General Council of the I.W.A. on the War. To the Members of the I.W.A. in Europe and the United States*, London, 23 July 1870.
16. MEW, XXXIII, pp. 40–41.
17. Letter to Kugelmann, 4 February 1871. ibid., p. 182.
18. F. Engels, *Notes on the War*, sixty articles on the war of 1870–71 in the *Pall Mall Gazette*, from 27 July to 18 February 1871.
19. MEW, XXXIII, p. 32.
20. 20 August 1870. ibid., p. 45.
21. Bakunin, *Œuvres*, IV, p. 499.
22. 'XXIXth Letter' from Paris, 25 January 1831. 1868. ed., VIII, p. 121.
23. To Ogarev, *Pisma*, p. 300; French version, Correspondance, p. 336.
24. To Albert Richard, 23 August 1870. J. Guillaume, II, p. 81.
25. Marx to Engels, 6 September 1870. MEW, XXXIII, pp. 54–5.
26. Marx to Engels, 10 September 1870. ibid., p. 59.
27. *Secret Address of the I.W.A. on the Franco-Prussian War*, London, 9 September 1870.
28. MEW, XXXIII, p. 140.
29. To Albert Richard, from London, 6 September 1870. cf. Oscar Testut, 1872; J. Guillaume, II, p. 100.

30. MEW, XXXIII, p. 158. On the role of the International at Lyons, cf. J. Rougerie, 1961.
31. Letter to Marx, 7 September 1870. MEW, XXXIII, p. 58.
32. ibid., pp. 61–2.
33. 20 August 1870. ibid., p. 45.
34. 4 February 1871. ibid., p. 183.
35. ibid., p. 58.
36. To Engels, 7 July 1868. MEW, XXXII, p. 115.
37. MEW, XXXIII, p. 54. He goes on to call him 'this 1848 toast-master, who now plays the Brutus'.
38. 19 and 25 September 1870; *Piśma*, pp. 304–6; *Correspondance*, pp. 338–9; J. Guillaume, II, p. 92.
39. 19 October 1870. MEW, XXXIII, p. 158.
40. 'The Freedom of the Press and of Debate in Germany.'
41. cf. note 18.
42. cf. 'Bibliographie de la Commune de Paris', article by J. Rougerie and G. Haupt, January–March 1962.
43. Letter to Louis Palix, 29 September 1870. *Œuvres*, IV, p. 78.
44. To Gaspard Sentiñon, 23 October 1870; quoted by J. Guillaume, Bakounine, *Œuvres*, II, p. 275.
45. The original text is quoted here; the first edition of the present work contained a somewhat different one, ending with the statement: 'Our revolution has not yet come, but we shall make it, and, when we are rid of the Prussians, we shall lay the foundations in a revolutionary fashion of the egalitarian society of which we dream.' This is a circular of the Paris federal council. It is addressed to provincial members of the International, informing them of the activities and participation in national defence of their Parisian colleagues, and can be dated from mid-September 1870.
46. On Lavrov in Paris, cf. *Parizhkaya Kommuna*, Petrograd, 1919; this letter is quoted on p. 80. See also Venturi, ch. XVIII.
47. 12 September 1874. MEW, XXXIII, p. 642.
48. Gambon had recently taken his seat in the National Assembly in Bordeaux. This radical with vaguely socialist leanings had figured on the list supported by the Paris members of the International. Like Pyat, another radical elected with the aid of the votes of members of the International, he consulted it on 'the course of action to be taken in the light of the attitude of the National Assembly'. cf. *Les Séances officielles de l'Internationale à Paris pendant le Siège et pendant la Commune*, Paris, E. Lachaud, 1872, p. 98. The reply quoted here is signed by 'one of the secretaries for France' (Henri Goullé) and was calmly accompanied by a summons to attend the session of 22 March.

49. 17 September 1874. MEW, XXXIII, p. 642.
50. 12 April 1871. ibid., p. 205.
51. ibid., p. 200.
52. To Leo Fränkel and Louis-Eugène Varlin, 13 May 1871, ibid., p. 226.
53. 22 February 1881. MEW, XXXV, p. 160.
54. 5 April 1871. J. Guillaume, II, p. 140.
55. ibid., p. 140 and p. 154.
56. Through an intermediary Marx sent the Communards details about the secret agreement between Bismarck and Jules Favre for joint action with a view to the 're-establishment of order in Paris', as well as 'advice' on how to thwart these plans. cf. the letter to Fränkel and Varlin of 13 May 1871 quoted above. In a letter to Beesly of 12 May 1871 Marx said he had this information from Bismarck's 'right hand' (according to MEW, Johannes Miquel, an ex-member of the Communist League). Through the agency of Engels, he sent them to Lafargue at Bordeaux. cf. MEW, XXXIII, pp. 226–8; *Chronik*, 1934, p. 300.
57. 12 April 1871. MEW, XXXI, p. 206.
58. Marx to Fränkel and Varlin, 13 May 1871. MEW, XXXIII, p. 226.
59. Minutes of the General Council. *Documents of the First International*, vol. IV, Moscow, undated, pp. 166 and 169.
60. 26 April 1871. MEW, XXXIII, p. 216.
61. All this material is available in French. cf. next note.
62. *Address of the General Council of the I.W.A. on the Civil War in France, 1871. To all the Members of the Association in Europe and the United States*. cf. also *La Guerre civile en France*, new ed., accompanied by Marx's preparatory work and press cuttings (18 March–1 May), Paris 1953.
63. 12 April 1871. MEW, XXXIII, p. 205.
64. In 1877 Marx took an interest in W. Bracke's translation into German of Lissagaray's *History of the Commune*, the MS of which he revised. See the correspondence with Bracke, MEW, XXXIV.

Chapter 20. The Decline of the International.

1. On this period, cf. M. Molnar, 1963.
2. To Kugelmann, 17 March 1868. MEW, XXXII, p. 540.
3. 18 June 1871. MEW, XXXIII, p. 238.
4. cf., for instance, the two interviews given by Marx after the Commune, published by M. Rubel, 1962.
5. Letter written in French but published in Flemish by *De Werker*, (8 April 1871), of which P. Coenen was the editor.
6. On how Marx was visualized by the French police, cf. H. Hirsch, 1955; and the evidence produced by J. Verdès in his article of April 1966.

7. Letter to Kugelmann, 17 April 1871. MEW, XXXIII, p. 209.

8. cf. Collins and Abramsky, 1965.

9. 'Konfidenzielle Mitteilung.' (MEW, XVI, pp. 409–20). Published in part in French, *Les Prétendues scissions* . . . , 1872 (cf. note 12). Enclosed with this letter of Marx's to the Brunswick committee of the German Social Democratic Party, dated 28 March 1870 and sent through Kugelmann, was a circular written by him in French, dated 1 January 1870, replying to Bakunin's attacks in *L'Égalité* (published by J. Guillaume, I, pp. 263–8). The 'Communication confidentielle contre Bakounine' and the circular are reprinted in *Lettres à Kugelmann*, Anthropos, Paris, 1968.

10. cf. Marx's and Engels's correspondence with W. Liebknecht, ed. G. Eckert, 1963. N. Riazanov, 1913 (Appendix IV).

11. cf. Bebel's memoirs. *Aus meinem Leben*, vol. II, p. 167 ff.

12. cf. the *Archives Bakounine*, II, *Michel Bakounine et les conflits dans l'Internationale, 1872.* J. Guillaume, vol. II; K. Marx and F. Engels, 'Les Prétendues scissions dans l'Internationale, circulaire privée du Conseil général de l'A.I.T.', Geneva, 1872; republished in *Le Mouvement socialiste*, July–August 1913; Archives Bakounine, II, 1965, pp. 269–96.

13. *Documents of the First International, 1870–1871*, vol. IV, p. 446.

14. cf. *L'Alliance de la Démocratie socialiste et l'A.I.T.*, op. cit. (ch. 18, note 12); also R. Cannac, 1961.

15. Published in Russian by A. N. Silov, *Borba Klassov*, Leningrad, 1924, nos. 1 and 2; reprinted in French in *Briefwechsel* (German translation of *Pisma*), 1895, pp. 374–80; recently reprinted in *Le Contrat social*, I, 1957, no. 2, pp. 122–6.

16. cf. R. Cannac, 1961.

17. Letter of 7 February 1870, published in *La Revue de Paris*, 1 September 1896.

18. cf. Appendix V.

19. 5 July 1870. MEW, XXXII, p. 520.

20. A Russian branch of the International was founded by Utin and Trussov (editor of the *Narodnoye Dielo*) in March 1870. A conference of the International in London in September 1871 authorized 'Citizen Utin' to publish an account of the Nechaiev trial in *L'Égalité*. See Marx's article, 'The International and Nechaiev', the *World*, 15 October 1871. cf. also J. Guillaume, vol. II, p. 201 ff.

21. 4 November 1871. MEW, XXXIII, p. 306.

22. Published in the *Neue Zeit* in 1893. cf. Adoratski, *Sammlung von Erinnerungen*, 1934, p. 186.

23. In a document referred to in note 12.

24. On the congress at The Hague, cf. Freymond, vol. II, ch. VII.

25. Documents published in the *Archives Bakounine* by A. Lehning

(vol. II); résumé in the Introduction, pp. XXXV–XXXVIII, pp. 108 and 112, and Appendix IX, 2.

26. Letter from Malon to Mathilde Roederer from Chiasso (Ticino), 19 August 1872. J. Guillaume, II, p. 314.

27. For what follows the minutes of the congress published in English by H. Gerth, 1958, may be consulted.

28. J. Guillaume, II, p. 321.

29. Documents of the Leipzig trial in K.-H. Ledigkeit, 1960.

30. This became article 7a of the statutes of the International, which had been drafted in 1864 (cf. above, pp. 282–3). La Pléiade, I, p. 471.

31. Report published in a Dutch newspaper, 10 October 1872, and in French in *La Liberté*, 15 September 1872. MEW, XVIII, p. 159–61 (translated from the French).

32. cf. Foreword, p. x.

33. F. Engels, 'Die Bakunisten an der Arbeit', *Der Volksstaat*, 31 October 1873. MEW, XVIII, p. 476 f.

34. 20 June 1873. MEW, XXXIII, p. 591. W. Blumenberg, 1965, reproduces Bebel's letters together with those of Engels, and provides valuable explanatory matter.

Chapter 21. The Last Ten Years.

1. 27 September 1873. MEW, XXXIII, p. 606.

2. 4 April 1874. ibid., p. 635.

3. Letter of 18 March 1872, La Pléiade, I, p. 543. It also contains information about this translation on pp. 537–41.

4. 30 August 1883. cf. La Pléiade, II, p. CXXI f.

5. This idea was frequently expressed by Engels. It occurs almost word for word in 'Die auswärtige Politik des Zarentums', *Die Neue Zeit*, VIII, May 1890, nos. 4 and 5. MEW XXII, pp. 13–41.

6. W. Liebknecht, *Zur orientalischen Frage, oder soll Europa kosakisch werden?* 2nd ed., Leipzig, 1878.

7. Marx to Sorge, 4 April 1874. MEW, XXXIII, p. 635.

8. Letters of 4 February 1874 and 11 February 1878. MEW, XXXIV, pp. 317–19, pp. 320–24. Liebknecht used these letters in the 2nd ed. of his pamphlet, op. cit., without mentioning the writer's name.

9. 27 September 1877. MEW, XXXIV, p. 296. See Appendix V.

10. ibid., p. 317.

11. MEW, XXXV, p. 179. On terrorism in Russia, cf. M. Slonim, 1933. Marx expressed himself as follows on the inevitable violence of revolutions in which reaction is dominant (statement to the *Chicago Tribune*, 5 January 1879): 'One does not have to be a socialist to foresee that Russia, Germany and probably Italy – if the Italians persist on their present path – will be the scenes of bloody revolution.

The events of the French Revolution could be repeated in those countries, which is obvious to anyone who understands politics. The revolutions will not be the work of a party, but of the whole nation.'

12. 16 December 1879. MEW, XXXIV, p. 341.
13. ibid., p. 464. N. F. Danielson, known as Nicolai-on. cf. Appendix V.
14. It is well known that Engels sharply criticized this programme in a letter to Bebel (28 March 1875) and that on 5 May 1875 Marx sent to W. Bracke his 'marginal comments', *Randglossen zum Programm der deutschen Arbeiterpartei*. This document was printed in 1891 and reprinted from the original MS by B. Nicolaievsky in 1921. MEW, XIX, pp. 15–32.
15. 14 November 1879. MEW, XXXIV, p. 421.
16. 31 July 1877. ibid., p. 284.
17. 24 November 1879. ibid., XXXIV, p. 425.
18. cf. a 'Circular to the leaders of Social Democracy', 17 September 1879, sent by Marx and Engels to Bebel and the social democrats in the Reichstag, denouncing opportunism and stressing the class struggle; the workers, they said, could not be 'liberated from above'. MEW, XXXIV, pp. 394–408. Two days later in a letter to Sorge Marx used the famous phrase: 'They are afflicted with parliamentary cretinism'.
19. 5 November 1881. MEW, XXXIV, p. 474.
20. cf. G. Eckert, 1965.
21. 25 October 1881. MEW, XXXV, p. 232. The Engels-Bernstein correspondence has recently been republished by H. Hirsch, 1967. The Engels-Lafargue correspondence is available in French. cf. Bibliography, 'Lafargue'.
22. cf. Marx's letter to Engels of 30 September 1882 drawing attention to 'tacit innuendoes . . . Marx is a German, indeed a Prussian'.
23. 'The self-styled "Marxism" in France is certainly a quite special product, to such an extent that Marx said to Lafargue: Ce qu'il y a de certain, c'est que moi, je ne suis pas marxiste' ('What is quite certain is that I am not a Marxist'). (Engels to Bernstein, 3 November 1882. MEW, XXXV, p. 388. cf. M. Dommanget, 1969.
24. 12 September 1882. MEW, XXXV, pp. 356–8.
25. 22 February 1881. cf. ch. 19, note 53.
26. Engels to Bernstein, 25 October 1881. MEW, XXXV, pp. 232–3.
27. H. M. Hyndman, 1911.
28. No doubt a reference to his daughter Eleanor and to Helene Demuth. Letter of 29 April 1881. MEW, XXXV, p. 186.
29. 15 March 1883. MEW, XXXV.
30. cf. Foreword, p. x.

Index